The Collected Poems of

LOUIS MACNEICE

By the same author

LOUIS MacNEICE

Collected Poems

faber and faber
LONDON · BOSTON

First published in 1966 by
Faber & Faber Limited
3 Queen Square London WC1N 3AU
First published in this edition 1979
Reprinted in 1986 and 1987
Printed in Great Britain by
Richard Clay Ltd, Bungay, Suffolk
All rights reserved

British Library Cataloguing in Publication Data

MacNeice, Louis
The collected poems of Louis MacNeice
I. Dodds, Eric Robertson
821'.9'12   PR6025.A316A17

ISBN 0–571–04985–0
ISBN 0–571–11353–2 Pbk

Contents

I

Juvenilia, 1925–1929

II

1931–1935

III

1933–1937

IV

1936–1938

XIV
1961–1963

XV
Translations

Author's Preface to
Collected Poems, 1925–1948

This collection includes the bulk of my published verse. While resisting the temptation to 'collect' only what I most admire I have omitted certain poems which I now dislike or which overlap others that I have kept; two or three, however, have been kept mainly at the request of my friends. There are a few poems here which have not appeared in my previous volumes while in Section II* I have reprinted a dozen poems from *Blind Fireworks* which might be called juvenilia. The arrangement of this collection should be clear from the Table of Contents; I thought it best to separate the shorter pieces from the longer while *Autumn Journal* falls naturally and not only on chronological grounds in the middle. Within each group the order of poems is not necessarily chronological. The earliest poem here is 'Genesis' (summer, 1925) and the latest, excepting the dedicatory sestina, 'The Window' (October, 1948). I have included no translations.

In preparing this book for the press I have also resisted the temptation to make many revisions, since I feel that after three or four years from the date of writing a poet should leave even not-so-well alone. Within that time limit I have to some extent revised; outside it I have merely altered titles where the original titles were makeshift and made a couple of word changes for the sake of factual accuracy; I have also cut three lines from the early poem 'Breaking Webs'.

The books in which these poems have previously appeared are the following: *Poems* (1935), *Out of the Picture* (1937), *Letters from Iceland* (1937), *The Earth Compels* (1938), *Autumn Journal* (1939), *Plant and Phantom* (1941), *Springboard* (1944), *Holes in the Sky* (1948)—all published by Faber and Faber—and *Blind Fireworks* (1929) published by Victor Gollancz.

---

* Section I in the present edition.

Editor's Preface

The editor of a posthumous volume of Collected Poems has three courses to choose from. He may attempt to gratify the modern passion for completeness by seeking out and printing every scrap of verse that his author ever wrote; he may follow his own judgement, or that of some contemporary, as to what is worth collecting; or he may accept the poet's judgement in so far as this is known. If he adopts the first course, he risks harming his author's reputation with small benefit to the common reader. If he adopts the second, he risks the censure of a later generation whose critical standards may be very different from his. And if he adopts either of these against the poet's known wishes, he infringes the dead man's moral right to do what he will with his own. The third course, where it is available, seems to me the proper one, unless the poet's judgement of his own writings is plainly eccentric.

MacNeice was in his maturity a severe but usually, I think, a just critic of his own earlier work. He put together in 1949 as much of his poetry up to that date as he wished to preserve, and I have obeyed his wishes. I have therefore followed him in discarding (a) most of the "juvenilia" published in *Blind Fireworks* when MacNeice was twenty-two, and (b) a further 31 pieces published in other volumes of verse; the titles are listed in Appendix I, together with the places where they can be found. Most of the rejected pieces in group (b) are either trivial or else repetitive of themes better handled elsewhere; a few are frankly bad; none in either group seems to me to approach the level of its author's best work. I have also excluded, *a fortiori*, those pieces—extant in periodicals or in manuscript—which MacNeice did not think worthy of inclusion in any of his published volumes. The great majority of these are early and may be viewed as discarded experiments.

After 1949 MacNeice published, with Faber & Faber, five more volumes of original verse—*Ten Burnt Offerings* (1952), *Autumn Sequel* (1954), *Visitations* (1957), *Solstices* (1961) and *The Burning Perch* (1963). His last (and as many think his best) volume went to press in January, 1963; he died in September of the same year; in the interval he was fully occupied in preparing his Clark Lectures, *Varieties of Parable*, and a number of radio programmes. It is therefore not surprising, though disappointing, that this final period has yielded only one new poem—'Thalassa', which was published posthumously in *The London Magazine* and is reprinted here. With its stoical reaffirmation of his underlying faith in life it makes a fitting conclusion to his life's work. My only other addition to the corpus of MacNeice's published verse is a small group of translations, only one of which has appeared in any previous collection. Translations were excluded from the *Collected Poems* of 1949, but there seemed to be a case for departing here from the rule of strict obedience: these pieces—most of them recent—illustrate both the breadth of MacNeice's sympathies and the equally wide range of his metrical versatility.

Order of poems. The earlier poems are here presented in the sequence adopted by MacNeice in the *Collected Poems* of 1949, save that I have restored the two earliest groups (1925–1929 and 1931–1935) to their chronological place at the beginning. The contents of the later volumes have been added in the order of their publication, and within each volume in the sequence chosen by their author.

Dates of composition. While the sequence of groups of poems in this book is thus broadly chronological, the pieces within each group are not for the most part arranged in order of composition. I have therefore thought it useful to date individual poems more exactly where this is possible, especially as the dates are often of biographical interest. In three of his volumes—*Poems*, Random House, 1937, *Plant and Phantom*, and *Eighty-Five Poems*—MacNeice gave the dates of composition of individual pieces; and a good many other poems can be securely dated from manuscript evidence.

Text. MacNeice's manuscript drafts show many corrections and rewritings; but once a poem was in print his general practice was to leave it alone. He did, however, make a few small changes—seldom affecting more than a word or two—in the *Collected Poems* of 1949, and a somewhat larger number in his later selection of *Eighty-Five Poems* (1959). The text printed here is in all cases the latest available, save for the occasional correction of an obvious misprint.

Titles. MacNeice had a trick of changing the titles of poems, to the confusion of future bibliographers. The titles given in the *Collected Poems* of 1949 have generally been adopted in this edition; but for the convenience of readers who might otherwise search in vain for some apparently missing favourite I have supplied in Appendix II an index of variant titles.

Second printing. I owe an especial debt of gratitude to Miss Robyn Marsack whose researches have enabled me to date a number of poems more exactly than in the previous printing. I am also indebted to her sharp eyes and to those of M. Adolphe Haberer and Dr. William McKinnon for the detection and removal of several unsightly misprints.

E. R. Dodds

Dedicatory Poem to
Collected Poems, 1925–1948

To Hedli

Acting younger than I am and thinking older
I have buried so many stray moments in this volume
That I feel shrunk; as though those April answers
Had withered off their Question and now turning,
As the year turns, I bind up ghost and image
To give them, Hedli, to you, a makeshift present.

For having lived, and too much, in the present,
Askance at the coming gods, estranged from those older
Who had created my fathers in their image,
I stand here now dumbfounded by the volume
Of angry sound which pours from every turning
On those who only so lately knew the answers.

So I lay my ear to the ground and no one answers
Though I know that the Word, like a bulb, is there, is present
And there the subterranean wheels keep turning
To make the world gush green when, we being older,
Others will be in their prime to drench a volume
In the full leaf of insight and bloom of image.

At one time I was content if things would image
Themselves in their own dazzle, if the answers
Came quick and smooth and the great depth and volume
Of the cold sea would wash me the chance present,
Bone or shell or message from some older
Castaway for whom there was no returning.

But now I am not content, the leaves are turning
And the gilt flaking from each private image
And all the poets I know, both younger and older,
Condemned to silence unless they divine the answers
Which our grim past has cached throughout our present
And which are no more than groped for in this volume.

Still at this point I tender you this volume
In hopes, my dearest, that your fingers turning
These pages may let fall, among those present,
Some greeting on my waifs and wraiths of image
And half-blind questions that still lack their answers,
Which lack grows no way less as I grow older.

Older and older. Which was the right turning?
Rhythm and image and still at best half answers
And at half volume. But take this; it is a present.

November, 1948

I
Juvenilia, 1925—1929

The Creditor

The quietude of a soft wind
Will not rescind
My debts to God, but gentle-skinned
His finger probes. I lull myself
In quiet in diet in riot in dreams,
In dopes in drams in drums in dreams
Till God retire and the door shut.
But
Now I am left in the fire-blaze
The peacefulness of the fire-blaze
Will not erase
My debts to God for His mind strays
Over and under and all ways
All days and always.

1929

Trains in the distance

Trains came threading quietly through my dozing childhood,
Gentle murmurs nosing through a summer quietude,
Drawing in and out, in and out, their smoky ribbons,
Parting now and then, and launching full-rigged galleons
And scrolls of smoke that hung in a shifting epitaph.
Then distantly the noise declined like a descending graph,
Sliding downhill gently to the bottom of the distance
(For now all things are there that all were here once);
And so we hardly noticed when that metal murmur came.
But it brought us assurance and comfort all the same,
And in the early night they soothed us to sleep,
And the chain of the rolling wheels bound us in deep
Till all was broken by that menace from the sea,
The steel-bosomed siren calling bitterly.

1926

Genesis

A million whirling spinning-wheels of flowing gossamer,
A million hammers jangling on the anvils of the sky,
The crisp chip of chisels and the murmuring of saws
And the flowing ripple of water from a million taps,

With the champ of griffin-horses with their heads in sacks of hay
And sawdust flitting to and fro in new-born fragrancy.
But not the same for all—flooding over weedy rocks
A green sea singing like a dream, and on the shore
Fair round pebbles with eggy speckles half transparent,
And brown sodden tangles of odorous wrack.

Summer, 1925

Glass falling

The glass is going down. The sun
Is going down. The forecasts say
It will be warm, with frequent showers.
We ramble down the showery hours
And amble up and down the day.
Mary will wear her black goloshes
And splash the puddles on the town;
And soon on fleets of macintoshes
The rain is coming down, the frown
Is coming down of heaven showing
A wet night coming, the glass is going
Down, the sun is going down.

1926

Poussin

In that Poussin the clouds are like golden tea,
And underneath the limbs flow rhythmically,
The cupids' blue feathers beat musically,
And we dally and dip our spoon in the golden tea.
The tea flows down the steps and up again,
An old-world fountain, pouring from sculptured lips,
And the chilly marble drop like sugar slips
And is lost in the dark gold depths, and the refrain
Of tea-leaves floats about and in and out,
And the motion is still as when one walks and the moon
Walks parallel but relations remain the same.
And thus we never reach the dregs of the cup,
Though we drink it up and drink it up and drink it up,
And thus we dally and dip our spoon.

4

Evening indoors

In this evening room there is no stir, no fuss;
The silken shade of the oil-light is diaphanous,
And so come other noises through the noise of the clock
Transparent as the shade, as a girl's frock.
There is no crease, no fold ruffling the room at all;
The glass fringe of the shade seems a summer waterfall,
Like August insects purring over mown grass
The flames blend and pass, incend and end and pass.
Like the calm blue marriage of the sky and sea,
Or a blue-veiled Madonna beaming vacancy,
See that Madonna snuff out the shaded light
And stroke with soothing hand asleep the night.

1927

Elephant trunk

Descending out of the grey
Clouds elephant trunk
Twitches away
Hat;
THAT
Was *not* what I expected,
A
Misdirected
Joke it seemed to me;
'What about a levitation?' I had said,
Preening head for halo,
All alert, combed, sanctified,
I thank Thee, Lord, I am not like other men
WHEN
Descending out of the grey
Clouds elephant trunk. . . .

(and so *ad nauseam*)

River in spate

The river falls and over the walls the coffins of cold funerals
Slide deep and sleep there in the close tomb of the pool,
And yellow waters lave the grave and pebbles pave its mortuary
And the river horses vault and plunge with their assault and battery,

5

And helter-skelter the coffins come and the drums beat and the waters flow,
And the panther horses lift their hooves and paw and shift and draw the bier,
The corpses blink in the rush of the river, and out of the water their chins they tip
And quaff the gush and lip the draught and crook their heads and crow,
Drowned and drunk with the cataract that carries them and buries them
And silts them over and covers them and lilts and chuckles over their bones;
The organ-tones that the winds raise will never pierce the water ways,
So all they will hear is the fall of hooves and the distant shake of harness,
And the beat of the bells on the horses' heads and the undertaker's laughter,
And the murmur that will lose its strength and blur at length to quietness,
And afterwards the minute heard descending, never ending heard,
And then the minute after and the minute after the minute after.

Candles

I

I have no clock, yet I can hear
The minutes pass while I sit here
Tired but free from tedium
And mark the waning cylinder.

To-morrow will be another day,
And to-day will then be yesterday,
To click the bonds of business
From Saturday to Saturday.

Another night will follow, but
My candle will then be a candle butt
And the door that is day and day's division
Will have opened once and shut.

Close your armoured books and mark
The waning cylinder that drips
Fluid time from pallid lips,
Making an island in the dark.

This island is too small, I fear;
Dark horses fret away the shore,
And I can build no breakwater
But only close a desperate ear
And mark the waning cylinder.

II

The candle in his white grave-clothes, always turning his cowled
   head,
Stood in his own shadow at the foot of my grave-bed;
Ho, said the candle with his rich dark beard,
How they howl like the dead!
And wagging his cowled head,
Ho, said the candle, they would make a body afeard.

1927

Nocturne

The dark blood of night-time
Foams among the ivy,
And leaps toward the lunelet
Of sea-chawn ivory,
And nowhere finds an outlet.

The wind goes fingering
His lantern. The wind goes
In his glistening oil-cape
Knocking at the windows,
Slouching round the landscape.

Sinisterly bend and dip
Those hulks of cloud canvas,
Probing through the elm-trees,
Past the house; and then pass
To a larger emptiness.

The lugubrious, salubrious seaside

The dogs' tails tick like metronomes,
Their barks encore the sticks you throw,
The sallow clouds yawn overhead,
The sagging deck-chairs yawn below.
I wish I had my marble clock
To race those minatory tails,
Or the fire-buckets at the Bank
To shame those proud enamelled pails,
Those wooden spades that dig the mind,
Unearthing memories of spades
When we were the protagonists
Flaunting down juvenile parades.
I hide my face in magazines
While children patronise the grave
Of mariners, while bathing girls
Deign to illuminate the wave.
That never-satisfied old maid, the sea,
Rehangs her white lace curtains ceaselessly.

Happy families

The room is all a stupid quietness,
Cajoled only by the fire's caress;
We loll severally about and sit
Severally and do our business severally,
For there's a little bit for everybody;
But that's not all there is to it.

Crusted in sandstone, while the wooden clock
Places two doctor fingers on his mouth,
We seem fossils in rock,
Or leaves turned mummies in drouth,
And garnered into a mouldy shrubbery corner
Where the wind has done with us. When we are old
The gardener will use us for leaf-mould.

Dutifully sitting on chair, lying on sofa,
Standing on hearth-rug, here we are again,
John caught the bus, Joshua caught the train,

And I took a taxi, so we all got somewhere;
No one deserted, no one was a loafer,
Nobody disgraced us, luckily for us
No one put his foot in it or missed the bus.

But the wind is a beggar and always
Raps at front door, back door, side door;
In spite of the neat placard that says
'No Hawkers Here' he knocks the more,
He blows loose paper into petulance
And ruffles the brazier's fiery hair; and once
He caught me suddenly surreptitiously
And heft me out of my shell. We'll pass that over
And forget about it and quietly sit
Knitting close, sitting close under cover.

Snuff out the candle, for the cap, I think,
Seems to fit, excellently fit.
Te saluto—in a fraction, half a wink—
But that's not all there is to it

1928

Breaking webs

The spider pendulously waits
Stranded in the unroaded air,
The spider's belly-mind creates
Thoroughfare on thoroughfare.

The fatally inquisitive moth
Wakes to ambition with a quiver,
Leaves its bed and board of cloth:
Wings of moth go flit and shiver.

And all the time on the window-pane
Shadow fingers of the trees
Wistfully grope and grope again
After the indoor mysteries.

Over asphalt, tar, and gravel
My racing model happily purrs,
Each charted road I yet unravel
Out of my mind's six cylinders.

Shutters of light, green and red,
Slide up and down. Like mingled cries,
Wind and sunlight clip and wed
Behind the canopy of my eyes.

. . . . .

Yet all the time on the window-pane
Shadow fingers of the trees
Grope, grope, grope again
After unseen fatalities.

1928

Mahavveray

*Scene: The corner of a great many streets, all very long, high, and ugly,
with windows boarded up; all quite empty; 2 policemen, A and B,
on point duty.*

A. Turn off the tap, Mahavveray, it's too cold here;
   Icicles all over the shop, it's no joke here.
   It's a bloody long time I've been waiting,
   For they all let me down and left me waiting.

B. You've been here a dozen and a half year
   Under the gutter and the grating. . . .

A. Turn off the tap, Mahavveray, it's too cold here.
   No one comes along this beat at all,
   With my baton and white gloves and all.

B. And no one will, never you fear;
   It's not their affair to loiter
   And patch up romances under a gutter;
   People might think they were queer. . . .

A. Turn off the tap, Mahavveray; it's cold here.

B. If they came along, what would You say,
   You old spec. of law and order?
   I bet you don't know how to look a bit gay,
   No one ever thought you were that sort of
   Fellow with his phiz out for the day.

A. That old woman in the pawnshop said
  She can't keep the drum-sticks off her head
  For the crossbones beat it about so. . . .

B. There was an old woman and she didn't know what to do,
  So she bought boots that cripples left off,
  She sold them to army majors for wagers,
  And when they died with the whooping-cough
  She stole the boots from their great cold feet
  And sold them to army majors for charity.

A. That old woman is doing her bit.

B. And she sold them to ladies of delicate distinction
  Saying they were a sure fit.

A. But all the time she throbbed like parchment,
  For she can't keep the crossbones off her skull. . . .

B. There was an old woman and she didn't know what to do,
  So she went out into the garden-plot to pull
  Dried peas for dinner, and she mixed them with buttons
  And stirred them up well and poured them down the sink,
  And when the family came home for supper they said, 'Well,
    well,
  There's not very much to eat or drink
  So you may go to Heaven.'

A. But that old woman was doing her bit
  To provide for the family in such a delicate position
  That they all broke down in a red fit.

B. There was an old woman and she didn't know what to do,
  She said, 'I'm going in for the beauty comp.'
  All the princes west o' the moon came to that show,
  And the Pope came with a certain amount of pomp,
  And they looked at her through field-glasses as she sat on a
    table,
  And the Pope said to the princes, 'What do you think of it?'
  And the princes said all at once, as well as they were able,
  'That old woman is doing her bit.'

Spring sunshine

In a between world, a world of amber,
The old cat on the sand-warm window-sill
Sleeps on the verge of nullity.

Spring sunshine has a quality
Transcending rooks and the hammering
Of those who hang new pictures,
Asking if it is worth it
To clamour and caw, to add stick to stick for ever.

If it is worth while really
To colonise any more the already populous
Tree of knowledge, to portion and reportion
Bits of broken knowledge brittle and dead,
Whether it would not be better
To hide one's head in the warm sand of sleep
And be embalmed without hustle or bother.

The rooks bicker heckle bargain always
And market carts lumber—
Let me in the calm of the all-humouring sun
Also indulge my humour
And bury myself beyond creaks and cawings
In a below world, a bottom world of amber.

April, 1929

Cradle song for Miriam

The clock's untiring fingers wind the wool of darkness
And we all lie alone, having long outgrown our cradles
(Sleep, sleep, Miriam)
And the flames like faded ladies always unheeded simper
And all is troubledness.

Soft the wool, dark the wool
Is gathered slowly, wholly up
Into a ball, all of it.

And yet in the back of the mind, lulled all else,
There is something unsleeping, un-tamperable-with

Something that whines and scampers
And like the ladies in the grate will not sleep nor forget itself,
Clawing at the wool like a kitten.

Sleep, sleep, Miriam.
And as for this animal of yours
He must be cradled also.
That he may not unravel this handiwork of forgetfulness,
That he may not philander with the flames before they die.

The world like a cradle rises and falls
On a wave of confetti and funerals
And sordor and stinks and stupid faces
And the deity making bored grimaces.

Oh what a muddle he has made of the wool,
(God will to-morrow have his hands full),
You must muzzle your beast, you must fasten him
For the whole of life—the interim.

Through the interim we pass
Everyone under an alias
Till they gather the strands of us together
And wind us up for ever and ever.

The clock's fingers wind, wind the wool of Lethe,
(Sleep, sleep, Miriam)
It glides across the floor drawn by hidden fingers
And the beast droops his head
And the fire droops its flounces
And winks a final ogle out of the fading embers
But no one pays attention;

This is too much, the flames say, insulted,
We who were once the world's beauties and now
No one pays attention
No one remembers us.

November, 1928

Mayfly

Barometer of my moods today, mayfly,
Up and down one among a million, one

13

The same at best as the rest of the jigging mayflies,
One only day of May alive beneath the sun.

The yokels tilt their pewters and the foam
Flowers in the sun beside the jewelled water.
Daughter of the South, call the sunbeams home
To nest between your breasts. The kingcups
Ephemeral are gay gulps of laughter.

Gulp of yellow merriment; cackle of ripples;
Lips of the river that pout and whisper round the reeds.
The mayfly flirting and posturing over the water
Goes up and down in the lift so many times for fun.

'When we are grown up we are sure to alter
Much for the better, to adopt solider creeds;
The kingcup will cease proffering his cup
And the foam will have blown from the beer and the heat no longer
     dance
And the lift lose fascination and the May
Change her tune to June—but the trouble with us mayflies
Is that we never have the chance to be grown up.'

They never have the chance, but what of time they have
They stretch out taut and thin and ringing clear;
So we, whose strand of life is not much more,
Let us too make our time elastic and
Inconsequently dance above the dazzling wave.

Nor put too much on the sympathy of things,
The dregs of drink, the dried cups of flowers,
The pathetic fallacy of the passing hours
When it is we who pass them—hours of stone,
Long rows of granite sphinxes looking on.

It is we who pass them, we the circus masters
Who make the mayflies dance, the lapwings lift their crests,
The show will soon shut down, its gay-rags gone,
But when this summer is over let us die together,
I want always to be near your breasts.

1929–34

14

II

1931—1935

διώκει παῖς ποτανὸν ὄρνιν

Belfast

The hard cold fire of the northerner
Frozen into his blood from the fire in his basalt
Glares from behind the mica of his eyes
And the salt carrion water brings him wealth.

Down there at the end of the melancholy lough
Against the lurid sky over the stained water
Where hammers clang murderously on the girders
Like crucifixes the gantries stand.

And in the marble stores rubber gloves like polyps
Cluster; celluloid, painted ware, glaring
Metal patents, parchment lampshades, harsh
Attempts at buyable beauty.

In the porch of the chapel before the garish Virgin
A shawled factory-woman as if shipwrecked there
Lies a bunch of limbs glimpsed in the cave of gloom
By us who walk in the street so buoyantly and glib.

Over which country of cowled and haunted faces
The sun goes down with a banging of Orange drums
While the male kind murders each its woman
To whose prayer for oblivion answers no Madonna.

September, 1931

Birmingham

Smoke from the train-gulf hid by hoardings blunders upward, the
  brakes of cars
Pipe as the policeman pivoting round raises his flat hand, bars
With his figure of a monolith Pharaoh the queue of fidgety machines
(Chromium dogs on the bonnet, faces behind the triplex screens).
Behind him the streets run away between the proud glass of shops,
Cubical scent-bottles artificial legs arctic foxes and electric mops,
But beyond this centre the slumward vista thins like a diagram:
There, unvisited, are Vulcan's forges who doesn't care a tinker's damn.

Splayed outwards through the suburbs houses, houses for rest
Seducingly rigged by the builder, half-timbered houses with lips
  pressed
So tightly and eyes staring at the traffic through bleary haws
And only a six-inch grip of the racing earth in their concrete claws;
In these houses men as in a dream pursue the Platonic Forms
With wireless and cairn terriers and gadgets approximating to the
  fickle norms
And endeavour to find God and score one over the neighbour
By climbing tentatively upward on jerry-built beauty and sweated
  labour.

The lunch hour: the shops empty, shopgirls' faces relax
Diaphanous as green glass, empty as old almanacs
As incoherent with ticketed gewgaws tiered behind their heads
As the Burne-Jones windows in St. Philip's broken by crawling leads;
Insipid colour, patches of emotion, Saturday thrills
(This theatre is sprayed with 'June')—the gutter take our old playbills,
Next week-end it is likely in the heart's funfair we shall pull
Strong enough on the handle to get back our money; or at any rate
  it is possible.

On shining lines the trams like vast sarcophagi move
Into the sky, plum after sunset, merging to duck's egg, barred with
  mauve
Zeppelin clouds, and Pentecost-like the cars' headlights bud
Out from sideroads and the traffic signals, crême-de-menthe or bull's
  blood,
Tell one to stop, the engine gently breathing, or to go on
To where like black pipes of organs in the frayed and fading zone
Of the West the factory chimneys on sullen sentry will all night wait
To call, in the harsh morning, sleep-stupid faces through the daily
  gate.

October, 1933

Turf-stacks

Among these turf-stacks graze no iron horses
Such as stalk, such as champ in towns and the soul of crowds,
Here is no mass-production of neat thoughts
No canvas shrouds for the mind nor any black hearses:
The peasant shambles on his boots like hooves
Without thinking at all or wanting to run in grooves.

18

But those who lack the peasant's conspirators,
The tawny mountain, the unregarded buttress,
Will feel the need of a fortress against ideas and against the
Shuddering insidious shock of the theory-vendors,
The little sardine men crammed in a monster toy
Who tilt their aggregate beast against our crumbling Troy.

For we are obsolete who like the lesser things
Who play in corners with looking-glasses and beads;
It is better we should go quickly, go into Asia
Or any other tunnel where the world recedes,
Or turn blind wantons like the gulls who scream
And rip the edge off any ideal or dream.

September, 1932

Upon this beach

Upon this beach the falling wall of the sea
Explodes its drunken marble
Amid gulls' gaiety.

Which ever-crumbling masonry, cancelling sum,
No one by any device can represent
In any medium.

Turn therefore inland, tripper, foot on the sea-holly,
Forget those waves' monstrous fatuity
And boarding bus be jolly.

September, 1932

Circe

'. . . *vitreamque Circen*'

Something of glass about her, of dead water,
Chills and holds us,
Far more fatal than painted flesh or the lodestone of live hair
This despair of crystal brilliance.
Narcissus' error
Enfolds and kills us—
Dazed with gazing on that unfertile beauty
Which is our own heart's thought.

19

Fled away to the beasts
One cannot stop thinking; Timon
Kept on finding gold.
In parrot-ridden forest or barren coast
A more importunate voice than bird or wave
Escutcheoned on the air with ice letters
Seeks and, of course, finds us
(Of course, being our echo).

Be brave, my ego, look into your glass
And realise that that never-to-be-touched
Vision is your mistress.

August, 1931

Spring voices

The small householder now comes out warily
Afraid of the barrage of sun that shouts cheerily,
Spring is massing forces, birds wink in air,
The battlemented chestnuts volley green fire,
The pigeons banking on the wind, the hoots of cars,
Stir him to run wild, gamble on horses, buy cigars;
Joy lies before him to be ladled and lapped from his hand—
Only that behind him, in the shade of his villa, memories stand
Breathing on his neck and muttering that all this has happened before,
Keep the wind out, cast no clout, try no unwarranted jaunts untried
   before,
But let the spring slide by nor think to board its car
For it rides West to where the tangles of scrap-iron are;
Do not walk, these voices say, between the bucking clouds alone
Or you may loiter into a suddenly howling crater, or fall, jerked back,
   garrotted by the sun.

April, 1933

Museums

Museums offer us, running from among the buses,
A centrally heated refuge, parquet floors and sarcophaguses,
Into whose tall fake porches we hurry without a sound
Like a beetle under a brick that lies, useless, on the ground.

Warmed and cajoled by the silence the cowed cypher revives,
Mirrors himself in the cases of pots, paces himself by marble lives,
Makes believe it was he that was the glory that was Rome,
Soft on his cheek the nimbus of other people's martyrdom,
And then returns to the street, his mind an arena where sprawls
Any number of consumptive Keatses and dying Gauls.

May, 1933

A contact

The trains pass and the trains pass, chains of lighted windows,
A register in an unknown language
For these are the trains in which one never goes.

The familiar rhythm but the unknown implications
Delight like a dead language
Which never shocks us by banal revelations.

So listening for the night express coming down the way
I receive the expected whistle of the engine
Sharp and straight on the ear like stigmata.

April, 1933

Nature morte

(Even so it is not so easy to be dead)

As those who are not athletic at breakfast day by day
Employ and enjoy the sinews of others vicariously,
Shielded by the upheld journal from their dream-puncturing wives
And finding in the printed word a multiplication of their lives,
So we whose senses give us things misfelt and misheard
Turn also, for our adjustment, to the pretentious word
Which stabilises the light on the sun-fondled trees
And, by photographing our ghosts, claims to put us at our ease;
Yet even so, no matter how solid and staid we contrive
Our reconstructions, even a still life is alive
And in your Chardin the appalling unrest of the soul
Exudes from the dried fish and the brown jug and the bowl.

July, 1933

To a Communist

Your thoughts make shape like snow; in one night only
The gawky earth grows breasts,
Snow's unity engrosses
Particular pettiness of stones and grasses.
But before you proclaim the millennium, my dear,
Consult the barometer—
This poise is perfect but maintained
For one day only.

1933

The individualist speaks

We with our Fair pitched among the feathery clover
Are always cowardly and never sober,
Drunk with steam-organs, thigh-rub and cream-soda
—We cannot remember enemies in this valley.

As chestnut candles turn to conkers, so we
Knock our brains together extravagantly
Instead of planting them to make more trees
—Who have not as yet sampled God's malice.

But to us urchins playing with paint and filth
A prophet scanning the road on the hither hills
Might utter the old warning of the old sin
—Avenging youth threatening an old war.

Crawling down like lava or termites
Nothing seduces, nothing dissolves, nothing affrights
You who scale off masks and smash the purple lights
—But I will escape, with my dog, on the far side of the Fair.

September, 1933

22

Sunday morning

Down the road someone is practising scales,
The notes like little fishes vanish with a wink of tails,
Man's heart expands to tinker with his car
For this is Sunday morning, Fate's great bazaar;
Regard these means as ends, concentrate on this Now,
And you may grow to music or drive beyond Hindhead anyhow,
Take corners on two wheels until you go so fast
That you can clutch a fringe or two of the windy past,
That you can abstract this day and make it to the week of time
A small eternity, a sonnet self-contained in rhyme.

But listen, up the road, something gulps, the church spire
Opens its eight bells out, skulls' mouths which will not tire
To tell how there is no music or movement which secures
Escape from the weekday time. Which deadens and endures.

May, 1933

August

The shutter of time darkening ceaselessly
Has whisked away the foam of may and elder
And I realise how now, as every year before,
Once again the gay months have eluded me.

For the mind, by nature stagey, welds its frame
Tomb-like around each little world of a day;
We jump from picture to picture and cannot follow
The living curve that is breathlessly the same.

While the lawn-mower sings moving up and down
Spirting its little fountain of vivid green,
I, like Poussin, make a still-bound fête of us
Suspending every noise, of insect or machine.

Garlands at a set angle that do not slip,
Theatrically (and as if for ever) grace
You and me and the stone god in the garden
And Time who also is shown with a stone face.

But all this is a dilettante's lie,
Time's face is not stone nor still his wings;
Our mind, being dead, wishes to have time die
For we, being ghosts, cannot catch hold of things.

August, 1933

The glacier

Just as those who gaze get higher than those who climb
A paradox unfolds on any who can tamper with time.
Where bus encumbers upon bus and fills its slot
Speed up the traffic in a quick motion film of thought
Till bus succeeds bus so identically sliding through
That you cannot catch the fraction of a chink between the two,
But they all go so fast, bus after bus, day after day,
Year after year, that you cannot mark any headway,
But the whole stream of traffic seems to crawl
Carrying its dead boulders down a glacier wall
And we who have always been haunted by the fear of becoming stone
Cannot bear to watch that catafalque creep down
And therefore turn away to seemingly slower things
And rejoice there to have found the speed of fins and wings
In the minnow-twisting of the latinist who alone
Nibbles and darts through the shallows of the lexicon
Or among plate-glass cases in sombre rooms where
Eyes appraise the glazen life of majolica ware
Or where a gardener with trowel and rheumatic pains
Pumps up the roaring sap of vegetables through their veins.

July, 1933

Perseus

Borrowed wings on his ankles,
Carrying a stone death,
The hero entered the hall,
All in the hall looked up,
Their breath frozen on them,
And there was no more shuffle or clatter in the hall at all.

So a friend of a man comes in
And leaves a book he is lending or flowers

24

And goes again, alive but as good as dead,
And you are left alive, no better than dead,
And you dare not turn the leaden pages of the book or touch the
  flowers, the hooded and arrested hours.

Close your eyes,
There are suns beneath your lids,
Or look in the looking-glass in the end room—
You will find it full of eyes,
The ancient smiles of men cut out with scissors and kept in mirrors.

Ever to meet me comes, in sun or dull,
The gay hero swinging the Gorgon's head
And I am left, with the dull drumming of the sun, suspended and
  dead,
Or the dumb grey-brown of the day is a leper's cloth,
And one feels the earth going round and round the globe of the
  blackening mantle, a mad moth.

August, 1934

An April manifesto

Our April must replenish the delightful wells,
Bucket's lip dipping, light on the sleeping cells,
Man from his vigil in the wintry chapel
Will card his skin with accurate strigil.
O frivolous and astringent spring
We never come full circle, never remember
Self behind self years without number,
A series of dwindling mirrors, but take a tangent line
And start again. Our April must replenish
Our bank-account of vanity and give our doors a coat of varnish.
Leave the tedium of audits and of finding correct
For the gaiety of places where people collect
For the paper rosettes of the stadium and the plaudits.
And you, let you paint your face and sleek your leg with silk
Which is your right to do
As gay trams run on rails and cows give milk.
Sharp sun-strop, surface-gloss, and momentary caprice
These are what we cherish
Caring not if the bridges and the embankments
Of past and future perish and cease;

Before the leaves grow heavy and the good days vanish
Hold out your glasses which our April must replenish.

April, 1934

Morning sun

Shuttles of trains going north, going south, drawing threads of blue,
The shining of the lines of trams like swords,
Thousands of posters asserting a monopoly of the good, the beautiful,
  the true,
Crowds of people all in the vocative, you and you,
The haze of the morning shot with words.

Yellow sun comes white off the wet streets but bright
Chromium yellows in the gay sun's light,
Filleted sun streaks the purple mist,
Everything is kissed and reticulated with sun
Scooped-up and cupped in the open fronts of shops
And bouncing on the traffic which never stops.

And the street fountain blown across the square
Rainbow-trellises the air and sunlight blazons
The red butcher's and scrolls of fish on marble slabs,
Whistled bars of music crossing silver sprays
And horns of cars, touché, touché, rapiers' retort, a moving cage,
A turning page of shine and sound, the day's maze.

But when the sun goes out, the streets go cold, the hanging meat
And tiers of fish are colourless and merely dead,
And the hoots of cars neurotically repeat and the tiptoed feet
Of women hurry and falter whose faces are dead;
And I see in the air but not belonging there
The blown grey powder of the fountain grey as the ash
That forming on a cigarette covers the red.

March, 1935

Cuckoo

Cuckoo across the poppies
    Making myth—
Simeon on his pillar
    Stands in the air alone

26

Without context
  Not looking down,
Personification
  Of distance.

Nothing to be seen
  But a stone posture,
The shape of the song
  Of the cuckoo.
                    June, 1935

Train to Dublin

Our half-thought thoughts divide in sifted wisps
Against the basic facts repatterned without pause,
I can no more gather my mind up in my fist
Than the shadow of the smoke of this train upon the grass—
This is the way that animals' lives pass.

The train's rhythm never relents, the telephone posts
Go striding backwards like the legs of time to where
In a Georgian house you turn at the carpet's edge
Turning a sentence while, outside my window here,
The smoke makes broken queries in the air.

The train keeps moving and the rain holds off,
I count the buttons on the seat, I hear a shell
Held hollow to the ear, the mere
Reiteration of integers, the bell
That tolls and tolls, the monotony of fear.

At times we are doctrinaire, at times we are frivolous,
Plastering over the cracks, a gesture making good,
But the strength of us does not come out of us.
It is we, I think, are the idols and it is God
Has set us up as men who are painted wood,

And the trains carry us about. But not consistently so,
For during a tiny portion of our lives we are not in trains,
The idol living for a moment, not muscle-bound
But walking freely through the slanting rain,
Its ankles wet, its grimace relaxed again.

All over the world people are toasting the King,
Red lozenges of light as each one lifts his glass,
But I will not give you any idol or idea, creed or king,
I give you the incidental things which pass
Outward through space exactly as each was.

I give you the disproportion between labour spent
And joy at random; the laughter of the Galway sea
Juggling with spars and bones irresponsibly,
I give you the toy Liffey and the vast gulls,
I give you fuschia hedges and whitewashed walls.

I give you the smell of Norman stone, the squelch
Of bog beneath your boots, the red bog-grass,
The vivid chequer of the Antrim hills, the trough of dark
Golden water for the cart-horses, the brass
Belt of serene sun upon the lough.

And I give you the faces, not the permanent masks,
But the faces balanced in the toppling wave—
His glint of joy in cunning as the farmer asks
Twenty per cent too much, or a girl's, forgetting to be suave,
A tiro choosing stuffs, preferring mauve.

And I give you the sea and yet again the sea's
Tumultuous marble,
With Thor's thunder or taking his ease akimbo,
Lumbering torso, but finger-tips a marvel
Of surgeon's accuracy.

I would like to give you more but I cannot hold
This stuff within my hands and the train goes on;
I know that there are further syntheses to which,
As you have perhaps, people at last attain
And find that they are rich and breathing gold.

September–October, 1934

Intimations of mortality

The shadows of the banisters march march,
The lovers linger under the arch,
On the beach the waves creep,
The little boy cannot go to sleep.

He is afraid of God and the Devil—
If he shuts his eyes they will draw level,
So he watches the half-open door and waits
For people on the stairs carrying lights.

Someone comes, carrying a lamp,
The shadows of the banisters march march,
All is above board, order is restored,
Time on horseback under a Roman arch.

Then the final darkness for eight hours
The murderous grin of toothy flowers,
The tick of his pulse in the pillow, the sick
Vertigo of falling in a fanged pit.

After one perfunctory kiss
His parents snore in conjugal bliss.
The night watchman with crossed thumbs
Grows an idol. The Kingdom comes. . . .

July, 1935

Wolves

I do not want to be reflective any more
Envying and despising unreflective things
Finding pathos in dogs and undeveloped handwriting
And young girls doing their hair and all the castles of sand
Flushed by the children's bedtime, level with the shore.

The tide comes in and goes out again, I do not want
To be always stressing either its flux or its permanence,
I do not want to be a tragic or philosophic chorus
But to keep my eye only on the nearer future
And after that let the sea flow over us.

Come then all of you, come closer, form a circle,
Join hands and make believe that joined
Hands will keep away the wolves of water
Who howl along our coast. And be it assumed
That no one hears them among the talk and laughter.

October, 1934

Aubade

Having bitten on life like a sharp apple
Or, playing it like a fish, been happy,

Having felt with fingers that the sky is blue,
What have we after that to look forward to?

Not the twilight of the gods but a precise dawn
Of sallow and grey bricks, and newsboys crying war.

November, 1934

Snow

The room was suddenly rich and the great bay-window was
Spawning snow and pink roses against it
Soundlessly collateral and incompatible:
World is suddener than we fancy it.

World is crazier and more of it than we think,
Incorrigibly plural. I peel and portion
A tangerine and spit the pips and feel
The drunkenness of things being various.

And the fire flames with a bubbling sound for world
Is more spiteful and gay than one supposes—
On the tongue on the eyes on the ears in the palms of one's hands—
There is more than glass between the snow and the huge roses.

January, 1935

III

1933—1937

An eclogue for Christmas

A. I meet you in an evil time.
B.   The evil bells
   Put out of our heads, I think, the thought of everything else.
A. The jaded calendar revolves,
   Its nuts need oil, carbon chokes the valves,
   The excess sugar of a diabetic culture
   Rotting the nerve of life and literature;
   Therefore when we bring out the old tinsel and frills
   To announce that Christ is born among the barbarous hills
   I turn to you whom a morose routine
   Saves from the mad vertigo of being what has been.
B. Analogue of me, you are wrong to turn to me,
   My country will not yield you any sanctuary,
   There is no pinpoint in any of the ordnance maps
   To save you when your towns and town-bred thoughts
      collapse,
   It is better to die *in situ* as I shall,
   One place is as bad as another. Go back where your instincts call
   And listen to the crying of the town-cats and the taxis again,
   Or wind your gramophone and eavesdrop on great men.
A. Jazz-weary of years of drums and Hawaiian guitar,
   Pivoting on the parquet I seem to have moved far
   From bombs and mud and gas, have stuttered on my feet
   Clinched to the streamlined and butter-smooth trulls of the
      élite,
   The lights irritating and gyrating and rotating in gauze—
   Pomade-dazzle, a slick beauty of gewgaws—
   I who was Harlequin in the childhood of the century,
   Posed by Picasso beside an endless opaque sea,
   Have seen myself sifted and splintered in broken facets,
   Tentative pencillings, endless liabilities, no assets,
   Abstractions scalpelled with a palette-knife
   Without reference to this particular life.
   And so it has gone on; I have not been allowed to be
   Myself in flesh or face, but abstracting and dissecting me
   They have made of me pure form, a symbol or a pastiche,
   Stylised profile, anything but soul and flesh:
   And that is why I turn this jaded music on
   To forswear thought and become an automaton.
B. There are in the country also of whom I am afraid—
   Men who put beer into a belly that is dead,

Women in the forties with terrier and setter who whistle and
swank
Over down and plough and Roman road and daisied bank,
Half-conscious that these barriers over which they stride
Are nothing to the barbed wire that has grown round their
pride.

A. And two there are, as I drive in the city, who suddenly per-
turb—
The one sirening me to draw up by the kerb
The other, as I lean back, my right leg stretched creating speed,
Making me catch and stamp, the brakes shrieking, pull up dead:
She wears silk stockings taunting the winter wind,
He carries a white stick to mark that he is blind.

B. In the country they are still hunting, in the heavy shires
Greyness is on the fields and sunset like a line of pyres
Of barbarous heroes smoulders through the ancient air
Hazed with factory dust and, orange opposite, the moon's glare,
Goggling yokel-stubborn through the iron trees,
Jeers at the end of us, our bland ancestral ease;
We shall go down like palaeolithic man
Before some new Ice Age or Genghiz Khan.

A. It is time for some new coinage, people have got so old,
Hacked and handled and shiny from pocketing they have made
bold
To think that each is himself through these accidents, being
blind
To the fact that they are merely the counters of an unknown
Mind.

B. A Mind that does not think, if such a thing can be,
Mechanical Reason, capricious Identity.
That I could be able to face this domination nor flinch—

A. The tin toys of the hawker move on the pavement inch by
inch
Not knowing that they are wound up; it is better to be so
Than to be, like us, wound up and while running down to
know—

B. But everywhere the pretence of individuality recurs—
A. Old faces frosted with powder and choked in furs.
B. The jutlipped farmer gazing over the humpbacked wall.
A. The commercial traveller joking in the urinal.
B. I think things draw to an end, the soil is stale.
A. And over-elaboration will nothing now avail,
The street is up again, gas, electricity or drains,
Ever-changing conveniences, nothing comfortable remains
Un-improved, as flagging Rome improved villa and sewer

(A sound-proof library and a stable temperature).
Our street is up, red lights sullenly mark
The long trench of pipes, iron guts in the dark,
And not till the Goths again come swarming down the hill
Will cease the clangour of the pneumatic drill.
But yet there is beauty narcotic and deciduous
In this vast organism grown out of us:
On all the traffic-islands stand white globes like moons,
The city's haze is clouded amber that purrs and croons,
And tilting by the noble curve bus after tall bus comes
With an osculation of yellow light, with a glory like chrysan-
      themums.

B. The country gentry cannot change, they will die in their shoes
From angry circumstance and moral self-abuse,
Dying with a paltry fizzle they will prove their lives to be
An ever-diluted drug, a spiritual tautology.
They cannot live once their idols are turned out,
None of them can endure, for how could they, possibly,
      without
The flotsam of private property, pekinese and polyanthus,
The good things which in the end turn to poison and pus,
Without the bandy chairs and the sugar in the silver tongs
And the inter-ripple and resonance of years of dinner-gongs?
Or if they could find no more that cumulative proof
In the rain dripping off the conservatory roof?
What will happen when the only sanction the country-
      dweller has—

A. What will happen to us, planked and panelled with jazz?
Who go to the theatre where a black man dances like an eel,
Where pink thighs flash like the spokes of a wheel, where we
      feel
That we know in advance all the jogtrot and the cake-walk
      jokes,
All the bumfun and the gags of the comedians in boaters and
      toques,
All the tricks of the virtuosos who invert the usual—

B. What will happen to us when the State takes down the manor
      wall,
When there is no more private shooting or fishing, when the
      trees are all cut down,
When faces are all dials and cannot smile or frown—

A. What will happen when the sniggering machine-guns in the
      hands of the young men
Are trained on every flat and club and beauty parlour and
      Father's den?

35

What will happen when our civilisation like a long-pent
    balloon—

B. What will happen will happen; the whore and the buffoon
    Will come off best; no dreamers, they cannot lose their dream
    And are at least likely to be reinstated in the new régime.
    But one thing is not likely—

A.   Do not gloat over yourself,
    Do not be your own vulture; high on some mountain shelf
    Huddle the pitiless abstractions bald about the neck
    Who will descend when you crumple in the plains a wreck.
    Over the randy of the theatre and cinema I hear songs
    Unlike anything—

B.   The lady of the house poises the silver tongs
    And picks a lump of sugar, 'ne plus ultra' she says
    'I cannot do otherwise, even to prolong my days'—

A. I cannot do otherwise either, to-night I will book my seat—

B. I will walk about the farm-yard which is replete
    As with the smell of dung so with memories—

A. I will gorge myself to satiety with the oddities
    Of every artiste, official or amateur,
    Who has pleased me in my rôle of hero-worshipper
    Who has pleased me in my rôle of individual man—

B. Let us lie once more, say 'What we think, we can'
    The old idealist lie—

A.   And for me before I die
    Let me go the round of the garish glare—

B.   And on the bare and high
    Places of England, the Wiltshire Downs and the Long Mynd
    Let the balls of my feet bounce on the turf, my face burn in the
        wind
    My eyelashes stinging in the wind, and the sheep like grey
        stones
    Humble my human pretensions—

A.   Let the saxophones and the xylophones
    And the cult of every technical excellence, the miles of canvas
        in the galleries
    And the canvas of the rich man's yacht snapping and tacking
        on the seas
    And the perfection of a grilled steak—

B.   Let all these so ephemeral things
    Be somehow permanent like the swallow's tangent wings:
    Goodbye to you, this day remember is Christmas, this morn
    They say, interpret it your own way, Christ is born.

December, 1933

Eclogue by a five-barred gate

(Death and two Shepherds)

D. There is no way here, shepherds, read the wooden sign,
Your road is a blind road, all this land is mine.
1. But your fields, mister, would do well for our sheep.
2. They could shelter from the sun where the low hills dip.
D. I have sheep of my own, see them over there.
1. There seems no nater in 'em, they look half dead.
2. They be no South Downs, they look so thin and bare.
D. More than half, shepherds, they are more than half dead.
But where are your own flocks you have been so talking of?
1. Right here at our elbow—
2.   Or they *was* so just now.
D. That's right, shepherd, they was so just now.
Your sheep are gone, they can't speak for you,
I must have your credentials, sing me who you are.
1. I am a shepherd of the Theocritean breed,
Been pasturing my songs, man and boy, this thirty year—
2. And for me too my pedigree acceptances
Have multiplied beside the approved streams.
D. This won't do, shepherds, life is not like that,
And when it comes to death I may say he is not like that.
Have you never thought of Death?
1.   Only off and on,
Thanatos in Greek, the accent proparoxytone—
2. That's not what he means, he means the thing behind the word
Same as took Alice White the time her had her third—
D. Cut out for once the dialect and the pedantry,
I thought a shepherd was a poet—
1.   On his flute—
2.   On his oat—
D. I thought he was a poet and could quote the prices
Of significant living and decent dying, could lay the rails level
    on the sleepers
To carry the powerful train of abstruse thought—
1. What an idea!
2.   But certainly poets are sleepers,
The sleeping beauty behind the many-coloured hedge—
D. All you do is burke the other and terrible beauty, all you do is
    hedge

And shirk the inevitable issue, all you do
Is shear your sheep to stop your ears.
Poetry you think is only the surface vanity,
The painted nails, the hips narrowed by fashion,
The hooks and eyes of words; but it is not that only,
And it is not only the curer sitting by the wayside,
Phials on his trestle, his palms grown thin as wafers
With blessing the anonymous heads;
And poetry is not only the bridging of two-banked rivers.

2. Who ever heard of a river without a further bank?
D. You two never heard of it.
Tell me now, I have heard the cuckoo, there is tar on your shoes,
I surmise that spring is here—

2.   Spring be here truly,
On Bank Holiday I wore canvas shoes,
Could feel the earth—

D.   And that being so, tell me
Don't you ever feel old?

2.   There's a question now.

1. It is a question we all have to answer,
And I may say that when I smell the beans or hear the thrush
I feel a wave intensely bitter-sweet and topped with silver—

D. There you go again, your self-congratulation
Blunts all edges, insulates with wool,
No spark of reality possible.
Can't you peel off for even a moment that conscious face?
All time is not your tear-off jotter, you cannot afford to
    scribble
So many so false answers.
This escapism of yours is blasphemy,
An immortal cannot blaspheme for one way or another
His trivialities will pattern in the end;
But for you your privilege and panic is to be mortal
And with Here and Now for your anvil
You must strike while the iron is hot—

2.   He is an old man,
That is why he talks so.

D.   Can't you understand me?
Look, I will set you a prize like any of your favourites,
Like any Tityrus or tired Damon;
Sing me, each in turn, what dream you had last night
And if either's dream rings true, to him I will open my gate.

2. Ho, here's talking.

1.   Let me collect myself.

D. Collect yourself in time for if you win my prize—

2. I'm going to sing first, I had a rare dream.
1. Your dream is nothing—
D.   The more nothing the better.
1. My dream will word well—
2.   But not wear well—
D. No dreams wear at all as dreams.
   Water appears tower only while in well—
   All from the same comes, the same drums sound
   In the pulsation of all the bulging suns,
   And no clock whatever, while winding or running down,
   Makes any difference to time however the long-legged weights
   Straggle down the cottage wall or the child grows leggy too—
1. I do not like your talking.
2.   It give giddiness
   Like the thrumming of the telephone wires in an east wind
   With the bellyache and headache and nausea.
D. It is not my nature to talk, so sing your pieces
   And I will try, what is repugnant too, to listen.
1. Last night as the bearded lips of sleep
   Closed with the slightest sigh on me and I sank through the
       blue soft caves
   Picked with light delicate as the chink of coins
   Or stream on the pebbles I was caught by hands
   And a face was swung in my eyes like a lantern
   Swinging on the neck of a snake.
   And that face I knew to be God and I woke,
   And now I come to look at yours, stranger,
   There is something in the lines of it—
D.   Your dream, shepherd,
   Is good enough of its kind. Now let us hear yours.
2. Well, I dreamt it was a hot day, the territorials
   Were out on melting asphalt under the howitzers,
   The brass music bounced on the houses. Come
   I heard cry as it were a water-nymph, come and fulfil me
   And I sped floating, my feet plashing in the tops of the wheat
   But my eyes were blind,
   I found her with my hands lying on the drying hay,
   Wet heat in the deeps of the hay as my hand delved,
   And I possessed her, gross and good like the hay,
   And she went and my eyes regained sight and the sky was full
       of ladders
   Angels ascending and descending with a shine like mackerel—
   Now I come to tell it it sounds nonsense.
D. Thank you, gentlemen, these two dreams are good,
   Better than your daytime madrigals.

If you really wish I will give you both the prize,
But take another look at my land before you choose it.
1. It looks colder now.
2.   The sheep have not moved.
1. I have a fancy there is no loving there
Even among sheep.
D.   They do not breed or couple.
1 & 2. And what about us, shall we enjoy it there?
D. *Enjoy what where?*
2.   Why, life in your land.
D. I will open this gate that you may see for yourselves.
1. You go first.
2.   Well, you come too.
1 & 2. We will go together to these pastures new . . .
D. So; they are gone; life in my land . . .
There is no life as there is no land.
They are gone and I am alone
With a gate the façade of a mirage.

                                                    May, 1934

Eclogue from Iceland

*Scene: The Arnarvatn Heath. Craven, Ryan and the ghost of
Grettir. Voice from Europe.*

R. This is the place, Craven, the end of our way;
Hobble the horses, we have had a long day.
C. The night is closing like a fist
And the long glacier lost in mist.
R. Few folk come this time of year.
What are those limping steps I hear?
C. Look, there he is coming now.
We shall have some company anyhow.
R. It must be the mist—he looks so big;
He is walking lame in the left leg.
G. Good evening, strangers. So you too
Are on the run? I welcome you.
I am Grettir Asmundson,

40

Dead many years. My day is done.
But you whose day is sputtering yet—
I forget. . . . What did I say?
We forget when we are dead
The blue and red, the grey and gay.
Your day spits with a damp wick,
Will fizzle out if you're not quick.
Men have been chilled to death who kissed
Wives of mist, forgetting their own
Kind who live out of the wind.
My memory goes, goes—Tell me
Are there men now whose compass leads
Them always down forbidden roads?
Greedy young men who take their pick
Of what they want but have no luck;
Who leap the toothed and dour crevasse
Of death on a sardonic phrase?
You with crowsfeet round your eyes
How are things where you come from?

c. Things are bad. There is no room
To move at ease, to stretch or breed—

G. And you with the burglar's underlip
In your land do things stand well?

R. In my land nothing stands at all
But some fly high and some lie low.

G. Too many people. My memory will go,
Lose itself in the hordes of modern people.
Memory is words; we remember what others
Say and record of ourselves—stones with the runes.
Too many people—sandstorm over the words.
Is your land also an island?
There is only hope for people who live upon islands
Where the Lowest Common labels will not stick
And the unpolluted hills will hold your echo.

R. I come from an island, Ireland, a nation
Built upon violence and morose vendettas.
My diehard countrymen like drayhorses
Drag their ruin behind them.
Shooting straight in the cause of crooked thinking
Their greed is sugared with pretence of public spirit.
From all which I am an exile.

c. Yes, we are exiles,
Gad the world for comfort.
This Easter I was in Spain before the Civil War
Gobbling the tripper's treats, the local colour,

Storks over Avila, the coffee-coloured waters of Ronda,
The comedy of the bootblacks in the cafés,
The legless beggars in the corridors of the trains,
Dominoes on marble tables, the architecture
Moorish mudejar churriguerresque,
The bullfight—the banderillas like Christmas candles,
And the scrawled hammer and sickle:
It was all copy—impenetrable surface.
I did not look for the sneer beneath the surface
Why should I trouble, an addict to oblivion
Running away from the gods of my own hearth
With no intention of finding gods elsewhere?

R. And so we came to Iceland—
C. Our latest joyride.
G. And what have you found in Iceland?
C. What have we found? More copy, more surface,
Vignettes as they call them, dead flowers in an album—
The harmoniums in the farms, the fine-bread and pancakes,
The pot of ivy trained across the window,
Children in gumboots, girls in black berets.
R. And dead craters and angled crags.
G. The crags which saw me jockey doom for twenty
Years from one cold hide-out to another;
The last of the saga heroes
Who had not the wisdom of Njal or the beauty of Gunnar
I was the doomed tough, disaster kept me witty;
Being born the surly jack, the ne'er-do-well, the loiterer
Hard blows exalted me.
When the man of will and muscle achieves the curule chair
He turns to a bully; better is his lot as outlaw
A wad of dried fish in his belt, a snatch of bilberries
And riding the sullen landscape far from friends
Through the jungle of lava, dales of frozen fancy,
Fording the gletcher, ducking the hard hail,
And across the easy pastures, never stopping
To rest among the celandines and bogcotton.
Under a curse I would see eyes in the night,
Always had to move on; craving company
In the end I lived on an island with two others.
To fetch fire I swam the crinkled fjord,
The crags were alive with ravens whose low croak
Told my ears what filtered in my veins—
The sense of doom. I wore it gracefully,
The fatal clarity that would not budge
But without false pride in martyrdom. For I,

Joker and dressy, held no mystic's pose,
Not wishing to die preferred the daily goods
The horse-fight, women's thighs, a joint of meat.

c. But this dyspeptic age of ingrown cynics
Wakes in the morning with a coated tongue
And whets itself laboriously to labour
And wears a blasé face in the face of death.
Who risk their lives neither to fill their bellies
Nor to avenge an affront nor grab a prize
But out of bravado or to divert ennui
Driving fast cars and climbing foreign mountains.
Outside the delicatessen shop the hero
With his ribbons and his empty pinned-up sleeve
Cadges for money while with turned-up collars
His comrades blow through brass the Londonderry Air
And silken legs and swinging buttocks advertise
The sale of little cardboard flags on pins.

g. Us too they sold
The women and the men with many sheep.
Graft and aggression, legal prevarication
Drove out the best of us,
Secured long life to only the sly and the dumb
To those who would not say what they really thought
But got their ends through pretended indifference
And through the sweat and blood of thralls and hacks
Cheating the poor men of their share of drift
The whale on Kaldbak in the starving winter.

r. And so to-day at Grimsby men whose lives
Are warped in Arctic trawlers load and unload
The shining tons of fish to keep the lords
Of the market happy with cigars and cars.

c. What is that music in the air—
Organ-music coming from far?

r. Honeyed music—it sounds to me
Like the Wurlitzer in the Gaiety.

g. I do not hear anything at all.

c. Imagine the purple light on the stage.

r. The melting moment of a stinted age

c. The pause before the film again
Bursts in a shower of golden rain.

g. I do not hear anything at all.

c. We shall be back there soon, to stand in queues
For entertainment and to work at desks,
To browse round counters of dead books, to pore
On picture catalogues and Soho menus,

To preen ourselves on the reinterpretation
Of the words of obsolete interpreters,
Collate delete their faded lives like texts,
Admire Flaubert, Cézanne—the tortured artists—
And leaning forward to knock out our pipes
Into the fire protest that art is good
And gives a meaning and a slant to life.

G. The dark is falling. Soon the air
Will stare with eyes, the stubborn ghost
Who cursed me when I threw him. Must
The ban go on for ever? I,
A ghost myself, have no claim now to die.

R. Now I hear the music again—
Strauss and roses—hear it plain.
The sweet confetti of music falls
From the high Corinthian capitals.

C. Her head upon his shoulder lies. . . .
Blend to the marrow as the music dies.

G. Brought up to the rough-house we took offence quickly
Were sticklers for pride, paid for it as outlaws—

C. Like Cavalcanti whose hot blood lost him Florence

R. Or the Wild Geese of Ireland in Mid-Europe.
Let us thank God for valour in abstraction
For those who go their own way, will not kiss
The arse of law and order nor compound
For physical comfort at the price of pride:
Soldiers of fortune, renegade artists, rebels and sharpers
Whose speech not cramped to Yea and Nay explodes
In crimson oaths like peonies, who brag
Because they prefer to taunt the mask of God,
Bid him unmask and die in the living lightning.
What is that voice maundering, meandering?

VOICE. Blues . . . blues . . . high heels and manicured hands
Always self-conscious of the vanity bag
And puritan painted lips that abnegate desire
And say 'we do not care' . . . 'we do not care'—
I don't care always in the air
Give my hips a shake always on thē make
Always on the mend coming around the bend
Always on the dance with an eye to the main
Chance, always taking the floor again—

C. There was Tchekov,
His haemorrhages drove him out of Moscow
The life he loved, not born to it, who thought
That when the windows blurred with smoke and talk

44

So that no-one could see out, then conversely
The giants of frost and satans of the peasant
Could not look in, impose the evil eye.

R. There was MacKenna
Spent twenty years translating Greek philosophy
Ill and tormented, unwilling to break contract,
A brilliant talker who left
The salon for the solo flight of Mind.

G. There was Onund Treefoot
Came late and lame to Iceland, made his way
Even though the land was bad and the neighbours jealous.

C. There was that dancer
Who danced the War, then falling into coma
Went with hunched shoulders through the ivory gate.

R. There was Connolly
Vilified now by the gangs of Catholic Action.

G. There was Egil
Hero and miser who when dying blind
Would have thrown his money among the crowd to hear
The whole world scuffle for his hoarded gold.

C. And there were many
Whose commonsense or sense of humour or mere
Desire for self-assertion won them through

R. But not to happiness. Though at intervals
They paused in sunlight for a moment's fusion
With friends or nature till the cynical wind
Blew the trees pale—

VOICE.   Blues, blues, sit back, relax
Let your self-pity swell with the music and clutch
Your tiny lavendered fetishes. Who cares
If floods depopulate China? I don't care
Always in the air sitting among the stars
Among the electric signs among the imported wines
Always on the spree climbing the forbidden tree
Tossing the peel of the apple over my shoulder
To see it form the initials of a new intrigue

G. Runes and runes which no one could decode

R. Wrong numbers on the 'phone—she never answered.

C. And from the romantic grille (Spanish baroque)
Only the eyes looked out which I see now.

G. You see them now?

C.   But seen before as well.

G. And many times to come, be sure of that.

R. I know them too
These eyes which hang in the northern mist, the brute

45

Stare of stupidity and hate, the most
Primitive and false of oracles.

C.   The eyes
That glide like snakes behind a thousand masks—
All human faces fit them, here or here:
Dictator, bullying schoolboy or common lout,
Acquisitive women, financiers, invalids,
Are capable all of that compelling stare
Stare which betrays the cosmic purposelessness
The nightmare noise of the scythe upon the hone,
Time sharpening his blade among high rocks alone.

R. The face that fate hangs as a figurehead
Above the truncheon or the nickelled death.

G. I won the fall. Though cursed for it, I won.

C. Which is why we honour you who working from
The common premisses did not end with many
In the blind alley where the trek began.

G. Though the open road is hard with frost and dark.

VOICE. Hot towels for the men, mud packs for the women
Will smooth the puckered minutes of your lives.
I offer you each a private window, a view
(The leper window reveals a church of lepers).

R. Do you believe him?

C. I don't know.
Do you believe him?

G. No.
You cannot argue with the eyes or voice;
Argument will frustrate you till you die
But go your own way, give the voice the lie,
Outstare the inhuman eyes. That is the way.
Go back to where you came from and do not keep
Crossing the road to escape them, do not avoid the ambush,
Take sly detours, but ride the pass direct.

C. But the points of axes shine from the scrub, the odds
Are dead against us. There are the lures of women
Who, half alive, invite to a fuller life
And never loving would be loved by others.

R. Who fortify themselves in pasteboard castles
And plant their beds with the cast-out toys of children,
Dead pines with tinsel fruits, nursery beliefs
And South Sea Island trinkets. Watch their years
The permutations of lapels and gussets,
Of stuffs—georgette or velvet or corduroy—
Of hats and eye-veils, of shoes, lizard or suède,
Of bracelets, milk or coral, of zip bags

46

Of compacts, lipstick, eyeshade and coiffures
All tributary to the wished ensemble,
The carriage of body that belies the soul.

C. And there are the men who appear to be men of sense,
Good company and dependable in a crisis,
Who yet are ready to plug you as you drink
Like dogs who bite from fear; for fear of germs
Putting on stamps by licking the second finger,
For fear of opinion overtipping in bars,
For fear of thought studying stupefaction.
It is the world which these have made where dead
Greek words sprout out in tin on sallow walls—
Clinic or polytechnic—a world of slums
Where any day now may see the Gadarene swine
Rush down the gullets of the London tubes
When the enemy, x or y, let loose their gas.

G. My friends, hounded like me, I tell you still
Go back to where you belong. I could have fled
To the Hebrides or Orkney, been rich and famous,
Preferred to assert my rights in my own country,
Mine which were hers for every country stands
By the sanctity of the individual will.

R. Yes, he is right.

C.   But we have not his strength

R. Could only abase ourselves before the wall
Of shouting flesh

C.   Could only offer our humble
Deaths to the unknown god, unknown but worshipped,
Whose voice calls in the sirens of destroyers.

G. Minute your gesture but it must be made—
Your hazard, your act of defiance and hymn of hate,
Hatred of hatred, assertion of human values,
Which is now your only duty.

C. Is it our only duty?

G.   Yes, my friends.
What did you say? The night falls now and I
Must beat the dales to chase my remembered acts.
Yes, my friends, it is your only duty.
And, it may be added, it is your only chance.

                                        1936

Eclogue between the motherless

A. What did you do for the holiday?
B.   I went home.
   What did you do?
A.   O, I went home for the holiday.
   Had a good time?
B.   Not bad as far as it went.
   What about you?
A.   O quite a good time on the whole—
(both) Quite a good time on the whole at home for the holiday
A. As far as it went—In a way it went too far,
   Back to childhood, back to the backwoods mind;
   I could not stand a great deal of it, bars on the brain
   And the blinds drawn in the drawing-room not to fade the
       chair covers
B. There were no blinds drawn in ours; my father has married
       again—
   A girl of thirty who had never had any lovers
   And wants to have everything bright
A.   That sounds worse than us.
   Our old house is just a grass-grown tumulus
   My father sits by himself with the bossed decanter,
   The garden is going to rack, the gardener
   Only comes three days, most of our money was in linen
B. My new stepmother is wealthy, you should see her in jodhpurs
   Brisking in to breakfast from a morning canter.
   I don't think he can be happy
A.   How can you tell?
   That generation is so different
B.   I suppose your sister
   Still keeps house for yours?
A.   Yes and she finds it hell.
   Nothing to do in the evenings.
B.   Talking of the evenings
   I can drop the ash on the carpet since my divorce.
   Never you marry, my boy. One marries only
   Because one thinks one is lonely—and so one was
   But wait till the lonely are two and no better
A.   As a matter
   Of fact I've got to tell you
B.   The first half year
   Is heaven come back from the nursery—swansdown kisses—
   But after that one misses something

48

A.   My dear,
    Don't depress me in advance; I've got to tell you—
B. My wife was warmth, a picture and a dance,
    Her body electric—silk used to crackle and her gloves
    Move where she left them. How one loves the surface
    But how one lacks the core—Children of course
    Might make a difference
A.   Personally I find
    I cannot go on any more like I was. Which is why
    I took this step in the dark
B.   What step?
A.   I thought
    I too might try what you
B.   Don't say that you
    And after all this time
A.   Let's start from the start.
    When I went home this time there was nothing to do
    And so I got haunted. Like a ball of wool
    That kittens have got at, all my growing up
    All the disposed-of process of my past
    Unravelled on the floor—One can't proceed any more
    Except on a static past; when the ice-floe breaks
    What's the good of walking? Talking of ice
    I remembered my mother standing against the sky
    And saying 'Go back in the house and change your shoes'
    And I kept having dreams and kept going back in the house.
    A sense of guilt like a scent—The day I was born
    I suppose that that same hour was full of her screams
B. You're run down
A.   Wait till you hear what I've done.
    It was not only dreams; even the crockery (odd
    It's not all broken by now) and the rustic seat in the rockery
    With the bark flaked off, all kept reminding me, binding
    My feet to the floating past. In the night at the lodge
    A dog was barking as when I was little in the night
    And I could not budge in the bed clothes. Lying alone
    I felt my legs were paralysed into roots
    And the same cracks in what used to be the nursery ceiling
    Gave me again the feeling I was young among ikons,
    Helpless at the feet of faceless family idols,
    Walking the tightrope over the tiger-pit,
    Running the gauntlet of inherited fears;
    So after all these years I turned in the bed
    And grasped the want of a wife and heard in the rain
    On the gravel path the steps of all my mistresses

And wondered which was coming or was she dead
And her shoes given to the char which tapped through London—
The black streets mirrored with rain and stained with lights.
I dreamed she came while a train
Was running behind the trees (with power progressing),
Undressing deftly she slipped cool knees beside me,
The clipped hair on her neck prickled my tongue
And the whole room swung like a ship till I woke with the
    window
Jittering in its frame from the train passing the garden
Carrying its load of souls to a different distance.
And of others, isolated by associations,
I thought—the scent of syringa or always wearing
A hat of fine white straw and never known in winter—
Splinters of memory. When I was little I sorted
Bits of lustre and glass from the heap behind the hen-house;
They are all distorted now the beautiful sirens
Mutilated and mute in dream's dissection,
Hanged from pegs in the Bluebeard's closet of the brain,
Never again nonchalantly to open
The doors of disillusion. Whom recording
The night marked time, the dog at the lodge kept barking
And as he barked the big cave opened of hell
Where all their voices were one and stuck at a point
Like a gramophone needle stuck on a notched record.
I thought 'Can I find a love beyond the family
And feed her to the bed my mother died in
Between the tallboys and the vase of honesty
On which I was born and groped my way from the cave
With a half-eaten fruit in my hand, a passport meaning
Enforced return for periods to that country?
Or will one's wife also belong to that country
And can one never find the perfect stranger?'
B. My complaint was that she stayed a stranger.
I remember her mostly in the car, stopping by the white
Moons of the petrol pumps, in a camelhair rug
Comfortable, scented and alien.

A.   That's what I want,
Someone immutably alien—
Send me a woman with haunches out of the jungle
And frost patterns for fancies,
The hard light of sun upon water in diamonds dancing
And the brute swagger of the sea; let her love be the drop
From the cliff of my dream, be the axe on the block
Be finesse of the ice on the panes of the heart

Be careless, be callous, be glass frolic of prisms
Be eyes of guns through lashes of barbed wire,
Be the gaoler's smile and all that breaks the past.
B. Odd ideals you have; all I wanted
Was to get really close but closeness was
Only a glove on the hand, alien and veinless,
And yet her empty gloves could move
A.   My next move
Is what I've got to tell you, I picked on the only
One who would suit and wrote proposing marriage
B. Who is she?
A.   But she can't have yet received it;
She is in India.
B.   India be damned.
What is her name?
A.   I said I cannot offer
Anything you will want
B.   Why?
A.   and I said
I know in two years' time it will make no difference.
I was hardly able to write it at the claw-foot table
Where my mother kept her diary. There I sat
Concocting a gambler's medicine; the afternoon was cool,
The ducks drew lines of white on the dull slate of the pool
And I sat writing to someone I hardly knew
And someone I shall never know well. Relying on that
I stuck up the envelope, walked down the winding drive,
All that was wanted a figurehead, passed by the lodge
Where the dog is chained and the gates, relying on my mood
To get it posted
B.   Who is the woman?
A.   relying
B. Who is the woman?
A.   She is dying
B.   Dying of what?
A. Only a year to live
B.   Forgive me asking
But
A.   Only a year and ten yards down the road
I made my goal where it has always stood
Waiting for the last
B.   You must be out of your mind;
If it were anyone else I should not mind
A. Waiting for the last collection before dark
The pillarbox like an exclamation mark.

Valediction

Their verdure dare not show ... their verdure dare not show ...
Cant and randy—the seals' heads bobbing in the tide-flow
Between the islands, sleek and black and irrelevant
They cannot depose logically what they want:
Died by gunshot under borrowed pennons,
Sniped from the wet gorse and taken by the limp fins
And slung like a dead seal in a boghole, beaten up
By peasants with long lips and the whisky-drinker's cough.
Park your car in the city of Dublin, see Sackville Street
Without the sandbags in the old photos, meet
The statues of the patriots, history never dies,
At any rate in Ireland, arson and murder are legacies
Like old rings hollow-eyed without their stones
Dumb talismans.
See Belfast, devout and profane and hard,
Built on reclaimed mud, hammers playing in the shipyard,
Time punched with holes like a steel sheet, time
Hardening the faces, veneering with a grey and speckled rime
The faces under the shawls and caps:
This was my mother-city, these my paps.
Country of callous lava cooled to stone,
Of minute sodden haycocks, of ship-sirens' moan,
Of falling intonations—I would call you to book
I would say to you, Look;
I would say, This is what you have given me
Indifference and sentimentality
A metallic giggle, a fumbling hand,
A heart that leaps to a fife band:
Set these against your water-shafted air
Of amethyst and moonstone, the horses' feet like bells of hair
Shambling beneath the orange cart, the beer-brown spring
Guzzling between the heather, the green gush of Irish spring.
Cursèd be he that curses his mother. I cannot be
Anyone else than what this land engendered me:
In the back of my mind are snips of white, the sails
Of the Lough's fishing-boats, the bellropes lash their tails
When I would peal my thoughts, the bells pull free—
Memory in apostasy.
I would tot up my factors
But who can stand in the way of his soul's steam-tractors?
I can say Ireland is hooey, Ireland is
A gallery of fake tapestries,

But I cannot deny my past to which my self is wed,
The woven figure cannot undo its thread.
On a cardboard lid I saw when I was four
Was the trade-mark of a hound and a round tower,
And that was Irish glamour, and in the cemetery
Sham Celtic crosses claimed our individuality,
And my father talked about the West where years back
He played hurley on the sands with a stick of wrack.
Park your car in Killarney, buy a souvenir
Of green marble or black bog-oak, run up to Clare,
Climb the cliff in the postcard, visit Galway city,
Romanticise on our Spanish blood, leave ten per cent of pity
Under your plate for the emigrant,
Take credit for our sanctity, our heroism and our sterile want
Columba Kevin and briny Brandan the accepted names,
Wolfe Tone and Grattan and Michael Collins the accepted names,
Admire the suavity with which the architect
Is rebuilding the burnt mansion, recollect
The palmy days of the Horse Show, swank your fill,
But take the Holyhead boat before you pay the bill;
Before you face the consequence
Of inbred soul and climatic maleficence
And pay for the trick beauty of a prism
In drug-dull fatalism.
I will exorcise my blood
And not to have my baby-clothes my shroud
I will acquire an attitude not yours
And become as one of your holiday visitors,
And however often I may come
Farewell, my country, and in perpetuum;
Whatever desire I catch when your wind scours my face
I will take home and put in a glass case
And merely look on
At each new fantasy of badge and gun.
Frost will not touch the hedge of fuchsias,
The land will remain as it was,
But no abiding content can grow out of these minds
Fuddled with blood, always caught by blinds;
The eels go up the Shannon over the great dam;
You cannot change a response by giving it a new name.
Fountain of green and blue curling in the wind
I must go east and stay, not looking behind,
Not knowing on which day the mist is blanket-thick
Nor when sun quilts the valley and quick
Winging shadows of white clouds pass

Over the long hills like a fiddle's phrase.
If I were a dog of sunlight I would bound
From Phoenix Park to Achill Sound,
Picking up the scent of a hundred fugitives
That have broken the mesh of ordinary lives,
But being ordinary too I must in course discuss
What we mean to Ireland or Ireland to us;
I have to observe milestone and curio
The beaten buried gold of an old king's bravado,
Falsetto antiquities, I have to gesture,
Take part in, or renounce, each imposture;
Therefore I resign, good-bye the chequered and the quiet hills
The gaudily-striped Atlantic, the linen-mills
That swallow the shawled file, the black moor where half
A turf-stack stands like a ruined cenotaph;
Good-bye your hens running in and out of the white house
Your absent-minded goats along the road, your black cows
Your greyhounds and your hunters beautifully bred
Your drums and your dolled-up Virgins and your ignorant dead.

January, 1934

Ode

To-night is so coarse with chocolate
   The wind blowing from Bournville
That I hanker after the Atlantic
   With a frivolous nostalgia
Like that which film-fans feel
   For their celluloid abstractions
The nifty hero and the deathless blonde
   And find escape by proxy
From the eight-hour day or the wheel
   Of work and bearing children.

If God is boundless as the sea or sky
The eye bounds both of them and Him,
We always have the horizon
Not to swim to but to see:
God is seen with shape and limit
More purple towards the rim,
This segment of His infinite extension
Is all the God of Him for me.

And you too, my love, my limit,
So palpable and your hair shot with red—
I do not want a hundred wives or lives
Any more than I want to be too well read
Or have money like the sand or ability like the hydra's heads
To flicker the tongues of self-engendering power,
I want a sufficient sample, the exact and framed
Balance of definite masses, the islanded hour.

I would pray for that island; mob mania in the air,
I cannot assume their easy bravery
Drugged with a slogan, chewing the old lie
That parallel lines will meet at infinity;
As I walk on the shore of the regular and rounded sea
I would pray off from my son the love of that infinite
Which is too greedy and too obvious; let his Absolute
Like any four-walled house be put up decently.

Let us turn to homeliness,
Born in the middle of May
Let him accumulate, corroborate while he may
The blessedness of fact
Which lives in the dancing atom and the breathing trees
And everywhere except in the fancy of man
Who daubs his slush on the hawthorn and the may.

Let him have five good senses
The feeling for symmetry
And the sense of the magnet,
His mind deft and unflustered
To change gear easily
And let not the blasphemy
Of dusty words deceive him.

May he hit the golden mean
Which contains the seasonal extreme,
May he riot in the diving sun
And die in the crystal dream,
May his good deeds flung forth
Like boomerangs return
To wear around his neck
As beads of definite worth.

May he pick up daintily
The ambiguous joys,

As a bee in May the blossom of fruit
Cross-fertilise his data and distil
From the drum balalaika fiddle and organ
From sun's gunnery splintering glass
More than the twanging dazzle or the dazzling noise.

To get permanence, to hear the personance
Of all the water-gullies and blackbirds' songs
Drained off or died twenty years back
To make one's flesh of them and so renounce the mask
Of the sham soul, the cask bobbing empty
On leaden waves, the veneer the years crack.

To ride two horses at once, a foot on each
Tilting outward on space abstract and packed
With the audience of the dead and the unborn,
To pay his debts to each
To beach his boat so that others can use it
To throw his bread on the waters, the best deposit.

That people are lovable is a strange discovery
And there are many conflicting allegiances;
The pedals of a chance bicycle
Make a gold shower turning in the sun,
Trains leave in all directions on wild rails
And for every act determined on and won
There is a possible world denied and lost.

Do not then turn maudlin or weathercock,
We must cut the throat of the hour
That it may not haunt us because our sentiments
Continued its existence to pollute
Its essence; bottled time turns sour upon the sill.

The children play in the park; the ducklings
Rise and scurry on the water, a car
Changes down, the sandwichmen
Move up and down with the never-changing news.
Do not brood too much on the forking paths.

The leaves dark green on top, light green under, seas of green
Had brought him on full flood, the colour laid on in slices
As by a mason's trowel or ice cream in sliders
Bought in dusty streets under the yellow-green beeches,
A little while ago the green was only peppered
But now we gape at a wealthy wave and a tidal tower of green.

Coral azalea and scarlet rhododendron
Syringa and pink horse-chestnut and laburnum
Solid as temples, niched with the song of birds,
Widen the eyes and nostrils, demand homage of words.
And we have to turn from them,
Compose ourselves, fit out an ethic:
Have I anything to hand my son,
Scarab or compass for his journey?

Only so far, so far as I can find, symbols;
No decalogue, no chemical formula;
Unanalysed scent and noise, the fly on the pane,
The tulips banked on the glass-and-black hearse
A memory of a cock crowing in the dark like a curse
The remembered hypnotism of an aeroplane in June—

Watching the cricket from between
Slabs of green and slabs of blue and slowly ladled clouds
We looked at the sky through straw hats,
The sky was turned into black and white small stars.
Then came, southward as always, the angel
His song like the heat dancing on the gravel
High above the bat-chock and the white umpires
Moving south while the clapping of a run turns chill in echo
And his own drone is whittled to the point of a pin
So that dozing boys fumbled the ghost of sound.

But this identical sound the then epitome
Of summer's athletic ease and the smell of cut grass
Will sometime be our augury of war
When these tiny flies like nibs will calmly draw our death
A dipping gradient on the graph of Europe
And over the hairy flatnesses of Russia
This sound when we have died will linger to a wisp
And the endless corn wave tiredly.

Humming and buzzing, the bomber and the fly on the pane
And the telephone wires hung on dead pines,
In Ireland once a string of bright-red haws
Hung, thrown up by children, on those wires:
Not to hang so, O God, between your iron spires!
The town-dweller like a rabbit in a greengrocer's
Who was innocent and integral once
Now, red with slit guts, hangs by the heels
Hangs by the heels gut-open against the fog
Between two spires that are not conscious of him.

Therefore let not my son, halving the truth
Be caught between jagged edges;
And let him not falsify the world
By taking it to pieces;

The marriage of Cause and Effect, Form and Content
Let him not part asunder.
Wisdom for him in the time of tulips
Monastic repose, martial élan,
Then the opening mouth a dragon or a voluptuary—
These moments let him retain like limbs
His time not crippled by flaws of faith or memory.

In the Birmingham Market Hall at this time
There are horseshoe wreaths of mauve stock
Fixed with wire and nailed with pale pink roses
The tribute to a life that ran on standard wheels—
May his life be more than this matter of wheels and wire.

I remember all the houses where parents
Have reared their children to be parents
(Cut box and privet and the parrot's voice)
To be clerks to total the flow of alien money
To be florists to design these wreaths and wedding bouquets.

I cannot draw up any code
    There are too many qualifications
Too many asterisk asides
    Too many crosses in the margin
But as others, forgetting the others,
    Run after the nostrums
Of science art and religion
    So would I mystic and maudlin
Dream of the both real and ideal
    Breakers of ocean.
I must put away this drug.

Must become the migrating bird following felt routes
The comet's superficially casual orbit kept
Not self-abandoning to sky-blind chutes
To climb miles and kiss the miles of foam
For nothing is more proud than humbly to accept
And without soaring or swerving win by ignoring
The endlessly curving sea and so come to one's home.
And so come to one's peace while the yellow waves are roaring.

1934

58

Homage to clichés

With all this clamour for progress
This hammering out of new phases and gadgets, new trinkets and
   phrases
I prefer the automatic, the reflex, the cliché of velvet.
The foreseen smile, sexual, maternal, or hail-fellow-met,
The cat's fur sparking under your hand
And the indolent delicacy of your hand
These fish coming in to the net
I can see them coming for yards
The way that you answer, the way that you dangle your foot
These fish that are rainbow and fat
One can catch in the hand and caress and return to the pool.
So five minutes spent at a bar
Watching the fish coming in, as you parry and shrug
This is on me or this is on me,
Or an old man momentously sharpens a pencil as though
He were not merely licking his fur like a cat—
The cat's tongue curls to the back of its neck, the fish swivel round
   by the side of their tails, on the abbey the arrows of gold
On the pinnacles shift in the wind—
This is on me this time
Watch how your flattery logic seduction or wit
Elicit the expected response
Each tiny hammer of the abbey chime
Beating on the outer shell of the eternal bell
Which hangs like a Rameses, does not deign to move
For Mahomet comes to the mountain and the fish come to the bell.
What will you have now? The same again?
A finger can pull these ropes,
A gin and lime or a double Scotch—
Watch the response, the lifting wrist the clink and smile
The fish come in, the hammered notes come out
From a filigree gothic trap.
These are the moments that are anaplerotic, these are the gifts to be
   accepted
Remembering the qualification
That everything is not true to type like these
That the pattern and the patina of these
Are superseded in the end.
Stoop your head, follow me through this door
Up the belfry stair.
What do you see in this gloom, this womb of stone?

I see eight bells hanging alone.
Eight black panthers, eight silences
On the outer shell of which our fingers via hammers
Rapping with an impertinent precision
Have made believe that this was the final music.
Final as if finality were the trend of fish
That always seek the net
As if finality were the obvious gag
The audience laughing in anticipation
As if finality were the angled smile
Drawn from the dappled stream of casual meetings
(Yet oh thank God for such)
But there is this much left over
There is very much left over:
The Rameses, the panther, the two-ton bell
Will never move his sceptre
Never spring, never swing
No, no, he will never move . . .
What will you have, my dear? The same again?
Two more double Scotch, watch the approved response
This is the preferred mode;
I have shut the little window that looks up the road
Towards the tombs of the kings
For I have heard that you meet people walking in granite
I have shut up the gates under padlock
For fear of wild beasts
And I have shut my ears to the possible peal of bells,
Every precaution—
What will you have, my dear? The same again?
Count up our fag-ends
This year next year sometime never
Next year is this year, sometime is next time, never is sometime
Never is the Bell, Never is the Panther, Never is Rameses
Oh the cold stone panic of Never—
The ringers are taking off their coats, the panther crouches
The granite sceptre is very slightly inclining
As our shoes tap against the bar and our glasses
Make two new rings of wet upon the counter
Somewhere behind us stands a man, a counter
A timekeeper with a watch and a pistol
Ready to shoot and with his shot destroy
This whole delightful world of cliché and refrain—
What will you have, my dear? The same again?

December, 1935

Letter to Graham and Anna

To Graham and Anna: from the Arctic Gate
I send this letter to N.W.8,
Hoping that Town is not the usual mess,
That Pauli is rid of worms, the new cook a success.
I have got here, you see, without being sick
On a boat of eight hundred tons to Reykjavik.
Came second-class—no air but many men;
Having seen the first-class crowd would do the same again.
Food was good, mutton and bits of fishes,
A smart line-up of Scandinavian dishes—
Beet, cheese, ham, jam, smoked salmon, gaffalbitar,
Sweet cucumber, German sausage, and Ryvita.
So I came here to the land the Romans missed,
Left for the Irish saint and the Viking colonist.
But what am I doing here? Qu'allais-je faire
Among these volcanic rocks and this grey air?
Why go north when Cyprus and Madeira
De jure if not de facto are much nearer?
The reason for hereness seems beyond conjecture,
There are no trees or trains or architecture,
Fruits and greens are insufficient for health,
Culture is limited by lack of wealth,
The tourist sights have nothing like Stonehenge,
The literature is all about revenge.
And yet I like it if only because this nation
Enjoys a scarcity of population
And cannot rise to many bores or hacks
Or paupers or poor men paying Super-Tax.
Yet further, if you can stand it, I will set forth
The obscure but powerful ethics of Going North.
Morris did it before, dropping the frills and fuss,
Harps and arbours, Tristram and Theseus,
For a land of rocks and sagas. And certain unknown
Old Irish hermits, holy skin and bone,
Camped on these crags in order to forget
Their blue-black cows in Kerry pastures wet.
Those Latin-chattering margin-illuminating monks
Fled here from home without kit-bags or trunks
To mortify their flesh—but we must mortify
Our blowsy intellects before we die,

Who feed our brains on backchat and self-pity
And always need a noise, the radio or the city,
Traffic and changing lights, crashing the amber,
Always on the move and so do not remember
The necessity of the silence of the islands,
The glacier floating in the distance out of existence,
The need to grip and grapple the adversary,
Knuckle on stony knuckle, to dot and carry
One and carry one and not give up the hunt
Till we have pinned the Boyg down to a point.
In England one forgets—in each performing troupe
Forgets what one has lost, there is no room to stoop
And look along the ground, one cannot see the ground
For the feet of the crowd, and the lost is never found.
I dropped something, I think, but I am not sure what
And cannot say if it mattered much or not,
So let us get on or we shall be late, for soon
The shops will close and the rush-hour be on.
This is the fret that makes us cat-like stretch
And then contract the fingers, gives the itch
To open the French window into the rain,
Walk out and never be seen at home again.
But where to go? No oracle for us,
Bible or Baedeker, can tell the terminus.
The songs of jazz have told us of a moon country
And we like to dream of a heat which is never sultry,
Melons to eat, champagne to drink, and a lazy
Music hour by hour depetalling the daisy.
Then Medici manuscripts have told of places
Where common sense was wedded to the graces,
Doric temples and olive-trees and such,
But broken marble no longer goes for much.
And there are some who scorn this poésie de départs
And say 'Escape by staying where you are;
A man is what he thinks he is and can
Find happiness within.' How nice to be born a man.
The tourist in space or time, emotion or sensation,
Meets many guides but none have the proper orientation.
We are not changing ground to escape from facts
But rather to find them. This complex world exacts
Hard work of simplifying; to get its focus
You have to stand outside the crowd and caucus.
This all sounds somewhat priggish. You and I
Know very well the immediate reason why
I am in Iceland. Three months ago or so

Wystan said that he was planning to go
To Iceland to write a book and would I come too;
And I said yes, having nothing better to do.
But all the same we never make any choice
On such a merely mechanical stimulus.
The match is not the cause of fire, so pause
And look for the formal as well as the efficient cause.
Aristotle's pedantic phraseology
Serves better than common sense or hand-to-mouth psychology
ἔσχε τὴν φύσιν—'found its nature'; the crude
Embryo rummages every latitude
Looking for itself, its nature, its final pattern,
Till the fairy godmother's wand touches the slattern
And turns her to a princess for a moment
Beyond definition or professorial comment.
We find our nature daily or try to find it,
The old flame gutters, leaves red flames behind it.
An interval of tuning and screwing and then
The symphony restarts, the creature lives again—
Blake's arabesques of fire; the subtle creature
Swings on Ezekiel's wheels, finding its nature.
In short we must keep moving to keep pace
Or else drop into Limbo, the dead place.
I have come north, gaily running away
From the grinding gears, the change from day to day,
The creaks of the familiar room, the smile
Of the cruel clock, the bills upon the file,
The excess of books and cushions, the high heels
That walk the street, the news, the newsboys' yells,
The flag-days and the cripple's flapping sleeve.
The ambushes of sex, the passion to retrieve
Significance from the river of passing people,
The attempt to climb the ever-climbing steeple
And no one knows what is at the top of it,
All is a raffle for caps which may not fit,
But all take tickets, keep moving; still we may
Move off from movement or change it for a day;
Here is a different rhythm, the juggled balls
Hang in the air—the pause before the soufflé falls.
Here we can take a breath, sit back, admire
Stills from the film of life, the frozen fire;
Among these rocks can roll upon the tongue
Morsels of thought, not jostled by the throng,
Or morsels of un-thought, which is still better,
(Thinking these days makes a suburban clatter).

Here we can practise forgetfulness without
A sense of guilt, fear of the tout and lout,
And here—but Wystan has butted in again
To say we must go out in the frightful rain
To see a man about a horse and so
I shall have to stop. For we soon intend to go
Around the Langjökull, a ten-days' ride,
Gumboots and stockfish. Probably you'll deride
This sissy onslaught on the open spaces.
I can see the joke myself; however the case is
Not to be altered, but please remember us
So high up here in this vertiginous
Crow's-nest of the earth. Perhaps you'll let us know
If anything happens in the world below?

The Hebrides

On those islands
The west wind drops its message of indolence,
No one hurries, the Gulf Stream warms the gnarled
Rampart of gneiss, the feet of the peasant years
Pad up and down their sentry-beat not challenging
Any comer for the password—only Death
Comes through unchallenged in his general's cape.
The houses straggle on the umber moors,
The Aladdin lamp mutters in the boarded room
Where a woman smoors the fire of fragrant peat.
No one repeats the password for it is known,
All is known before it comes to the lips—
Instinctive wisdom. Over the fancy vases
The photos with the wrinkles taken out,
The enlarged portraits of the successful sons
Who married wealth in Toronto or New York,
Console the lonely evenings of the old
Who live embanked by memories of labour
And child-bearing and scriptural commentaries.
On those islands
The boys go poaching their ancestral rights—
The Ossianic salmon who take the yellow
Tilt of the river with a magnet's purpose—
And listen breathless to the tales at the ceilidh

Among the peat-smoke and the smells of dung
That fill the felted room from the cave of the byre.
No window opens of the windows sunk like eyes
In a four-foot wall of stones casually picked
From the knuckly hills on which these houses crawl
Like black and legless beasts who breathe in their sleep
Among the piles of peat and pooks of hay—
A brave oasis in the indifferent moors.
And while the stories circulate like smoke,
The sense of life spreads out from the one-eyed house
In wider circles through the lake of night
In which articulate man has dropped a stone—
In wider circles round the black-faced sheep,
Wider and fainter till they hardly crease
The ebony heritage of the herded dead.
On those islands
The tinkers whom no decent girl will go with,
Preserve the Gaelic tunes unspoiled by contact
With the folk-fancier or the friendly tourist,
And preserve the knowledge of horse-flesh and preserve
The uncompromising empire of the rogue.
On those islands
The tethered cow grazes among the orchises
And figures in blue calico turn by hand
The ground beyond the plough, and the bus, not stopping,
Drops a parcel for the lonely household
Where men remembering stories of eviction
Are glad to have their land though mainly stones—
The honoured bones which still can hoist a body.
On those islands
There is echo of the leaping fish, the identical
Sound that cheered the chiefs at ease from slaughter;
There is echo of baying hounds of a lost breed
And echo of MacCrimmon's pipes lost in the cave;
And seals cry with the voices of the drowned.
When men go out to fish, no one must say 'Good luck'
And the confidences told in a boat at sea
Must be as if printed on the white ribbon of a wave
Withdrawn as soon as printed—so never heard.
On those islands
The black minister paints the tour of hell
While the unregenerate drink from the bottle's neck
In gulps like gauntlets thrown at the devil's head
And spread their traditional songs across the hills
Like fraying tapestries of fights and loves,

The boar-hunt and the rope let down at night—
Lost causes and lingering home-sickness.
On those islands
The fish come singing from the drunken sea,
The herring rush the gunwales and sort themselves
To cram the expectant barrels of their own accord—
Or such is the dream of the fisherman whose wet
Leggings hang on the door as he sleeps returned
From a night when miles of net were drawn up empty.
On those islands
A girl with candid eyes goes out to marry
An independent tenant of seven acres
Who goes each year to the south to work on the roads
In order to raise a rent of forty shillings,
And all the neighbours celebrate their wedding
With drink and pipes and the walls of the barn reflect
The crazy shadows of the whooping dancers.
On those islands
Where many live on the dole or on old-age pensions
And many waste with consumption and some are drowned
And some of the old stumble in the midst of sleep
Into the pot-hole hitherto shunned in dreams
Or falling from the cliff among the shrieks of gulls
Reach the bottom before they have time to wake—
Whoever dies on the islands and however,
The whole of the village goes into three-day mourning,
The afflicted home is honoured and the shops are shut
For on those islands
Where a few surnames cover a host of people
And the art of being a stranger with your neighbour
Has still to be imported, death is still
No lottery ticket in a public lottery—
The result to be read on the front page of a journal—
But a family matter near to the whole family.
On those islands
Where no train runs on rails and the tyrant time
Has no clock-towers to signal people to doom
With semaphore ultimatums tick by tick,
There is still peace though not for me and not
Perhaps for long—still peace on the bevel hills
For those who still can live as their fathers lived
On those islands.

1937

IV
1936—1938

δυσέρωτες δὴ φαινόμεθ᾽ ὄντες
τοῦδ᾽ ὅ τι τοῦτο στίλβει κατὰ γῆν

Carrickfergus

I was born in Belfast between the mountain and the gantries
   To the hooting of lost sirens and the clang of trams:
Thence to Smoky Carrick in County Antrim
   Where the bottle-neck harbour collects the mud which jams

The little boats beneath the Norman castle,
   The pier shining with lumps of crystal salt;
The Scotch Quarter was a line of residential houses
   But the Irish Quarter was a slum for the blind and halt.

The brook ran yellow from the factory stinking of chlorine,
   The yarn-mill called its funeral cry at noon;
Our lights looked over the lough to the lights of Bangor
   Under the peacock aura of a drowning moon.

The Norman walled this town against the country
   To stop his ears to the yelping of his slave
And built a church in the form of a cross but denoting
   The list of Christ on the cross in the angle of the nave.

I was the rector's son, born to the anglican order,
   Banned for ever from the candles of the Irish poor;
The Chichesters knelt in marble at the end of a transept
   With ruffs about their necks, their portion sure.

The war came and a huge camp of soldiers
   Grew from the ground in sight of our house with long
Dummies hanging from gibbets for bayonet practice
   And the sentry's challenge echoing all day long;

A Yorkshire terrier ran in and out by the gate-lodge
   Barred to civilians, yapping as if taking affront:
Marching at ease and singing 'Who Killed Cock Robin?'
   The troops went out by the lodge and off to the Front.

The steamer was camouflaged that took me to England—
   Sweat and khaki in the Carlisle train;
I thought that the war would last for ever and sugar
   Be always rationed and that never again

Would the weekly papers not have photos of sandbags
   And my governess not make bandages from moss

And people not have maps above the fireplace
  With flags on pins moving across and across—

Across the hawthorn hedge the noise of bugles,
  Flares across the night,
Somewhere on the lough was a prison ship for Germans,
  A cage across their sight.

I went to school in Dorset, the world of parents
  Contracted into a puppet world of sons
Far from the mill girls, the smell of porter, the salt-mines
  And the soldiers with their guns.

1937

Iceland

No shields now
  Cross the knoll,
The hills are dull
  With leaden shale,
Whose arms could squeeze
  The breath from time
And the climb is long
  From cairn to cairn.

Houses are few
  But decorous
In a ruined land
  Of sphagnum moss;
Corrugated iron
  Farms inherit
The spirit and phrase
  Of ancient sagas.

Men have forgotten
  Anger and ambush,
To make ends meet
  Their only business:
The lover riding
  In the lonely dale
Hears the plover's
  Single pipe

And feels perhaps
    But undefined
The drift of death
    In the sombre wind
Deflating the trim
    Balloon of lust
In a grey storm
    Of dust and grit.

So we who have come
    As trippers North
Have minds no match
    For this land's girth;
The glacier's licking
    Tongues deride
Our pride of life,
    Our flashy songs.

But the people themselves
    Who live here
Ignore the brooding
    Fear, the sphinx;
And the radio
    With tags of tune
Defies their pillared
    Basalt crags.

Whose ancestors
    Thought that at last
The end would come
    To a blast of horns
And gods would face
    The worst in fight,
Vanish in the night
    The last, the first

Night which began
    Without device
In ice and rocks,
    No shade or shape;
Grass and blood,
    The strife of life,
Were an interlude
    Which soon must pass

71

And all go back
   Relapse to rock
Under the shawl
   Of the ice-caps,
The cape which night
   Will spread to cover
The world when the living
   Flags are furled.

1936

Passage steamer

Upon the decks they take beef tea
   Who are so free, so free, so free,
But down the ladder in the engine-room
   (Doom, doom, doom, doom)
The great cranks rise and fall, repeat,
The great cranks plod with their Assyrian feet
   To match the monotonous energy of the sea.

Back from a journey I require
   Some new desire, desire, desire
But I find in the open sea and sun
   None, none, none, none;
The gulls that bank around the mast
Insinuate that nothing we pass is past,
   That all our beginnings were long since begun.

And when I think of you, my dear,
   Who were so near, so near, so near,
The barren skies from wall to wall
   Appal, appal, pall, pall,
The spray no longer gilds the wave,
The sea looks nothing more nor less than a grave
   And the world and the day are grey and that is all.

1937

Postscript to Iceland
for W. H. Auden

Now the winter nights begin
Lonely comfort walls me in;
So before the memory slip
I review our Iceland trip—

Not for me romantic nor
Idyll on a mythic shore
But a fancy turn, you know,
Sandwiched in a graver show.

Down in Europe Seville fell,
Nations germinating hell,
The Olympic games were run—
Spots upon the Aryan sun.

And the don in me set forth
How the landscape of the north
Had educed the saga style
Plodding forward mile by mile.

And the don in you replied
That the North begins inside,
Our ascetic guts require
Breathers from the Latin fire.

So although no ghost was scotched
We were happy while we watched
Ravens from their walls of shale
Cruise around the rotting whale,

Watched the sulphur basins boil,
Loops of steam uncoil and coil,
While the valley fades away
To a sketch of Judgment Day.

So we rode and joked and smoked
With no miracles evoked,
With no levitations won
In the thin unreal sun;

In that island never found
Visions blossom from the ground,
No conversions like St. Paul,
No great happenings at all.

Holidays should be like this,
Free from over-emphasis,
Time for soul to stretch and spit
Before the world comes back on it,

Before the chimneys row on row
Sneer in smoke, 'We told you so'
And the fog-bound sirens call
Ruin to the long sea-wall.

Rows of books around me stand,
Fence me round on either hand;
Through that forest of dead words
I would hunt the living birds—

Great black birds that fly alone
Slowly through a land of stone,
And the gulls who weave a free
Quilt of rhythm on the sea.

Here in Hampstead I sit late
Nights which no one shares and wait
For the 'phone to ring or for
Unknown angels at the door;

Better were the northern skies
Than this desert in disguise—
Rugs and cushions and the long
Mirror which repeats the song.

For the litany of doubt
From these walls comes breathing out
Till the room becomes a pit
Humming with the fear of it

With the fear of loneliness
And uncommunicableness;
All the wires are cut, my friends
Live beyond the severed ends.

So I write these lines for you
Who have felt the death-wish too,
But your lust for life prevails—
Drinking coffee, telling tales.

Our prerogatives as men
Will be cancelled who knows when;
Still I drink your health before
The gun-butt raps upon the door.

1936

Sand in the air

Books, do not look at me,
    Clock, do not stare;
The fire's ashes fidget,
    There is sand in the air;
Drums tell its coming—
    The sandstorm that blows
From the desert of darkness—
    O in the desert of darkness
        Where is she walking?

Otherwise regular
    Quickening their beat
The marchers of madness
    Pick up their feet,
Make for my table
    And the empty chair
That faces me—Where,
    Where and why is she absent
        Leaving it empty?

Dial her number,
    None will reply;
In the shrivelled world
    There is only I;
Her voice is frozen,
    Hangs in my brain
On the crags of memory—
    O my dear, go away
        From the crags of memory.

75

Now that the shapes of mist

Now that the shapes of mist like hooded beggar-children
Slink quickly along the middle of the road
And the lamps draw trails of milk in ponds of lustrous lead
I am decidedly pleased not to be dead.

Or when wet roads at night reflect the clutching
Importunate fingers of trees and windy shadows
Lunge and flounce on the windscreen as I drive
I am glad of the accident of being alive.

There are so many nights with stars or close-
ly interleaved with battleship-grey or plum,
So many visitors whose Buddha-like palms are pressed
Against the windowpanes where people take their rest.

Whose favour now is yours to screen your sleep—
You need not hear the strings that are tuning for the dawn—
Mingling, my dear, your breath with the quiet breath
Of sleep whom the old writers called the brother of Death.

1936

Hidden ice

There are few songs for domesticity
For routine work, money-making or scholarship
Though these are apt for eulogy or for tragedy.

And I would praise our adaptability
Who can spend years and years in offices and beds
Every morning twirling the napkin ring,
A twitter of inconsequent vitality.

And I would praise our inconceivable stamina
Who work to the clock and calendar and maintain
The equilibrium of nerves and notions,
Our mild bravado in the face of time.

Those who ignore disarm. The domestic ambush
The pleated lampshade the defeatist clock
May never be consummated and we may never
Strike on the rock beneath the calm upholstering.

But some though buoyed by habit, though convoyed
By habitual faces and hands that help the food
Or help one with one's coat, have lost their bearings
Struck hidden ice or currents no one noted.

One was found like Judas kissing flowers
And one who sat between the clock and the sun
Lies like a Saint Sebastian full of arrows
Feathered from his own hobby, his pet hours.

January, 1936

From *Out of the picture*

I

The Oracle

The oracle
   High between the cliffs,
The tripod over
   The mephitic cleft,
Or the sybil's cave
   Where the winds blow
The dead leaf answers
   To and fro:
Where shall we find truth in an oracle?

The oracle
   Among the talking oaks,
The flight of birds,
   The examination of guts,
Luck of the cards,
   Lines of the hand,
Call of the raven
   In a sallow land:
Where shall we find truth in an oracle?

Riding in cars

Riding in cars
   On tilting roads
We have left behind
   Our household gods,
We have left behind
   The cautious clause,
The laws of the over-
   rational mind.

Frost on the window,
   Skater's figures,
Gunmen fingering
   Anxious triggers,
Stocks and shares
   (The ribbon of the rich),
The favourite down
   At the blind ditch.

Forgotten now
   The early days,
Youth's idyllic
   And dawdling ways;
Cruising along
   On the long road
We do not notice
   The limping god.

Swinging between
   Crutches he comes
To an overture
   Of buried drums;
His eyes will turn
   Our hands to stone,
His name is Time,
   He walks alone.

III

War heroes

When the heroes came back from the ten-years' war
(But no war now will last ten years)
They struck a port they seemed to have seen before.
There were old men sitting on the bollards
Puffing smoke across the sea,
There were dead men hanging in the gantries,
There was a lame bird limping on the quay.
When were we here before? one of them said.
The captain answered: This is where we were born
And where we have now returned. Dead to the Dead.

IV

Pindar is dead

There are hikers on all the roads—
  Pindar is dead—
The petrol pumps are doing a roaring business,
Motors are tuning up for the Easter races,
Building companies are loaning to the newly married—
  Pindar is dead and that's no matter.

There are climbers on all the hills—
  Pindar is dead—
With oiled boots and ropes they are tackling Snowdon,
The swimming baths are filled for Easter Monday,
Doctored with chlorine to prevent infection—
  Pindar is dead and that's no matter.

There is money on all the horses—
  Pindar is dead—
One belongs to a proud and a plethoric peer,
One to a maharajah, one to a midland magnate,
One to a dago count and one to a tweeded spinster—
  Pindar is dead and that's no matter.

There are flowers in all the markets—
  Pindar is dead—
Daffodils, tulips, and forced roses,

New potatoes and green peas for Easter,
Wreaths of moss and primrose for the churches
But no wreaths for runners, whether of olive or laurel—
    Pindar is dead and that's no matter.

V

Les neiges d'antan

What's become of all the glory and the grandeur of the gold-men and
    the gunmen,
The long breakers topped with silver of expanding power and profits,
Of the well-upholstered mansion, seven flights of stairs for the servants
Carrying coal from six in the morning?
What's become of the squadron of butlers, valets, grooms and second
    housemaids?
Gone like the carriage-horse and cabhorse that once dunged the streets
    of London.
What's become of the oracles in beards and whiskers, beauty in
    bustles?
What's become of Mr. Gladstone or of grandpa's roll-top desk,
Waterloo Bridge and General Gordon?
What's become of them? What's becoming of us?
Look ahead, Long-Sighted Jim,
What do you see in the future dim?
    I look ahead and what do I see?
    I see a pageant, a Lord Mayor's procession,
    The Aldermen and the flunkeys, the carnival giants,
    The tableaux on lorries, the flags and the coaches,
    And every single one of the people who make that procession
    Carries a white stick to show that he is blind.
What's become of the light of day, the golden spokes of the sun's
    wheels,
What's become of the fingers of light that picked the locks of the dark
    places,
What's become of all our private sentinels?
    Answer: The sentry has gone.
    He will not come back.
    The pavement was worn by his feet
    But moss will grow over the tracks.
    Anyone now can approach
    The door of your house without fear.
    The burglar, the beggar, the drunk,

The murdering madman, the whore,
The prophet in sackcloth, the priest,
The jackal, the tiger, the snake,
All have their eye on your door.
Close all the doors, bar all the shutters,
Be ready with revolver and electric torch,
Fire extinguisher and telephone directory,
Bible, cheque book, and *savoir faire*:
The vultures are gathered together,
Their hooked wings carve the urban air.
When the golden cycle is over, the wise men said,
Fire will consume the lot, the game resume,
And feathers of the birds of prey will singe as they tear the prey,
And the corpses roast where they fell
And the small blue flames will play
Like kittens with a ball of wool . . .
   FIRE   FIRE   FIRE   FIRE . . .
Fire in Troy, fire in Babylon, fire in Nineveh, fire in London,
   FIRE   FIRE   FIRE   FIRE
The buckets are empty of water, the hoses are punctured,
The city main is cut off, the holy well is dry,
There is no succour in the dusty ground, the metallic sky,
No rock will spout with water at the prophet's rod,
Nor fate repeat the legendary flood,
There is nothing to stem the mechanical march of fire,
Nothing to assuage the malice of the drunken fire.
   FIRE   FIRE   FIRE   FIRE

VI

Empty shoes

Someone said that shoes had personality,
That when you die your shoes. . . .
That the frozen overflow of personality
Hangs on in jags after the general thaw
When a man has died.
Icicles, acroteria.
In a corner, in a cloakroom, among rackets and rods
An old pair of brogues
With criss-cross wrinkles like an old man's face.
Or when a girl has died
Her shoes are lined up, spruce as soldiers,

81

Waiting for the word Dismiss.
And in hotels at night passing from door to door
There is something terrible in all those empty shoes.

November, 1934

VII

The jingles of the morning

Shall we remember the jingles of the morning,
The pipers the pedlars and the brass farthings,
The buds of music, the imagined darlings?
  No, we shall *not* remember.

Shall we remember the games with puffball and plantain,
Searching for the lost handle to the silent fountain,
Hiding in the shrubbery, shutting our eyes and counting?

Shall we remember the marigolds parading,
Smell of grass and noise of the corncrake railing
And the fun of dragging a stick along the paling?

And after that shall we remember the races,
The broken tape, the clamour of companions' voices,
The schoolboy's callow joys in smut and curses?

And shall we remember our early adult pleasure,
The dive in love's lagoons of brilliant azure,
The gay martyrdom, the brave fantasia?

Shall we remember the kick of inspired religion,
The visions in drink, the feel of the homing pigeon
Drawn by a magnet to an intuited region?

Shall we remember the noise of the moving nations
Or shall we remember the gusty sun's creations,
The night and the never-to-be-climbed-to constellations?
  No, we shall *not* remember.

VIII
Finale

It is not enough
To have winning ways,
   The trimmed wick burns clear,
To follow with an indolent eye
The flicker-pattern of the days,
   For here ends our hoarded oil.

The acquisitive arts
Are not enough,
   The trimmed wick burns clear,
It is a little and a tired time
To be making money or love,
   Here ends our hoarded oil.

A kiss, a cuddle,
A crossed cheque,
   The trimmed wick burns clear,
Walk among statues in the dark,
The odds are you will break your neck—
   Here ends our hoarded oil.

Taken for granted

Taken for granted
   The household orbit in childhood
The punctual sound of the gong
   The round of domestic service.

The lamps were trimmed at six,
   Sticks were lavish for firewood,
The cat made bread of my knees,
   The housewife shopped in the morning.

The shops were fragrant, the blistered
   Vagrant peered in the windows
At tripes like deep-sea plants,
   Sausages in ropes of marble.

83

On the knees of bountiful gods
        We lived in the ease of acceptance
Taking until we were twenty
        God's plenty for granted.

The brandy glass

Only let it form within his hands once more—
The moment cradled like a brandy glass.
Sitting alone in the empty dining hall . . .
From the chandeliers the snow begins to fall
Piling around carafes and table legs
And chokes the passage of the revolving door.
The last diner, like a ventriloquist's doll
Left by his master, gazes before him, begs:
'Only let it form within my hands once more.'
                                                1937

The sunlight on the garden

        The sunlight on the garden
        Hardens and grows cold,
        We cannot cage the minute
        Within its nets of gold,
        When all is told
        We cannot beg for pardon.

        Our freedom as free lances
        Advances towards its end;
        The earth compels, upon it
        Sonnets and birds descend;
        And soon, my friend,
        We shall have no time for dances.

        The sky was good for flying
        Defying the church bells
        And every evil iron
        Siren and what it tells:
        The earth compels,
        We are dying, Egypt, dying

And not expecting pardon,
Hardened in heart anew,
But glad to have sat under
Thunder and rain with you,
And grateful too
For sunlight on the garden.

1937

June thunder

The Junes were free and full, driving through tiny
Roads, the mudguards brushing the cowparsley,
Through fields of mustard and under boldly embattled
 Mays and chestnuts

Or between beeches verdurous and voluptuous
Or where broom and gorse beflagged the chalkland—
All the flare and gusto of the unenduring
 Joys of a season

Now returned but I note as more appropriate
To the maturer mood impending thunder
With an indigo sky and the garden hushed except for
 The treetops moving.

Then the curtains in my room blow suddenly inward,
The shrubbery rustles, birds fly heavily homeward,
The white flowers fade to nothing on the trees and rain comes
 Down like a dropscene.

Now there comes the catharsis, the cleansing downpour
Breaking the blossoms of our overdated fancies
Our old sentimentality and whimsicality
 Loves of the morning.

Blackness at half-past eight, the night's precursor,
Clouds like falling masonry and lightning's lavish
Annunciation, the sword of the mad archangel
 Flashed from the scabbard.

If only you would come and dare the crystal
Rampart of rain and the bottomless moat of thunder,
If only now you would come I should be happy
　　Now if now only.

1937

The heated minutes

The heated minutes climb
The anxious hill,
The tills fill up with cash,
The tiny hammers chime
The bells of good and ill,
And the world piles with ash
From fingers killing time.

If you were only here
Among these rocks,
I should not feel the dull
The taut and ticking fear
That hides in all the clocks
And creeps inside the skull—
If you were here, my dear.

1937

Leaving Barra

The dazzle on the sea, my darling,
Leads from the western channel,
A carpet of brilliance taking
My leave for ever of the island.

I never shall visit that island
Again with its easy tempo—
The seal sunbathing, the circuit
Of gulls on the wing for garbage.

I go to a different garbage
And scuffle for scraps of notice,

Pretend to ignore the stigma
That stains my life and my leisure.

For fretful even in leisure
I fidget for different values,
Restless as a gull and haunted
By a hankering after Atlantis.

I do not know that Atlantis
Unseen and uncomprehended,
Dimly divined but keenly
Felt with a phantom hunger.

If only I could crush the hunger
If only I could lay the phantom
Then I should no doubt be happy
Like a fool or a dog or a buddha.

O the self-abnegation of Buddha
The belief that is disbelieving
The denial of chiaroscuro
Not giving a damn for existence!

But I would cherish existence
Loving the beast and the bubble
Loving the rain and the rainbow,
Considering philosophy alien.

For all the religions are alien
That allege that life is a fiction,
And when we agree in denial
The cock crows in the morning.

If only I could wake in the morning
And find I had learned the solution,
Wake with the knack of knowledge
Who as yet have only an inkling.

Though some facts foster the inkling—
The beauty of the moon and music,
The routine courage of the worker,
The gay endurance of women,

And you who to me among women
Stand for so much that I wish for,

I thank you, my dear, for the example
Of living like a fugue and moving.

For few are able to keep moving,
They drag and flag in the traffic;
While you are alive beyond question
Like the dazzle on the sea, my darling.

1937

Trilogy for X

I

When clerks and navvies fondle
   Beside canals their wenches,
In rapture or in coma
   The haunches that they handle,
And the orange moon sits idle
   Above the orchard slanted—
Upon such easy evenings
   We take our loves for granted.

But when, as now, the creaking
   Trees on the hills of London
Like bison charge their neighbours
   In wind that keeps us waking
And in the draught the scalloped
   Lampshade swings a shadow,
We think of love bound over—
   The mortgage on the meadow.

And one lies lonely, haunted
   By limbs he half remembers,
And one, in wedlock, wonders
   Where is the girl he wanted;
And some sit smoking, flicking
   The ash away and feeling
For love gone up like vapour
   Between the floor and ceiling.

But now when winds are curling
  The trees do you come closer,
Close as an eyelid fasten
  My body in darkness, darling;
Switch the light off and let me
  Gather you up and gather
The power of trains advancing
  Further, advancing further.

II

And love hung still as crystal over the bed
  And filled the corners of the enormous room;
The boom of dawn that left her sleeping, showing
  The flowers mirrored in the mahogany table.

O my love, if only I were able
  To protract this hour of quiet after passion,
Not ration happiness but keep this door for ever
  Closed on the world, its own world closed within it.

But dawn's waves trouble with the bubbling minute,
  The names of books come clear upon their shelves,
The reason delves for duty and you will wake
  With a start and go on living on your own.

The first train passes and the windows groan,
  Voices will hector and your voice become
A drum in tune with theirs, which all last night
  Like sap that fingered through a hungry tree
Asserted our one night's identity.

III

  March gave clear days,
    Gave unaccustomed sunshine,
  Prelude to who knows
    What dead end or downfall;
  O my love, to
    Browse in the painted prelude.

  Regent's Park was
    Gay with ducks and deck-chairs,

Omens were absent,
Cooks bought cloves and parsley;
O my love, to
Stop one's ear to omens.

Pigeons courting, the cock
Like an eighteenth-century marquis
Puffing his breast and dragging
His fantail waltzwise;
O my love, the
Southward trains are puffing.

Nursemaids gossiped,
Sun was bright on pram-paint,
Gold in the breeze the arrow
Swivelled on church-tops;
But Living drains the living
Sieve we catch our gold in.

Toy sail skidding on Whitestone
Pond at the peak of London,
Challenge of bells at morning,
Crocus and almond;
O my love, my
Thoughts avoid the challenge.

But the rumbling summer rolls
A register behind us—
March to April to May
To denser summer—
And the road is dusty, the goal
Unknown we march to.

Rampant on Europe headlines
Herald beasts of fable;
Backward the eyes to ancient
Codes—vellum and roseleaf;
From the moving train of time the
Fields move backward.

And now the searchlights
Play their firemen's hoses,
Evil their purport
Though their practice lovely,
Defence and death being always
Collateral, coeval.

And now the soldier
　　Tightens belt and outlook,
Eyes on the target,
　　Mind in the trigger-finger,
And a flight of lead connecting
　　Self and horizon.

And now, and last, in London
　　Poised on the edge of absence
I ask for a moment's mention
　　Of days the days will cancel,
Though the long run may also
　　Bring what we ask for.
　　　　　　　　　Summer, 1938

Chess

At the penultimate move, their saga nearly sung,
They have worked so hard to prove what lads they were when young,
Have looked up every word in order to be able to say
The gay address unheard when they were dumb and gay.
Your Castle to King's Fourth under your practised hand!
What is the practice worth, so few being left to stand?
Better the raw levies jostling in the square
Than two old men in a crevice sniping at empty air;
The veterans on the pavement puff their cheeks and blow
The music of enslavement that echoes back 'I told you so';
The chapped hands fumble flutes, the tattered posters cry
Their craving for recruits who have not had time to die.
While our armies differ they move and feel the sun,
The victor is a cypher once the war is won.
Choose your gambit, vary the tactics of your game,
You move in a closed ambit that always ends the same.

Circus

I

Trapezists

Intricacy of engines,
Delicacy of darkness;
They rise into the tent's
Top like deep-sea divers

And hooked from the mouth like fish
Frame their frolic
Above the silent music
And the awed audience,

Hang by their teeth
Beneath the cone of canvas,
The ring beneath them
An eye that is empty

Who live in a world
Of aery technic
Like dolls or angels
Sexless and simple

Our fear their frame,
Hallowed by handclaps,
Honoured by eyes
Upward in incense.

On the tent's walls
Fourfold shadowed
In a crucifixion's
Endless moment

Intricacy of,
Delicacy of,
Darkness and engines.

II
Horses

The long whip lingers,
Toys with the sawdust;
The horses amble
On a disc of dreams.

The drumsticks flower
In pink percussion
To mix with the metal
Petals of brass.

The needle runs
In narrower circles;
The long whip leaps
And leads them inward.

Piebald horses
And ribald music
Circle around
A spangled lady.

III
Clowns

Clowns, Clowns and
Clowns
A firm that furthers
Nobody's business

Zanies by royal
Charter and adept
At false addition
And gay combustion

With bladders for batons
And upright eyebrows
Flappers for feet
And figs for no one.

The child's face pops
Like ginger beer
To see the air
Alive with bowlers.

Bric-a-brac
Pick-a-back
Spillbucket
Splits.

IV

Elephants

Tonnage of instinctive
Wisdom in tinsel,
Trunks like questions
And legs like tree trunks

On each forehead
A buxom blonde
And round each leg
A jangle of bells,

Deep in each brain
A chart of tropic
Swamp and twilight
Of creepered curtains,

Shamble in shoddy
Finery forward
And make their salaams
To the tiers of people—

Dummies with a reflex
Muscle of laughter
When they see the mountains
Come to Mahomet . . .

Efficacy of engines,
Obstinacy of darkness.

Christmas shopping

Spending beyond their income on gifts for Christmas—
Swing doors and crowded lifts and draperied jungles—
What shall we buy for our husbands and sons
   Different from last year?

Foxes hang by their noses behind plate glass—
Scream of macaws across festoons of paper—
Only the faces on the boxes of chocolates are free
   From boredom and crowsfeet.

Sometimes a chocolate-box girl escapes in the flesh,
Lightly manoeuvres the crowd, trilling with laughter;
After a couple of years her feet and her brain will
   Tire like the others.

The great windows marshal their troops for assault on the purse
Something-and-eleven the yard, hoodwinking logic,
The eleventh hour draining the gurgling pennies
   Down to the conduits

Down to the sewers of money—rats and marshgas—
Bubbling in maundering music under the pavement;
Here go the hours of routine, the weight on our eyelids—
   Pennies on corpses'.

While over the street in the centrally heated public
Library dwindling figures with sloping shoulders
And hands in pockets, weighted in the boots like chessmen,
   Stare at the printed

Columns of ads, the quickset road to riches,
Starting at a little and temporary but once we're
Started who knows whether we shan't continue,
   Salaries rising,

Rising like a salmon against the bullnecked river,
Bound for the spawning-ground of care-free days—
Good for a fling before the golden wheels run
   Down to a standstill.

And Christ is born—The nursery glad with baubles,
Alive with light and washable paint and children's

Eyes, expects as its due the accidental
    Loot of a system.

Smell of the South—oranges in silver paper,
Dates and ginger, the benison of firelight,
The blue flames dancing round the brandied raisins,
    Smiles from above them,

Hands from above them as of gods but really
These their parents, always seen from below, them-
Selves are always anxious looking across the
    Fence to the future—

Out there lies the future gathering quickly
Its blank momentum; through the tubes of London
The dead winds blow the crowds like beasts in flight from
    Fire in the forest.

The little firtrees palpitate with candles
In hundreds of chattering households where the suburb
Straggles like nervous handwriting, the margin
    Blotted with smokestacks.

Further out on the coast the lighthouse moves its
Arms of light through the fog that wads our welfare,
Moves its arms like a giant at Swedish drill whose
    Mind is a vacuum.

Bagpipe music

It's no go the merrygoround, it's no go the rickshaw,
All we want is a limousine and a ticket for the peepshow.
Their knickers are made of crêpe-de-chine, their shoes are made of
    python,
Their halls are lined with tiger rugs and their walls with heads of
    bison.

John MacDonald found a corpse, put it under the sofa,
Waited till it came to life and hit it with a poker,
Sold its eyes for souvenirs, sold its blood for whisky,
Kept its bones for dumb-bells to use when he was fifty.

It's no go the Yogi-Man, it's no go Blavatsky,
All we want is a bank balance and a bit of skirt in a taxi.

Annie MacDougall went to milk, caught her foot in the heather,
Woke to hear a dance record playing of Old Vienna.
It's no go your maidenheads, it's no go your culture,
All we want is a Dunlop tyre and the devil mend the puncture.

The Laird o' Phelps spent Hogmanay declaring he was sober,
Counted his feet to prove the fact and found he had one foot over.
Mrs. Carmichael had her fifth, looked at the job with repulsion,
Said to the midwife 'Take it away; I'm through with over-
   production'.

It's no go the gossip column, it's no go the Ceilidh,
All we want is a mother's help and a sugar-stick for the baby.

Willie Murray cut his thumb, couldn't count the damage,
Took the hide of an Ayrshire cow and used it for a bandage.
His brother caught three hundred cran when the seas were lavish,
Threw the bleeders back in the sea and went upon the parish.

It's no go the Herring Board, it's no go the Bible,
All we want is a packet of fags when our hands are idle.

It's no go the picture palace, it's no go the stadium,
It's no go the country cot with a pot of pink geraniums,
It's no go the Government grants, it's no go the elections,
Sit on your arse for fifty years and hang your hat on a pension.

It's no go my honey love, it's no go my poppet;
Work your hands from day to day, the winds will blow the profit.
The glass is falling hour by hour, the glass will fall for ever,
But if you break the bloody glass you won't hold up the weather.

1937

V

1938

Note

I am aware that there are over-statements in this poem—e.g. in the passages dealing with Ireland, the Oxford by-election or my own more private existence. There are also inconsistencies. If I had been writing a didactic poem proper, it would have been my job to qualify or eliminate these over-statements and inconsistencies. But I was writing what I have called a Journal. In a journal or a personal letter a man writes what he feels at the moment; to attempt scientific truthfulness would be—paradoxically— dishonest. The truth of a lyric is different from the truths of science, and this poem is something half-way between the lyric and the didactic poem. In as much as it is half-way towards a didactic poem I trust that it contains some 'criticism of life' or implies some standards which are not merely personal. I was writing it from August 1938 until the New Year and have not altered any passages relating to public events in the light of what happened after the time of writing. Thus the section about Barcelona having been written before the fall of Barcelona, I should consider it dishonest to have qualified it retrospectively by my reactions to the later event. Nor am I attempting to offer what so many people now demand from poets—a final verdict or a balanced judgment. It is the nature of this poem to be neither final nor balanced. I have certain beliefs which, I hope, emerge in the course of it but which I have refused to abstract from their context. For this reason I shall probably be called a trimmer by some and a sentimental extremist by others. But poetry in my opinion must be honest before anything else and I refuse to be 'objective' or clear-cut at the cost of honesty.

March, 1939

Autumn journal

I

Close and slow, summer is ending in Hampshire,
    Ebbing away down ramps of shaven lawn where close-clipped yew
Insulates the lives of retired generals and admirals
      And the spyglasses hung in the hall and the prayer-books ready
        in the pew
And August going out to the tin trumpets of nasturtiums
    And the sunflowers' Salvation Army blare of brass
And the spinster sitting in a deck-chair picking up stitches
    Not raising her eyes to the noise of the 'planes that pass

Northward from Lee-on-Solent. Macrocarpa and cypress
  And roses on a rustic trellis and mulberry trees
And bacon and eggs in a silver dish for breakfast
  And all the inherited assets of bodily ease
And all the inherited worries, rheumatism and taxes,
  And whether Stella will marry and what to do with Dick
And the branch of the family that lost their money in Hatry
  And the passing of the *Morning Post* and of life's climacteric
And the growth of vulgarity, cars that pass the gate-lodge
  And crowds undressing on the beach
And the hiking cockney lovers with thoughts directed
  Neither to God nor Nation but each to each.
But the home is still a sanctum under the pelmets,
  All quiet on the Family Front,
Farmyard noises across the fields at evening
  While the trucks of the Southern Railway dawdle . . . shunt
Into poppy sidings for the night—night which knows no
    passion
  No assault of hands or tongue
For all is old as flint or chalk or pine-needles
  And the rebels and the young
Have taken the train to town or the two-seater
  Unravelling rails or road,
Losing the thread deliberately behind them—
  Autumnal palinode.
And I am in the train too now and summer is going
  South as I go north
Bound for the dead leaves falling, the burning bonfire,
  The dying that brings forth
The harder life, revealing the trees' girders,
  The frost that kills the germs of *laissez-faire*;
West Meon, Tisted, Farnham, Woking, Weybridge,
  Then London's packed and stale and pregnant air.
My dog, a symbol of the abandoned order,
  Lies on the carriage floor,
Her eyes inept and glamorous as a film star's,
  Who wants to live, i.e. wants more
Presents, jewellery, furs, gadgets, solicitations
  As if to live were not
Following the curve of a planet or controlled water
  But a leap in the dark, a tangent, a stray shot.
It is this we learn after so many failures,
  The building of castles in sand, of queens in snow,
That we cannot make any corner in life or in life's beauty,
  That no river is a river which does not flow.

Surbiton, and a woman gets in, painted
  With dyed hair but a ladder in her stocking and eyes
Patient beneath the calculated lashes,
  Inured for ever to surprise;
And the train's rhythm becomes the *ad nauseam* repetition
  Of every tired aubade and maudlin madrigal,
The faded airs of sexual attraction
  Wandering like dead leaves along a warehouse wall:
'I loved my love with a platform ticket,
  A jazz song,
A handbag, a pair of stockings of Paris Sand—
  I loved her long.
I loved her between the lines and against the clock,
  Not until death
But till life did us part I loved her with paper money
  And with whisky on the breath.
I loved her with peacock's eyes and the wares of Carthage,
  With glass and gloves and gold and a powder puff
With blasphemy, camaraderie, and bravado
  And lots of other stuff.
I loved my love with the wings of angels
  Dipped in henna, unearthly red,
With my office hours, with flowers and sirens,
  With my budget, my latchkey, and my daily bread.'
And so to London and down the ever-moving
  Stairs
Where a warm wind blows the bodies of men together
  And blows apart their complexes and cares.

II

Spider, spider, twisting tight—
  But the watch is wary beneath the pillow—
I am afraid in the web of night
  When the window is fingered by the shadows of branches,
When the lions roar beneath the hill
  And the meter clicks and the cistern bubbles
And the gods are absent and the men are still—
  Noli me tangere, my soul is forfeit.
Some now are happy in the hive of home,
  Thigh over thigh and a light in the night nursery,
And some are hungry under the starry dome
  And some sit turning handles.

103

Glory to God in the Lowest, peace beneath the earth,
  Dumb and deaf at the nadir;
I wonder now whether anything is worth
  The eyelid opening and the mind recalling.
And I think of Persephone gone down to dark,
  No more a virgin, gone the garish meadow,
But why must she come back, why must the snowdrop
  mark
  That life goes on for ever?
There are nights when I am lonely and long for love
  But to-night is quintessential dark forbidding
Anyone beside or below me; only above
  Pile high the tumulus, good-bye to starlight.
Good-bye the Platonic sieve of the Carnal Man
  But good-bye also Plato's philosophising;
I have a better plan
  To hit the target straight without circumlocution.
If you can equate Being in its purest form
  With denial of all appearance,
Then let me disappear—the scent grows warm
  For pure Not-Being, Nirvana.
Only the spider spinning out his reams
  Of colourless thread says Only there are always
Interlopers, dreams,
  Who let no dead dog lie nor death be final;
Suggesting, while he spins, that to-morrow will outweigh
  To-night, that Becoming is a match for Being,
That to-morrow is also a day,
  That I must leave my bed and face the music.
As all the others do who with a grin
  Shake off sleep like a dog and hurry to desk or engine
And the fear of life goes out as they clock in
  And history is reasserted.
Spider, spider, your irony is true;
  Who am I—or I—to demand oblivion?
I must go out to-morrow as the others do
  And build the falling castle;
Which has never fallen, thanks
  Not to any formula, red tape or institution,
Not to any creeds or banks,
  But to the human animal's endless courage.
Spider, spider, spin
  Your register and let me sleep a little,
Not now in order to end but to begin
  The task begun so often.

III

August is nearly over, the people
  Back from holiday are tanned
With blistered thumbs and a wallet of snaps and a little
  Joie de vivre which is contraband;
Whose stamina is enough to face the annual
  Wait for the annual spree,
Whose memories are stamped with specks of sunshine
  Like faded *fleurs de lys.*
Now the till and the typewriter call the fingers,
  The workman gathers his tools
For the eight-hour day but after that the solace
  Of films or football pools
Or of the gossip or cuddle, the moments of self-glory
  Or self-indulgence, blinkers on the eyes of doubt,
The blue smoke rising and the brown lace sinking
  In the empty glass of stout.
Most are accepters, born and bred to harness,
  And take things as they come,
But some refusing harness and more who are refused it
  Would pray that another and a better Kingdom come,
Which now is sketched in the air or travestied in slogans
  Written in chalk or tar on stucco or plaster-board
But in time may find its body in men's bodies,
  Its law and order in their heart's accord,
Where skill will no longer languish nor energy be trammelled
  To competition and graft,
Exploited in subservience but not allegiance
  To an utterly lost and daft
System that gives a few at fancy prices
  Their fancy lives
While ninety-nine in the hundred who never attend the banquet
  Must wash the grease of ages off the knives.
And now the tempter whispers 'But you also
  Have the slave-owner's mind,
Would like to sleep on a mattress of easy profits,
  To snap your fingers or a whip and find
Servants or houris ready to wince and flatter
  And build with their degradation your self-esteem;
What you want is not a world of the free in function
  But a niche at the top, the skimmings of the cream.'
And I answer that that is largely so for habit makes me
  Think victory for one implies another's defeat,

That freedom means the power to order, and that in order
    To preserve the values dear to the élite
The élite must remain a few. It is so hard to imagine
    A world where the many would have their chance without
A fall in the standard of intellectual living
    And nothing left that the highbrow cared about.
Which fears must be suppressed. There is no reason for thinking
    That, if you give a chance to people to think or live,
The arts of thought or life will suffer and become rougher
    And not return more than you could ever give.
And now I relapse to sleep, to dreams perhaps and reaction
    Where I shall play the gangster or the sheikh,
Kill for the love of killing, make the world my sofa,
    Unzip the women and insult the meek.
Which fantasies no doubt are due to my private history,
    Matter for the analyst,
But the final cure is not in his past-dissecting fingers
    But in a future of action, the will and fist
Of those who abjure the luxury of self-pity
    And prefer to risk a movement without being sure
If movement would be better or worse in a hundred
    Years or a thousand when their heart is pure.
None of our hearts are pure, we always have mixed motives.
    Are self deceivers, but the worst of all
Deceits is to murmur 'Lord, I am not worthy'
    And, lying easy, turn your face to the wall.
But may I cure that habit, look up and outwards
    And may my feet follow my wider glance
First no doubt to stumble, then to walk with the others
    And in the end—with time and luck—to dance.

IV

September has come and I wake
    And I think with joy how whatever, now or in future, the system
Nothing whatever can take
    The people away, there will always be people
For friends or for lovers though perhaps
    The conditions of love will be changed and its vices diminished
And affection not lapse
    To narrow possessiveness, jealousy founded on vanity.
September has come, it is *hers*
    Whose vitality leaps in the autumn,

Whose nature prefers
  Trees without leaves and a fire in the fire-place;
So I give her this month and the next
  Though the whole of my year should be hers who has rendered
    already
So many of its days intolerable or perplexed
  But so many more so happy;
Who has left a scent on my life and left my walls
  Dancing over and over with her shadow,
Whose hair is twined in all my waterfalls
  And all of London littered with remembered kisses.
So I am glad
  That life contains her with her moods and moments
More shifting and more transient than I had
  Yet thought of as being integral to beauty;
Whose mind is like the wind on a sea of wheat,
  Whose eyes are candour,
And assurance in her feet
  Like a homing pigeon never by doubt diverted.
To whom I send my thanks
  That the air has become shot silk, the streets are music,
And that the ranks
  Of men are ranks of men, no more of cyphers.
So that if now alone
  I must pursue this life, it will not be only
A drag from numbered stone to numbered stone
  But a ladder of angels, river turning tidal.
Off-hand, at times hysterical, abrupt,
  You are one I always shall remember,
Whom cant can never corrupt
  Nor argument disinherit.
Frivolous, always in a hurry, forgetting the address,
  Frowning too often, taking enormous notice
Of hats and backchat—how could I assess
  The thing that makes you different?
You whom I remember glad or tired,
  Smiling in drink or scintillating anger,
Inopportunely desired
  On boats, on trains, on roads when walking.
Sometimes untidy, often elegant,
  So easily hurt, so readily responsive,
To whom a trifle could be an irritant
  Or could be balm and manna.
Whose words would tumble over each other and pelt
  From pure excitement,

Whose fingers curl and melt
  When you were friendly.
I shall remember you in bed with bright
  Eyes or in a café stirring coffee
Abstractedly and on your plate the white
  Smoking stub your lips had touched with crimson.
And I shall remember how your words could hurt
  Because they were so honest
And even your lies were able to assert
  Integrity of purpose.
And it is on the strength of knowing you
  I reckon generous feeling more important
Than the mere deliberating what to do
  When neither the pros nor cons affect the pulses.
And though I have suffered from your special strength
  Who never flatter for points nor fake responses
I should be proud if I could evolve at length
  An equal thrust and pattern.

V

To-day was a beautiful day, the sky was a brilliant
  Blue for the first time for weeks and weeks
But posters flapping on the railings tell the fluttered
  World that Hitler speaks, that Hitler speaks
And we cannot take it in and we go to our daily
  Jobs to the dull refrain of the caption 'War'
Buzzing around us as from hidden insects
  And we think 'This must be wrong, it has happened before,
Just like this before, we must be dreaming;
  It was long ago these flies
Buzzed like this, so why are they still bombarding
  The ears if not the eyes?'
And we laugh it off and go round town in the evening
  And this, we say, is on me;
Something out of the usual, a Pimm's Number One, a Picon—
  But did you see
The latest? You mean whether Cobb has bust the record
  Or do you mean the Australians have lost their last by ten
Wickets or do you mean that the autumn fashions—
  No, we don't mean anything like that again.
No, what we mean is Hodza, Henlein, Hitler,
  The Maginot Line,

The heavy panic that cramps the lungs and presses
    The collar down the spine.
And when we go out into Piccadilly Circus
    They are selling and buying the late
Special editions snatched and read abruptly
    Beneath the electric signs as crude as Fate.
And the individual, powerless, has to exert the
    Powers of will and choice
And choose between enormous evils, either
    Of which depends on somebody else's voice.
The cylinders are racing in the presses,
    The mines are laid,
The ribbon plumbs the fallen fathoms of Wall Street,
    And you and I are afraid.
To-day they were building in Oxford Street, the mortar
    Pleasant to smell,
But now it seems futility, imbecility,
    To be building shops when nobody can tell
What will happen next. What will happen
    We ask and waste the question on the air;
Nelson is stone and Johnnie Walker moves his
    Legs like a cretin over Trafalgar Square.
And in the Corner House the carpet-sweepers
    Advance between the tables after crumbs
Inexorably, like a tank battalion
    In answer to the drums.
In Tottenham Court Road the tarts and negroes
    Loiter beneath the lights
And the breeze gets colder as on so many other
    September nights.
A smell of French bread in Charlotte Street, a rustle
    Of leaves in Regent's Park
And suddenly from the Zoo I hear a sea-lion
    Confidently bark.
And so to my flat with the trees outside the window
    And the dahlia shapes of the lights on Primrose
        Hill
Whose summit once was used for a gun emplacement
    And very likely will
Be used that way again. The bloody frontier
    Converges on our beds
Like jungle beaters closing in on their destined
    Trophy of pelts and heads.
And at this hour of the day it is no good saying
    'Take away this cup';

Having helped to fill it ourselves it is only logic
   That now we should drink it up.
Nor can we hide our heads in the sands, the sands have
   Filtered away;
Nothing remains but rock at this hour, this zero
   Hour of the day.
Or that is how it seems to me as I listen
   To a hooter call at six
And then a woodpigeon calls and stops but the wind continues
   Playing its dirge in the trees, playing its tricks.
And now the dairy cart comes clopping slowly—
   Milk at the doors—
And factory workers are on their way to factories
   And charwomen to chores.
And I notice feathers sprouting from the rotted
   Silk of my black
Double eiderdown which was a wedding
   Present eight years back.
And the linen which I lie on came from Ireland
   In the easy days
When all I thought of was affection and comfort,
   Petting and praise.
And now the woodpigeon starts again denying
   The values of the town
And a car having crossed the hill accelerates, changes
   Up, having just changed down.
And a train begins to chug and I wonder what the morning
   Paper will say,
And decide to go quickly to sleep for the morning already
   Is with us, the day is to-day.

VI

And I remember Spain
   At Easter ripe as an egg for revolt and ruin
Though for a tripper the rain
   Was worse than the surly or the worried or the haunted faces
With writings on the walls—
   Hammer and sickle, Boicot, Viva, Muerra;
With café-au-lait brimming the waterfalls,
   With sherry, shellfish, omelettes.
With fretted stone the Moor
   Had chiselled for effects of sun and shadow;

With shadows of the poor,
  The begging cripples and the children begging.
The churches full of saints
  Tortured on racks of marble—
The old complaints
  Covered with gilt and dimly lit with candles.
With powerful or banal
  Monuments of riches or repression
And the Escorial
  Cold for ever within like the heart of Philip.
With ranks of dominoes
  Deployed on café tables the whole of Sunday;
With cabarets that call the tourist, shows
  Of thighs and eyes and nipples.
With slovenly soldiers, nuns,
  And peeling posters from the last elections
Promising bread or guns
  Or an amnesty or another
Order or else the old
  Glory veneered and varnished
As if veneer could hold
  The rotten guts and crumbled bones together.
And a vulture hung in air
  Below the cliffs of Ronda and below him
His hook-winged shadow wavered like despair
  Across the chequered vineyards.
And the boot-blacks in Madrid
  Kept us half an hour with polish and pincers
And all we did
  In that city was drink and think and loiter.
And in the Prado half-
  wit princes looked from the canvas they had paid for
(Goya had the laugh—
  But can what is corrupt be cured by laughter?)
And the day at Aranjuez
  When the sun came out for once on the yellow river
With Valdepeñas burdening the breath
  We slept a royal sleep in the royal gardens;
And at Toledo walked
  Around the ramparts where they throw the garbage
And glibly talked
  Of how the Spaniards lack all sense of business.
And Avila was cold
  And Segovia was picturesque and smelly
And a goat on the road seemed old

As the rocks or the Roman arches.
And Easter was wet and full
  In Seville and in the ring on Easter Sunday
A clumsy bull and then a clumsy bull
  Nodding his banderillas died of boredom.
And the standard of living was low
  But that, we thought to ourselves, was not our business;
All that the tripper wants is the *status quo*
  Cut and dried for trippers.
And we thought the papers a lark
  With their party politics and blank invective;
And we thought the dark
  Women who dyed their hair should have it dyed more often.
And we sat in trains all night
  With the windows shut among civil guards and peasants
And tried to play piquet by a tiny light
  And tried to sleep bolt upright;
And cursed the Spanish rain
  And cursed their cigarettes which came to pieces
And caught heavy colds in Cordova and in vain
  Waited for the right light for taking photos.
And we met a Cambridge don who said with an air
  'There's going to be trouble shortly in this country,'
And ordered anis, pudgy and debonair,
  Glad to show off his mastery of the language.
But only an inch behind
  This map of olive and ilex, this painted hoarding,
Careless of visitors the people's mind
  Was tunnelling like a mole to day and danger.
And the day before we left
  We saw the mob in flower at Algeciras
Outside a toothless door, a church bereft
  Of its images and its aura.
And at La Linea while
  The night put miles between us and Gibraltar
We heard the blood-lust of a drunkard pile
  His heaven high with curses;
And next day took the boat
  For home, forgetting Spain, not realising
That Spain would soon denote
  Our grief, our aspirations;
Not knowing that our blunt
  Ideals would find their whetstone, that our spirit
Would find its frontier on the Spanish front,
  Its body in a rag-tag army.

Conferences, adjournments, ultimatums,
    Flights in the air, castles in the air,
The autopsy of treaties, dynamite under the bridges,
    The end of *laissez faire*.
After the warm days the rain comes pimpling
    The paving stones with white
And with the rain the national conscience, creeping,
    Seeping through the night.
And in the sodden park on Sunday protest
    Meetings assemble not, as so often, now
Merely to advertise some patent panacea
    But simply to avow
The need to hold the ditch; a bare avowal
    That may perhaps imply
Death at the doors in a week but perhaps in the long run
    Exposure of the lie.
Think of a number, double it, treble it, square it,
    And sponge it out
And repeat *ad lib.* and mark the slate with crosses;
    There is no time to doubt
If the puzzle really has an answer. Hitler yells on the wireless,
    The night is damp and still
And I hear dull blows on wood outside my window;
    They are cutting down the trees on Primrose Hill.
The wood is white like the roast flesh of chicken,
    Each tree falling like a closing fan;
No more looking at the view from seats beneath the branches,
    Everything is going to plan;
They want the crest of this hill for anti-aircraft,
    The guns will take the view
And searchlights probe the heavens for bacilli
    With narrow wands of blue.
And the rain came on as I watched the territorials
    Sawing and chopping and pulling on ropes like a team
In a village tug-of-war; and I found my dog had vanished
    And thought 'This is the end of the old régime,'
But found the police had got her at St. John's Wood station
    And fetched her in the rain and went for a cup
Of coffee to an all-night shelter and heard a taxi-driver
    Say 'It turns me up
When I see these soldiers in lorries'—rumble of tumbrils
    Drums in the trees

Breaking the eardrums of the ravished dryads—
    It turns me up; a coffee, please.
And as I go out I see a windscreen-wiper
    In an empty car
Wiping away like mad and I feel astounded
    That things have gone so far.
And I come back here to my flat and wonder whether
    From now on I need take
The trouble to go out choosing stuff for curtains
    As I don't know anyone to make
Curtains quickly. Rather one should quickly
    Stop the cracks for gas or dig a trench
And take one's paltry measures against the coming
    Of the unknown Uebermensch.
But one—meaning I—is bored, am bored, the issue
    Involving principle but bound in fact
To squander principle in panic and self-deception—
    Accessories after the act,
So that all we foresee is rivers in spate sprouting
    With drowning hands
And men like dead frogs floating till the rivers
    Lose themselves in the sands.
And we who have been brought up to think of 'Gallant Belgium'
    As so much blague
Are now preparing again to essay good through evil
    For the sake of Prague;
And must, we suppose, become uncritical, vindictive,
    And must, in order to beat
The enemy, model ourselves upon the enemy,
    A howling radio for our paraclete.
The night continues wet, the axe keeps falling,
    The hill grows bald and bleak
No longer one of the sights of London but maybe
    We shall have fireworks here by this day week.

VIII

Sun shines easy, sun shines gay
    On bug-house, warehouse, brewery, market,
On the chocolate factory and the B.S.A.,
    On the Greek town hall and Josiah Mason;
On the Mitchells and Butlers Tudor pubs,
    On the white police and the one-way traffic

And glances off the chromium hubs
  And the metal studs in the sleek macadam.
Eight years back about this time
  I came to live in this hazy city
To work in a building caked with grime
  Teaching the classics to Midland students;
Virgil, Livy, the usual round,
  Principal parts and the lost digamma;
And to hear the prison-like lecture room resound
  To Homer in a Dudley accent.
But Life was comfortable, life was fine
  With two in a bed and patchwork cushions
And checks and tassels on the washing-line,
  A gramophone, a cat, and the smell of jasmine.
The steaks were tender, the films were fun,
  The walls were striped like a Russian ballet,
There were lots of things undone
  But nobody cared, for the days were early.
Nobody niggled, nobody cared,
  The soul was deaf to the mounting debit,
The soul was unprepared
  But the firelight danced on the ply-wood ceiling.
We drove round Shropshire in a bijou car—
  Bewdley, Cleobury Mortimer, Ludlow—
And the map of England was a toy bazaar
  And the telephone wires were idle music.
And sun shone easy, sun shone hard
  On quickly dropping pear-tree blossom
And pigeons courting in the cobbled yard
  With flashing necks and notes of thunder.
We slept in linen, we cooked with wine,
  We paid in cash and took no notice
Of how the train ran down the line
  Into the sun against the signal.
We lived in Birmingham through the slump—
  Line your boots with a piece of paper—
Sunlight dancing on the rubbish dump,
  On the queues of men and the hungry chimneys.
And the next election came—
  Labour defeats in Erdington and Aston;
And life went on—for us went on the same;
  Who were we to count the losses?
Some went back to work and the void
  Took on shape while others climbing
The uphill nights of the unemployed

Woke in the morning to factory hooters.
Little on the plate and nothing in the post;
    Queue in the rain or try the public
Library where the eye may coast
    Columns of print for a hopeful harbour.
But roads ran easy, roads ran gay
    Clear of the city and we together
Could put on tweeds for a getaway
    South or west to Clee or the Cotswolds;
Forty to the gallon; into the green
    Fields in the past of English history;
Flies in the bonnet and dust on the screen
    And no look back to the burning city.
That was then and now is now,
    Here again on a passing visit,
Passing through but how
    Memory blocks the passage.
Just as in Nineteen-Thirty-One
    Sun shines easy but I no longer
Docket a place in the sun—
    No wife, no ivory tower, no funk-hole.
The night grows purple, the crisis hangs
    Over the roofs like a Persian army
And all of Xenophon's parasangs
    Would take us only an inch from danger.
Black-out practice and A.R.P.,
    Newsboys driving a roaring business,
The flapping paper snatched to see
    If anything has, or has not, happened.
And I go to the Birmingham Hippodrome
    Packed to the roof and primed for laughter
And beautifully at home
    With the ukulele and the comic chestnuts;
'As pals we meet, as pals we part'—
    Embonpoint and a new tiara;
The comedian spilling the apple-cart
    Of *doubles entendres* and doggerel verses
And the next day begins
    Again with alarm and anxious
Listening to bulletins
    From distant, measured voices
Arguing for peace
    While the zero hour approaches,
While the eagles gather and the petrol and oil and grease
    Have all been applied and the vultures back the eagles.

But once again
    The crisis is put off and things look better
And we feel negotiation is not vain—
    Save my skin and damn my conscience.
And negotiation wins,
    If you can call it winning,
And here we are—just as before—safe in our skins;
    Glory to God for Munich.
And stocks go up and wrecks
    Are salved and politicians' reputations
Go up like Jack-on-the-Beanstalk; only the Czechs
    Go down and without fighting.

IX

Now we are back to normal, now the mind is
    Back to the even tenor of the usual day
Skidding no longer across the uneasy camber
    Of the nightmare way.
We are safe though others have crashed the railings
    Over the river ravine; their wheel-tracks carve the bank
But after the event all we can do is argue
    And count the widening ripples where they sank.
October comes with rain whipping around the ankles
    In waves of white at night
And filling the raw clay trenches (the parks of London
    Are a nasty sight).
In a week I return to work, lecturing, coaching,
    As impresario of the Ancient Greeks
Who wore the chiton and lived on fish and olives
    And talked philosophy or smut in cliques;
Who believed in youth and did not gloze the unpleasant
    Consequences of age;
What is life, one said, or what is pleasant
    Once you have turned the page
Of love? The days grow worse, the dice are loaded
    Against the living man who pays in tears for breath;
Never to be born was the best, call no man happy
    This side death.
Conscious—long before Engels—of necessity
    And therein free
They plotted out their life with truism and humour
    Between the jealous heaven and the callous sea.
And Pindar sang the garland of wild olive

And Alcibiades lived from hand to mouth
Double-crossing Athens, Persia, Sparta,
  And many died in the city of plague, and many of drouth
In Sicilian quarries, and many by the spear and arrow
  And many more who told their lies too late
Caught in the eternal factions and reactions
  Of the city-state.
And free speech shivered on the pikes of Macedonia
  And later on the swords of Rome
And Athens became a mere university city
  And the goddess born of the foam
Became the kept hetaera, heroine of Menander,
  And the philosopher narrowed his focus, confined
His efforts to putting his own soul in order
  And keeping a quiet mind.
And for a thousand years they went on talking,
  Making such apt remarks,
A race no longer of heroes but of professors
  And crooked business men and secretaries and clerks
Who turned out dapper little elegiac verses
  On the ironies of fate, the transience of all
Affections, carefully shunning an over-statement
  But working the dying fall.
The Glory that was Greece: put it in a syllabus, grade it
  Page by page
To train the mind or even to point a moral
  For the present age:
Models of logic and lucidity, dignity, sanity,
  The golden mean between opposing ills
Though there were exceptions of course but only exceptions—
  The bloody Bacchanals on the Thracian hills.
So the humanist in his room with Jacobean panels
  Chewing his pipe and looking on a lazy quad
Chops the Ancient World to turn a sermon
  To the greater glory of God.
But I can do nothing so useful or so simple;
  These dead are dead
And when I should remember the paragons of Hellas
  I think instead
Of the crooks, the adventurers, the opportunists,
  The careless athletes and the fancy boys,
The hair-splitters, the pedants, the hard-boiled sceptics
  And the Agora and the noise
Of the demagogues and the quacks; and the women pouring
  Libations over graves

And the trimmers at Delphi and the dummies at Sparta and lastly
    I think of the slaves.
And how one can imagine oneself among them
    I do not know;
It was all so unimaginably different
    And all so long ago.

X

And so return to work—the M.A. gown,
    Alphas and Betas, central heating, floor-polish,
Demosthenes on the Crown
    And Oedipus at Colonus.
And I think of the beginnings of other terms
    Coming across the sea to unknown England
And memory reaffirms
    That alarm and exhilaration of arrival:
White wooden boxes, clatter of boots, a smell
    Of changing-rooms—Lifebuoy soap and muddy flannels—
And over all a bell
    Dragooning us to dormitory or classroom,
Ringing with a tongue of frost across the bare
    Benches and desks escutcheoned with initials;
We sat on the hot pipes by the wall, aware
    Of the cold in our bones and the noise and the bell impending.
A fishtail gas-flare in the dark latrine;
    Chalk and ink and rows of pegs and lockers;
The War was on—maize and margarine
    And lessons on the map of Flanders.
But we had our toys—our electric torches, our glass
    Dogs and cats, and plasticine and conkers,
And we had our games, we learned to dribble and pass
    In jerseys striped like tigers.
And we had our makebelieve, we had our mock
    Freedom in walks by twos and threes on Sunday,
We dug out fossils from the yellow rock
    Or drank the Dorset distance.
And we had our little tiptoe minds, alert
    To jump for facts and fancies and statistics
And our little jokes of Billy Bunter dirt
    And a heap of home-made dogma.
The Abbey chimes varnished the yellow street,
    The water from the taps in the bath was yellow,
The trees were full of owls, the sweets were sweet
    And life an expanding ladder.

119

And reading romances we longed to be grown up,
   To shoot from the hip and marry lovely ladies
And smoke cigars and live on claret cup
   And lie in bed in the morning;
Taking it for granted that things would still
   Get better and bigger and better and bigger and better,
That the road across the hill
   Led to the Garden of Eden;
Everything to expect and nothing to deplore,
   Cushy days beyond the dumb horizon
And nothing to doubt about, to linger for
   In the halfway house of childhood.
And certainly we did not linger, we went on
   Growing and growing, gluttons for the future,
And four foot six was gone
   And we found it was time to be leaving
To be changing school, sandstone changed for chalk
   And ammonites for the flinty husks of sponges,
Another lingo to talk
   And jerseys in other colours.
And still the acquiring of unrelated facts,
   A string of military dates for history,
And the Gospels and the Acts
   And logarithms and Greek and the Essays of Elia;
And still the exhilarating rhythm of free
   Movement swimming or serving at tennis,
The fives-courts' tattling repartee
   Or rain on the sweating body.
But life began to narrow to what was done—
   The dominant gerundive—
And Number Two must mimic Number One
   In bearing, swearing, attitude and accent.
And so we jettisoned all
   Our childish fantasies and anarchism;
The weak must go to the wall
   But strength implies the system;
You must lose your soul to be strong, you cannot stand
   Alone on your own legs or your own ideas;
The order of the day is complete conformity and
   An automatic complacence.
Such was the order of the day; only at times
   The Fool among the yes-men flashed his motley
To prick their pseudo-reason with his rhymes
   And drop his grain of salt on court behaviour.
And sometimes a whisper in books

Would challenge the code, or a censored memory sometimes,
Sometimes the explosion of rooks,
    Sometimes the mere batter of light on the senses.
And the critic jailed in the mind would peep through the grate
    And husky from long silence, murmur gently
That there is something rotten in the state
    Of Denmark but the state is not the whole of Denmark,
And a spade is still a spade
    And the difference is not final between a tailored
Suit and a ready-made
    And knowledge is not—necessarily—wisdom;
And a cultured accent alone will not provide
    A season ticket to the Vita Nuova;
And there are many better men outside
    Than ever answered roll-call.
But the critic did not win, has not won yet
    Though always reminding us of points forgotten;
We hasten to forget
    As much as he remembers.
And school was what they always said it was,
    An apprenticeship to life, an initiation,
And all the better because
    The initiates were blindfold;
The reflex action of a dog or sheep
    Being enough for normal avocations
And life rotating in an office sleep
    As long as things are normal.
Which it was assumed that they would always be;
    On that assumption terms began and ended;
And now, in Nineteen-Thirty-Eight A.D.,
    Term is again beginning.

XI

But work is alien; what do I care for the Master
    Of those who know, of those who know too much?
I am too harassed by my familiar devils,
    By those I cannot see, by those I may not touch;
Knowing perfectly well in the mind, on paper,
    How wasteful and absurd
Are personal fixations but yet the pulse keeps thrumming
    And her voice is faintly heard
Through walls and walls of indifference and abstraction
    And across the London roofs

And every so often calls up hopes from nowhere,
  A distant clatter of hoofs,
And my common sense denies she is returning
  And says, if she does return, she will not stay;
And my pride, in the name of reason, tells me to cut my losses
  And call it a day.
Which, if I had the cowardice of my convictions,
  I certainly should do
But doubt still finds a loophole
  To gamble on another rendezvous.
And I try to feel her in fancy but the fancy
  Dissolves in curls of mist
And I try to summarise her but how can hungry
  Love be a proper analyst?
For suddenly I hate her and would murder
  Her memory if I could
And then of a sudden I see her sleeping gently
  Inaccessible in a sleeping wood
But thorns and thorns around her
  And the cries of night
And I have no knife or axe to hack my passage
  Back to the lost delight.
And then I think of the others and jealousy riots
  In impossible schemes
To kill them with all the machinery of fact and with all the
  Tortures of dreams.
But yet, my dear, if only for my own distraction,
  I have to try to assess
Your beauty of body, your paradoxes of spirit,
  Even your taste in dress.
Whose emotions are an intricate dialectic,
  Whose eagerness to live
A many-sided life might be deplored as fickle,
  Unpractical, or merely inquisitive.
A superficial comment; for your instinct
  Sanctions all you do,
Who know that truth is nothing in abstraction,
  That action makes both wish and principle come true;
Whose changes have the logic of a prism,
  Whose moods create,
Who never linger haggling on the threshold,
  To weigh the pros and cons until it is too late.
At times intractable, virulent, hypercritical,
  With a bitter tongue;
Over-shy at times, morose, defeatist,

At times a token that the world is young;
Given to over-statement, careless of caution,
   Quick to sound the chimes
Of delicate intuition, at times malicious
   And generous at times.
Whose kaleidoscopic ways are all authentic,
   Whose truth is not of a statement but of a dance
So that even when you deceive your deceits are merely
   Technical and of no significance.
And so, when I think of you, I have to meet you
   In thought on your own ground;
To apply to you my algebraic canons
   Would merely be unsound;
And, having granted this, I cannot balance
   My hopes or fears of you in pros and cons;
It has been proved that Achilles cannot catch the Tortoise,
   It has been proved that men are automatons,
Everything wrong has been proved. I will not bother
   Any more with proof;
I see the future glinting with your presence
   Like moon on a slate roof,
And my spirits rise again. It is October,
   The year-god dying on the destined pyre
With all the colours of a scrambled sunset
   And all the funeral elegance of fire
In the grey world to lie cocooned but shaping
   His gradual return;
No one can stop the cycle;
   The grate is full of ash but fire will always burn.
Therefore, listening to the taxis
   (In which you never come) so regularly pass,
I wait content, banking on the spring and watching
   The dead leaves canter over the dowdy grass.

XII

These days are misty, insulated, mute
   Like a faded tapestry and the soft pedal
Is down and the yellow leaves are falling down
   And we hardly have the heart to meddle
Any more with personal ethics or public calls;
   People have not recovered from the crisis,
Their faces are far away, the tone of the words
   Belies their thesis.

123

For they say that now it is time unequivocally to act,
  To let the pawns be taken,
That criticism, a virtue previously,
  Now can only weaken
And that when we go to Rome
  We must do as the Romans do, cry out together
For bread and circuses; put on your togas now
  For this is Roman weather.
Circuses of death and from the topmost tiers
  A cataract of goggling, roaring faces;
On the arena sand
  Those who are about to die try out their paces.
Now it is night, a cold mist creeps, the night
  Is still and damp and lonely;
Sitting by the fire it is hard to realise
  That the legions wait at the gates and that there is only
A little time for rest though not by rights for rest,
  Rather for whetting the will, for calculating
A compromise between necessity and wish,
  Apprenticed late to learn the trade of hating.
Remember the sergeant barking at bayonet practice
  When you were small;
To kill a dummy you must act a dummy
  Or you cut no ice at all.
Now it is morning again, the 25th of October,
  In a white fog the cars have yellow lights;
The chill creeps up the wrists, the sun is sallow,
  The silent hours grow down like stalactites.
And reading Plato talking about his Forms
  To damn the artist touting round his mirror,
I am glad that I have been left the third best bed
  And live in a world of error.
His world of capital initials, of transcendent
  Ideas is too bleak;
For me there remain to all intents and purposes
  Seven days in the week
And no one Tuesday is another and you destroy it
  If you subtract the difference and relate
It merely to the Form of Tuesday. This is Tuesday
  The 25th of October, 1938.
Aristotle was better who watched the insect breed,
  The natural world develop,
Stressing the function, scrapping the Form in Itself,
  Taking the horse from the shelf and letting it gallop.
Education gives us too many labels

And clichés, cuts too many Gordian knots;
Trains us to keep the roads nor reconnoitre
    Any of the beauty-spots or danger-spots.
Not that I would rather be a peasant; the Happy Peasant
    Like the Noble Savage is a myth;
I do not envy the self-possession of an elm-tree
    Nor the aplomb of a granite monolith.
All that I would like to be is human, having a share
    In a civilised, articulate and well-adjusted
Community where the mind is given its due
    But the body is not distrusted.
As it is, the so-called humane studies
    May lead to cushy jobs
But leave the men who land them spiritually bankrupt
    Intellectual snobs.
Not but what I am glad to have my comforts,
    Better authentic mammon than a bogus god;
If it were not for Lit.Hum. I might be climbing
    A ladder with a hod.
And seven hundred a year
    Will pay the rent and the gas and the 'phone and the grocer;
(The Emperor takes his seat beneath the awning,
    Those who are about to die . . .) Come, pull the curtains closer.

XIII

Which things being so, as we said when we studied
    The classics, I ought to be glad
That I studied the classics at Marlborough and Merton,
    Not everyone here having had
The privilege of learning a language
    That is incontrovertibly dead,
And of carting a toy-box of hall-marked marmoreal phrases
    Around in his head.
We wrote compositions in Greek which they said was a lesson
    In logic and good for the brain;
We marched, counter-marched to the field-marshal's blue-pencil
        baton,
    We dressed by the right and we wrote out the sentence again.
We learned that a gentleman never misplaces his accents,
    That nobody knows how to speak, much less how to write
English who has not hob-nobbed with the great-grandparents of
        English,
    That the boy on the Modern Side is merely a parasite

But the classical student is bred to the purple, his training in syntax
   Is also a training in thought
And even in morals; if called to the bar or the barracks
   He always will do what he ought.
And knowledge, besides, should be prized for the sake of knowledge:
   Oxford crowded the mantelpiece with gods—
Scaliger, Heinsius, Dindorf, Bentley and Wilamowitz—
   As we learned our genuflexions for Honour Mods.
And then they taught us philosophy, logic and metaphysics,
   The Negative Judgment and the Ding an Sich,
And every single thinker was powerful as Napoleon
   And crafty as Metternich.
And it really was very attractive to be able to talk about tables
   And to ask if the table *is*,
And to draw the cork out of an old conundrum
   And watch the paradoxes fizz.
And it made one confident to think that nothing
   Really was what it seemed under the sun,
That the actual was not real and the real was not with us
   And all that mattered was the One.
And they said 'The man in the street is so naïve, he never
   Can see the wood for the trees;
He thinks he knows he sees a thing but cannot
   Tell you how he knows the thing he thinks he sees.'
And oh how much I liked the Concrete Universal,
   I never thought that I should
Be telling them vice-versa
   That they can't see the trees for the wood.
But certainly it was fun while it lasted
   And I got my honours degree
And was stamped as a person of intelligence and culture
   For ever wherever two or three
Persons of intelligence and culture
   Are gathered together in talk
Writing definitions on invisible blackboards
   In non-existent chalk.
But such sacramental occasions
   Are nowadays comparatively rare;
There is always a wife or a boss or a dun or a client
   Disturbing the air.
Barbarians always, life in the particular always,
   Dozens of men in the street,
And the perennial if unimportant problem
   Of getting enough to eat.
So blow the bugles over the metaphysicians,

Let the pure mind return to the Pure Mind;
I must be content to remain in the world of Appearance
   And sit on the mere appearance of a behind.
But in case you should think my education was wasted
   I hasten to explain
That having once been to the University of Oxford
   You can never really again
Believe anything that anyone says and that of course is an asset
   In a world like ours;
Why bother to water a garden
   That is planted with paper flowers?
O the Freedom of the Press, the Late Night Final,
   To-morrow's pulp;
One should not gulp one's port but as it isn't
   Port, I'll gulp it if I want to gulp
But probably I'll just enjoy the colour
   And pour it down the sink
For I don't call advertisement a statement
   Or any quack medicine a drink.
Good-bye now, Plato and Hegel,
   The shop is closing down;
They don't want any philosopher-kings in England,
   There ain't no universals in this man's town.

XIV

The next day I drove by night
   Among red and amber and green, spears and candles,
Corkscrews and slivers of reflected light
   In the mirror of the rainy asphalt
Along the North Circular and the Great West roads
   Running the gauntlet of impoverished fancy
Where housewives bolster up their jerry-built abodes
   With *amour propre* and the habit of Hire Purchase.
The wheels whished in the wet, the flashy strings
   Of neon lights unravelled, the windscreen-wiper
Kept at its job like a tiger in a cage or a cricket that sings
   All night through for nothing.
Factory, a site for a factory, rubbish dumps,
   Bungalows in lath and plaster, in brick, in concrete,
And shining semi-circles of petrol pumps
   Like intransigent gangs of idols.
And the road swings round my head like a lassoo

Looping wider and wider tracts of darkness
And the country succeeds the town and the country too
Is damp and dark and evil.
And coming over the Chilterns the dead leaves leap
    Charging the windscreen like a barrage of angry
Birds as I take the steep
    Plunge to Henley or Hades.
And at the curves of the road the telephone wires
    Shine like strands of silk and the hedge solicits
My irresponsible tyres
    To an accident, to a bed in the wet grasses.
And in quiet crooked streets only the village pub
    Spills a golden puddle
Over the pavement and trees bend down and rub
    Unopened dormer windows with their knuckles.
Nettlebed, Shillingford, Dorchester—each unrolls
    The road to Oxford; *Qu'allais-je faire* to-morrow
Driving voters to the polls
    In that home of lost illusions?
And what am I doing it for?
    Mainly for fun, partly for a half-believed-in
Principle, a core
    Of fact in a pulp of verbiage,
Remembering that this crude and so-called obsolete
    Top-heavy tedious parliamentary system
Is our only ready weapon to defeat
    The legions' eagles and the lictors' axes;
And remembering that those who by their habit hate
    Politics can no longer keep their private
Values unless they open the public gate
    To a better political system.
That Rome was not built in a day is no excuse
    For *laissez-faire*, for bowing to the odds against us;
What is the use
    Of asking what is the use of one brick only?
The perfectionist stands for ever in a fog
    Waiting for the fog to clear; better to be vulgar
And use your legs and leave a blank for Hogg
    And put a cross for Lindsay.
There are only too many who say 'What difference does it make
    One way or the other?
To turn the stream of history will take
    More than a by-election.'
So Thursday came and Oxford went to the polls
    And made its coward vote and the streets resounded

To the triumphant cheers of the lost souls—
  The profiteers, the dunderheads, the smarties.
And I drove back to London in the dark of the morning, the trees
  Standing out in the headlights cut from cardboard;
Wondering which disease
  Is worse—the Status Quo or the Mere Utopia.
For from now on
  Each occasion must be used, however trivial,
To rally the ranks of those whose chance will soon be gone
  For even guerrilla warfare.
The nicest people in England have always been the least
  Apt to solidarity or alignment
But all of them must now align against the beast
  That prowls at every door and barks in every headline.
Dawn and London and daylight and last the sun:
  I stop the car and take the yellow placard
Off the bonnet; that little job is done
  Though without success or glory.
The plane-tree leaves come sidling down
  (Catch my guineas, catch my guineas)
And the sun caresses Camden Town,
  The barrows of oranges and apples.

XV

Shelley and jazz and lieder and love and hymn-tunes
  And day returns too soon;
We'll get drunk among the roses
  In the valley of the moon.
Give me an aphrodisiac, give me lotus,
  Give me the same again;
Make all the erotic poets of Rome and Ionia
  And Florence and Provence and Spain
Pay a tithe of their sugar to my potion
  And ferment my days
With the twang of Hawaii and the boom of the Congo,
  Let the old Muse loosen her stays
Or give me a new Muse with stockings and suspenders
  And a smile like a cat,
With false eyelashes and finger-nails of carmine
  And dressed by Schiaparelli, with a pill-box hat.
Let the aces run riot round Brooklands,
  Let the tape-machines go drunk,

Turn on the purple spotlight, pull out the Vox Humana,
    Dig up somebody's body in a cloakroom trunk.
Give us sensations and then again sensations—
    Strip-tease, fireworks, all-in wrestling, gin;
Spend your capital, open your house and pawn your padlocks,
    Let the critical sense go out and the Roaring Boys come in.
Give me a houri but houris are too easy,
    Give me a nun;
We'll rape the angels off the golden reredos
    Before we're done.
Tiger-women and Lesbos, drums and entrails,
    And let the skies rotate,
We'll play roulette with the stars, we'll sit out drinking
    At the Hangman's Gate.
O look who comes here. I cannot see their faces
    Walking in file, slowly in file;
They have no shoes on their feet, the knobs of their ankles
    Catch the moonlight as they pass the stile
And cross the moor among the skeletons of bog-oak
    Following the track from the gallows back to the town;
Each has the end of a rope around his neck. I wonder
    Who let these men come back, who cut them down—
And now they reach the gate and line up opposite
    The neon lights on the medieval wall
And underneath the sky-signs
    Each one takes his cowl and lets it fall
And we see their faces, each the same as the other,
    Men and women, each like a closed door,
But something about their faces is familiar;
    Where have we seen them before?
Was it the murderer on the nursery ceiling
    Or Judas Iscariot in the Field of Blood
Or someone at Gallipoli or in Flanders
    Caught in the end-all mud?
But take no notice of them, out with the ukulele,
    The saxophone and the dice;
They are sure to go away if we take no notice;
    Another round of drinks or make it twice.
That was a good one, tell us another, don't stop talking,
    Cap your stories; if
You haven't any new ones tell the old ones,
    Tell them as often as you like and perhaps those horrible stiff
People with blank faces that are yet familiar
    Won't be there when you look again, but don't
Look just yet, just give them time to vanish. I said to vanish;

What do you mean—they won't?
Give us the songs of Harlem or Mitylene—
    Pearls in wine—
There can't be a hell unless there is a heaven
    And a devil would have to be divine
And there can't be such things one way or the other;
    That we know;
You can't step into the same river twice so there can't be
    Ghosts; thank God that rivers always flow.
Sufficient to the moment is the moment;
    Past and future merely don't make sense
And yet I thought I had seen them . . .
    But *how*, if there is only a present tense?
Come on, boys, we aren't afraid of bogies,
    Give us another drink;
This little lady has a fetish,
    She goes to bed in mink.
This little pig went to market—
    Now I think you may look, I think the coast is clear.
Well, why don't you answer?
    I can't answer because they are still there.

XVI

Nightmare leaves fatigue:
    We envy men of action
Who sleep and wake, murder and intrigue
    Without being doubtful, without being haunted.
And I envy the intransigence of my own
    Countrymen who shoot to kill and never
See the victim's face become their own
    Or find his motive sabotage their motives.
So reading the memoirs of Maud Gonne,
    Daughter of an English mother and a soldier father,
I note how a single purpose can be founded on
    A jumble of opposites:
Dublin Castle, the vice-regal ball,
    The embassies of Europe,
Hatred scribbled on a wall,
    Gaols and revolvers.
And I remember, when I was little, the fear
    Bandied among the servants
That Casement would land at the pier

With a sword and a horde of rebels;
And how we used to expect, at a later date,
    When the wind blew from the west, the noise of shooting
Starting in the evening at eight
    In Belfast in the York Street district;
And the voodoo of the Orange bands
    Drawing an iron net through darkest Ulster,
Flailing the limbo lands—
    The linen mills, the long wet grass, the ragged hawthorn.
And one read black where the other read white, his hope
    The other man's damnation:
Up the Rebels, To Hell with the Pope,
    And God Save—as you prefer—the King or Ireland.
The land of scholars and saints:
    Scholars and saints my eye, the land of ambush,
Purblind manifestoes, never-ending complaints,
    The born martyr and the gallant ninny;
The grocer drunk with the drum,
    The land-owner shot in his bed, the angry voices
Piercing the broken fanlight in the slum,
    The shawled woman weeping at the garish altar.
Kathaleen ni Houlihan! Why
    Must a country, like a ship or a car, be always female,
Mother or sweetheart? A woman passing by,
    We did but see her passing.
Passing like a patch of sun on the rainy hill
    And yet we love her for ever and hate our neighbour
And each one in his will
    Binds his heirs to continuance of hatred.
Drums on the haycock, drums on the harvest, black
    Drums in the night shaking the windows:
King William is riding his white horse back
    To the Boyne on a banner.
Thousands of banners, thousands of white
    Horses, thousands of Williams
Waving thousands of swords and ready to fight
    Till the blue sea turns to orange.
Such was my country and I thought I was well
    Out of it, educated and domiciled in England,
Though yet her name keeps ringing like a bell
    In an under-water belfry.
Why do we like being Irish? Partly because
    It gives us a hold on the sentimental English
As members of a world that never was,
    Baptised with fairy water;

And partly because Ireland is small enough
    To be still thought of with a family feeling,
And because the waves are rough
    That split her from a more commercial culture;
And because one feels that here at least one can
    Do local work which is not at the world's mercy
And that on this tiny stage with luck a man
    Might see the end of one particular action.
It is self-deception of course;
    There is no immunity in this island either;
A cart that is drawn by somebody else's horse
    And carrying goods to somebody else's market.
The bombs in the turnip sack, the sniper from the roof,
    Griffith, Connolly, Collins, where have they brought us?
Ourselves alone! Let the round tower stand aloof
    In a world of bursting mortar!
Let the school-children fumble their sums
    In a half-dead language;
Let the censor be busy on the books; pull down the Georgian slums;
    Let the games be played in Gaelic.
Let them grow beet-sugar; let them build
    A factory in every hamlet;
Let them pigeon-hole the souls of the killed
    Into sheep and goats, patriots and traitors.
And the North, where I was a boy,
    Is still the North, veneered with the grime of Glasgow,
Thousands of men whom nobody will employ
    Standing at the corners, coughing.
And the street-children play on the wet
    Pavement—hopscotch or marbles;
And each rich family boasts a sagging tennis-net
    On a spongy lawn beside a dripping shrubbery.
The smoking chimneys hint
    At prosperity round the corner
But they make their Ulster linen from foreign lint
    And the money that comes in goes out to make more money.
A city built upon mud;
    A culture built upon profit;
Free speech nipped in the bud,
    The minority always guilty.
Why should I want to go back
    To you, Ireland, my Ireland?
The blots on the page are so black
    That they cannot be covered with shamrock.
I hate your grandiose airs,

Your sob-stuff, your laugh and your swagger,
Your assumption that everyone cares
    Who is the king of your castle.
Castles are out of date,
    The tide flows round the children's sandy fancy;
Put up what flag you like, it is too late
    To save your soul with bunting.
Odi atque amo:
    Shall we cut this name on trees with a rusty dagger?
Her mountains are still blue, her rivers flow
    Bubbling over the boulders.
She is both a bore and a bitch;
    Better close the horizon,
Send her no more fantasy, no more longings which
    Are under a fatal tariff.
For common sense is the vogue
    And she gives her children neither sense nor money
Who slouch around the world with a gesture and a brogue
    And a faggot of useless memories.

XVII

From the second floor up, looking north, having breakfast
    I see the November sun at nine o'clock
Gild the fusty brickwork of rows on rows of houses
    Like animals asleep and breathing smoke,
And savouring Well-being
    I light my first cigarette, grow giddy and blink,
Glad of this titillation, this innuendo,
    This make-believe of standing on a brink;
For all our trivial daily acts are altered
    Into heroic or romantic make-believe
Of which we are hardly conscious—Who is it calls me
    When the cold draught picks my sleeve?
Or sneezing in the morning sunlight or smelling the bonfire
    Over the webbed lawn and the naked cabbage plot?
Or stepping into a fresh-filled bath with strata
    Of cold water and hot?
We lie in the bath between tiled walls and under
    Ascending scrolls of steam
And feel the ego merge as the pores open
    And we lie in the bath and dream;
And responsibility dies and the thighs are happy

And the body purrs like a cat
But this lagoon grows cold, we have to leave it, stepping
    On to a check rug on a cork mat.
The luxury life is only to be valued
    By those who are short of money or pressed for time
As the cinema gives the poor their Jacob's ladder
    For Cinderellas to climb.
And Plato was right to define the bodily pleasures
    As the pouring water into a hungry sieve
But wrong to ignore the rhythm which the intercrossing
    Coloured waters permanently give.
And Aristotle was right to posit the Alter Ego
    But wrong to make it only a halfway house:
Who could expect—or want—to be spiritually self-supporting,
    Eternal self-abuse?
Why not admit that other people are always
    Organic to the self, that a monologue
Is the death of language and that a single lion
    Is less himself, or alive, than a dog and another dog?
Virtue going out of us always; the eyes grow weary
    With vision but it is vision builds the eye;
And in a sense the children kill their parents
    But do the parents die?
And the beloved destroys like fire or water
    But water scours and sculps and fire refines
And if you are going to read the testaments of cynics,
    You must read between the lines.
A point here and a point there: the current
    Jumps the gaps, the ego cannot live
Without becoming other for the Other
    Has got yourself to give.
And even the sense of taste provides communion
    With God as plant or beast;
The sea in fish, the field in a salad of endive,
    A sacramental feast.
The soul's long searchlight hankers for a body,
    The single body hungers for its kind,
The eye demands the light at the risk of blindness
    And the mind that did not doubt would not be mind
And discontent is eternal. In luxury or business,
    In family or sexual love, in purchases or prayers,
Our virtue is invested, the self put out at interest,
    The returns are never enough, the fact compares
So badly with the fancy yet fancy itself is only
    A divination of fact

And if we confine the world to the prophet's tripod
　　The subjects of our prophecy contract.
Open the world wide, open the senses,
　　Let the soul stretch its blind enormous arms,
There is vision in the fingers only needing waking,
　　Ready for light's alarms.
O light, terror of light, hoofs and ruthless
　　Wheels of steel and brass
Dragging behind you lacerated captives
　　Who also share your triumph as you pass.
Light which is time, belfry of booming sunlight,
　　The ropes run up and down,
The whole town shakes with the peal of living people
　　Who break and build the town.
Aristotle was right to think of man-in-action
　　As the essential and really existent man
And man means men in action; try and confine your
　　Self to yourself if you can.
Nothing is self-sufficient, pleasure implies hunger
　　But hunger implies hope:
I cannot lie in this bath for ever, clouding
　　The cooling water with rose geranium soap.
I cannot drug my life with the present moment;
　　The present moment may rape—but all in vain—
The future, for the future remains a virgin
　　Who must be tried again.

XVIII

In the days that were early the music came easy
　　On cradle and coffin, in the corn and the barn
Songs for the reaping and spinning and only the shepherd
　　Then as now was silent beside the tarn:
Cuffs of foam around the beer-brown water,
　　Crinkled water and a mackerel sky;
It is all in the day's work—the grey stones and heather
　　And the sheep that breed and break their legs and die.
The uplands now as then are fresh but in the valley
　　Polluted rivers run—the Lethe and the Styx;
The soil is tired and the profit little and the hunchback
　　Bobs on a carthorse round the sodden ricks.
Sing us no more idylls, no more pastorals,
　　No more epics of the English earth;

The country is a dwindling annexe to the factory,
    Squalid as an after-birth.
This England is tight and narrow, teeming with unwanted
    Children who are so many, each is alone;
Niobe and her children
    Stand beneath the smokestack turned to stone.
And still the church-bells brag above the empty churches
    And the Union Jack
Thumps the wind above the law-courts and the barracks
    And in the allotments the black
Scarecrow holds a fort of grimy heads of cabbage
    Besieged by grimy birds
Like a hack politician fighting the winged aggressor
    With yesterday's magic coat of ragged words.
Things were different when men felt their programme
    In the bones and pulse, not only in the brain,
Born to a trade, a belief, a set of affections;
    That instinct for belief may sprout again,
There are some who have never lost it
    And some who foster or force it into growth
But most of us lack the right discontent, contented
    Merely to cavil. Spiritual sloth
Creeps like lichen or ivy over the hinges
    Of the doors which never move;
We cannot even remember who is behind them
    Nor even, soon, shall have the chance to prove
If anyone at all is behind them—
    The Sleeping Beauty or the Holy Ghost
Or the greatest happiness of the greatest number;
    All we can do at most
Is press an anxious ear against the keyhole
    To hear the Future breathing; softly tread
In the outer porch beneath the marble volutes—
    Who knows if God, as Nietzsche said, is dead?
There is straw to lay in the streets; call the hunchback,
    The gentleman farmer, the village idiot, the Shropshire Lad,
To insulate us if they can with coma
    Before we all go mad.
What shall we pray for, Lord? Whom shall we pray to?
    Shall we give like decadent Athens the benefit of the doubt
To the Unknown God or smugly pantheistic
    Assume that God is everywhere round about?
But if we assume such a God, then who the devil
    Are these with empty stomachs or empty smiles?
The blind man's stick goes tapping on the pavement

137

For endless glittering miles
Beneath the standard lights; the paralytic winding
    His barrel-organ sprays the passers-by
With April music; the many-ribboned hero
    With half a lung or a leg waits his turn to die.
God forbid an Indian acquiescence,
    The apotheosis of the status quo;
If everything that happens happens according
    To the nature and wish of God, then God must go:
Lay your straw in the streets and go about your business
    An inch at a time, an inch at a time,
We have not even an hour to spend repenting
    Our sins; the quarters chime
And every minute is its own alarum clock
    And what we are about to do
Is of vastly more importance
    Than what we have done or not done hitherto.
It is December now, the trees are naked
    As the three crosses on the hill;
Through the white fog the face of the orange sun is cryptic
    Like a lawyer making the year's will.
The year has little to show, will leave a heavy
    Overdraft to its heir;
Shall we try to meet the deficit or passing
    By on the other side continue *laissez-faire*?
International betrayals, public murder,
    The devil quoting scripture, the traitor, the coward, the thug
Eating dinner in the name of peace and progress,
    The doped public sucking a dry dug;
Official recognition of rape, revival of the ghetto
    And free speech gagged and free
Energy scrapped and dropped like surplus herring
    Back into the barren sea;
Brains and beauty festering in exile,
    The shadow of bars
Falling across each page, each field, each raddled sunset,
    The alien lawn and the pool of nenuphars;
And hordes of homeless poor running the gauntlet
    In hostile city streets of white and violet lamps
Whose flight is without a terminus but better
    Than the repose of concentration camps.
Come over, they said, into Macedonia and help us
    But the chance is gone;
Now we must help ourselves, we can leave the vulture
    To pick the corpses clean in Macedon.

No wonder many would renounce their birthright,
    The responsibility of moral choice,
And sit with a mess of pottage taking orders
    Out of a square box from a mad voice—
Lies on the air endlessly repeated
    Turning the air to fog,
Blanket on blanket of lie, no room to breathe or fidget
    And nobody to jog
Your elbow and say 'Up there the sun is rising;
    Take it on trust, the sun will always shine.'
The sun may shine no doubt but how many people
    Will see it with their eyes in Nineteen-Thirty-Nine?
Yes, the earlier days had their music,
    We have some still to-day,
But the orchestra is due for the bonfire
    If things go on this way.
Still there are still the seeds of energy and choice
    Still alive even if forbidden, hidden,
And while a man has voice
    He may recover music.

XIX

The pigeons riddle the London air,
    The shutter slides from the chain-store window
The frock-coat statue stands in the square
    Caring for no one, caring for no one.
The night-shift men go home to bed,
    The kettle sings and the bacon sizzles;
Some are hungry and some are dead—
    A wistful face in a faded photo.
Under the stairs is a khaki cap;
    That was Dad's, Dad was a plumber—
You hear that dripping tap?
    He'd have had it right in no time.
No time now; Dad is dead,
    He left me five months gone or over;
Tam cari capitis, for such a well-loved head
    What shame in tears, what limit?
It is the child I mean,
    Born prematurely, strangled;
Dad was off the scene,
    He would have made no difference.

The stretchers run from ward to ward,
  The telephone rings in empty houses,
The torn shirt soaks on the scrubbing board,
  O what a busy morning.
Baby Croesus crawls in a pen
  With alphabetical bricks and biscuits;
The doll-dumb file of sandwichmen
  Carry lies from gutter to gutter.
The curate buys his ounce of shag,
  The typist tints her nails with coral,
The housewife with her shopping bag
  Watches the cleaver catch the naked
New Zealand sheep between the legs—
  What price now New Zealand?
The cocker spaniel sits and begs
  With eyes like a waif on the movies.
O what a busy morning,
  Engines start with a roar,
All the wires are buzzing,
  The tape-machines vomit on the floor.
And I feel that my mind once again is open,
  The lady is gone who stood in the way so long,
The hypnosis is over and no one
  Calls encore to the song.
When we are out of love, how were we ever in it?
  Where are the mountains and the mountain skies,
That heady air instinct with
  A strange sincerity which winged our lies?
The peaks have fallen in like dropping pastry:
  Now I could see her come
Around the corner without the pulse responding,
  The flowery orator in the heart is dumb,
His bag of tricks is empty, his over-statements,
  Those rainbow bubbles, have burst:
When we meet, she need not feel embarrassed,
  The cad with the golden tongue has done his worst
And has no orders from me to mix his phrases rich,
  To make the air a carpet
For her to walk on; I only wonder which
  Day, which hour, I found this freedom.
But freedom is not so exciting,
  We prefer to be drawn
In the rush of the stars as they circle—
  A traffic that ends with dawn.
Now I am free of the stars

And the word 'love' makes no sense, this history is almost
Ripe for the mind's museum—broken jars
    That once held wine or perfume.
Yet looking at their elegance on the stands
    I feel a certain pride that only lately
(And yet so long ago) I held them in my hands
    While they were full and fragrant.
So on this busy morning I hope, my dear,
    That you are also busy
With another vintage of another year;
    I wish you luck and I thank you for the party—
A good party though at the end my thirst
    Was worse than at the beginning
But never to have drunk no doubt would be the worst;
    Pain, they say, is always twin to pleasure.
Better to have these twins
    Than no children at all, very much better
To act for good and bad than have no sins
    And take no action either.
You were my blizzard who had been my bed.
    But taking the whole series of blight and blossom
I would not choose a simpler crop instead;
    Thank you, my dear—dear against my judgment.

XX

Nelson stands on a black pillar,
    The electric signs go off and on—
Distilleries and life insurance companies—
    The traffic circles, coming and gone,
Past the National Gallery closed and silent
    Where in their frames
Other worlds persist, the passions of the artist
    Caught like frozen flames:
The Primitives distilling from the cruel
    Legend a faith that is almost debonair,
Sebastian calmly waiting the next arrow,
  . The crucifixion in the candid air:
And Venice lolling in wealth for ever under glass,
    Pearls in her hair, panther and velvet:
And the rococo picnic on the grass
    With wine and lutes and banter:
And the still life proclaiming with aplomb

The self-content of bread or fruit or vases
And personality like a silent bomb
   Lurking in the formal portrait.
Here every day the visitors walk slowly
   Rocking along the parquet as if on a ship's deck
Feeling a vague affinity with the pictures
   Yet wary of these waves which gently peck
The side of the boat in passing; they are anxious
   To end the voyage, to land in their own time;
The sea of the past glimmers with white horses,
   A paradigm
Of life's successions, treacheries, recessions;
   The unfounded confidence of the dead affronts
Our own system of values
   Like airmen doing their stunts
Over our private garden; these arrogant Old Masters
   Swoop and loop and lance us with a quick
Shadow; we only want to cultivate our garden,
   Not for us the virtuoso, slick
Tricks of the airy region,
   For our part our feet are on the ground,
They should not be allowed to fly so low above us,
   Their premises are unsound
And history has refuted them and yet
   They cast their shadows on us like aspersions;
Propellers and white horses,
   Movement, movement, can we never forget
The movements of the past which should be dead?
   The mind of Socrates still clicks like scissors
And Christ who should lie quiet in the garden
   Flowered in flame instead.

   .   .   .   .

A week to Christmas, cards of snow and holly,
   Gimcracks in the shops,
Wishes and memories wrapped in tissue paper,
   Trinkets, gadgets and lollipops
And as if through coloured glasses
   We remember our childhood's thrill
Waking in the morning to the rustling of paper,
   The eiderdown heaped in a hill
Of wogs and dogs and bears and bricks and apples
   And the feeling that Christmas Day
Was a coral island in time where we land and eat our lotus
   But where we can never stay.
There was a star in the East, the magi in their turbans

Brought their luxury toys
In homage to a child born to capsize their values
    And wreck their equipoise.
A smell of hay like peace in the dark stable—
    Not peace however but a sword
To cut the Gordian knot of logical self-interest,
    The fool-proof golden cord;
For Christ walked in where no philosopher treads
    But armed with more than folly,
Making the smooth place rough and knocking the heads
    Of Church and State together.
In honour of whom we have taken over the pagan
    Saturnalia for our annual treat
Letting the belly have its say, ignoring
    The spirit while we eat.
And Conscience still goes crying through the desert
    With sackcloth round his loins:
A week to Christmas—hark the herald angels
    Beg for copper coins.

XXI

And when we clear away
    All this debris of day-to-day experience,
What comes out to light, what is there of value
    Lasting from day to day?
I sit in my room in comfort
    Looking at enormous flowers—
Equipment purchased with my working hours,
    A daily mint of perishable petals.
The figures of the dance repeat
    The unending cycle of making and spending money,
Eating our daily bread in order to earn it
    And earning in order to eat.
And is that all the story,
    The mainspring and the plot,
Or merely a mechanism without which not
    Any story could be written?
        Sine qua non!
    Sine qua non indeed, we cannot ever
Live by soul alone; the soul without the stomach
    Would find its glory gone.
But the total cause outruns the mere condition,

143

There is more to it than that;
Life would be (as it often seems) flat
    If it were merely a matter of not dying.
For each individual then
    Would be fighting a losing battle
But with life as collective creation
    The rout is rallied, the battle begins again.
Only give us the courage of our instinct,
    The will to truth and love's initiative,
Then we could hope to live
    A life beyond the self but self-completing.
And, as the emperor said, What is the use
    Of the minor loyalty—'Dear city of Cecrops',
Unless we have also the wider franchise, can answer
    'Dear city of Zeus'?
And so when the many regrets
    Trouble us for the many lost affections,
Let us take the wider view before we count them
    Hopelessly bad debts.
For Cecrops has his rights as Zeus has his
    And every tree is a tree of branches
And every wood is a wood of trees growing
    And what has been contributes to what is.
So I am glad to have known them,
    The people or events apparently withdrawn;
The world is round and there is always dawn
    Undeniably somewhere.
'Praised be thou, O Lord, for our brother the sun'
    Said the grey saint, laving his eyes in colour;
Who creates and destroys for ever
    And his cycle is never done.
In this room chrysanthemums and dahlias
    Like brandy hit the heart; the fire,
A small wild animal, furthers its desire
    Consuming fuel, self-consuming.
And flames are the clearest cut
    Of shapes and the most transient:
O fire, my spendthrift,
    May I spend like you, as reckless but
Giving as good return—burn the silent
    Into running sound, deride the dark
And jump to glory from a single spark
    And purge the world and warm it.
The room grows cold, the flicker fades,
    The sinking ashes whisper, the fickle

Eye forgets but later will remember
  The radiant cavalcades.
The smoke has gone from the chimney,
  The water has flowed away under the bridge,
The silhouetted lovers have left the ridge,
  The flower has closed its calyx.
The crow's-feet have come to stay,
  The jokes no longer amuse, the palate
Rejects milk chocolate and Benedictine—
  Yesterday and the day before yesterday.
But oh, not now my love, but oh my friend,
  Can you not take it merely on trust that life is
The only thing worth living and that dying
  Had better be left to take care of itself in the end?
For to have been born is in itself a triumph
  Among all that waste of sperm
And it is gratitude to wait the proper term
  Or, if not gratitude, duty.
I know that you think these phrases highfalutin
  And, when not happy, see no claim or use
For staying alive; the quiet hands seduce
  Of the god who is god of nothing.
And while I sympathise
  With the wish to quit, to make the great refusal,
I feel that such a defeat is also treason,
  That deaths like these are lies.
A fire should be left burning
  Till it burns itself out:
We shan't have another chance to dance and shout
  Once the flames are silent.

XXII

December the nineteenth: over the black roofs
  And the one black paint-brush poplar
The white steam rises and deploys in puffs
  From the house-hidden railway, a northern
Geyser erupting in a land of lava,
  But white can be still whiter for now
The dun air starts to jig with specks that circle
  Like microbes under a lens; this is the first snow;
And soon the specks are feathers blandly sidling

Inconsequent as the fancies of young girls
And the air has filled like a dance-hall,
  A waltz of white dresses and strings of pearls.
And the papers declare the snow has come to stay,
  A new upholstery on roof and garden
Refining, lining, underlining the day,
  And the sombre laurels break parole and blossom
In enormous clumps of peonies; and the cars
  Turn animal, moving slowly
In their white fur like bears,
  And the white trees fade into the hill behind them
As negroes' faces fade in a dark background,
  Our London world
Grown all of a piece and peaceful like the Arctic,
  The sums all cancelled out and the flags furled.
At night we sleep behind stockades of frost,
  Nothing alive in the streets to run the gauntlet
Of this unworldly cold except the lost
  Wisps of steam from the gratings of the sewers.
It is holiday time, time for the morning snack,
  Time to be leaving the country:
I have taken my ticket south, I will not look back,
  The pipes may burst for all I care, the gutter
Dribble with dirty snow, the Christmas party
  Be ruined by catarrh;
Let us flee this country and leave its complications
  Exactly where they (the devil take them) are.
So Dover to Dunkerque:
  The Land of Cockayne begins across the Channel.
The hooter cries to hell with the year's work,
  The snowflakes flirt with the steam of the steamer.
But the train in France is cold, the window
  Frosted with patterns of stars and fern,
And when we scrape a peephole on the window
  There is nothing new to learn;
Nothing but snow and snow all the way to Paris,
  No roast pigs walk this way
And any snatched half-hour of self-indulgence
  Is an intercalary day.
Sweet, my love, my dear, whoever you are or were,
  I need your company on this excursion
For, where there is the luxury of leisure, there
  There should also be the luxury of women.
I do not need you on my daily job
  Nor yet on any spiritual adventure,

146

Not when I earn my keep but when I rob
    Time of his growth of tinsel:
No longer thinking you or any other
    Essential to my life—soul-mate or dual star;
All I want is an elegant and witty playmate
    At the perfume counter or the cocktail bar.
So here where tourist values are the only
    Values, where we pretend
That eating and drinking are more important than thinking
    And looking at things than action and a casual friend
Than a colleague and that work is a dull convenience
    Designed to provide
Money to spend on amusement and that amusement
    Is an eternal bride
Who will never sink to the level of a wife, that gossip
    Is the characteristic of art
And that the sensible man must keep his aesthetic
    And his moral standards apart—
Here, where we think all this, I need you badly,
    Whatever your name or age or the colour of your hair;
I need your surface company (what happens
    Below the surface is my own affair).
And I feel a certain pleasurable nostalgia
    In sitting alone, drinking, wondering if you
Will suddenly thread your way among these vulcanite tables
    To a mutually unsuspected rendezvous
Among these banal women with feathers in their hats and halos
    Of evanescent veils
And these bald-at-thirty Englishmen whose polished
    Foreheads are the tombs of record sales;
Where alcohol, anchovies and shimmying street-lamps
    Knock the stolid almanac cock-a-hoop,
Where reason drowns and the senses
    Foam, flame, tingle and loop the loop.
And striking red or green matches to light these loose
    Cigarettes of black tobacco I need you badly—
The age-old woman apt for all misuse
    Whose soul is out of the picture.
How I enjoy this bout of cynical self-indulgence,
    Of glittering and hard-boiled make-believe;
The cynic is a creature of overstatements
    But an overstatement is something to achieve.
And how (with a grain of salt) I enjoy hating
    The world to which for ever I belong,
This hatred, this escape, being equally factitious—

A passing song.
For I cannot stay in Paris
    And, if I did, no doubt I should soon be bored
For what I see is not the intimate city
    But the brittle dance of lights in the Place de la Concorde.
So much for Christmas: I must go further south
    To see the New Year in on hungry faces
But where the hungry mouth
    Refuses to deny the heart's allegiance.
Look: the road winds up among the prickly vineyards
    And naked winter trees;
Over there are pain and pride beyond the snow-lit
    Sharp annunciation of the Pyrenees.

XXIII

The road ran downhill into Spain,
    The wind blew fresh on bamboo grasses,
The white plane-trees were bone-naked
    And the issues plain:
We have come to a place in space where shortly
    All of us may be forced to camp in time:
The slender searchlights climb,
    Our sins will find us out, even our sins of omission.
When I reached the town it was dark,
    No lights in the streets but two and a half millions
Of people in circulation
    Condemned like the beasts in the ark
With nothing but water around them:
    Will there ever be a green tree or a rock that is dry?
The shops are empty and in Barceloneta the eye-
    Sockets of the houses are empty.
But still they manage to laugh
    Though they have no eggs, no milk, no fish, no fruit, no tobacco,
        no butter,
Though they live upon lentils and sleep in the Metro,
    Though the old order is gone and the golden calf
Of Catalan industry shattered;
    The human values remain, purged in the fire,
And it appears that every man's desire
    Is life rather than victuals.
Life being more, it seems, than merely the bare
    Permission to keep alive and receive orders,

Humanity being more than a mechanism
    To be oiled and greased and for ever unaware
Of the work it is turning out, of why the wheels keep turning;
    Here at least the soul has found its voice
Though not indeed by choice;
    The cost was heavy.
They breathe the air of war and yet the tension
    Admits, beside the slogans it evokes,
An interest in philately or pelota
    Or private jokes.
And the sirens cry in the dark morning
    And the lights go out and the town is still
And the sky is pregnant with ill-will
    And the bombs come foxing the fated victim
As pretty as a Guy Fawkes show—
    Silver sprays and tracer bullets—
And in the pauses of destruction
    The cocks in the centre of the town crow.
The cocks crow in Barcelona
    Where clocks are few to strike the hour;
Is it the heart's reveille or the sour
    Reproach of Simon Peter?
The year has come to an end,
    Time for resolutions, for stock-taking;
Felice Nuevo Año!
    May God, if there is one, send
As much courage again and greater vision
    And resolve the antinomies in which we live
Where man must be either safe because he is negative
    Or free on the edge of a razor.
Give those who are gentle strength,
    Give those who are strong a generous imagination,
And make their half-truth true and let the crooked
    Footpath find its parent road at length.
I admit that for myself I cannot straiten
    My broken rambling track
Which reaches so irregularly back
    To burning cities and rifled rose-bushes
And cairns and lonely farms
    Where no one lives, makes love or begets children,
All my heredity and my upbringing
    Having brought me only to the Present's arms—
The arms not of a mistress but of a wrestler,
    Of a God who straddles over the night sky;
No wonder Jacob halted on his thigh—

          The price of a drawn battle.
For never to begin
     Anything new because we know there is nothing
New, is an academic sophistry—
     The original sin.
I have already had friends
     Among things and hours and people
But taking them one by one—odd hours and passing people;
     Now I must make amends
And try to correlate event with instinct
     And me with you or you and you with all,
No longer think of time as a waterfall
     Abstracted from a river.
I have loved defeat and sloth,
     The tawdry halo of the idle martyr;
I have thrown away the roots of will and conscience,
     Now I must look for both,
Not any longer act among the cushions
     The Dying Gaul;
Soon or late the delights of self-pity must pall
     And the fun of cursing the wicked
World into which we were born
     And the cynical admission of frustration
('Our loves are not full measure,
     There are blight and rooks on the corn').
Rather for any measure so far given
     Let us be glad
Nor wait on purpose to be wisely sad
     When doing nothing we find we have gained nothing.
For here and now the new valkyries ride
     The Spanish constellations
As over the Plaza Cataluña
     Orion lolls on his side;
Droning over from Majorca
     To maim or blind or kill
The bearers of the living will,
     The stubborn heirs of freedom
Whose matter-of-fact faith and courage shame
     Our niggling equivocations—
We who play for safety,
     A safety only in name.
Whereas these people contain truth, whatever
     Their nominal façade.
Listen: a whirr, a challenge, an aubade—
     It is the cock crowing in Barcelona.

Sleep, my body, sleep, my ghost,
 Sleep, my parents and grand-parents,
And all those I have loved most:
 One man's coffin is another's cradle.
Sleep, my past and all my sins,
 In distant snow or dried roses
Under the moon for night's cocoon will open
 When day begins.
Sleep, my fathers, in your graves
 On upland bogland under heather;
What the wind scatters the wind saves,
 A sapling springs in a new country.
Time is a country, the present moment
 A spotlight roving round the scene;
We need not chase the spotlight,
 The future is the bride of what has been.
Sleep, my fancies and my wishes,
 Sleep a little and wake strong,
The same but different and take my blessing—
 A cradle-song.
And sleep, my various and conflicting
 Selves I have so long endured,
Sleep in Asclepius' temple
 And wake cured.
And you with whom I shared an idyll
 Five years long,
Sleep beyond the Atlantic
 And wake to a glitter of dew and to bird-song.
And you whose eyes are blue, whose ways are foam,
 Sleep quiet and smiling
And do not hanker
 For a perfection which can never come.
And you whose minutes patter
 To crowd the social hours,
Curl up easy in a placid corner
 And let your thoughts close in like flowers.
And you, who work for Christ, and you, as eager
 For a better life, humanist, atheist,
And you, devoted to a cause, and you, to a family,
 Sleep and may your beliefs and zeal persist.
Sleep quietly, Marx and Freud,
 The figure-heads of our transition.
Cagney, Lombard, Bing and Garbo,

Sleep in your world of celluloid.
Sleep now also, monk and satyr,
  Cease your wrangling for a night.
Sleep, my brain, and sleep, my senses,
  Sleep, my hunger and my spite.
Sleep, recruits to the evil army,
  Who, for so long misunderstood,
Took to the gun to kill your sorrow;
  Sleep and be damned and wake up good.
While we sleep, what shall we dream?
  Of Tir nan Og or South Sea islands,
Of a land where all the milk is cream
  And all the girls are willing?
Or shall our dream be earnest of the real
  Future when we wake,
Design a home, a factory, a fortress
  Which, though with effort, we can really make?
What is it we want really?
  For what end and how?
If it is something feasible, obtainable,
  Let us dream it now,
And pray for a possible land
  Not of sleep-walkers, not of angry puppets,
But where both heart and brain can understand
  The movements of our fellows;
Where life is a choice of instruments and none
  Is debarred his natural music,
Where the waters of life are free of the ice-blockade of hunger
  And thought is free as the sun,
Where the altars of sheer power and mere profit
  Have fallen to disuse,
Where nobody sees the use
  Of buying money and blood at the cost of blood and money,
Where the individual, no longer squandered
  In self-assertion, works with the rest, endowed
With the split vision of a juggler and the quick lock of a taxi,
  Where the people are more than a crowd.
So sleep in hope of this—but only for a little;
  Your hope must wake
While the choice is yours to make,
  The mortgage not foreclosed, the offer open.
Sleep serene, avoid the backward
  Glance; go forward, dreams, and do not halt
(Behind you in the desert stands a token
  Of doubt—a pillar of salt).

Sleep, the past, and wake, the future,
    And walk out promptly through the open door;
But you, my coward doubts, may go on sleeping,
    You need not wake again—not any more.
The New Year comes with bombs, it is too late
    To dose the dead with honourable intentions:
If you have honour to spare, employ it on the living;
    The dead are dead as Nineteen-Thirty-Eight.
Sleep to the noise of running water
    To-morrow to be crossed, however deep;
This is no river of the dead or Lethe,
    To-night we sleep
On the banks of Rubicon—the die is cast;
    There will be time to audit
The accounts later, there will be sunlight later
    And the equation will come out at last.

VI

1939—1940

ein Zwiespalt und Zwitter von
Pflanze und von Gespenst

NIETZSCHE

Prognosis

Goodbye, Winter,
The days are getting longer,
The tea-leaf in the teacup
Is herald of a stranger.

Will he bring me business
Or will he bring me gladness
Or will he come for cure
Of his own sickness?

With a pedlar's burden
Walking up the garden
Will he come to beg
Or will he come to bargain?

Will he come to pester,
To cringe or to bluster,
A promise in his palm
Or a gun in his holster?

Will his name be John
Or will his name be Jonah
Crying to repent
On the Island of Iona?

Will his name be Jason
Looking for a seaman
Or a mad crusader
Without rhyme or reason?

What will be his message—
War or work or marriage?
News as new as dawn
Or an old adage?

Will he give a champion
Answer to my question
Or will his words be dark
And his ways evasion?

Will his name be Love
And all his talk be crazy?

Or will his name be Death
And his message easy?
                    Spring, 1939

Stylite

The saint on the pillar stands,
The pillar is alone,
He has stood so long
That he himself is stone;
Only his eyes
Range across the sand
Where no one ever comes
And the world is banned.

Then his eyes close,
He stands in his sleep,
Round his neck there comes
The conscience of a rope,
And the hangman counting
Counting to ten—
At nine he finds
He has eyes again.

The saint on the pillar stands,
The pillars are two,
A young man opposite
Stands in the blue,
A white Greek god,
Confident, with curled
Hair above the groin
And his eyes on the world.
                    March, 1940

Entirely

If we could get the hang of it entirely
    It would take too long;
All we know is the splash of words in passing
    And falling twigs of song,

And when we try to eavesdrop on the great
    Presences it is rarely
That by a stroke of luck we can appropriate
    Even a phrase entirely.

If we could find our happiness entirely
    In somebody else's arms
We should not fear the spears of the spring nor the city's
    Yammering fire alarms
But, as it is, the spears each year go through
    Our flesh and almost hourly
Bell or siren banishes the blue
    Eyes of Love entirely.

And if the world were black or white entirely
    And all the charts were plain
Instead of a mad weir of tigerish waters,
    A prism of delight and pain,
We might be surer where we wished to go
    Or again we might be merely
Bored but in brute reality there is no
    Road that is right entirely.

March, 1940

Plant and phantom

Man: a flutter of pages,
Leaves in the Sibyl's cave,
Shadow changing from dawn to twilight,
Murmuration of corn in the wind,
A shaking of hands with hallucinations,
Hobnobbing with ghosts, a pump of blood,
Mirage, a spider dangling
Over chaos and man a chaos.

Who cheats the pawky Fates
By what he does, not is,
By what he makes, imposing
On flux an architectonic—
Cone of marble, calyx of ice,
Spandrel and buttress, iron
Loops across the void,
Stepping stones in the random.

159

Man: a dance of midges,
Gold glass in the sunlight,
Prattle of water, palaver
Of starlings in a disused
Chimney, a gimcrack castle,
Seaweed tugging the rocks,
Guttering candles, the Northern
Lights and the Seventh Wave.

Whose life if a bluff, professing
To follow the laws of Nature,
In fact a revolt, a mad
Conspiracy and usurpation,
Smuggling over the frontier
Of fact a sense of value,
Metabolism of death,
Re-orchestration of world.

Man: a riot of banners,
Bulge in the wind, a prism,
Organ-pipes in the sunset,
Orgy of brains and glands,
Thunder-crackle and the bounce of hail,
Wink of wings and fog's delusion,
A rampant martyr, a midnight
Echo, a forest fire.

Who felt with his hands in empty
Air for the Word and did not
Find it but felt the aura,
Dew on the skin, could not forget it.
Ever since has fumbled, intrigued,
Clambered behind and beyond, and learnt
Words of blessing and cursing, hoping
To find in the end the Word Itself.

September, 1940

The British Museum Reading Room

Under the hive-like dome the stooping haunted readers
Go up and down the alleys, tap the cells of knowledge—
Honey and wax, the accumulation of years—

Some on commission, some for the love of learning,
Some because they have nothing better to do
Or because they hope these walls of books will deaden
    The drumming of the demon in their ears.

Cranks, hacks, poverty-stricken scholars,
In pince-nez, period hats or romantic beards
    And cherishing their hobby or their doom
Some are too much alive and some are asleep
Hanging like bats in a world of inverted values,
Folded up in themselves in a world which is safe and silent:
    This is the British Museum Reading Room.

Out on the steps in the sun the pigeons are courting,
Puffing their ruffs and sweeping their tails or taking
    A sun-bath at their ease
And under the totem poles—the ancient terror—
Between the enormous fluted Ionic columns
There seeps from heavily jowled or hawk-like foreign faces
    The guttural sorrow of the refugees.

July, 1939

London rain

The rain of London pimples
The ebony street with white
And the neon-lamps of London
Stain the canals of night
And the park becomes a jungle
In the alchemy of night.

My wishes turn to violent
Horses black as coal—
The randy mares of fancy,
The stallions of the soul—
Eager to take the fences
That fence about my soul.

Across the countless chimneys
The horses ride and across
The country to the channel
Where warning beacons toss,

161

To a place where God and No-God
Play at pitch and toss.

Whichever wins I am happy
For God will give me bliss
But No-God will absolve me
From all I do amiss
And I need not suffer conscience
If the world was made amiss.

Under God we can reckon
On pardon when we fall
But if we are under No-God
Nothing will matter at all,
Arson and rape and murder
Must count for nothing at all.

So reinforced by logic
As having nothing to lose
My lust goes riding horseback
To ravish where I choose,
To burgle all the turrets
Of beauty as I choose.

But now the rain gives over
Its dance upon the town,
Logic and lust together
Come dimly tumbling down,
And neither God nor No-God
Is either up or down.

The argument was wilful,
The alternatives untrue,
We need no metaphysics
To sanction what we do
Or to muffle us in comfort
From what we did not do.

Whether the living river
Began in bog or lake,
The world is what was given,
The world is what we make
And we only can discover
Life in the life we make.

So let the water sizzle
Upon the gleaming slates,
There will be sunshine after
When the rain abates
And rain returning duly
When the sun abates.

My wishes now come homeward,
Their gallopings in vain,
Logic and lust are quiet,
Once more it starts to rain.
Falling asleep I listen
To the falling London rain.

July, 1939

The closing album

I

Dublin

Grey brick upon brick,
Declamatory bronze
On sombre pedestals—
O'Connell, Grattan, Moore—
And the brewery tugs and the swans
On the balustraded stream
And the bare bones of a fanlight
Over a hungry door
And the air soft on the cheek
And porter running from the taps
With a head of yellow cream
And Nelson on his pillar
Watching his world collapse.

This was never my town,
I was not born nor bred
Nor schooled here and she will not
Have me alive or dead
But yet she holds my mind
With her seedy elegance,
With her gentle veils of rain

And all her ghosts that walk
And all that hide behind
Her Georgian façades—
The catcalls and the pain,
The glamour of her squalor,
The bravado of her talk.

The lights jig in the river
With a concertina movement
And the sun comes up in the morning
Like barley-sugar on the water
And the mist on the Wicklow hills
Is close, as close
As the peasantry were to the landlord,
As the Irish to the Anglo-Irish,
As the killer is close one moment
To the man he kills,
Or as the moment itself
Is close to the next moment.

She is not an Irish town
And she is not English,
Historic with guns and vermin
And the cold renown
Of a fragment of Church latin,
Of an oratorical phrase.
But oh the days are soft,
Soft enough to forget
The lesson better learnt,
The bullet on the wet
Streets, the crooked deal,
The steel behind the laugh,
The Four Courts burnt.

Fort of the Dane,
Garrison of the Saxon,
Augustan capital
Of a Gaelic nation,
Appropriating all
The alien brought,
You give me time for thought
And by a juggler's trick
You poise the toppling hour—
O greyness run to flower,
Grey stone, grey water,
And brick upon grey brick.

II

Cushendun

Fuchsia and ragweed and the distant hills
Made as it were out of clouds and sea:
All night the bay is plashing and the moon
  Marks the break of the waves.

Limestone and basalt and a whitewashed house
With passages of great stone flags
And a walled garden with plums on the wall
  And a bird piping in the night.

Forgetfulness: brass lamps and copper jugs
And home-made bread and the smell of turf or flax
And the air a glove and the water lathering easy
  And convolvulus in the hedge.

Only in the dark green room beside the fire
With the curtains drawn against the winds and waves
There is a little box with a well-bred voice:
  What a place to talk of War.

III

Sligo and Mayo

In Sligo the country was soft; there were turkeys
  Gobbling under sycamore trees
And the shadows of clouds on the mountains moving
  Like browsing cattle at ease.

And little distant fields were sprigged with haycocks
  And splashed against a white
Roadside cottage a welter of nasturtium
  Deluging the sight,

And pullets pecking the flies from around the eyes of heifers
    Sitting in farmyard mud
Among hydrangeas and the falling ear-rings
    Of fuchsias red as blood.

But in Mayo the tumbledown walls went leap-frog
    Over the moors,
The sugar and salt in the pubs were damp in the casters
    And the water was brown as beer upon the shores

Of desolate loughs, and stumps of hoary bog-oak
    Stuck up here and there
And as the twilight filtered on the heather
    Water-music filled the air,

And when the night came down upon the bogland
    With all-enveloping wings
The coal-black turfstacks rose against the darkness
    Like the tombs of nameless kings.

IV

Galway

O the crossbones of Galway,
The hollow grey houses,
The rubbish and sewage,
The grass-grown pier,
And the dredger grumbling
All night in the harbour:
The war came down on us here.

Salmon in the Corrib
Gently swaying
And the water combed out
Over the weir
And a hundred swans
Dreaming on the harbour:
The war came down on us here.

The night was gay
With the moon's music
But Mars was angry
On the hills of Clare
And September dawned
Upon willows and ruins:
The war came down on us here

V

Why, now it has happened,
Should the clock go on striking to the firedogs
And why should the rooks be blown upon the evening
Like burnt paper in a chimney?

And why should the sea maintain its turbulence,
    its elegance,
And draw a film of muslin down the sand
With each receding wave?

And why, now it has happened,
Should the atlas still be full of the maps of countries
We never shall see again?

And why, now it has happened,
And doom all night is lapping at the door,
Should I remember that I ever met you—
Once in another world?

August–September, 1939

Meeting point

Time was away and somewhere else,
There were two glasses and two chairs
And two people with the one pulse
(Somebody stopped the moving stairs):
Time was away and somewhere else.

And they were neither up nor down;
The stream's music did not stop
Flowing through heather, limpid brown,
Although they sat in a coffee shop
And they were neither up nor down.

The bell was silent in the air
Holding its inverted poise—
Between the clang and clang a flower,
A brazen calyx of no noise:
The bell was silent in the air.

The camels crossed the miles of sand
That stretched around the cups and plates;
The desert was their own, they planned
To portion out the stars and dates:
The camels crossed the miles of sand.

Time was away and somewhere else.
The waiter did not come, the clock
Forgot them and the radio waltz
Came out like water from a rock:
Time was away and somewhere else.

Her fingers flicked away the ash
That bloomed again in tropic trees:
Not caring if the markets crash
When they had forests such as these,
Her fingers flicked away the ash.

God or whatever means the Good
Be praised that time can stop like this,
That what the heart has understood
Can verify in the body's peace
God or whatever means the Good.

Time was away and she was here
And life no longer what it was,
The bell was silent in the air
And all the room one glow because
Time was away and she was here.

April, 1939

A toast

The slurred and drawled and crooning sounds,
The blurred and suave and sidling smells,
The webs of dew, the bells of buds,
The sun going down in crimson suds—
   This is on me and these are yours.

The bland and sculped and urgent beasts,
The here and there and nowhere birds,
The tongues of fire, the words of foam,
The curdling stars in the night's dome—
   This is on me and these are yours.

The face and grace and muscle of man,
The balance of his body and mind,
Who keeps a trump behind his brain
Till instinct flicks it out again—
   This is on me and these are yours.

The courage of eyes, the craft of hands,
The gay feet, the pulse of hope,
The will that flings a rope—though hard—
To catch the future off its guard—
   This is on me and these are yours.

The luck and pluck and plunge of blood,
The wealth and spilth and sport of breath,
And sleep come down like death above
The fever and the peace of love—
   This is on me and these are yours.

May, 1939

Order to view

It was a big house, bleak;
Grass on the drive;
We had been there before
But memory, weak in front of
A blistered door, could find
Nothing alive now;

The shrubbery dripped, a crypt
Of leafmould dreams; a tarnished
Arrow over an empty stable
Shifted a little in the tenuous wind,

And wishes were unable
To rise; on the garden wall
The pear trees had come loose
From rotten loops; one wish,
A rainbow bubble, rose,
Faltered, broke in the dull
Air—What was the use?
The bell-pull would not pull
And the whole place, one might
Have supposed, was deadly ill:
The world was closed,

And remained closed until
A sudden angry tree
Shook itself like a setter
Flouncing out of a pond
And beyond the sombre line
Of limes a cavalcade
Of clouds rose like a shout of
Defiance. Near at hand
Somewhere in a loose-box
A horse neighed
And all the curtains flew out of
The windows; the world was open.
March, 1940

Novelettes

I

The Old Story

The old story is true of charms fading;
He knew her first before her charm was mellow—
Slim; surprise in her eyes; like a woodland creature
Crept abroad who found the world amazing,

Who, afterwards maturing, yet was dainty,
Light on her feet and gentle with her fingers;

Put on a little flesh, became an easy
Spreadeagled beauty for Renaissance painters.

And then she went; he did not see her after
Until by the shore of a cold sea in winter
With years behind her and the waves behind her
Drubbing the memory up and down the pebbles.

Flotsam and wrack; the bag of old emotions;
Watch in the swirl her ten years back reflections—
White as a drowning hand, then gone for ever;
Here she stands who was twenty and is thirty.

The same but different and he found the difference
A surgeon's knife without an anaesthetic;
He had known of course that this happens
But had not guessed the pain of it or the panic,

And could not say 'My love', could hardly
Say anything at all, no longer knowing
Whom he was talking to but watched the water
Massing for action on the cold horizon.

Summer, 1939

II

Les Sylphides

Life in a day: he took his girl to the ballet;
Being shortsighted himself could hardly see it—
    The white skirts in the grey
    Glade and the swell of the music
    Lifting the white sails.

Calyx upon calyx, canterbury bells in the breeze
The flowers on the left mirror to the flowers on the right
    And the naked arms above
    The powdered faces moving
    Like seaweed in a pool.

Now, he thought, we are floating—ageless, oarless—
Now there is no separation, from now on
    You will be wearing white
    Satin and a red sash
    Under the waltzing trees.

But the music stopped, the dancers took their curtain,
The river had come to a lock—a shuffle of programmes—
   And we cannot continue down
   Stream unless we are ready
   To enter the lock and drop.

So they were married—to be the more together—
And found they were never again so much together,
   Divided by the morning tea,
   By the evening paper,
   By children and tradesmen's bills.

Waking at times in the night she found assurance
Due to his regular breathing but wondered whether
   It was really worth it and where
   The river had flowed away
   And where were the white flowers.

Summer, 1939

III

The Gardener

He was not able to read or write,
He did odd jobs on gentlemen's places
Cutting the hedge or hoeing the drive
With the smile of a saint,
With the pride of a feudal chief,
For he was not quite all there.

Crippled by rheumatism
By the time his hair was white,
He would reach the garden by twelve
His legs in soiled puttees,
A clay pipe in his teeth,
A tiny flag in his cap,
A white cat behind him,
And his eyes a cornflower blue.

And between the clack of the shears
Or the honing of the scythe
Or the rattle of the rake on the gravel
He would talk to amuse the children,

He would talk to himself or the cat
Or the robin waiting for worms
Perched on the handle of the spade;
Would remember snatches of verse
From the elementary school
About a bee and a wasp
Or the cat by the barndoor spinning;
And would talk about himself for ever—
You would never find his like—
Always in the third person;
And would level his stick like a gun
(With a glint in his eye)
Saying 'Now I'm a Frenchman'—
He was not quite right in the head.

He believed in God—
The Good Fellow Up There—
And he used a simile of Homer
Watching the falling leaves,
And every year he waited for the Twelfth of July,
Cherishing his sash and his fife
For the carnival of banners and drums.
He was always claiming but never
Obtaining his old age pension,
For he did not know his age.

And his rheumatism at last
Kept him out of the processions.
And he came to work in the garden
Later and later in the day,
Leaving later at night;
In the damp dark of the night
At ten o'clock or later
You could hear him mowing the lawn,
The mower moving forward,
And backward, forward and backward
For he mowed while standing still;
He was not quite up to the job.

But he took a pride in the job,
He kept a bowl of cold
Tea in the crotch of a tree,
Always enjoyed his food
And enjoyed honing the scythe
And making the potato drills

And putting the peasticks in;
And enjoyed the noise of the corncrake,
And the early hawthorn hedge
Peppered black and green,
And the cut grass dancing in the air—
Happy as the day was long.

Till his last sickness took him
And he could not leave his house
And his eyes lost their colour
And he sat by the little range
With a finch in a cage and a framed
Certificate of admission
Into the Orange Order,
And his speech began to wander
And memory ebbed
Leaving upon the shore
Odd shells and heads of wrack
And his soul went out on the ebbing
Tide in a trim boat
To find the Walls of Derry
Or the land of the Ever Young.

Summer, 1939

IV

Christina

It all began so easy
With bricks upon the floor
Building motley houses
And knocking down your houses
And always building more.

The doll was called Christina,
Her under-wear was lace,
She smiled while you dressed her
And when you then undressed her
She kept a smiling face.

Until the day she tumbled
And broke herself in two

And her legs and arms were hollow
And her yellow head was hollow
Behind her eyes of blue.

. . . . .

He went to bed with a lady
Somewhere seen before,
He heard the name Christina
And suddenly saw Christina
Dead on the nursery floor.

July, 1939

V

Provence

It is a decade now since he and she
Spent September in Provence: the vineyard
Was close about the house; mosquitoes and cicadas
Garrulous day and night; and by the sea
Thighs and shoulders tanning themselves and one
Gay old man in particular who never
Missed a day, a glutton for the sun,
But did not bathe. He and she with swimming
Every noon were wild for food; a Basque
Woman cooked on charcoal—aubergine with garlic,
And there were long green grapes exploding on the palate
And smelling of eau de Cologne. They had nothing to ask
Except that it should go on. Watching the vintage—
A file of bullock carts and the muzzle of each
Animal munching purple—he suddenly said
'We must get married soon.' Down on the beach,
His wife and three of his three children dead,
An old man lay in the sun, perfectly happy.

September, 1940

VI

The Preacher

He carried a ball of darkness with him, unrolled it
To find his way by in streets and rooms,
Every train or boat he took was Charon's ferry,
He never left the Catacombs;

He never smiled but spun his strands of black
Among the secular crowd who, when he tripped their feet,
Saw their own faces in the wet street, saw
Their hell beneath the street.

Among old iron, cinders, sizzling dumps,
A world castrated, amputated, trepanned,
He walked in the lost acres crying 'Repent
For the Kingdom of Death is at hand'.

He took the books of pagan art and read
Between the lines or worked them out to prove
Humanism a palimpsest and God's
Anger a more primal fact than love.

And in the city at night where drunken song
Climbed the air like tendrils of vine
He bared a knife and slashed the roots and laid
Another curse on Cain. The sign

Of the cross between his eyes, his mouth drawn down,
He passed the flower-sellers and all
The roses reeked of an abattoir, the gardenias
Became the décor of a funeral.

His hands were always clenched, an eagle
Riveted on a world of vice;
Going upstairs he built, block upon block
An Aztec pyramid of sacrifice.

Going upstairs to die in a bare room
He tried to square his accounts; lying in bed
He summoned home his deeds, drew back
Sixty years' expended thread,

Pulled it in through the chink beneath the door,
Wrapped it around him, all
His faith and his despair a ball of black
And he himself at the centre of the ball.

March, 1940

Débâcle

They had built it up—but not for this the lean
And divinatory years,
The red-eyed pioneers
Facing the dark and making the desert green.

Not for this the pale inventor's lamp
Alight till dawn, the hands
Weary with sifting sands,
The burst of nuggets on the miners' camp.

Vision and sinew made it of light and stone;
Not grateful nor enchanted
Their heirs took it for granted
Having a world—a world that was all their own.

At sundown now the windows had gone gold
For half an hour; a quick
Chill came off the brick
Walls and the flesh was suddenly old and cold.

Crumbling between the fingers, under the feet,
Crumbling behind the eyes,
Their world gives way and dies
And something twangs and breaks at the end of the street.

September, 1940

Death of an actress

I see from the paper that Florrie Forde is dead—
Collapsed after singing to wounded soldiers,
At the age of sixty-five. The American notice
Says no doubt all that need be said

About this one-time chorus girl; whose rôle
For more than forty stifling years was giving
Sexual, sentimental, or comic entertainment,
A gaudy posy for the popular soul.

Plush and cigars: she waddled into the lights,
Old and huge and painted, in velvet and tiara,

Her voice gone but around her head an aura
Of all her vanilla-sweet forgotten vaudeville nights.

With an elephantine shimmy and a sugared wink
She threw a trellis of Dorothy Perkins roses
Around an audience come from slum and suburb
And weary of the tea-leaves in the sink;

Who found her songs a rainbow leading west
To the home they never had, to the chocolate Sunday
Of boy and girl, to cowslip time, to the never-
Ending weekend Islands of the Blest.

In the Isle of Man before the war before
The present one she made a ragtime favourite
Of 'Tipperary', which became the swan-song
Of troop-ships on a darkened shore;

And during Munich sang her ancient quiz
Of *Where's Bill Bailey?* and the chorus answered,
Muddling through and glad to have no answer:
Where's Bill Bailey? How do *we* know where he is!

Now on a late and bandaged April day
In a military hospital Miss Florrie
Forde has made her positively last appearance
And taken her bow and gone correctly away.

Correctly. For she stood
For an older England, for children toddling
Hand in hand while the day was bright. Let the wren and robin
Gently with leaves cover the Babes in the Wood.

                                        May, 1940

Bar-room matins

> Popcorn peanuts clams and gum:
> We whose Kingdom has not come
> Have mouths like men but still are dumb

> Who only deal with Here and Now
> As circumstances may allow:
> The sponsored programme tells us how.

And yet the preachers tell the pews
What man misuses God can use:
Give us this day our daily news

That we may hear behind the brain
And through the sullen heat's migraine
The atavistic voice of Cain:

'Who entitled you to spy
From your easy heaven? Am I
My brother's keeper? Let him die.'

And God in words we soon forget
Answers through the radio set:
'The curse is on his forehead yet.'

Mass destruction, mass disease:
We thank thee, Lord, upon our knees
That we were born in times like these

When with doom tumbling from the sky
Each of us has an alibi
For doing nothing—Let him die.

Let him die, his death will be
A drop of water in the sea,
A journalist's commodity.

Pretzels crackers chips and beer:
Death is something that we fear
But it titillates the ear.

Anchovy almond ice and gin:
All shall die though none can win;
Let the Untergang begin—

Die the soldiers, die the Jews,
And all the breadless homeless queues.
Give us this day our daily news.

July, 1940

Flight of the heart

Heart, my heart, what will you do?
There are five lame dogs and one deaf-mute
All of them with demands on you.

    I will build myself a copper tower
    With four ways out and no way in
    But mine the glory, mine the power.

And what if the tower should shake and fall
With three sharp taps and one big bang?
What would you do with yourself at all?

    I would go in the cellar and drink the dark
    With two quick sips and one long pull,
    Drunk as a lord and gay as a lark.

But what when the cellar roof caves in
With one blue flash and nine old bones?
How, my heart, will you save your skin?

    I will go back where I belong
    With one foot first and both eyes blind
    I will go back where I belong
    In the fore-being of mankind.

October, 1940

Refugees

With prune-dark eyes, thick lips, jostling each other
These, disinterred from Europe, throng the deck
To watch their hope heave up in steel and concrete
Powerful but delicate as a swan's neck,

Thinking, each of them, the worst is over
And we do not want any more to be prominent or rich,
Only to be ourselves, to be unmolested
And make ends meet—an ideal surely which

Here if anywhere is feasible. Their glances
Like wavering antennae feel

Around the sliding limber towers of Wall Street
And count the numbered docks and gingerly steal

Into the hinterland of their own future
Behind this excessive annunciation of towers,
Tracking their future selves through a continent of strangeness.
The liner moves to the magnet; the quay flowers

With faces of people's friends. But these are mostly
Friendless and all they look to meet
Is a secretary who holds his levée among ledgers,
Tells them to take a chair and wait . . .

And meanwhile the city will go on, regardless
Of any new arrival, trains like prayers
Radiating from stations haughty as cathedrals,
Tableaux of spring in milliners' windows, great affairs

Being endorsed on a vulcanite table, lines of washing
Feebly garish among grimy brick and dour
Iron fire-escapes; barrows of cement are rumbling
Up airy planks; a florist adds a flower

To a bouquet that is bound for somebody's beloved
Or for someone ill; in a sombre board-room great
Problems wait to be solved or shelved. The city
Goes on but you, you will probably find, must wait

Till something or other turns up. Something-or-Other
Becomes an expected angel from the sky;
But do not trust the sky, the blue that looks so candid
Is non-committal, frigid as a harlot's eye.

Gangways—the handclasp of the land. The resurrected,
The brisk or resigned Lazaruses, who want
Another chance, go trooping ashore. But chances
Are dubious. Fate is stingy, recalcitrant

And officialdom greets them blankly as they fumble
Their foreign-looking baggage; they still feel
The movement of the ship while through their imagination
The known and the unheard-of constellations wheel.

September, 1940

Jehu

Peace on New England, on the shingled white houses, on golden
Rod and the red Turkey carpet spikes of sumach. The little
American flags are flapping in the graveyard. Continuous
   Chorus of grasshoppers. Fleece
Of quiet around the mind. Honey-suckle, phlox and smoke-bush,
Hollyhocks and nasturtium and corn on the cob. And the pine wood
   Smelling of outmoded peace.

A king sat over the gate looking to the desert. A spiral
Of dust came toward him, a special messenger asking
Anxiously 'Is it peace?' The heavy eyebrows lowered,
   He answered 'What have I
To do with peace?' and the messenger mopped the sweat and obedient
Took his place behind the king who still sat scanning
   Miles of desert and sky.

Negative prospect; sand in the lungs; blood in the sand; deceiving
Mirage of what were once ideals or even motives
And in this desert even a ghost can hardly
   Live—but in the long run what
Have I to do with life? He got up blandly, harnessed his horses
And furiously drove, his eyeballs burning and the chariot's
   Axles burning hot.

Someone sat in a window with a new coiffure, her raddled
Face, a Muse's possibly once but now a harlot's,
Smirked at the charioteer who, looking past her, signalled
   To the maids to throw her down
And they threw her down and the wheels went over her ribs and the
    carcase,
The one-time inspiration of artists, the toast of kings, was abandoned
   To the scavenger dogs of the town.

And now the sand blows over Kent and Wales where we may shortly
Learn the secret of the desert's purge, of the mad driving,
The cautery of the gangrened soul, though we are not certain
   Whether we shall stand beside
The charioteer, the surgeon, or shall be one with the pampered
Queen who tittered in the face of death, unable to imagine
   The meaning of the flood tide.

August, 1940

The death-wish

It being in this life forbidden to move
Too lightly, people, over-cautious, contrive
To save their lives by weighting them with dead
Habits, hopes, beliefs, anything not alive,
Till all this ballast of unreality sinks
The boat and all our thinking gurgles down
Into the deep sea that never thinks.

Which being so, it is not surprising that
Some in their impatience jump the rails,
Refusing to wait the communal failure, preferring
The way the madman or the meteor fails,
Deceiving themselves to think their death uncommon,
And mad to possess the unpossessable sea
As a man in spring desires to die in woman.

May, 1940

Autobiography

In my childhood trees were green
And there was plenty to be seen.

Come back early or never come.

My father made the walls resound,
He wore his collar the wrong way round.

Come back early or never come.

My mother wore a yellow dress;
Gently, gently, gentleness.

Come back early or never come.

When I was five the black dreams came;
Nothing after was quite the same.

Come back early or never come.

The dark was talking to the dead;
The lamp was dark beside my bed.

Come back early or never come.

When I woke they did not care;
Nobody, nobody was there.

Come back early or never come.

When my silent terror cried,
Nobody, nobody replied.

Come back early or never come.

I got up; the chilly sun
Saw me walk away alone.

Come back early or never come.
September, 1940

Conversation

Ordinary people are peculiar too:
Watch the vagrant in their eyes
Who sneaks away while they are talking with you
Into some black wood behind the skull,
Following un-, or other, realities,
Fishing for shadows in a pool.

But sometimes the vagrant comes the other way
Out of their eyes and into yours
Having mistaken you perhaps for yesterday
Or for to-morrow night, a wood in which
He may pick up among the pine-needles and burrs
The lost purse, the dropped stitch.

Vagrancy however is forbidden; ordinary men
Soon come back to normal, look you straight
In the eyes as if to say 'It will not happen again',
Put up a barrage of common sense to baulk
Intimacy but by mistake interpolate
Swear-words like roses in their talk.
March, 1940

The ear

There are many sounds which are neither music nor voice,
There are many visitors in masks or in black glasses
Climbing the spiral staircase of the ear. The choice
Of callers is not ours. Behind the hedge
Of night they wait to pounce. A train passes,
The thin and audible end of a dark wedge.

We should like to lie alone in a deaf hollow
Cocoon of self where no person or thing would speak:
In fact we lie and listen as a man might follow
A will o' the wisp in an endless eyeless bog,
Follow the terrible drone of a cockchafer, or the bleak
Oracle of a barking dog.

April, 1940

Evening in Connecticut

Equipoise: becalmed
Trees, a dome of kindness;
Only the scissory noise of the grasshoppers;
Only the shadows longer and longer.

The lawn a raft
In a sea of singing insects,
Sea without waves or mines or premonitions:
Life on a china cup.

But turning. The trees turn
Soon to brocaded autumn.
Fall. The fall of dynasties; the emergence
Of sleeping kings from caves—

Beard over the breastplate,
Eyes not yet in focus, red
Hair on the back of the hands, unreal
Heraldic axe in the hands.

Unreal but still can strike.
And in defence we cannot call on the evening

185

Or the seeming-friendly woods—
Nature is not to be trusted,

Nature whose falls of snow,
Falling softer than catkins,
Bury the lost and over their grave a distant
Smile spreads in the sun.

Not to be trusted, no,
Deaf at the best; she is only
And always herself, Nature is only herself,
Only the shadows longer and longer.

September, 1940

Entered in the minutes

I

Barcelona in Wartime

In the Paralelo a one-legged
Man sat on the ground,
His one leg out before him,
Smiling. A sudden sound

Of crazy laughter shivered
The sunlight; overhead
A parrot in a window of aspidistras
Was laughing like the dead.

II

Business Men

The two men talking business
So easily in the train
Project themselves upon me
Just as the window pane

Reflects their faces, and I
Find myself in a trance
To hear two strangers talking
The same language for once.

III
Night Club

After the legshows and the brandies
And all the pick-me-ups for tired
Men there is a feeling
Something more is required.

The lights go down and eyes
Look up across the room;
Salome comes in, bearing
The head of God knows whom.

IV
Didymus

Refusing to fall in love with God, he gave
Himself to the love of created things,
Accepting only what he could see, a river
Full of the shadows of swallows' wings

That dipped and skimmed the water; he would not
Ask where the water ran or why.
When he died a swallow seemed to plunge
Into the reflected, the wrong, sky.

October–November, 1939

Plain speaking

In the beginning and in the end the only decent
Definition is tautology: man is man,
Woman woman, and tree tree, and world world,
Slippery, self-contained; catch as catch can.

Which when caught between the beginning and end
Turn other than themselves, their entities unfurled,
Flapping and overlapping—a tree becomes
A talking tower, and a woman becomes world.

Catch them in nets, but either the thread is thin
Or the mesh too big or, thirdly, the fish die
And man from false communion dwindles back
Into a mere man under a mere sky.

But dream was dream and love was love and what
Happened happened—even if the judge said
It should have been otherwise—and glitter glitters
And I am I although the dead are dead.

March, 1940

Perdita

The glamour of the end attic, the smell of old
Leather trunks—Perdita, where have you been
Hiding all these years? Somewhere or other a green
Flag is waving under an iron vault
And a brass bell is the herald of green country
And the wind is in the wires and the broom is gold.

Perdita, what became of all the things
We said that we should do? The cobwebs cover
The labels of Tyrol. The time is over-
Due and in some metropolitan station
Among the clank of cans and the roistering files
Of steam the caterpillars wait for wings.

March, 1940

The dowser

An inkling only, whisper in the bones
Of strange weather on the way,
Twitch of the eyelid, shadow of a passing bird.
It is coming some time soon.

What? or who? An inkling only,
Adumbration of unknown glory
Drew to the feet of Saint Francis where the waves
Broke, an army of fish.

Humming wires; feel of a lost limb
Cut off in another life;
Trance on the tripod; effulgence
Of headlights beyond the rise in the road.

And the hazel rod bent, dipping, contorting,
Snake from sleep; they were right
Who remembered some old fellow
(Dead long ago) who remembered the well.

'Dig', he said, 'dig',
Holding the lantern, the rod bent double,
And we dug respecting his knowledge,
Not waiting for morning, keenly

Dug: the clay was heavy
Two hours heavy, before
The clink of a spade revealed
What or whom? We expected a well—

A well? A mistake somewhere . . .
More of a tomb . . . Anyhow we backed away
From the geyser suddenly of light that erupted, sprayed
Rocketing over the sky azaleas and gladioli.

September, 1940

The return

All the lost interpretations,
All the unconsummated consummations,
All the birds that flew and left the big sky empty,
Come back throwing shadows on our patience.

Bethlehem is desolate and the stables
Cobwebbed, mute; below each Tower of Babel's
Sentrydom of night, inside the bleak
Glass of cafés chairs are piled on tables.

Notwithstanding which, notwithstanding
The hospital—the icicles round the landing—
Expecting Birth, we know that it will come
Sooner or later, banding

Together the good daemons, the defiance
And lolloping vulcanite of sea-lions,
The harlequinade of water through a sluice,
Tigers in the air, and in the teeth of science

The acclamation of earth's returning daughter,
Jonquils out of hell, and after
Hell the imperative of joy, the dancing
Fusillade of sunlight on the water.

February, 1940

Cradle song for Eleanor

Sleep, my darling, sleep;
   The pity of it all
Is all we compass if
   We watch disaster fall.
Put off your twenty-odd
   Encumbered years and creep
Into the only heaven,
   The robbers' cave of sleep.

The wild grass will whisper,
   Lights of passing cars
Will streak across your dreams
   And fumble at the stars;
Life will tap the window
   Only too soon again,
Life will have her answer—
   Do not ask her when.

When the winsome bubble
   Shivers, when the bough
Breaks, will be the moment
   But not here or now.
Sleep and, asleep, forget
   The watchers on the wall
Awake all night who know
   The pity of it all.

October, 1940

VII

1941—1944

To Hedli

Because the velvet image,
Because the lilting measure,
No more convey my meaning
I am compelled to use
Such words as disabuse
My mind of casual pleasure
And turn it towards a centre—
A zone which others too
And you
May choose to enter.

Prayer before birth

I am not yet born; O hear me.
Let not the bloodsucking bat or the rat or the stoat or the
    club-footed ghoul come near me.

I am not yet born, console me.
I fear that the human race may with tall walls wall me,
    with strong drugs dope me, with wise lies lure me,
        on black racks rack me, in blood-baths roll me.

I am not yet born; provide me
With water to dandle me, grass to grow for me, trees to talk
    to me, sky to sing to me, birds and a white light
        in the back of my mind to guide me.

I am not yet born; forgive me
For the sins that in me the world shall commit, my words
    when they speak me, my thoughts when they think me,
        my treason engendered by traitors beyond me,
            my life when they murder by means of my
            hands, my death when they live me.

I am not yet born; rehearse me
In the parts I must play and the cues I must take when
    old men lecture me, bureaucrats hector me, mountains
        frown at me, lovers laugh at me, the white
            waves call me to folly and the desert calls
                me to doom and the beggar refuses
                    my gift and my children curse me.

I am not yet born; O hear me,
Let not the man who is beast or who thinks he is God
    come near me.

I am not yet born; O fill me
With strength against those who would freeze my
    humanity, would dragoon me into a lethal automaton,
        would make me a cog in a machine, a thing with
            one face, a thing, and against all those
                who would dissipate my entirety, would
                    blow me like thistledown hither and
                      thither or hither and thither
                        like water held in the
                          hands would spill me.

Let them not make me a stone and let them not spill me.
Otherwise kill me.

1944

Precursors

O that the rain would come—the rain in big battalions—
Or thunder flush the hedge a more clairvoyant green
Or wind walk in and whip us and strip us or booming
Harvest moon transmute this muted scene.

But all is flat, matt, mute, unlivened, unexpectant,
And none but insects dare to sing or pirouette;
That Man is a dancer is an anachronism—
Who has forgotten his steps or hardly learnt them yet.

Yet one or two we have known who had the gusto
Of wind or water-spout, and one or two
Who carry an emerald lamp behind their faces
And—during thunder-storms—the light comes shining through.

c. 1944

Explorations

The whale butting through scarps of moving marble,
The tapeworm probing the intestinal darkness,
The swallows drawn collectively to their magnet,
    These are our prototypes and yet,
Though we may envy them still, they are merely patterns
    To wonder at—and forget.

For the ocean-carver, cumbrous but unencumbered,
Who tired of land looked for his freedom and frolic in water,
Though he succeeded, has failed; it is only instinct
    That plots his graph and he,
Though appearing to us a free and a happy monster, is merely
    An appanage of the sea.

And the colourless blind worm, triumphantly self-degraded,
Who serves as an image to men of the worst adjustment—

Oxymoron of parasitical glory—
  Cannot even be cursed,
Lacking the only pride of his way of life, not knowing
  That he has chosen the worst.

So even that legion of birds who appear so gladly
Purposeful, with air in their bones, enfranchised
Citizens of the sky and never at odds with
  The season or out of line,
Can be no model to us; their imputed purpose
  Is a foregone design—

And ours is not. For we are unique, a conscious
Hoping and therefore despairing creature, the final
Anomaly of the world, we can learn no method
  From whales or birds or worms;
Our end is our own to be won by our own endeavour
  And held on our own terms.

Mutations

If there has been no spiritual change of kind
Within our species since Cro-Magnon Man
And none is looked for now while the millennia cool,
Yet each of us has known mutations in the mind
When the world jumped and what had been a plan
Dissolved and rivers gushed from what had seemed a pool.

For every static world that you or I impose
Upon the real one must crack at times and new
Patterns from new disorders open like a rose
And old assumptions yield to new sensation;
The Stranger in the wings is waiting for his cue,
The fuse is always laid to some annunciation.

Surprises keep us living: as when the first light
Surprised our infant eyes or as when, very small,
Clutching our parents' hands we toddled down a road
Where all was blank and windless both to touch and sight
Had we not suddenly raised our eyes which showed
The long grass blowing wild on top of the high wall.

For it is true, surprises break and make,
As when the baton falls and all together the hands
On the fiddle-bows are pistons, or when crouched above
His books the scholar suddenly understands
What he has thought for years—or when the inveterate rake
Finds for once that his lust is becoming love.

Brother Fire

When our brother Fire was having his dog's day
Jumping the London streets with millions of tin cans
Clanking at his tail, we heard some shadow say
'Give the dog a bone'—and so we gave him ours;
Night after night we watched him slaver and crunch away
The beams of human life, the tops of topless towers.

Which gluttony of his for us was Lenten fare
Who mother-naked, suckled with sparks, were chill
Though cotted in a grille of sizzling air
Striped like a convict—black, yellow and red;
Thus were we weaned to knowledge of the Will
That wills the natural world but wills us dead.

O delicate walker, babbler, dialectician Fire,
O enemy and image of ourselves,
Did we not on those mornings after the All Clear,
When you were looting shops in elemental joy
And singing as you swarmed up city block and spire,
Echo your thoughts in ours? 'Destroy! Destroy!'

November, 1942

The Trolls

(Written after an air-raid, April 1941)

(i)

In the misty night humming to themselves like morons
They ramble and rumble over the roof-tops, stumble and shamble
    from pile to pillar,

In clodhopping boots that crunch the stars
And a blank smirk on their faces:
    Pretty Polly won't die yet.

Skittle-alley horseplay, congurgitation . . . they don't know
    what they are doing,
All they can do is stutter and lurch, riding their hobby, grinding
Their hobnails into our bodies, into our brains, into the domed
Head where the organ music lingers:
    Pretty Polly won't die yet.

Here they come—I thought we had lost them—
Here they come once more and once too many with their rough
    and
Tumble antics, here they
Are, they are, they ARE:
    Pretty Polly won't die yet,
    Oh, won't she?

(ii)

Than which not any could be found other
And outside which is less than nothing—
This, as they call it, life.
But such as it is, gurgling and tramping, licking their thumbs
    before they
Turn the pages over, tear them out, they
Wish it away, they
Puff with enormous cheeks, put paid to
Hours and minutes—thistledown in the void.

(iii)

Death has a look of finality;
We think we lose something but if it were not for
Death we should have nothing to lose, existence
Because unlimited would merely be existence
Without incarnate value. The trolls can occasion
Our death but they are not able
To use it as we can use it.
Fumbling and mumbling they try to
Spell out Death correctly; they are not able.

Than which not any. Time
Swings on the poles of death
And the latitude and the longitude of life
Are fixed by death, and the value
Of every organism, act and moment
Is, thanks to death, unique.

(v)

This then is our answer under
The crawl of lava, a last
Shake of the fist at the vanishing sky, at the hulking
Halfwit demons who rape and slobber, who assume
That when we are killed no more will be heard of us—
Silence of men and trolls' triumph.
A wrong—in the end—assumption.
Barging and lunging out of the clouds, a daft
Descent of no-good gods, they think to
Be rid for ever of the voice of men but they happen
To be trying what even trolls
Can never accomplish, they happen
To be—for all their kudos—
Wrong, wrong in the end.

Troll's courtship

I am a lonely Troll after my gala night;
I have knocked down houses and stamped my feet on the people's
    heart,
I have trundled round the sky with the executioner's cart
And dropped my bait for corpses, watched them bite,
But I am a lonely Troll—nothing in the end comes right.

In a smoking and tinkling dawn with fires and broken glass
I am a lonely Troll; my tributes are in vain
To Her to whom if I had even a human brain
I might have reached but, as it is, the epochs pass
And leave me unfulfilled, no further than I was.

Because I cannot accurately conceive
Any ideal, even ideal Death,
My curses and my boasts are merely a waste of breath,
My lusts and lonelinesses grunt and heave
And blunder round among the ruins that I leave.

Yet from the lubber depths of my unbeing I
Aspire to Her who was my Final Cause but who
Is always somewhere else and not to be spoken to,
Is always nowhere: which is in the long run why
I make for nowhere, make a shambles of the sky.

Nostalgia for the breasts that never gave nor could
Give milk or even warmth has desolated me,
Clutching at shadows of my nullity
That slink and mutter through the leafless wood
Which thanks to me is dead, is dead for good.

A cone of ice enclosing liquid fire,
Utter negation in a positive form,
That would be how She is, the nadir and the norm
Of dissolution and the constant pyre
Of all desirable things—that is what I desire

And therefore cry to Her with the voice of broken bells
To come, visibly, palpably, to come,
Gluing my ear to gutted walls but walls are dumb,
All I can catch is a gurgle as of the sea in shells
But not Her voice—for She is always somewhere else.

May, 1941

The revenant

*(The last lyric from a Song Cycle: a girl speaks
to her dead lover)*

The nearness of remoteness like a lion's eye,
    So near in a cage yet so far away,
In this death we are proud to die—
    The yellow eye of a beast of prey.

To die in a moment is a small thing
  Like a sea-shell in a quiet room,
Yet from that shell the sea will fling
  The thunder of uncharted doom.

So large, so small, so near, so far,
  So stark a prison, yet so free—
Nothing now can mend nor mar
  This death you have brought home to me.

The windows of our life were placed
  So that their panes were blurred with breath,
We never saw which way they faced
  But now they open wide on death.

The yellow eye of the beast will close,
  The stolen shell return to the sea;
I thank you, my love, for this repose,
  For the death you have brought home to me.

                                    c. 1944

Convoy

Together, keeping in line, slow as if hypnotised
Across the blackboard sea in sombre echelon
The food-ships draw their wakes. No Euclid could have devised
Neater means to a more essential end—
Unless the chalk breaks off, the convoy is surprised.

The cranks go up and down, the smoke-trails tendril out,
The precious cargoes creak, the signals clack,
All is under control and nobody need shout,
We are steady as we go, and on our flanks
The little whippet warships romp and scurry about.

This is a bit like us: the individual sets
A course for all his soul's more basic needs
Of love and pride-of-life, but sometimes he forgets
How much their voyage home depends upon pragmatic
And ruthless attitudes—destroyers and corvettes.

                                    December, 1942

Whit Monday

Their feet on London, their heads in the grey clouds,
The Bank (if you call it a holiday) Holiday crowds
Stroll from street to street, cocking an eye
For where the angel used to be in the sky;
But the Happy Future is a thing of the past and the street
Echoes to nothing but their dawdling feet.
The Lord's my shepherd—familiar words of myth
Stand up better to bombs than a granite monolith,
Perhaps there is something in them. *I'll not want*—
Not when I'm dead. *He makes me down to lie*—
Death my christening and fire my font—
The quiet (Thames, or Don's or Salween's) *waters by.*

June, 1942

Swing-song

I'm only a wartime working girl,
The machine shop makes me deaf,
I have no prospects after the war
And *my* young man is in the R.A.F.
   K for Kitty calling P for Prue . . .
   Bomb Doors Open . . .
   Over to You.

Night after night as he passes by
I wonder what he's gone to bomb
And I fancy in the jabber of the mad machines
That I hear him talking on the intercomm.
   K for Kitty calling P for Prue . . .
   Bomb Doors Open . . .
   Over to You.

So there's no one in the world, I sometimes think,
Such a wallflower as I
For I must talk to myself on the ground
While he is talking to his friends in the sky:
   K for Kitty calling P for Prue . . .
   Bomb Doors Open . . .
   Over to You.

November, 1942

Bottleneck

Never to fight unless from a pure motive
And for a clear end was his unwritten rule
Who had been in books and visions to a progressive school
And dreamt of barricades, yet being observant
Knew that that was not the way things are:
This man would never make a soldier or a servant.

When I saw him last, carving the longshore mist
With an ascetic profile, he was standing
Watching the troopship leave, he did not speak
But from his eyes there peered a furtive footsore envy
Of these who sailed away to make an opposed landing
So calm because so young, so lethal because so meek.

Where he is now I could not say; he will,
The odds are, always be non-combatant
Being too violent in soul to kill
Anyone but himself, yet in his mind
A crowd of odd components mutter and press
For compromise with fact, longing to be combined
Into a working whole but cannot jostle through
The permanent bottleneck of his highmindedness.

December, 1942

Neutrality

The neutral island facing the Atlantic,
The neutral island in the heart of man,
Are bitterly soft reminders of the beginnings
That ended before the end began.

Look into your heart, you will find a County Sligo,
A Knocknarea with for navel a cairn of stones,
You will find the shadow and sheen of a moleskin mountain
And a litter of chronicles and bones.

Look into your heart, you will find fermenting rivers,
Intricacies of gloom and glint,
You will find such ducats of dream and great doubloons of ceremony
As nobody to-day would mint.

But then look eastward from your heart, there bulks
A continent, close, dark, as archetypal sin,
While to the west off your own shores the mackerel
Are fat—on the flesh of your kin.

September, 1942

The conscript

Being so young he feels the weight of history
Like clay around his boots; he would, if he could, fly
In search of a future like a sycamore seed
But is prevented by his own Necessity,
His own yet alien, which, whatever he may plead,
To every question gives the same reply.

Choiceless therefore, driven from pillar to post,
Expiating his pedigree, fulfilling
An oracle whose returns grow less and less,
Bandied from camp to camp to practise killing
He fails even so at times to remain engrossed
And is aware, at times, of life's largesse.

From camp to camp, from Eocene to chalk,
He lives a paradox, lives in a groove
That runs dead straight to an ordained disaster
So that in two dimensions he must move
Like an automaton, yet his inward stalk
Vertically aspires and makes him his own master.

Hence, though on the flat his life has no
Promise but of diminishing returns,
By feeling down and upwards he can divine
That dignity which far above him burns
In stars that yet are his and which below
Stands rooted like a dolmen in his spine.

The news-reel

Since Munich, what? A tangle of black film
Squirming like bait upon the floor of my mind
And scissors clicking daily. I am inclined
    To pick these pictures now but will hold back

203

Till memory has elicited from this blind
Drama its threads of vision, the intrusions
Of value upon fact, that sudden unconfined
Wind of understanding that blew out
From people's hands and faces, undesigned
Evidence of design, that change of climate
Which did not last but happens often enough
To give us hope that fact is a façade
And that there is an organism behind
Its brittle littleness, a rhythm and a meaning,
Something half-conjectured and half-divined,
Something to give way to and so find.

Nuts in May

May come up with bird-din
And May come up with sun-dint,
May come up with water-wheels
  And May come up with iris.

In the sun-peppered meadow the shepherds are old,
Their flutes are broken and their tales are told,
And their ears are deaf when the guns unfold
The new philosophy over the wold.

May come up with pollen of death,
May come up with cordite,
May come up with a chinagraph
  And May come up with a stopwatch.

In the high court of heaven Their tail-feathers shine
With cowspit and bullspit and spirits of wine,
They know no pity, being divine,
And They give no quarter to thine or mine.

May come up with Very lights,
May come up with duty,
May come up with a bouncing cheque,
  An acid-drop and a bandage.

Yes, angels are frigid and shepherds are dumb,
There is no holy water when the enemy come,

The trees are askew and the skies are a-hum
And you have to keep mum and go to it and die for your life
and keep mum.

May come up with fiddle-bows,
May come up with blossom,
May come up the same again,
The same again but different.

1943

The mixer

With a pert moustache and a ready candid smile
He has played his way through twenty years of pubs,
Deckchairs, lounges, touchlines, junctions, homes,
And still as ever popular, he roams
Far and narrow, mimicking the style
Of other people's leisure, scattering stubs.

Colourless, when alone, and self-accused,
He is only happy in reflected light
And only real in the range of laughter;
Behind his eyes are shadows of a night
In Flanders but his mind long since refused
To let that time intrude on what came after.

So in this second war which is fearful too,
He cannot away with silence but has grown
Almost a cipher, like a Latin word
That many languages have made their own
Till it is worn and blunt and easy to construe
And often spoken but no longer heard.

Nostalgia

In cock-wattle sunset or grey
Dawn when the dagger
Points again of longing
For what was never home
We needs must turn away
From the voices that cry 'Come'—
That under-sea ding-donging.

Dingle-dongle, bells and bluebells,
Snapdragon solstice, lunar lull,
The wasp circling the honey
Or the lamp soft on the snow—
These are the times at which
The will is vulnerable,
The trigger-finger slow,
The spirit lonely.

These are the times at which
Aloneness is too ripe
When homesick for the hollow
Heart of the Milky Way
The soundless clapper calls
And we would follow
But earth and will are stronger
And nearer—and we stay.

October, 1942

Babel

There was a tower that went before a fall.
    Can't we ever, my love, speak in the same language?
Its nerves grew worse and worse as it grew tall.
    Have we no aims in common?

As children we were bickering over beads—
    Can't we ever, my love, speak in the same language?
The more there are together, Togetherness recedes.
    Have we no aims in common?

Exiles all as we are in a foreign city,
    Can't we ever, my love, speak in the same language?
We cut each other's throats out of our great self-pity—
    Have we no aims in common?

Patriots, dreamers, die-hards, theoreticians, all,
    Can't we ever, my love, speak in the same language,
Or shall we go, still quarrelling over words, to the wall?
    Have we no aims in common?

December, 1942

Schizophrene

Hearing offstage the taps filling the bath
The set dissolves to childhood—in her cot
Hearing that ominous relentless noise
Which the grown-ups have started, who are not,
She knows, aware of what it means; it means
The Dark, the Flood, the Malice. It destroys
All other meanings—dolls or gingerbread;
It means a Will that wills all children dead.

Hearing the gasfire breathe monotonously
She waits for words but no words come, she lifts
A soapstone hand to smooth her hair and feels
The hand is someone else's—the scene shifts
To a cold desert where the wind has dropped
And the earth's movement stopped and something steals
Up from the grit through nerve and bone and vein
To flaunt its iron tendrils in her brain.

Hearing again the telegraph wires again
Humming again and always, she must lean
Against the humming post and search her mind
For what it is they say; in some latrine
She knows she wrote it first upon the wall
In self-incrimination, duly signed;
And, unrevoked since then, that signature
Runs round the world on wires, accusing her.

Hearing the church-bells too, she knows at once
That only she can hear them for it is no
Church or even belfry where they hang,
There are no ropes attached or ringers down below,
These bells are disembodied, they express
The claims of frozen Chaos and will clang
Till this and every other world shall melt
And Chaos be Itself and nothing felt.

Lastly, hearing the cock in the grey dawn
Crow once, crow twice, she shivers and dissolves
To someone else who in the hour of trial
Denied his Master and his guilt devolves
On her head only. If she could speak up,

She might even now atone for that denial
But the grey cock still crows and she knows why;
For she must still deny, deny, deny.

Alcohol

On golden seas of drink, so the Greek poet said,
Rich and poor are alike. Looking around in war
We watch the many who have returned to the dead
Ordering time-and-again the same-as-before:

Those Haves who cannot bear making a choice,
Those Have-nots who are bored with having nothing to choose,
Call for their drinks in the same tone of voice,
Find a factitious popular front in booze.

Another drink: Bacchylides was right
And self-deception golden—Serve him quick,
The siphon stutters in the archaic night,
The flesh is willing and the soul is sick.

Another drink: Adam is back in the Garden.
Another drink: the snake is back on the tree.
Let your brain go soft, your arteries will harden;
If God's a peeping tom he'll see what he shall see.

Another drink: Cain has slain his brother.
Another drink: Cain, they say, is cursed.
Another and another and another—
The beautiful ideologies have burst.

A bottle swings on a string. The matt-grey iron ship,
Which ought to have been the Future, sidles by
And with due auspices descends the slip
Into an ocean where no auspices apply.

Take away your slogans; give us something to swallow,
Give us beer or brandy or schnapps or gin;
This is the only road for the self-betrayed to follow—
The last way out that leads not out but in.

December, 1942

The libertine

In the old days with married women's stockings
Twisted round his bedpost he felt himself a gay
Dog but now his liver has begun to groan,
Now that pick-ups are the order of the day:
O leave me easy, leave me alone.

Voluptuary in his 'teens and cynic in his twenties,
He ran through women like a child through growing hay
Looking for a lost toy whose capture might atone
For his own guilt and the cosmic disarray:
O leave me easy, leave me alone.

He never found the toy and has forgotten the faces,
Only remembers the props . . . a scent-spray
Beside the bed or a milk-white telephone
Or through the triple ninon the acrid trickle of day:
O leave me easy, leave me alone.

Long fingers over the gunwale, hair in a hair-net,
Furs in January, cartwheel hats in May,
And after the event the wish to be alone—
Angels, goddesses, bitches, all have edged away:
O leave me easy, leave me alone.

So now, in middle age, his erotic programme
Torn in two, if after such a delay
An accident should offer him his own
Fulfilment in a woman, still he would say:
O leave me easy, leave me alone.

1943

Epitaph for liberal poets

If in the latter
End—which is fairly soon—our way of life goes west
And some shall say *So What* and some *What Matter*,
Ready under new names to exploit or be exploited,
What, though better unsaid, would we have history say
Of us who walked in our sleep and died on our Quest?

We who always had, but never admitted, a master,
Who were expected—and paid—to be ourselves,
Conditioned to think freely, how can we
Patch up our broken hearts and modes of thought in plaster
And glorify in chromium-plated stories
Those who shall supersede us and cannot need us—
The tight-lipped technocratic Conquistadores?

The Individual has died before; Catullus
Went down young, gave place to those who were born old
And more adaptable and were not even jealous
Of his wild life and lyrics. Though our songs
Were not so warm as his, our fate is no less cold.

Such silence then before us, pinned against the wall,
Why need we whine? There is no way out, the birds
Will tell us nothing more; we shall vanish first,
Yet leave behind us certain frozen words
Which some day, though not certainly, may melt
And, for a moment or two, accentuate a thirst.

December, 1942

The satirist

Who is that man with the handshake? Don't you know;
He is the pinprick master, he can dissect
All your moods and manners, he can discover
A selfish motive for anything—and collect
His royalties as recording angel. No
Reverence here for hero, saint or lover.

Who is that man so deftly filling his pipe
As if creating something? That's the reason:
He is not creative at all, his mind is dry
And bears no blossoms even in the season,
He is an onlooker, a heartless type,
Whose hobby is giving everyone else the lie.

Who is that man with eyes like a lonely dog?
Lonely is right. He knows that he has missed
What others miss unconsciously. Assigned
To a condemned ship he still must keep the log
And so fulfil the premises of his mind
Where large ideals have bred a satirist.

This way out

You're not going yet? I must; I have to work.
Though no one better relished halcyon days
Behind his eyes the winch of will was busy
And dizzy ways led zigzag through the murk.

So deprecatingly he blew a nought
In smoke and threw the stub into the purring grate
And left us, as he always did, to follow
His colonising fate through Africas of thought.

He always broke off so, abrupt but shy
In knowledge of his mission, veered and tacked
To his own breezes—till as a variation
His explanation cracked and threw the words awry:
You're not going yet? I must; I have to die.

Thyestes

When the King sat down to the feast and the golden lid revealed
The human cutlets and the Graces sang
Their lays of love returned and lovers meeting,
Did his blood tell him what his mind concealed?
Didn't he know—or did he—what he was eating?

Thus Here and We, neither of which is what
The mind and map admit, in perfidy are linked;
This green foam frets away our sense of duty
While we, who watch it blossom and bulge, are not
Spectators in our hearts but murderers of beauty.

Cannibalism and incest: such is time,
A trail of shaking candles, such are we
Who garnish to pollute and breed to kill—
Messmates in the eucharist of crime
And heirs to two of those three black crosses on the hill.

1943

Prayer in mid-passage

O Thou my monster, Thou my guide,
Be with me where the bluffs divide
Nor let me contemplate return
To where my backward chattels burn
In haunts of friendship and untruth—
The Cities of the Plain of Youth.

O pattern of inhuman good,
Hard critic of our thought and blood,
By whose decree there is no zone
Where man can live by men alone,
Unveil Thyself that all may see
Thy fierce impersonality.

We were the past—and doomed because
We were a past that never was;
Yet grant to men that they may climb
This time-bound ladder out of time
And by our human organs we
Shall thus transcend humanity.

Take therefore, though Thou disregard,
This prayer, this hymn, this feckless word,
O Thou my silence, Thou my song,
To whom all focal doubts belong
And but for whom this breath were breath—
Thou my meaning, Thou my death.

c. 1943

Prospect

Though loves languish and sour
Fruit puts the teeth on edge,
Though the ragged nests are empty of song
In the barbed and blistered hedge,

Though old men's lives and children's bricks
Spell out a Machiavellian creed,
Though the evil Past is ever present
And the happy Present is past indeed,

Though the stone grows and grows
That we roll up the hill
And the hill grows and grows
And gravity conquers still,

Though Nature's laws exploit
And defeat anarchic men,
Though every sandcastle concept
Being *ad hoc* must crumble again,

And though to-day is arid,
We know—and knowing bless—
That rooted in futurity
There is a plant of tenderness.

The springboard

He never made the dive—not while I watched.
High above London, naked in the night
Perched on a board. I peered up through the bars
Made by his fear and mine but it was more than fright
That kept him crucified among the budding stars.

Yes, it was unbelief. He knew only too well
That circumstances called for sacrifice
But, shivering there, spreadeagled above the town,
His blood began to haggle over the price
History would pay if he were to throw himself down.

If it would mend the world, that would be worth while
But he, quite rightly, long had ceased to believe
In any Utopia or in Peace-upon-Earth;
His friends would find in his death neither ransom nor reprieve
But only a grain of faith—for what it was worth.

And yet we know he knows what he must do.
There above London where the gargoyles grin
He will dive like a bomber past the broken steeple,
One man wiping out his own original sin
And, like ten million others, dying for the people.

June, 1942

213

When we were children

When we were children words were coloured
(Harlot and murder were dark purple)
And language was a prism, the light
    A conjured inlay on the grass,
Whose rays to-day are concentrated
    And language grown a burning-glass.

When we were children Spring was easy,
Dousing our heads in suds of hawthorn
And scrambling the laburnum tree—
    A breakfast for the gluttonous eye;
Whose winds and sweets have now forsaken
    Lungs that are black, tongues that are dry.

Now we are older and our talents
Accredited to time and meaning,
To handsel joy requires a new
    Shuffle of cards behind the brain
Where meaning shall remarry colour
    And flowers be timeless once again.
                                    June, 1944

VIII

1944—1947

What is truth? says Pilate,
Waits for no answer;
Double your stakes, says the clock
To the ageing dancer;
Double the guard, says Authority,
Treble the bars;
Holes in the sky, says the child
Scanning the stars.

The streets of Laredo

O early one morning I walked out like Agag,
Early one morning to walk through the fire
Dodging the pythons that leaked on the pavements
With tinkle of glasses and tangle of wire;

When grimed to the eyebrows I met an old fireman
Who looked at me wryly and thus did he say:
'The streets of Laredo are closed to all traffic,
We won't never master this joker to-day.

'O hold the branch tightly and wield the axe brightly,
The bank is in powder, the banker's in hell,
But loot is still free on the streets of Laredo
And when we drive home we drive home on the bell.'

Then out from a doorway there sidled a cockney,
A rocking-chair rocking on top of his head:
'O fifty-five years I been feathering my love-nest
And look at it now—why, you'd sooner be dead.'

At which there arose from a wound in the asphalt,
His big wig a-smoulder, Sir Christopher Wren
Saying: 'Let them make hay of the streets of Laredo;
When your ground-rents expire I will build them again.'

Then twangling their bibles with wrath in their nostrils
From Bonehill Fields came Bunyan and Blake:
'Laredo the golden is fallen, is fallen;
Your flame shall not quench nor your thirst shall not slake.'

'I come to Laredo to find me asylum',
Says Tom Dick and Harry the Wandering Jew;
'They tell me report at the first police station
But the station is pancaked—so what can I do?'

Thus eavesdropping sadly I strolled through Laredo
Perplexed by the dicta misfortunes inspire
Till one low last whisper inveigled my earhole—
The voice of the Angel, the voice of the fire:

O late, very late, have I come to Laredo
A whimsical bride in my new scarlet dress

217

But at last I took pity on those who were waiting
To see my regalia and feel my caress.

Now ring the bells gaily and play the hose daily,
Put splints on your legs, put a gag on your breath;
O you streets of Laredo, you streets of Laredo,
Lay down the red carpet—My dowry is death.

July, 1945

Hiatus

The years that did not count—Civilians in the towns
Remained at the same age as in Nineteen-Thirty-Nine,
Saying last year, meaning the last of peace;
Yet eyes began to pucker, mouth to crease,
The hiatus was too packed with fears and frowns,
The would-be absent heart came forth a magnetic mine.

As if the weekly food queue were to stretch,
Absorb all future Europe. Or as if
The sleepers in the Tube had come from Goya's Spain
Or Thucydides' Corcyra—a long way to fetch
People to prove that civilization is vain,
Wrapped in old quilts; no wonder they wake stiff.

Yes, we wake stiff and older; especially when
The schoolboys of the Thirties reappear,
Fledged in the void, indubitably men,
Having kept vigil on the Unholy Mount
And found some dark and tentative things made clear,
Some clear made dark, in the years that did not count.

July, 1945

Corner seat

Suspended in a moving night
The face in the reflected train
Looks at first sight as self-assured
As your own face—But look again:

Windows between you and the world
Keep out the cold, keep out the fright;
Then why does your reflection seem
So lonely in the moving night?

Aftermath

Shuffle and cut. What was so large and one
Is now a pack of dog's-eared chances—Oh
Where is the Fear that warmed us to the gun,
That moved the cock to tousle the night and crow
In the gaps between the bombs? In this new round
The joker that could have been any moment death
Has been withdrawn, the cards are what they say
And none is wild; the bandaging dark which bound
This town together is loosed and in the array
Of bourgeois lights man's love can save its breath:
Their ransomed future severs once more the child
Of luck from the child of lack—and none is wild.

February, 1946

Twelfth night

Snow-happy hicks of a boy's world—
O crunch of bull's-eyes in the mouth,
O crunch of frost beneath the foot—
If time would only remain furled
In white, and thaw were not for certain
And snow would but stay put, stay put!

When the pillar-box wore a white bonnet—
O harmony of roof and hedge,
O parity of sight and thought—
And each flake had your number on it
And lives were round for not a number
But equalled nought, but equalled nought!

But now the sphinx must change her shape—
O track that reappears through slush,
O broken riddle, burst grenade—
And lives must be pulled out like tape
To measure something not themselves,
Things not given but made, but made.

For now the time of gifts is gone—
O boys that grow, O snows that melt,
O bathos that the years must fill—

219

Here is dull earth to build upon
Undecorated; we have reached
Twelfth Night or what you will . . . you will.

Bluebells

She, who last felt young during the war,
This Easter has no peace to be waiting for;
Though coining dandelions from her eyes
Has lost the old enrichment of surprise
And though her man is back, yet feels he has brought
The Desert with him, making her cheeks taut.

So both wake early, listen without words
To the now foreign badinage of birds,
And in the twilight when only the bats fly
They miss those engines overbrimming the sky,
For all green Nature has gone out of gear
Since they were apart and hoping, since last year.

Sun is too bright and brittle, wheat is too quick,
She turns from them to the wood where the slow thick
Shade is becalmed and chill and as a glacial stream
Meeting the sea inlays and weaves a milky gleam
Through the dark waste, so here the bluebells flow
Athwart the undergrowth, a merger of blue snow.

'Oh in this dark beneathness where he and I
Live, let a delta of flowers atone for the sky
Which we cannot face and from my ice-cap, oh,
Let one river at least unfreeze and flow
And through that brine so deep and yet so dim
Let my cold gentleness irradiate him.'

1946

Tam cari capitis

That the world will never be quite—what a cliché—the same again
Is what we only learn by the event
When a friend dies out on us and is not there
To share the periphery of a remembered scent

Or leave his thumb-print on a shared ideal;
Yet it is not at floodlit moments we miss him most,
Not intervolution of wind-rinsed plumage of oat-field
Nor curragh dancing off a primeval coast

Nor the full strings of passion; it is in killing
Time where he could have livened it, such as the drop-by-drop
Of games like darts or chess, turning the faucet
On full at a threat to the queen or double top.

July, 1946

The National Gallery

The kings who slept in the caves are awake and out,
The pictures are back in the Gallery; Old Masters twirl their cadenzas,
  whisper and shout,
Hundreds of windows are open again on a vital but changeless world—
  a day-dream free from doubt.

Here are the angels playing their lutes at the Birth—
Clay become porcelain; the pattern, the light, the ecstasy which make
  sense of the earth;
Here is Gethsemane scooped like a glacier, here is Calvary calmly
  assured of its own worth.

Here are the gold haloes, opaque as coins,
The pink temple of icing-sugar, the blandly scalloped rock which joins
Primitive heaven and earth; here is our Past wiping the smuts from his
  eyes, girding his loins.

Here saint may be gorgeous, hedonist austere,
The soul's nativity drawn of the earth and earthy, our brother the
  Ass being near,
The petty compartments of life thrown wind-wide open, our lop-
  sided instincts and customs atoned for here.

Here only too have the senses unending joy:
Draperies slip but slip no further and expectation cannot cloy;
The great Venetian buttocks, the great Dutch bosoms, remain in their
  time—their prime—beyond alloy.

And the Painter's little daughter, far-off-eyed,
Still stretches for the cabbage white, her sister dawdling at her side;
That she grew up to be mad does not concern us, the idyl and the
  innocent poise abide.

Aye; the kings are back from their caves in the Welsh hills,
Refreshed by darkness, armed with colour, sleight-of-hand and
    imponderables,
Armed with Uccello's lances, with beer-mugs, dragons' tongues,
    peacocks' eyes, bangles and spangles and flounces and frills;

Armed with the full mystique of the commonplace,
The lusts of the eye, the gullet, the loins, the memory—grace after
    living and grace
Before some plain-clothes death grabs at the artist's jemmy,
    leaves us yet one more half-solved case.

For the quickness of the heart deceives the eye,
Reshuffling the themes: a Still Life lives while portrayed flesh and
    feature die
Into fugues and subterfuges of being as enveloping and as aloof as a
    frosty midnight sky.

So fling wide the windows, this window and that, let the air
Blowing from times unconfined to Then, from places further and
    fuller than There,
Purge our particular time-bound unliving lives, rekindle a pentecost in
    Trafalgar Square.

October, 1945

Littoral

Indigo, mottle of purple and amber, ink,
Damson whipped with cream, improbable colours of sea
And unanalysable rhythms—fingering foam
Tracing, erasing its runes, regardless
Of you and me
And whether we think it escape or the straight way home.

The sand here looks like metal, it feels there like fur,
The wind films the sand with sand;
This hoary beach is burgeoning with minutiae
Like a philosopher
Who, thinking, makes cat's-cradles with string—or a widow
Who knits for her sons but remembers a tomb in another land.

Brain-bound or heart-bound sea—old woman or old man—
To whom we are ciphers, creatures to ignore,
We poach from you what images we can,

Luxuriously afraid
To plump the Unknown in a bucket with a spade—
Each child his own seashore.

1945

The Cromlech

From trivia of froth and pollen
White tufts in the rabbit warren
And every minute like a ticket
Nicked and dropped, nicked and dropped,
Extracters and abstracters ask
What emerges, what survives,
And once the stopper is unstopped
What was the essence in the flask
And what is Life apart from lives
And where, apart from fact, the value.

To which we answer, being naïve,
Wearing the world upon our sleeve,
That to dissect a given thing
Unravelling its complexity
Outrages its simplicity
For essence is not merely core
And each event implies the world,
A centre needs periphery.

This being so, at times at least
Granted the sympathetic pulse
And granted the perceiving eye
Each pregnant with a history,
Appearance and appearances—
In spite of the philosophers
With their jejune dichotomies—
Can be at times reality.

So Tom and Tessy holding hands
(Dare an abstraction steal a kiss?)
Cannot be generalized away,
Reduced by bleak analysis
To pointers demonstrating laws
Which drain the colour from the day;

Not mere effects of a crude cause
But of themselves significant,
To rule-of-brain recalcitrant,
This that they are and do is This . . .

Tom is here, Tessy is here
At this point in a given year
With all this hour's accessories,
A given glory—and to look
That gift-horse in the mouth will prove
Or disprove nothing of their love
Which is as sure intact a fact,
Though young and supple, as what stands
Obtuse and old, in time congealed,
Behind them as they mingle hands—
Self-contained, unexplained,
The cromlech in the clover field.

June, 1945

Carrick revisited

Back to Carrick, the castle as plumb assured
As thirty years ago—Which war was which?
Here are new villas, here is a sizzling grid
But the green banks are as rich and the lough as hazily lazy
And the child's astonishment not yet cured.

Who was—and am—dumbfounded to find myself
In a topographical frame—here, not there—
The channels of my dreams determined largely
By random chemistry of soil and air;
Memories I had shelved peer at me from the shelf.

Fog-horn, mill-horn, corncrake and church bell
Half-heard through boarded time as a child in bed
Glimpses a brangle of talk from the floor below
But cannot catch the words. Our past we know
But not its meaning—whether it meant well.

Time and place—our bridgeheads into reality
But also its concealment! Out of the sea
We land on the Particular and lose
All other possible bird's-eye views, the Truth
That is of Itself for Itself—but not for me.

Torn before birth from where my fathers dwelt,
Schooled from the age of ten to a foreign voice,
Yet neither western Ireland nor southern England
Cancels this interlude; what chance misspelt
May never now be righted by my choice.

Whatever then my inherited or acquired
Affinities, such remains my childhood's frame
Like a belated rock in the red Antrim clay
That cannot at this era change its pitch or name—
And the pre-natal mountain is far away.

June, 1945

Slum song

O the slums of Dublin fermenting with children
   Wander far and near
The growing years are a cruel squadron
And poverty is a rusty cauldron
   Wander near and far.

The youths play cards by the broken fanlight
   Wander far and near
The Jack looks greasy in the sunlight
As hands will fumble in the moonlight
   Wander near and far.

And the grown man must play the horses
   Wander far and near
Some do better on different courses
But the black will remain to draw the hearses
   Wander near and far.

The bowsey in his second childhood
   Wander far and near
Thumbs his pipe of peace and briarwood
But lacks a light to relight his manhood
   Wander near and far.

Near and far, far and near,
The street-lamp winks, the mutes are here,
Above the steeple hangs a star
So near and far . . . far.

July, 1945

The Strand

White Tintoretto clouds beneath my naked feet,
This mirror of wet sand imputes a lasting mood
To island truancies; my steps repeat

Someone's who now has left such strands for good
Carrying his boots and paddling like a child,
A square black figure whom the horizon understood—

My father. Who for all his responsibly compiled
Account books of a devout, precise routine
Kept something in him solitary and wild,

So loved the western sea and no tree's green
Fulfilled him like these contours of Slievemore
Menaun and Croaghaun and the bogs between.

Sixty-odd years behind him and twelve before,
Eyeing the flange of steel in the turning belt of brine
It was sixteen years ago he walked this shore

And the mirror caught his shape which catches mine
But then as now the floor-mop of the foam
Blotted the bright reflections—and no sign

Remains of face or feet when visitors have gone home.

1945

Last before America

A spiral of green hay on the end of a rake:
The moment is sweat and sun-prick—children and old women
Big in a tiny field, midgets against the mountain,
So toy-like yet so purposed you could take
This for the Middle Ages.

At night the accordion melts in the wind from the sea
From the bourne of emigrant uncle and son, a defeated
Music that yearns and abdicates; chimney-smoke and spindrift
Mingle and part as ghosts do. The decree
Of the sea's divorce is final.

Pennsylvania or Boston? It was another name,
A land of a better because an impossible promise
Which split these families; it was to be a journey
Away from death—yet the travellers died the same
As those who stayed in Ireland.

Both myth and seismic history have been long suppressed
Which made and unmade Hy Brasil—now an image
For those who despise charts but find their dream's endorsement
In certain long low islets snouting towards the west
Like cubs that have lost their mother.

1945

Under the mountain

Seen from above
The foam in the curving bay is a goose-quill
That feathers . . . unfeathers . . . itself.

Seen from above
The field is a flap and the haycocks buttons
To keep it flush with the earth.

Seen from above
The house is a silent gadget whose purpose
Was long since obsolete.

But when you get down
The breakers are cold scum and the wrack
Sizzles with stinking life.

When you get down
The field is a failed or a worth-while crop, the source
Of back-ache if not heartache.

And when you get down
The house is a maelstrom of loves and hates where you—
Having got down—belong.

No more sea

Dove-melting mountains, ridges gashed with water,
Itinerant clouds whose rubrics never alter,
Give, without oath, their testimony of silence
To islanders whose hearts themselves are islands;

For whom, if the ocean bed should silt up later
And living thoughts coagulate in matter,
An age of mainlanders, that dare not fancy
Life out of uniform, will feel no envy—

No envy unless some atavistic scholar
Plodding that dry and tight-packed world discover
Some dusty relic that once could swim, a fossil
Mind in its day both its own king and castle,

And thence conceive a vague inaccurate notion
Of what it meant to live embroiled with ocean
And between moving dunes and beyond reproving
Sentry-boxes to have been self-moving.

October, 1944

Godfather

Elusive
This godfather who mostly forgets one's birthday,
Perusing
Old schoolbooks when he should be reading the papers
Or, when he does
Glance at a daily, snooping between the headlines.

Revolving
Doors whisk him away as you enter a café,
Clopping
Hoofs of black horses drown his steps in the High Street;
He signs
Huge cheques without thinking, never is overdrawn.

The air-raids
Found him lying alone on his back and blowing
Carefree
Smoke-rings—a pipe-dream over the burning city;
At the crack
Of dawn he would lounge away, his hands in his pockets.

Adept
At all surprises, disguises, to conjure a Christmas
Packet
Into a stocking unnoticed or make without fussing
His first call ever and leave
Pale stone tablets like visiting cards in the churchyard.

February, 1946

Aubade for infants

Snap the blind; I am not blind,
I must spy what stalks behind
Wall and window—Something large
Is barging up beyond the down,
Chirruping, hooting, hot of foot.

Beyond that wall what things befall?
My eye can fly though I must crawl.
Dance and dazzle—Something bright
Ignites the dumps of sodden cloud,
Loud and laughing, a fiery face . . .

Whose broad grimace (the voice is bass)
Makes nonsense of my time and place—
Maybe you think that I am young?
I who flung before my birth
To mother earth the dawn-song too!

And you—
However old and deaf this year—
Were near me when that song was sung.

July, 1945

The cyclist

Freewheeling down the escarpment past the unpassing horse
Blazoned in chalk the wind he causes in passing
Cools the sweat of his neck, making him one with the sky,
In the heat of the handlebars he grasps the summer
Being a boy and to-day a parenthesis
Between the horizon's brackets; the main sentence

Waits to be picked up later but these five minutes
Are all to-day and summer. The dragonfly
Rises without take-off, horizontal,
Underlining itself in a sliver of peacock light.

And glaring, glaring white
The horse on the down moves within his brackets,
The grass boils with grasshoppers, a pebble
Scutters from under the wheel and all this country
Is spattered white with boys riding their heat-wave,
Feet on a narrow plank and hair thrown back

And a surf of dust beneath them. Summer, summer—
They chase it with butterfly nets or strike it into the deep
In a little red ball or gulp it lathered with cream
Or drink it through closed eyelids; until the bell
Left-right-left gives his forgotten sentence
And reaching the valley the boy must pedal again
Left-right-left but meanwhile
For ten seconds more can move as the horse in the chalk
Moves unbeginningly calmly
Calmly regardless of tenses and final clauses
Calmly unendingly moves.

July, 1946

Woods

My father who found the English landscape tame
Had hardly in his life walked in a wood,
Too old when first he met one; Malory's knights,
Keats's nymphs or the Midsummer Night's Dream
Could never arras the room, where he spelled out True and Good
With their interleaving of half-truths and not-quites.

While for me from the age of ten the socketed wooden gate
Into a Dorset planting, into a dark
But gentle ambush, was an alluring eye;
Within was a kingdom free from time and sky,
Caterpillar webs on the forehead, danger under the feet,
And the mind adrift in a floating and rustling ark

Packed with birds and ghosts, two of every race,
Trills of love from the picture-book—Oh might I never land
But here, grown six foot tall, find me also a love
Also out of the picture-book; whose hand
Would be soft as the webs of the wood and on her face
The wood-pigeon's voice would shaft a chrism from above.

So in a grassy ride a rain-filled hoof-mark coined
By a finger of sun from the mint of Long Ago
Was the last of Lancelot's glitter. Make-believe dies hard;
That the rider passed here lately and is a man we know
Is still untrue, the gate to Legend remains unbarred,
The grown-up hates to divorce what the child joined.

Thus from a city when my father would frame
Escape, he thought, as I do, of bog or rock
But I have also this other, this English, choice
Into what yet is foreign; whatever its name
Each wood is the mystery and the recurring shock
Of its dark coolness is a foreign voice.

Yet in using the word tame my father was maybe right,
These woods are not the Forest; each is moored
To a village somewhere near. If not of to-day
They are not like the wilds of Mayo, they are assured
Of their place by men; reprieved from the neolithic night
By gamekeepers or by Herrick's girls at play.

And always we walk out again. The patch
Of sky at the end of the path grows and discloses
An ordered open air long ruled by dyke and fence,
With geese whose form and gait proclaim their consequence,
Pargetted outposts, windows browed with thatch,
And cow pats—and inconsequent wild roses.

1946

Elegy for minor poets

Who often found their way to pleasant meadows
Or maybe once to a peak, who saw the Promised Land,
Who took the correct three strides but tripped their hurdles,
Who had some prompter they barely could understand,
Who were too happy or sad, too soon or late,
I would praise these in company with the Great;

For if not in the same way, they fingered the same language
According to their lights. For them as for us
Chance was a coryphaeus who could be either
An angel or an *ignus fatuus*.
Let us keep our mind open, our fingers crossed;
Some who go dancing through dark bogs are lost.

Who were lost in many ways, through comfort, lack of
    knowledge,
Or between women's breasts, who thought too little, too much,
Who were the world's best talkers, in tone and rhythm
Superb, yet as writers lacked a sense of touch,
So either gave up or just went on and on—
Let us salute them now their chance is gone;

And give the benefit of the doubtful summer
To those who worshipped the sky but stayed indoors
Bound to a desk by conscience or by the spirit's
Hayfever. From those office and study floors
Let the sun clamber on to the notebook, shine,
And fill in what they groped for between each line.

Who were too carefree or careful, who were too many
Though always few and alone, who went the pace
But ran in circles, who were lamed by fashion,
Who lived in the wrong time or the wrong place,
Who might have caught fire had only a spark occurred,
Who knew all the words but failed to achieve the Word—

Their ghosts are gagged, their books are library flotsam,
Some of their names—not all—we learnt in school
But, life being short, we rarely read their poems,
Mere source-books now to point or except a rule,
While those opinions which rank them high are based
On a wish to be different or on lack of taste.

In spite of and because of which, we later
Suitors to their mistress (who, unlike them, stays young)
Do right to hang on the grave of each a trophy
Such as, if solvent, he would himself have hung
Above himself; these debtors preclude our scorn—
Did we not underwrite them when we were born?

April, 1946

232

Autolycus

In his last phase when hardly bothering
To be a dramatist, the Master turned away
From his taut plots and complex characters
To tapestried romances, conjuring
With rainbow names and handfuls of sea-spray
And from them turned out happy Ever-afters.

Eclectic always, now extravagant,
Sighting his matter through a timeless prism
He ranged his classical bric-à-brac in grottos
Where knights of Ancient Greece had Latin mottoes
And fishermen their flapjacks—none should want
Colour for lack of an anachronism.

A gay world certainly though pocked and scored
With childish horrors and a fresh world though
Its mainsprings were old gags—babies exposed,
Identities confused and queens to be restored;
But when the cracker bursts it proves as you supposed—
Trinket and moral tumble out just so.

Such innocence—In his own words it was
Like an old tale, only that where time leaps
Between acts three and four there was something born
Which made the stock-type virgin dance like corn
In a wind that having known foul marshes, barren steeps,
Felt therefore kindly towards Marinas, Perditas . . .

Thus crystal learned to talk. But Shakespeare balanced it
With what we knew already, gabbing earth
Hot from Eastcheap—Watch your pockets when
That rogue comes round the corner, he can slit
Purse-strings as quickly as his maker's pen
Will try your heartstrings in the name of mirth.

O master pedlar with your confidence tricks,
Brooches, pomanders, broadsheets and what-have-you,
Who hawk such entertainment but rook your client
And leave him brooding, why should we forgive you
Did we not know that, though more self-reliant
Than we, you too were born and grew up in a fix?

August, 1945

233

Street scene

Between March and April when barrows of daffodils butter the
    pavement,
The colossus of London stretches his gaunt legs, jerking
The smoke of his hair back from his eyes and puffing
Smoke-rings of heavenward pigeons over Saint Paul's,
While in each little city of each individual person
The black tree yearns for green confetti and the black kerb for yellow
    stalls.

Ave Maria! A sluice is suddenly opened
Making Orphan Street a conduit for a fantastic voice;
The Canadian sergeant turns to stone in his swagger,
The painted girls, the lost demobbed, the pinstriped accountant listen
As the swan-legged cripple straddled on flightless wings of crutches
Hitting her top note holds our own lame hours in equipoise,

Then waddles a yard and switches *Cruising down the river*
Webbed feet hidden, the current smooth *On a Sunday afternoon*
Sunshine fortissimo; some young man from the Desert
Fumbles, new from battle-dress, for his pocket,
Drops a coin in that cap she holds like a handbag,
Then slowly walks out of range of *A sentimental tune*

Which cruising down—repeat—cruises down a river
That has no source nor sea but is each man's private dream
Remote as his listening eyes; repeat for all will listen
Cruising away from thought with *An old accordion playing*
Not that it is, her accompanist plucks a banjo
On a Sunday afternoon. She ends. And the other stream

Of Orphan Street flows back—instead of silence racket,
Brakes gears and sparrows; the passers-by pass by,
The swan goes home on foot, a girl takes out her compact—
Silence instead of song; the Canadian dives for the pub
And a naval officer on the traffic island
Unsees the buses with a mid-ocean eye.

1946

Relics

Obsolete as books in leather bindings
Buildings in stone like talkative ghosts continue
   Their well-worn anecdotes
As here in Oxford shadow the dark-weathered
Astrakhan rustication of the arches
   Puts a small world in quotes:

While high in Oxford sunlight playfully crocketed
Pinnacles, ripe as corn on the cob, look over
   To downs where once without either wheel or hod
Ant-like, their muscles cracking under the sarsen,
Shins white with chalk and eyes dark with necessity,
   The Beaker People pulled their weight of God.

March, 1947

The drunkard

His last train home is Purgatory in reverse,
A spiral back into time and down towards Hell
Clutching a quizzical strap where wraiths of faces
Contract, expand, revolve, impinge; disperse
On a sickly wind which drives all wraiths pell-mell
Through tunnels to their appointed, separate places,

And he is separate too, who had but now ascended
Into the panarchy of created things
Wearing his halo cocked, full of good will
That need not be implemented; time stood still
As the false coin rang and the four walls had wings
And instantly the Natural Man was mended.

Instantly and it would be permanently
God was uttered in words and gulped in gin,
The barmaid was a Madonna, the adoration
Of the coalman's breath was myrrh, the world was We
And pissing under the stars an act of creation
While the low hills lay purring round the inn.

Such was the absolute moment, to be displaced
By moments; the clock takes over—time to descend
Where Time will brief us, briefed himself to oppress
The man who looks and finds Man human and not his friend
And whose tongue feels around and around but cannot taste
That hour-gone sacrament of drunkenness.

March, 1946

Hands and eyes

In a high wind
Gnarled hands cup to kindle an old briar,
From a frilled cot
Twin sea anemones grope for a hanging lamp,
In a foul cage
Old coal-gloves dangle from dejected arms.

Of which three pairs of hands the child's are helpless
(Whose wheels barely engage)
And the shepherd's from his age are almost bloodless
While the chimpanzee's are hopeless
Were there not even a cage.

In a dark room
Docile pupils grow to their full for prey,
Down a long bar
Mascara scrawls a gloss on a torn leaf,
On a high col
The climber's blue marries the blue he climbs.

Of which three pairs of eyes the tart's are mindless
(Who pawned her mind elsewhere)
And the black cat's, in gear with black, are heartless
While the alpinist's are timeless
In gear with timeless air.

In a cold church
It flickers in the draught, then burns erect;
In a loud mob
It bugles, merges, feels with a start alone;
In a bright beam
It waltzes dust to dust with its chance loves.

Of which three souls the praying one is selfless
But only for a span
And the gregarious man's is rudderless, powerless,
While the soul in love is luckless,
Betrays what chance it can.

And still the wind
Blows, the ape is marooned, the lamp ungrasped;
Woman and cat
Still wait to pounce and the climber waits to fall;
As each soul burns
The best it may, in foul or blustering air.
Oh would He, were there a God, have mercy on us all?

May/June, 1946

Place of a skull

Earth water stars and flesh—the seamless coat
Which is the world, he left; who from to-day
Had no more need to wear it. The remote
Metropolis yawned, the parchment flapped away,

Away, the blood dried in the sand. The bored
Soldiers played for the leavings but even they,
Though trained to carve up continents with the sword,
Approved the weaver who had made night and day

And time and mind a tegument, therefore swore
To hazard it as one lot. The dice were gay
And someone won: *Why the first time I wore
That dead man's coat it frayed I cannot say.*

Slow movement

Waking, he found himself in a train, andante,
With wafers of early sunlight blessing the unknown fields
And yesterday cancelled out, except for yesterday's papers
    Huddling under the seat.

237

It is still very early, this is a slow movement;
The viola-player's hand like a fish in a glass tank
Rises, remains quivering, darts away
    To nibble invisible weeds.

Great white nebulae lurch against the window
To deploy across the valley, the children are not yet up
To wave us on—we pass without spectators,
    Braiding a voiceless creed.

And the girl opposite, name unknown, is still
Asleep and the colour of her eyes unknown
Which might be wells of sun or moons of wish
    But it is still very early.

The movement ends, the train has come to a stop
In buttercup fields, the fiddles are silent, the whole
Shoal of silver tessellates the aquarium
    Floor, not a bubble rises . . .

And what happens next on the programme we do not know,
If, the red line topped on the gauge, the fish will go mad in
    the tank
Accelerando con forza, the sleeper open her eyes
    And, so doing, open ours.

November, 1945

Carol

To end all carols, darling,
    To end all carols now,
Let us walk through the cloister
    With a thoughtful brow,

Pruning what was grafted
    Through ages of blind faith—
The rubrics and the finials
    Drift away like breath.

From Bethlehem the sheep-bells
    Grew to a steepled peal,
The joists of the stable
    Spread an ashlar chill,

The rafters of the stable
  Hooped themselves on high
And coveys of boys' voices
  Burst on a stone sky;

While the wrinkled, whimpering image
  Wrapped in his mother's shawl
Was carried between pillars
  Down endless aisles and all

The doors opened before him
  In every holy place
And the doors came to behind him,
  Left him in cold space.

Beyond our prayers and knowing,
  Many light-years away—
So why sing carols, darling?
  To-day is to-day.

Then answered the angel:
  To-day is to-day
And the Son of God is vanished
  But the sons of men stay

And man is a spirit
  And symbols are his meat,
So pull not down the steeple
  In your monied street.

For money chimes feebly,
  Matter dare not sing—
Man is a spirit,
  Let the bells ring.

Ring all your changes, darling,
  Save us from the slough;
Begin all carols, darling,
  Begin all carols now.

                    January, 1946

IX
1940—1948

Plurality

It is patent to the eye that cannot face the sun
The smug philosophers lie who say the world is one;
World is other and other, world is here and there,
Parmenides would smother life for lack of air
Precluding birth and death; his crystal never breaks—
No movement and no breath, no progress nor mistakes,
Nothing begins or ends, no one loves or fights,
All your foes are friends and all your days are nights
And all the roads lead round and are not roads at all
And the soul is muscle-bound, the world a wooden ball.
The modern monist too castrates, negates our lives
And nothing that we do, make or become survives,
His terror of confusion freezes the flowing stream
Into mere illusion, his craving for supreme
Completeness means he chokes each orifice with tight
Plaster as he evokes a dead ideal of white
All-white Universal, refusing to allow
Division or dispersal—Eternity is now
And Now is therefore numb, a fact he does not see
Postulating a dumb static identity
Of Essence and Existence which could not fuse without
Banishing to a distance belief along with doubt,
Action along with error, growth along with gaps;
If man is a mere mirror of God, the gods collapse.
No, the formula fails that fails to make it clear
That only change prevails, that the seasons make the year,
That a thing, a beast, a man is what it is because
It is something that began and is not what it was,
Yet is itself throughout, fluttering and unfurled,
Not to be cancelled out, not to be merged in world,
Its entity a denial of all that is not it,
Its every move a trial through chaos and the Pit,
An absolute and so defiant of the One
Absolute, the row of noughts where time is done,
Where nothing goes or comes and Is is one with Ought
And all the possible sums alike resolve to nought.
World is not like that, world is full of blind
Gulfs across the flat, jags against the mind,
Swollen or diminished according to the dice,
Foaming, never finished, never the same twice.
You talk of Ultimate Value, Universal Form—
Visions, let me tell you, that ride upon the storm

And must be made and sought but cannot be maintained,
Lost as soon as caught, always to be regained,
Mainspring of our striving towards perfection, yet
Would not be worth achieving if the world were set
Fair, if error and choice did not exist, if dumb
World should find its voice for good and God become
Incarnate once for all. No, perfection means
Something but must fall unless there intervenes
Between that meaning and the matter it should fill
Time's revolving hand that never can be still.
Which being so and life a ferment, you and I
Can only live by strife in that the living die,
And, if we use the word Eternal, stake a claim
Only to what a bird can find within the frame
Of momentary flight (the value will persist
But as event the night sweeps it away in mist).
Man is man because he might have been a beast
And is not what he was and feels himself increased,
Man is man in as much as he is not god and yet
Hankers to see and touch the pantheon and forget
The means within the end and man is truly man
In that he would transcend and flout the human span:
A species become rich by seeing things as wrong
And patching them, to which I am proud that I belong.
Man is surely mad with discontent, he is hurled
By lovely hopes or bad dreams against the world,
Raising a frail scaffold in never-ending flux,
Stubbornly when baffled fumbling the stubborn crux
And so he must continue, raiding the abyss
With aching bone and sinew, conscious of things amiss,
Conscious of guilt and vast inadequacy and the sick
Ego and the broken past and the clock that goes too quick,
Conscious of waste of labour, conscious of spite and hate,
Of dissension with his neighbour, of beggars at the gate,
But conscious also of love and the joy of things and the power
Of going beyond and above the limits of the lagging hour,
Conscious of sunlight, conscious of death's inveigling touch,
Not completely conscious but partly—and that is much.

August, 1940

The casualty

(in memoriam G.H.S.)

'Damn!' you would say if I were to write the best
Tribute I could to you, 'All clichés', and you would grin
Dwindling to where that faded star allures
Where no time presses and no days begin—
Turning back shrugging to the misty West
Remembered out of Homer but now yours.

Than whom I do not expect ever again
To find a more accordant friend, with whom
I could be silent knowledgeably; you never
Faked or flattered or time-served. If ten
Winds were to shout you down or twenty oceans boom
Above the last of you, they will not sever

That thread of so articulate silence. How
You died remains conjecture; instantaneous
Is the most likely—that the shutter fell
Congealing the kaleidoscope at Now
And making all your past contemporaneous
Under that final chord of the mid-Atlantic swell.

So now the concert is over, the seats vacated,
Eels among the footlights, water up to the roof
And the gilded cherubs crumbling—and you come in
Jaunty as ever but with a half-frustrated
Look on your face, you expect the show to begin
But you are too late and cannot accept the proof

That you are too late because you have died too early
And this is under sea. Puzzled but gay
You still come in, come in, and the waves distort
Your smile and chivvy your limbs through a maze of pearly
Pillars of ocean death—and yet you force your way
In on my dreams as if you had something still to report.

How was it then? How is it? You and I
Have often since we were children discussed death
And sniggered at the preacher and wondered how
He can talk so big about mortality
And immortality more. But you yourself could now
Talk big as any—if you had the breath.

However since you cannot from this date
Talk big or little, since you cannot answer
Even what alive you could, but I let slip
The chance to ask you, I can correlate
Only of you what memories dart and trip
Through freckling lights and stop like a forgetful dancer.

Archaic gusto sprouted from a vase
Of dancing satyrs, lips of a Gothic imp
Laughing down from a church-top, inky fingers
Jotting notes on notes, and piccolo and tymp
Importunate at the circus—but there lingers
Also a scent of awe, a cosmic pause;

For you were a good mixer and could laugh
With Rowlandson or Goya and you liked
Bijoux and long-eared dogs and silken legs
And titivated rooms but more than half
Your story lay outside beyond the spiked
Railing where in the night some old blind minstrel begs.

He begged and you responded, being yourself,
Like Raftery or Homer, of his kind—
Creative not for the counter or the shelf
But innocently whom the world bewilders
And so they observe and love it till their mind
May turn them from mere students into builders.

Of which high humble company were you,
Outside the cliques, unbothered with the fashion,
And self-apprenticed to the grinding trade
Of thinking things anew, stropping the blade
You never used, your multicoloured passion
Having been merged by death in universal Blue.

So what you gave were inklings: trivial signs
Of some momentous truth, a footprint here and there
In melting snow, a marginal caress
Of someone else's words, a gentleness
In greeting, a panache of heady wines
Or children's rockets vanishing in air.

Look at these snapshots; here you see yourself
Spilling a paint-pot on a virgin wall
Or boisterous in a sailing-boat or bubbling

At a Punch-and-Judy show or a music-hall
Or lugging Clausewitz from a public shelf
To make your private notes, thumbing and doubling

His corseted pages back. Yes, here and here
You see yourself spilling across the border
Of nice convention, here at a students' dance
Pinching a girl's behind—to reappear
A small boy twined in bracken and aprance
Like any goatfoot faun to propagate disorder.

Here you are swapping gags in winking bars
With half an eye on the colour clash of beet
Lobster and radish, here you are talking back
To a caged baboon and here the Wiltshire sleet
Riddles your football jersey—here the sack
Of night pours down on you Provençal stars.

Here you are gabbling Baudelaire or Donne,
Here you are mimicking that cuckoo clock,
Here you are serving a double fault for set,
Here you are diving naked from a Dalmatian rock,
Here you are barracking the sinking sun,
Here you are taking Proust aboard your doomed corvette.

Yes, all you gave were inklings; even so
Invaluable—such as I remember
Out of your mouth or only in your eyes
On walks in blowsy August, Brueghel-like December,
Or when the gas was hissing and a glow
Of copper jugs gave back your lyrical surprise.

For above all that was your gift—to be
Surprised and therefore sympathetic, warm
Towards things as well as people, you could see
The integrity of differences—O did you
Make one last integration, find a Form
Grow out of formlessness when the Atlantic hid you?

Whether you did or not, the fact remains
(Which I, for all your doubts, could have no doubt of)
That your whole life till then showed an endeavour
Towards a discovery—and if your pains

Were lost the loss is ours as well; for you are out of
This life and cannot start any more hares for ever.

c. 1943

The Kingdom

I

Under the surface of flux and of fear there is an underground
   movement,
Under the crust of bureaucracy, quiet behind the posters,
Unconscious but palpably there—the Kingdom of individuals.

   And of these is the Kingdom—
Equal in difference, interchangeably sovereign—
The incorruptible souls who work without a commission,
The pairs of hands that are peers of hearts, the eyes that marry with
   eyes,
The candid scholar, the unselfish priest, the uncomplaining mothers
   of many,
The active men who are kind, the contemplative who give,
The happy-go-lucky saint and the peace-loving buccaneer.

These, as being themselves, are apart from not each other
But from such as being false are merely other,
So these are apart as parts within a pattern
Not merged nor yet excluded, members of a Kingdom
Which has no king except each subject, therefore
Apart from slaves and tyrants and from every
Community of mere convenience; these are
Apart from those who drift and those who force,
Apart from partisan order and egotistical anarchy,
Apart from the easy religion of him who would find in God
A boss, a ponce, an alibi, and apart from
The logic of him who arrogates to himself
The secret of the universe, the whole
Choreography of atoms; these are humble
And proud at once, working within their limits
And yet transcending them. These are the people
Who vindicate the species. And they are many. For go,
Go wherever you choose, among tidy villas or terrible
Docks, dumps and pitheads, or through the spangled moors
Or along the vibrant narrow intestines of great ships

Or into those countries of which we know very little—
Everywhere you will discover the men of the Kingdom
Loyal by intuition, born to attack, and innocent.

II

Take this old man with the soldierly straight back
Dressed in tweeds like a squire but he has not a squire's presumption,
His hands are gentle with wild flowers, his memory
Latticed with dialect and anecdotes
And wisps of nature poetry; he is of the Kingdom,
A country-lover and very English, the cadence
Of Christmas bells in his voice, his face like Cotswold stone
Severe but warm, a sureness in his walk
And his blood attuned to the seasons—whether it is the glyptic
Winter turning feathered twigs to stone
And making the Old Bill pollards monuments
Beside the dyke of Lethe—or if it is the frantic
Calf-love and early oratory of spring—
Or peony-time with the midges dancing—or later, sweeter,
That two-in-one of clarity and mist,
Of maidenlight and ripeness, which is autumn:
Every case is new and yet he knows the answers
For he is of the Kingdom. Through the serene and chequered
Fields that he knows he walks like a fallen angel
Whose fall has made him a man. Ladders of cirrhus cloud
Lead down as well as up, the ricochet of rain
Makes the clay smell sweet and snow in sunlight
Affirms the tussocks under it. Such changes—
The hedgerow stippled with hips or lathered with elder—
To him are his own rhythm like his breathing
And intimate as dreams. Hirsute or fluted earth,
Squares of plough and stubble, oatcake and corduroy,
Russet and emerald, and the shot-silk evening
And all the folk-song stars—these are his palette
And it is he who blends them with the brush-strokes
Of long experience and sudden insight,
Being mature and yet naïve, a lover
Of what is not himself—but it becomes himself
And he repays it interest, so has had
A happy life and will die happy; more—
Belongs, though he never knew it, to the Kingdom.

When she had her stroke the china dogs
Did not even flinch, although they might have guessed
That to-morrow no one would dust them, but the family
Felt that this was an Act of God and did not see
The syllogism slouched across the kitchen table,
The inevitable caller; given poverty,
Given two on the dole and one a cripple,
Given the false peace and the plight of England,
And given her matriarchal pride, her bones
That would not rest, her arrogation of every
Job in the house to herself, given her grim
Good humour—her daily tonic against despair,
Given her wakeful nights trying to balance the budget
And given her ignorance of her own frailty,
What other end was coming? They propped her up
While the canary fidgeted with his seed
And the clock hiccupped, being about to strike,
And someone ran for the doctor: 'Our Mother is taken bad.'
Everything in that house was mutually possessive:
She was Our Mother, Dad was called Our Dad,
Connie Our Connie and the cat Our Tiger
But now the most possessing and the most possessed
Was on her way to leave them. They did not see
Even that this was so, they did not see
The tall clock stretch his arms like a rising Cross
Or see the steam of the kettle turn to incense;
Our Mother is taken bad—and that was all.
They did not see that the only cable was broken
That held them together, self-respecting and sane,
And that chaos was now on the move. For they did not know,
Except at times by inklings, that their home
Remained a rebel island in the sea
Of authorised disgust only because their mother
Who thought herself resigned, was a born rebel
Against the times and loyal to a different
Order, being enfranchised of the Kingdom.

'Drunk again! Where do you think you are?'
'I think I am somewhere where I don't belong;
I chanced in here from the Kingdom.' And he crashed

His heavyweight hand among the chipped and dinted
Vessels of false good-fellowship, went out
Into the night with his chin like a bulldozer
Churning a trough of fury; then the Night
Being herself archaic and instinctive
Welcomed his earthy anger, clapped him on the back
And told him stories that were not wit but humour,
Not smut but satyr-talk, not clever but wise,
Not elegant but poetry. And his mouth relaxed,
His head went back and he laughed, hearing the bugle
That blows to-morrow morning, blows for a hard routine,
Blows for the life automatic, for spit and polish and jargon
And deference to fools, but blows also for comrades,
Blows for a gay and a brave unforced solidarity,
Blows for the elemental community, blows for
Knowledge of shared emotion past and future,
(Blows for the static life that suddenly comes to
Life with the smell at dawn of running engines)
And blows as well—to those who have ears to hear
And hands to strike—for the Kingdom.

V

Too large in feature for a world of cuties,
Too sculptured for a cocktail lounge flirtation,
This girl is almost awkward, carrying off
The lintel of convention on her shoulders,
A Doric river-goddess with a pitcher
Of ice-cold wild emotions. Pour them where she will
The pitcher will not empty nor the stream grow warm
But is so cold it burns. Vitality and fear
Are marbled in her eyes, from hour to hour
She changes like the sky—one moment is so gay
That all her words are laughter but the next
Moment she is puzzled, her own Sphinx,
Made granite by her destiny, encumbered
With the dour horoscopes of dying nations
Deduced from dying stars.
So what can you expect? Behind that classic
Forehead, under that smooth Renaissance dome,
The Gothic devils revel around a corpse
Allegedly a saint's and snuff the holy candles
And cackle and deny—and their denial

Torments her with a doubt. She raises once again
Her pitcher, tilts it—Will the water flow?—
And see, it flows, it flows ice-cold as ever,
Anarchic, pure and healing. For she filled it
One day that is not dead at a lost well
Between two rocks under a sombre ilex
In the grey dawn in a deserted corner
Of the remembered Kingdom.

VI

A little dapper man but with shiny elbows
And short keen sight, he lived by measuring things
And died like a recurring decimal
Run off the page, refusing to be curtailed;
Died as they say in harness, still believing
In science, reason, progress. Left his work
Unfinished *ipso facto* which, continued,
Will supersede his name in the next text-book
And relegate him to the anonymous crowd
Of small discoverers in lab or cloister
Who link us with the Ice Age. Obstinately
He canalised his fervour, it was slow
The task he set himself but plotting points
On graph paper he felt the emerging curve
Like the first flutterings of an embryo
In somebody's first pregnancy; resembled
A pregnant woman too in that his logic
Yet made that hidden child the centre of the world
And almost a messiah; so that here,
Even here, over the shining test-tubes
The spirit of the alchemist still hovered
Hungry for magic, for the philosopher's stone.
And Progress—is that magic too? He never
Would have conceded it, not even in these last
Years of endemic doubt; in his perspective
Our present tyrants shrank into parochial
Lords of Misrule, cross eddies in a river
That has to reach the sea. But has it? Who
Told him the sea was there?
Maybe he told himself and the mere name
Of Progress was a shell to hold to the ear

And hear the breakers burgeon. Rules were rules
And all induction checked but in the end
His reasoning hinged on faith and the first axiom
Was oracle or instinct. He was simple
This man who flogged his brain, he was a child;
And so, whatever progress means in general,
He in his work meant progress. Patiently
As Stone Age man he flaked himself away
By blocked-out patterns on a core of flint
So that the core which was himself diminished
Until his friends complained that he had lost
Something in charm or interest. But conversely
His mind developed like an ancient church
By the accretion of side-aisles and the enlarging of lights
Till all the walls are windows and the sky
Comes in, if coloured; such a mind . . . a man . . .
Deserves a consecration; such a church
Bears in its lines the trademark of the Kingdom.

VII

All is well, said the voice from the tiny pulpit,
All is well with the child. And the voice cracked
For the preacher was very old and the coffin down in the aisle
Held the body of one who had been his friend and colleague
For forty years and was dead in daffodil time
Before it had come to Easter. All is well with
One who believed and practised and whose life
Presumed the Resurrection. What that means
He may have felt he knew; this much is certain—
The meaning filled his actions, made him courteous
And lyrical and strong and kind and truthful,
A generous puritan. Above whose dust
About this time each year the spendthrift plants
Will toss their trumpets heralding a life
That shows itself in time but remains timeless
As is the heart of music. So to-day
These yellow fanfares in the trench re-echo,
Before the spades get busy, the same phrase
The preacher lost his voice on. All is well,
The flowers say, with the child; and so it must be
For, it is said, the children are of the Kingdom.

VIII

Over the roofs and cranes, blistered cupola and hungry smokestack,
   over the moored balloons and the feathery tufts of searchlights,
Over the cold transmitters jabbering under the moon,
Over the hump of the ocean big with wrecks and over
Our hide-bound fog-bound lives the hosts of the living collect
Like migrant birds, or bees to the sound of a gong:
Subjects all of the Kingdom but each in himself a king.
These are the people who know in their bones the answer
To the statesman's quiz and the false reformer's crude
Alternatives and ultimatums. These have eyes
And can see each other's goodness, do not need salvation
By whip, brochure, sterilisation or drugs,
Being incurably human; these are the catalytics
To break the inhuman into humanity; these are
The voices whose words, whether in code or in clear,
Are to the point and can be received apart from
The buzz of jargon. Apart from the cranks, the timid,
The self-deceiving realist, the self-seeking
Altruist, the self-indulgent penitent,
Apart from all the frauds are these who have the courage
Of their own vision and their friends' good will
And have not lost their cosmic pride, responding
Both to the simple lyrics of blood and the architectonic fugues of reason.
These have their faults like all creators, like
The hero who must die or like the artist who
Himself is like a person with one hand
Working it into a glove; yes, they have faults
But are the chosen—because they have chosen, being
Beautiful if grotesque and wise though wilful
And hard as meteorites. Of these, of such is
Your hope, your clue, your cue, your snowball letter
That makes your soft flakes hard, your aspirations active;
Of such is your future if it is to be fruitful,
Of such is your widow's cruse, your Jacob's ladder,
Of such is the garden of souls, the orchestration of instinct,
The fertilisation of mind, of such are your beacons,
Your breaking of bread, your dance of desire, your North-West passage,
Of such is the epilogue to your sagas of bronze and steel,
Your amnesty, your advent, your Rebirth,
The archetype and the vindication of history;
The hierarchy of the equal—the Kingdom of Earth.

c. 1943

Western landscape

In doggerel and stout let me honour this country
Though the air is so soft that it smudges the words
And herds of great clouds find the gaps in the fences
Of chance preconceptions and foam-quoits on rock-points
At once hit and miss, hit and miss.
So the kiss of the past is narcotic, the ocean
Lollingly lullingly over-insidiously
Over and under crossing the eyes
And docking the queues of the teetotum consciousness
Proves and disproves what it wants.
For the western climate is Lethe,
The smoky taste of cooking on turf is lotus,
There are affirmation and abnegation together
From the broken bog with its veins of amber water,
From the distant headland, a sphinx's fist, that barely grips the sea,
From the taut-necked donkey's neurotic-asthmatic-erotic lamenting,
From the heron in trance and in half-mourning,
From the mitred mountain weeping shale.

O grail of emerald passing light
And hanging smell of sweetest hay
And grain of sea and loom of wind
Weavingly laughingly leavingly weepingly —
Webs that will last and will not.
But what
Is the hold upon, the affinity with
Ourselves of such a light and line,
How do we find continuance
Of our too human skeins of wish
In this inhuman effluence?
O relevance of cloud and rock—
If such could be our permanence!
The flock of mountain sheep belong
To tumbled screes, to tumbling seas
The ribboned wrack, and moor to mist;
But we who savour longingly
This plenitude of solitude
Have lost the right to residence,
Can only glean ephemeral
Ears of our once beatitude.
Caressingly cajolingly—
Take what you can for soon you go—

Consolingly, coquettishly,
The soft rain kisses and forgets,
Silken mesh on skin and mind;
A deaf-dumb siren that can sing
With fingertips her falsities,
Welcoming, abandoning.

O Brandan, spindrift hermit, who
Hankering roaming un-homing up-anchoring
From this rock wall looked seawards to
Knot the horizon round your waist,
Distil that distance and undo
Time in quintessential West:
The best negation, round as nought,
Stiller than stolen sleep—though bought
With mortification, voiceless choir
Where all were silent as one man
And all desire fulfilled, unsought.
Thought:
The curragh went over the wave and dipped in the trough
When that horny-handed saint with the abstract eye set off
Which was fourteen hundred years ago—maybe never—
And yet he bobs beyond that next high crest for ever.
Feeling:
Sea met sky, he had neither floor nor ceiling,
The rising blue of turf-smoke and mountain were left behind,
Blue neither upped nor downed, there was blue all round the mind.
Emotion:
One thought of God, one feeling of the ocean,
Fused in the moving body, the unmoved soul,
Made him a part of a not to be parted whole.
Whole.
And the West was all the world, the lonely was the only,
The chosen—and there was no choice—the Best,
For the beyond was here . . .

                                        But for us now
The beyond is still out there as on tiptoes here we stand
On promontories that are themselves a-tiptoe
Reluctant to be land. Which is why this land
Is always more than matter—as a ballet
Dancer is more than body. The west of Ireland
Is brute and ghost at once. Therefore in passing
Among these shadows of this permanent show
Flitting evolving dissolving but never quitting—

This arbitrary and necessary Nature
Both bountiful and callous, harsh and wheedling—
Let now the visitor, although disfranchised
In the constituencies of quartz and bog-oak
And ousted from the elemental congress,
Let me at least in token that my mother
Earth was a rocky earth with breasts uncovered
To suckle solitary intellects
And limber instincts, let me, if a bastard
Out of the West by urban civilization
(Which unwished father claims me—so I must take
What I can before I go) let me who am neither Brandan
Free of all roots nor yet a rooted peasant
Here add one stone to the indifferent cairn . . .
With a stone on the cairn, with a word on the wind, with a prayer in the
  flesh let me honour this country.

July, 1945

The Stygian banks

Like a strange soul upon the Stygian banks
Staying for waftage

TROILUS AND CRESSIDA

I

To keep themselves young—Is that why people have children?
To try and catch up with the ghosts of their own discoveries,
A light that has gone into space? Unscrolling history,
To slip back through the New Learning of adolescence
Into those Middle Ages of nursery masons
Where all the bricks were gay; the rondel of the years
Never changing its burden, only the leader
Changing his lines and time changing the leader.
Now it is Spring, O follow your leader, follow your
Child in his fourteenth-century dance; the wool trade
Is booming still, wool is building churches
And the Black Death has not come. Now it is Spring
And the half-grown wheat in the wind is a ripple of satin,
Let you in your child who is only lately articulate
Throw the lassoo of his sight to the height of some green thing,
  christen it

With a new name which no one has ever used
And call a tree a tree.
                                  Oh, we know that the word merry
Is vulgarised and Chaucer's England was not
All cakes and ale nor all our childhood happy;
Still there is something lost. The very limitedness
Of childhood, its ignorance, its impotence,
Made every cockcrow a miracle after the ogre's night
And every sunbeam glad—as the medieval winter
Slow and dense with cold made March a golden avatar,
April Adam's innocence and May maiden's gaiety;
Nor did the burden change though the blossoms fell,
Alison is for ever aged fifteen
Though leasing different bodies. So let your child
Bowl your own life in his hoop; a wandering clerk yourself
Have you not in your time stolen a love-song
And written it down in an abbey? A different body
Yours from your father's and your child's from yours
But now it is Spring and the roll of the drums of the Judgement
Muffled with foliage, so you can fool yourself justly,
Playing the jongleur; that your songs are an artifice
Is of your nature; that the blossom must fall
Is what keeps it fresh; that lives and pieces of lives
Are cut off is needed to shape them, time is a chisel,
So what was is. If it were not cut off,
Youth would not be youth. This granted take your stance
Under the high window which will not open—
You have a right to fool yourself; though your children
Cannot keep either you or themselves young
They *are* themselves in passing and the aubade
Though—no, because—the window will not open
Will find itself in the air, cut off as it must be
By sudden cry of alarm from the turreted watchman
Which also rhymes. Cut off like a piece of sculpture.
This is the dawn. Reality. Fantasy holds.

II

Fantasy holds the child in the man, the lover in the monk, the monk in
    the lover,
The arbour in the abbey, the ages together,
But as notes are together in music—no merging of history;
The aisles of this church have their intervals. Father and son

Do not repeat; this child has different totems
From that one and from his father's. The slab in the floor of the nave
Makes one family a sonnet, each name with a line to itself,
But the lines, however the bones may be jumbled beneath,
Merge no more than the lives did. We must avoid
That haunting wish to fuse all persons together;
To *be* my neighbour is banned—and if I could be,
I could neither know him nor love him. Each of us carries
His own ground with him to walk on. Look at your child
Bowling his hoop along that arterial road
Where he cannot read the signpost; as he trundles,
It may, as they say, ring some bell from your past
Or, as Aristotle would put it, by an analogy
Match his private theme with themes of your own
As a waft of roses for one, of beans for another,
Will waft him back not to a general love
But to some girl with a name, herself and no other.
Analogy, correspondence, metaphor, harmonics—
We have no word for the bridges between our present
Selves and our past selves or between ourselves and others
Or between one part of ourselves and another part,
Yet we must take it as spoken, the bridge is there
Or how could your child's hoop cross it? Strike the right note
And the wine-glasses will ring. I am alone
And you are alone and he and she are alone
But in that we carry our grounds we can superimpose them,
No more fusing them than a pack of cards is fused
Yet the Jack comes next to the Queen. Though when they are dealt
You will often fail of the sequence; only you know
That there were such cards in the pack, there *are* other people
And moss-roses and beanfields and in yourself
Monk and lover and a battered hoop
With you for once behind it—and a coffin
With you for once inside it. All these active,
Even that compère of wax who now it is Spring
Jogs your elbow as the blossom falls
Whispering: 'Fulfil yourself. But renounce the temptation
To imbrue the world with self and thus blaspheme
All other selves by merging them. Rather fill,
Fulfil yourself with the Give and Take of the Spring
And honour the green of the grass, the rights of the others,
Taking what they can give, giving what they can take,
Not random pigments muddled and puddled together
But a marriage of light reflected.' Thus from the coffin
The retired life warns us against retiring

Now it is Spring and the roll of the drums of the Judgement
Can still be assumed far off. The hoops are running
A cow-parsley gauntlet, white as though for a wedding,
Alison is fifteen, the labourer's arm
Ripples with muscle, the green corn with wind,
And the glasses chime to a note that we cannot hear
For the frequency is too high. Within us a monk
Copies a love-song but remains a monk
And out there beyond our eyes Tom-Dick-and-Harry
Remain respectively Tom and Dick and Harry
Clapping backs in the sunshine. Granted the word merry
Is out of favour, it is the word's fault,
The thing itself yet sprouts and spouts before you
Calling for a communion. Fill your glasses;
When they are emptied again, the note may be higher yet
And your own glass may break.

III

And what when the glass breaks when the Note sounds?
What when the wind blows and the bough breaks?
Will each life seem a lullaby cut off
And no humanity adult? From the tree-top
Where all our conversation was *Why* and *Mine*
The answer now being *Why Not? Not Yours!*
If so, if we have by a sense no right to be here,
Trespassers, propertyless, never of age,
Branded by thoughts, born with a silver spoon—
With the power of words—in the mouth and smuggling in
To a world of foregone conclusions the heresy of choice,
If, to sum all, to be born man is wrong,
Breaking a closed circle, then let us break it clean
And make two wrongs a right, using the contraband
The genes got past the customs, putting it out at interest
And in the face of Nature's ritual of reflex actions
Riding our heresy high. Look, love! Now it is Spring
And the wind blows, pick what buds you fancy,
Fill your wine-glass, rockabye baby, break the circular world wide
    open;
It is your birthright never to be grown up
But always growing, never yourself completed
As are the brutes and therefore, unlike the brutes,
Able to shape something outside yourself
Finding completion only in othernesses

Whether perceived started without you
Or conceived within you, ending beyond you;
For things that you do or make can win a final pattern
But never yourself—never at least until
The velocity of a wind, the frequency of a note,
End in a topple, a clink, a shutter released
And the dead man gets his exposure. But now it is Spring
And we need not be camera-conscious, we are still doing and making
Not to display our muscles but to elicit
A rhythm, a value, implicit in something beyond us.
Rockabye baby! The wind that whitens the cornfield
And lilts in the telephone wires is tilting the tree-top
Further and further—but sing in your cradle,
You can outplay that wind which cutting off your song
Can never cut off itself, merely repeats itself
Where yours will end and find itself in the air
Unlike your body not returning to earth
But There—like a piece of sculpture.
                              Yes, let the teacher of ethics
Reduce all acts to selfishness, let the economist
Confuse conditions and causes and the psychologist
Prove and disprove the rose from manure and the scientist
Explain all value away by material fact—
What do I care? It is Spring and it always will be
However the blossoms fall; and however impure
Our human motives, we can sheer off sometimes
On the purity of a tangent. Let the wind
Lunge like a trombone, draw back his hand to his mouth,
Then lunge again and further; he is welcome
And time and all particulars are welcome
And death which rounds the song. Fill your glasses;
There *is* a distinction between vintages
And heretics must have courage. There *is* a despair
Which the animals do not know, it is chiefly exhaustion
When the bull kneels down in the ring; but our despair
Need not exhaust, it is our privilege—
Our paradox—to recognize the insoluble
And going up with an outstretched hand salute it.
For we, unlike the bull, have a matador within us
More titivated still, more cruel still,
Whom we have known for years and the holiday crowd
Have been waiting there for years and the sand is smooth
And the sun will not go in till the show is over. Yes,
We too are in a ring and gaudy banderillas
May quiver in our flanks; the paradox

Is that we can break out—being about to die
We can salute our death, the consciousness
Of what must be ennobling that arena
Where we have defied what must be.

                                        Now it is Spring
And the blossoms fall like sighs but we can hold them
Each as a note in the air, a chain of defiance,
Making the transient last by having Seen it
And so distilled value from mere existence;
Thus when our own existence is cut off
That stroke will put a seal upon our value.
The eye will close but the vision that it borrowed
Has sealed the roses red.

IV

That roses are red is home—and homesickness.
As that men are alive is living—and deathwish;
And that men are dead is a name and a cause.
The hoop takes different turnings, Alison different bodies,
The burden does not change;
Though the spokesman may simulate progress
It must be within that unchanging framework,
Drilling the peas and beans in the garden but not seeing over the
    wall,
The mellow grass-grown wall encircling and forbidding
Too high to climb and no birds fly across it;
Only an incoming wind which unlike the winds of the garden
(The winds which threaten the new-born child in the tree-top
But only can share the name of This by analogy)
Flutters no paper tag on a stick in a plot,
Moves no leaf; the dandelion puff balls
Ignore it and we often. Often—but why are that lover's
Eyes of a sudden distant? He does not raise them—
One cannot see over the wall—Not one hair on his head
Is blown out of place but he ceases to give, give out;
Does not even widen his focus for here is
A movement only inwards, intake of distance.
Until she speaks and the wall is back in its place
Rounding off their vision again with words,
Unchanging burden to which the bees assent
And the thrush with a snail in its beak. A 'real' wind
Yawns—and flicks a tree-top nonchalantly
As if to say 'Look, though half in my sleep,
I can do more than that Other.' So all is well. As it was.

The voices of pigeons are grinding their delicate mills of lust,
Arkwright and Hargreaves are busy changing England,
The hooter sounds at eight, Darwin will sweep away
One code and give us a new one; all is well
As the girl sees in her lover's eyes returning—
'I am so glad you are here. I am so glad you are back.
Now you must stay for ever. Do not be foolish;
Even if a wind from over the wall can reach you,
It is a one-way traffic.' And saying this she smiles
And smiling this she lies and lying knows it,
There is a fleck of distance in her eyes too,
But the mill must grind. Why is it people have children?
So take London to-day: the queues of itching minds
Waiting for news that they do not want, for nostrums
They only pretend to believe in; most of their living
Is grinding mills that are not even their own.
The pigeons are luckier in their significant ritual,
And the dome of Saint Paul's more overt in its significance
But what to these does the word significant signify,
Who are neither autonomous crystals nor willing notes
In any symphonic whole? What they achieve of value
Is mainly in spasms, might be ascribed to chance
Did we not know that all men, even apparent ciphers
Rough out their own best moments. Moments too rare
For most of these in the queue. Granted the garden,
There are distinctions in soil and in what comes out of it
(To consider means is not mean, so long as a gadget
Is not set up for an end, so long as an end
Can infiltrate into means); but still, above all,
To raise a value gardens must be gardened
Which is where choice comes in. Then will. Then sweat.
And—in the last resort—there is something else comes in
That does not belong and yet—You see that wall?
Many will tell you that is what protects us,
What makes in fact the garden, saves it from not-being
So that, now it is there, we need not think beyond it;
But look at the eyes of that tired man in the queue
In whom fatigue dulling the senses has rendered
Some other part of him sensitive—Intake of distance.
What is it that comes in? Can it be that the wall
Is really a stepping-stone? So that what is beyond it
(That which as well perhaps could be called what is Not)
Is the sanction itself of the wall and so of the garden?
Do we owe these colours and shapes to something which seems their
 death?

It does not bear thinking of; that was not a thought came in
To the tired man's eyes—Look back at him now; he has lost it,
Perhaps we only imagined that *he* imagined—
No matter, the queue is moving. Move along there;
If you want a system the public address is a good one
And you need not ask how came this mechanical voice
Nor by what right it tells you to move along there.
The blue cock pigeon is courting again. The hooter
Will sound at eight. That is the end of the news.

V

That is the end of the news. The humanist
Thinks he has heard something new and the man in the street
Passing the garish but dowdy hoarding dodges the dripping brush
While his brother changes the posters. Now it is Spring
But the know-all blonde on the poster will never know it
For only a few projections of human minds
Are able to give and take. For all that, now it is Spring—
Foaming white edges of roads, white hedges, white
Alison walking the rim of a classical text
Lovingly copied by monks who misunderstood it
But in her arms are flowers, long hours of flowers,
And her smile serene as young and the horned head-dress
Cuts the enamel sky. People have children,
One might say, to be childlike. Munching salad
Your child can taste the colour itself—the green—
And the colour of radish—the red; his jaded parents,
Wise to the fallacy, foster it (for we begin with
A felt unity and, they presume, shall end with
An unfelt ditto but all between is by proxy,
So the more mouthfuls of cress he takes the better,
For *we* can remember . . . can we? . . .) Glory is what?
The remembrance of an effulgence that was illusion?
Or is the illusion now in burnishing the past?
Or building up, in the catch-phrase, for the future
Which, with a capital F, is a catch-phrase too? Nostalgia
Implies having a home. Which heroes die for—
But can they without having seen it? The hackneyed songs
Mislead us—Home Sweet Rose, Last Home of Summer—
The paradox of a sentimentalist
Insisting on clinging to what he insists is gone;
When now is the opposite paradox now it is Spring
And what we insist remains we insist on leaving
After exchange of courtesies. Let the blossom

Fall, that is fact but the fact can be retranslated
To value of blossom and also to value of fall;
While we, who recognize both, must turn our backs on the orchard
To follow the road of facts which we make ourselves
Where others, men, will help us to conjure value
In passing and out of passing but always turning
Our backs on the road we have made
Until—which has value too—at a certain point we fall
And the hoop topples into the ditch. The well-worn symbols
Of quests and inns and pilgrims' progresses
Do correspond; the inn-sign clanks in the night
And the windows gild the cobbles—which is merry,
All the more because we meet it in transit
And the next morning Tom and Dick as to-day
May clap each other on the back and Harry may still stare down
Into the tawny well in the pewter mug—
Or so we think having left them but in fact
They too are for the road, they too have heard
The roll of recruiting drums beyond the horizon
However the woods of spring may blur the reverberations
As in the little church the fresco above the rood-loft
Has lost its percussive colours but though faded
The bearded Judge and the horned figures with prongs
Unlike the blonde in the poster still can give. And take.

VI

And take me then! In the dawn under the high window
The burden is the same. And on the black embankment
The lost man watching the lights jig in the water
And choosing the spot to plunge has the same burden
But the lines between are gone; his own invention
They slipped his memory sooner. So the lover,
Once the watchman cries, must kiss his hand
Up to the grille and go. And the lisping child
Envious of a bird stretches his arms to fly
Or to embrace the sea, loving it at first sight:
O air, O water, take me! Thus there are some
Who when the wind which is not like any wind known
Brings to their ears from ahead the drums of the Judgement
Slacken their pace and, not to be taken by That,
Implore all others to take them. As if those others could answer

In the absolute terms required. It is only silence
Could answer them as they want, only the wind
Which they dread, the wind which passes Alison by
Without even ruffling her dress, yet once in a way
Passes not by but into her. Ancient Athens
Was a sparrow-chatter of agora-gibes and eristic
But in the mind of Socrates beneath
His quizzical voice was the daemon, a cone of silence;
And in Imperial Rome in the roaring bloody arena
Linking the man with the net and the man with the sword
Was a circuit of silence, electric. The Middle Ages
Were rowdy with earth and hell, yet in Alison's poise in the orchard,
Dripping from the pen of the monk, the lance of the Lanzknecht,
Was a silence, drop by drop. But here to-day in London
Can we—we cannot have—lost it? Talking so much
Our optimism and pessimism are both
Corrupted dialects, divorced from grammar,
Almost indeed from meaning. The hooter sounds,
The busker sings to the queue, grinding of gears,
But if we stopped haggling, stopped as we did in the raids,
The gap in our personal racket, as in the gunfire,
Should become positive, crystal; which is the end of the news
Which is the beginning of wisdom. No captions and no jargon,
No diminution, distortion or sterilization of entity,
But calling a tree a tree. For this wisdom
Is not an abstraction, a wordiness, but being silence
Is love of the chanting world.

VII

So let the world chant on. There is harsh fruit in the garden
But flowers are flowers and, what is more, can be tended
And here we stay and communicate, joining hands
To share the burden while each in turn can throw
His own lines in between; friar and wandering tumbler
Smuggle a pollen of culture into the villages
And Socrates stands by the sun-dial, talking away
But his soul is calm, moving, not seeming to move,
Like the pointer of shadow and silent. Yes, here we stay—for a little—
Strange souls in the daylight. Troilus
Patrols the Stygian banks, eager to cross,
But the value is not on the further side of the river,
The value lies in his eagerness. No communion
In sex or elsewhere can be reached and kept

Perfectly or for ever. The closed window,
The river of Styx, the wall of limitation
Beyond which the word beyond loses its meaning,
Are the fertilizing paradox, the grille
That, severing, joins, the end to make us begin
Again and again, the infinite dark that sanctions
Our growing flowers in the light, our having children;
The silence behind our music. The very silence
Which the true martyr hears on the pyre to darken
The hissing motley flames and the jeers, to make him
In spite of logic a phoenix. From that silence
Are borrowed ear and voice and from that darkness
We borrow vision, seal the roses red.
The hooter will sound at eight till the wall falls
But in the meantime—which is time—it is ours
To practise a faith which is heresy and by defying
Our nature to raise a flag on it. Come, let us laugh
As the animals cannot, laugh in the mind for joy;
Let the west wind lather the tree-top, toss the cradle,
Let the young decant the spring for us, banners of wine
While the Jack sits next to the Queen, let us busily gaily
Build us a paean, mixing for need is the metaphors,
Munching the green and the red, becoming as little children
Whose curls are falling blossom, using the eye
And the ear to fill the orchestra, plant the garden,
Bowling a hoop, braiding a love-song, fighting
A fire that cannot be seen; heretics all
Who unlike anything else that breathes in the world
When feeling pain can be lyrical and despairing
Can choose what we despair of. Glory is what?
We cannot answer in words though every verb is a hint of it
And even Die is a live word. Nor can we answer
In any particular action for each is adulterate coin
However much we may buy with it. No answer
Is ours—yet we are unique
In putting the question at all and a false coin
Presumes a true mint somewhere. Your child's hoop,
Though far from a perfect circle, holds the road
And the road is far from straight, yet like a bee
Can pollinate the towns for the towns though ugly
Have blossom in them somewhere. Far from perfect
Presumes perfection *where*? A catechism the drums
Asseverate day-long, night-long: Glory is what?
A question! . . . Now it is Spring.

May, 1946

Letter from India
for Hedli

Our letters cross by nosing silver
Place of a skull, skull of a star,
Each answer coming late and little,
The air-mail being no avatar,
And whence I think I know you are
I feel divided as for ever.

For here where men as fungi burgeon
And each crushed puffball dies in dust
This plethoric yet phantom setting
Makes yours remote so that even lust
Can take no tint nor curve on trust
Beyond these plains' beyondless margin.

You are north-west but what is Western
Assurance here where words are snakes
Gulping their tails, flies that endemic
In mosque and temple, morgue and jakes,
Eat their blind fill of man's mistakes
And yet each carcase proves eternal?

Here where the banyan weeps her children,
Where pavements flower with wounds and fins
And kite and vulture hold their vigil
Which never ends, never begins
To end, this world which spins and grins
Seems a mere sabbath of bacilli;

So that, for all the beauties hoarded
In Buddhist stupa, Mogul tomb,
In flick of hand and fold of sari,
In chant and scripture which illume
The soul's long night, I find no room
For our short night in this miasma

Where smiling, sidling, cuddling hookahs
They breed and broil, breed and brawl,
Their name being legend while their lifewish

Verging on deathwise founders all
This colour in one pool, one pall,
Granting no incense and no lotus.

Whereas though Europe founder likewise
Too close acquaintance leaves us blind
Who by aloofness, by selection,
Have written off what looms behind
The fragile fences of our mind,
Have written off the flood, the jungle.

So cast up here this India jolts us
Awake to what engrossed our sleep;
This was the truth and now we see it,
This was the horror—it is deep;
The lid is off, the things that creep
Down there are we, we were there always.

And always also, doubtless, ruthless
Doubt made us grope for the same clue,
We too sat cross-legged, eyes on navel,
Deaf to the senses and we too
Saw the Beyond—but now the view
Is of the near, the too near only.

I have seen Sheikhupura High School
Fester with glaze-eyed refugees
And the bad coin of fear inverted
Under Purana Kila's trees
And like doomed oxen those and these
Cooped by their past in a blind circle;

And day by day, night upon nightmare,
Have spied old faults and sores laid bare,
Line upon lineless, measureless under
Pretended measure, and no air
To feed such premises as where
A private plot would warrant shelter.

For even should humanism always
Have been half-impotent, debased,
How for all that can her own children
Break from the retina encased
In which our vision here must waste,
Meeting but waste, the chance of Vision?

And a Testator half-forgotten
Still with his will sways you and me
Presuming Jack and Jill so sacred
That though all rivers reach the sea
His course through land's diversity
Is still for us what makes a river.

What wonder then if from this maelstrom
Of persons where no person counts
I should feel frail trusting the ether
With love in weighed and staid amounts
And as the liaising aircraft mounts
Can think its chartered speed illusion?

For though to me an absolute person
Yet even you and even by me
Being clamped by distance in a *burqa*
Cannot be seen, still less can see
How in this earlier century
Dark children daub the skies with arson.

And the small noises that invest me,
The sweepers' early morning slow
Swishing, the electric fans, the crickets,
Plait a dense hedge between us so
That your voice rings of long ago,
Beauty asleep in a Grimm story.

Yet standing here and notwithstanding
Our severance, need I think it loss
If from this past you are my future
As in all spite of gulf and gloss
However much their letters cross
East and West are wed and welcome;

And both of us are both, in either
An India sleeps below our West,
So you for me are proud and finite
As Europe is, yet on your breast
I could find too that undistressed
East which is east and west and neither?

1947

The North Sea

But not for a king's daughter? Here where Sir Patrick Spens
Went down to survive as a shiver on the scalp, a name,
I forage among the smearbread in the steamer
For the same snacks as a year ago and the same
Gull flies past the porthole while the immense
Eye of this Nordic sea outstares the dreamer,

Until he doubts whether the time between
These trips held any content; until he doubts
Whether the space between is not his all
And Bergen and Tynehead merely ins and outs,
The touch or the dead ball line, since these green
Waves are the only field of play for the ball,

Which makes one think (Sir Patrick went down playing
And a loud laugh laughed he) the laugh is on us
Who assert we are going to or from say Norway,
Who assume (*a quo* or *ad quem*) a terminus,
Who count this course between a mere delaying
And the cold vast between a stooge, a doorway.

Doorway? No more so than your office hours.
Doorway? No more so than your hours in bed
Alone or with a companion. And stooge no more
Than any counted or discounted flowers
Or stars which you might breed or weed or wed
Or grope for through strange lenses—or ignore.

For this, while we are in it, is an arena,
A perfect blue, green, grey, or pepper-and-salted nought,
In which beneath an indifferent sky the ghosts
Of Vikings board and grapple and the coasts
Which they were briefed to raid shrink to an idle thought
And each long dragon ship like an amphisbaena

Stings with both head and tail—but like a bee
Leaves her sting in time and thereby dies
And thereby lives in legend. The rover drowned
On a Thursday lives on a Thor's Day, the waves agree
To differ in Old Norse, the years rebound
To souse us in a lather of battle cries

And, as these top and vex our engines' pulse,
So hull-down on the horizon we can divine
A chain of round bright shields on a long gunwale
Itching to give the lie to screw and funnel,
To caterpillar up the scarps of brine
Like a tank's bogies, proving progress false.

Thus the Dark Ages like a traversing gun
Cover our own and we are in their sights,
Halvars and Olafs jostle our Esquires
And blood-lust our conventions; what we have done
Elsewhere is nowhere when the North Sea night's
Black single eye turns round on us and fires;

And we the target are the pupil too,
Sighted and sighting, are the central point
Round which the master's hand in strident chalk
Has roughed a circle in the pointless blue
Which timelessly is true like the great auk
But within time the times are out of joint,

And no ideal can be drawn to the life
And no eye gaze on it and never blink;
We saw the new world late yestreen with the old
Troll in her arms and now, shrill as a fife,
The wind is rising, the king's daughter is cold
As well she might be for this ship must sink.

And though Sir Patrick Spens were a man of iron
And master of his craft, he must conform
To the sea's routine; a wife in every port
Is nothing to that unconscionable siren
Whose arms are the lifting skylines and to court
Whom is to court the end, the deadly storm.

A Viking's last battle, their proverb ran,
Is always a defeat (not literally
True but true); just so the skipper's last
Trip is a wreck, settling down equitably
To drown in the arms of his mistress and mother, a fast
Lock of ill luck, an ending where he began.

Thus the wheel of the sea, of life, comes full circle, the gun
Swings in the swinging turret and finds her range
To illuminate, to annihilate, in a flash

Our timebound cargo and in a flash to change
The morse of the mind to changelessness—dot and dash
Be ended and the circle and point be one.

And so between firth and fro Sir Patrick must make his call
To find say a northern queen, say Understanding,
And make her take ship home with him—as must we—
And should our fate preclude both home and landing
Yet to have even embarked her, though not all,
Is all most men can hope for in such a sea.

1948

Mahabalipuram

All alone from his dark sanctum the lingam fronts, affronts the sea,
The world's dead weight of breakers against sapling, bull and candle
          Where worship comes no more,
Yet how should these cowherds and gods continue to dance in the rock
All the long night along ocean in this lost border between
That thronging gonging mirage of paddy and toddy and dung
          And this uninhabited shore?

Silent except for the squadrons of water, the dark grim chargers
      launched from Australia,
Dark except for their manes of phosphorus, silent in spite of the
      rockhewn windmill
          That brandishes axe and knife—
The many-handed virgin facing, abasing the Oaf, the Demon;
Dark in spite of the rockhewn radiance of Vishnu and Shiva and silent
In spite of the mooing of Krishna's herds; yet in spite of this darkness
      and silence
          Behold what a joy of life—

Which goes with an awe and a horror; the innocence which sur-
      mounted the guilt
Thirteen centuries back when an artist eyeing this litter of granite
          Saw it for waste and took
A header below the rockface, found there already like a ballet of fishes
Passing, repassing each other, these shapes of gopi and goblin,
Of elephant, serpent and antelope, saw them and grasped his mallet
          And cried with a clear stroke: Look!

273

And now we look, we to whom mantra and mudra mean little,
And who find in this Hindu world a zone that is ultra-violet
          Balanced by an infra-red,
Austerity and orgy alike being phrased, it seems, in a strange dead
    language
But now that we look without trying to learn and only look in the
    act of leaping
After the sculptor into the rockface, now we can see, if not hear, those
    phrases
          To be neither strange nor dead.

Not strange for all their ingrown iconography, not so strange as our
    own dreams
Because better ordered, these are the dreams we have needed
          Since we forgot how to dance;
This god asleep on the snake is the archetype of the sleep that we lost
When we were born, and these wingless figures that fly
Merely by bending the knee are the earnest of what we aspire to
          Apart from science and chance.

And the largest of all these reliefs, forty foot high by a hundred,
Is large in more senses than one, including both heaven and the animal
    kingdom
          And a grain of salt as well
For the saint stands always above on one leg fasting
Acquiring power while the smug hypocritical cat beneath him
Stands on his hindlegs too admired by the mice
          Whom the sculptor did not tell.

Nor did he tell the simple and beautiful rustics
Who saved from their doom by Krishna are once more busy and happy
          Absorbed in themselves and Him,
That trapped in this way in the rock their idyl would live to excite
And at once annul the lust and the envy of tourists
Taking them out of themselves and to find themselves in a world
          That has neither rift nor rim:

A monochrome world that has all the indulgence of colour,
A still world whose every harmonic is audible,
          Largesse of spirit and stone;
Created things for once and for all featured in full while for once and
    never
The creator who is destroyer stands at the last point of land
Featureless; in a dark cell, a phallus of granite, as abstract
          As the North Pole; as alone.

But the visitor must move on and the waves assault the temple,
Living granite against dead water, and time with its weathering action
      Make phrase and feature blurred;
Still from to-day we know what an avatar is, we have seen
God take shape and dwell among shapes, we have felt
Our ageing limbs respond to those ageless limbs in the rock
      Reliefs. Relief is the word.

                            1948

The window

I

Neck of an hour-glass on its side—
   Hermitage, equilibrium.
The slightest tilt and a grain would glide
   Away from you or towards you;
So without tremolo hold this moment
   Where in this window two worlds meet
Or family voices from the room behind you
Or canned music from beyond the garden
   Will irrupt, disrupt, delete.

Between this room and the open air
   Flowers in a vase imponderably—
The painter knew who set them there
   The knack of closed and open;
With highlights upon bloom and bulge
   He hung this bridge in timelessness
Preventing traffic hence and hither
And claimed his own authority
   To span, to ban, to bless.

The sands of light within, without,
   Equated and inviolable,
Allow no footprint and no doubt
   Of savagery or trespass
Where art enhancing yet revoking
   The random lives on which it drew
Has centred round one daub of ochre,
Has garnered in one square of canvas
   Something complete and new.

So there it rests the clump of flowers,
    Suspension bridge and talisman,
Not his nor hers nor yours not ours
    But everyone's and no one's,
Against the light, flanked by the curtains
    No draught nor chatter can discompose
For this is a window we cannot open
A hair's breadth more, this is a window
    Impossible to close.

Thus pictures (windows themselves) preclude
    Both ventilation and burglary—
No entrance to their solitude,
    No egress to adventure,
For life that lives from mind to moment,
    From mouth to mouth, from none to now,
Must never, they say, infringe that circle,
At most may sense it at a tangent
    And without knowing how.

II

How, yes how! To achieve in a world of flux and bonfires
Something of art's coherence, in a world of wind and hinges
An even approximate poise, in a world of beds and hunger
    A fullness more than the feeding a sieve?
For the windows here admit draughts and the bridges may not be
    loitered on
And what was ecstasy there would be quietism here and the people
    Here have to live.

Beginning your life with an overdraft, born looking out on a surge of
    eroding
Objects, your cradle a coracle, your eyes when they start to focus
Traitors to the king within you, born in the shadow of an hourglass
    But vertical (this is not art),
You feel like the tides the tug of a moon, never to be reached, interfer-
    ing always,
And always you suffer this two-way traffic, impulses outward and
    images inward
    Distracting the heart.

And the infant's eyes are drawn to the blank of light, the window,
The small boy cranes out to spit on the pavement, the student tosses

His midnight thoughts to the wind, the schoolgirl ogles the brilliantined
  Head that dazzles the day
While the bedridden general stares and stares, embarking
On a troopship of cloud for his youth or for Landikotal, evading
  The sneer of the medicine tray.

Take-off outwards and over and through the same channel an intake—
Thistledown, dust in the sun, fritillaries, homing pigeons,
All to which senses and mind like sea anemones open
  In this never private pool;
The waves of other men's bodies and minds galumphing in, voices
  demanding
To be heard or be silenced, complied with, competed with, answered,
  Voices that flummox and fool,

That nonchalantly beguile or bark like a sergeant-major,
Narcotic voices like bees in a buddleia bush or neurotic
Screaming of brakes and headlines, voices that grab through the
  window
  And chivvy us out and on
To make careers, make love, to dunk our limbs in tropical
Seas, or to buy and sell in the temple from which the angry
  Man with the whip has gone.

He has gone and the others go too but still there is often a face at your
  window—
The Welsh corporal who sang in the pub, the girl who was always
  at a cross purpose,
The pilot doodling at his last briefing, the Catalan woman clutching
  the soup bowl,
  The child that has not been born:
All looking in and their eyes meet yours, the hour-glass turns over and
  lies level,
The stopwatch clicks, the sand stops trickling, what was remote and
  raw is blended
  And mended what was torn.

And how between inrush and backwash such a betrothal should
  happen
Of tethered antennae and drifting vanishing filament
We do not know nor who keeps the ring and in passing
  Absolves us from time and tide
And from our passing selves, who salves from the froth of otherness
These felt and delectable Others; we do not know for we lose ourselves
  In finding a world outside.

Loss and discovery, froth and fulfilment, this is our medium,
A second best, an approximate, frameless, a sortie, a tentative
Counter attack on the void, a launching forth from the window
  Of a raven or maybe a dove
And we do not know what they will find but gambling on their
    fidelity
And on other islanded lives we keep open the window and fallibly
  Await the return of love.

III

How, yes how? In this mirrored maze—
  Paradox and antinomy—
To card the bloom off falling days,
  To reach the core that answers?
And how on the edge of senselessness
  To team and build, to mate and breed,
Forcing the mud to dance a ballet,
Consigning an old and doubtful cargo
  To a new and wayward seed?

But, hows apart, this we affirm
  (Pentecost or sacrament?)
That though no frame will hold, no term
  Describe our Pyrrhic salvoes,
Yet that which art gleaning, congealing,
  Sets in antithesis to life
Is what in living we lay claim to,
Is what gives light and shade to living
  Though not with brush or knife.

The painted curtain never stirs—
  Airlessness and hourlessness—
And a dead painter still demurs
  When we intrude our selfhood;
But even as he can talk by silence
  So, blinkered and acquisitive,
Even at the heart of lust and conflict
We can find form, our lives transcended
  While and because we live.

But here our jargon fails; no word,
   'Miracle' or 'catalysis',
Will fit what dare not have occurred
   But does occur regardless;
Let then the poet like the parent
   Take it on trust and, looking out
Through his own window to where others
Look out at him, be proudly humbled
   And jettison his doubt.

The air blows in, the pigeons cross—
   Communication. Alchemy.
Here is profit where was loss
   And what was dross is golden,
Those are friends who once were foreign
   And gently shines the face of doom,
The pot of flowers inspires the window.
The air blows in, the vistas open
   And a sweet scent pervades the room.

October, 1948

X

March 1950—April 1951

Every voyage is a death,
Every action is a loss,
Every poem drees its weird,
Carries its meaning like a cross;
Yet the burnt poet loves the fire
Which gulps what pittance he can give—
Dry words dying, dying, dead,
Burning that the Word may live.

Suite for recorders

*... it strikes a man more dead than
a great reckoning in a little room.*

AS YOU LIKE IT

I

If shepherd to nymph were the whole story
Dying in holocausts of blossom,
No midwife and no middleman
Would contravene the upright sun.

If Raleigh to Marlowe on the other
Hand were an uncontested audit,
Then Thames need only flow to mock
A death in tavern or on block;

Nor swimming Hellespont nor climbing
Starwards could answer the inquiring
Blade that would spill each threaded bead,
Each grace-note of a broken reed;

While far sou'wested Eldorado,
Old pipe-dream in the Tower of London,
Would be no more than history claims—
A long axe handle spliced for James.

But if—that If!—to die while swearing
Be lambing time and back to living
They leap the gap, some black, some white—
What matter so the heart be right?

They leap the gap, these pets of northern
Adventurers in their idler moments,
And call from arrogant eyes and mouth
A smile to greet a borrowed South,

Where close-cropped vines, though but black fingers,
Cock snooks at time, acre on acre
Proclaiming with a million Ayes
The long-dead shepherd worth his prize.

And though Black Jenny spin her coarsest
Pall on Persepolis and Mayday,
Though Time drive ships from sail to steam,
Though what was vision shrink to dream,

Yet Thames flows on beneath the traitors'
Bodiless heads and Spenser's carefree
Swans are found loyal to their creed
That deathbed comforts bridal bed.

Great reckonings come, yet cheat nor schemer
Outlives, outdies, his early beauty,
Black fingers will bear fruit and spring
Put paid to every reckoning.

II

In a little room, a little plot, a little lifetime,
Hark, the shrill recorders after meat; the Elizabethan
Mayflies in a silver web which dangled over chaos,
    Twirling round and round,
Waited for the silent headsman, countering his silence
    With arabesques of sound.

Courtier with the knife behind the smile, ecclesiastic
With faggots in his eyes, tight-lipped scholar with forbidden
Fruit in his back garden, all were conscious in their bowels
    Of the web and whose it was
And beneath it of the void where not old faith nor yet new learning
    Dare breathe the word Because.

Chancing, dancing, in the threads of life, time, death, at least of
    something,
Though always over nothing, Spanish gold, high ruffs, carved cross-
    bones,
All were solid—like stage props—to men and women only players,
    Only women, only men,
Briefed to make one first if last appearance more or less word-perfect,
    Having no chance again.

Golden age? Age of discovery? Age of madrigals and liars,
Age when men died young. We envy what we think an innocent
    ardour,

What in fact was staged revolt upon a tightrope, a creative
  Despair, a blithe despair of youth,
Which in that swivelling dubious web essayed its white lies in defiance
  Of the black void of truth.

Violent men with salt in their nostrils, blood on their hands, whose
    gentler moments
Conjured up, for lack of sleep, a land which ancient literati,
Careless of the starved and sweaty facts, had filled with mimic
  Shepherds fluting to their sheep
For Spenser, Sidney, Kit and Will to loll and count and then recounting
  Their antics fall asleep.

Life as a game? An art? An orgy? Something of each; a mortification
Also. Prematurely dead—or dumb—they left behind them
What for us? A bed of flowers? A second best? A starting point? Or
  Blind end, blind spring, spring of a trap?
Yet still they pipe and still from No Man's Pastures trip their white,
    their ringstraked,
  Their black sheep through the gap.

III

Pride in your history is pride
In living what your fathers died,
Is pride in taking your own pulse
And counting in you someone else.

Which someone, though long dead before,
Scrabbles and chirps on your own floor;
The orange he can hardly hold
Contains a world of Spanish gold.

Members one of another? Who
Could prove by reason that gag true?
But reason, if it were a lie,
Should counsel us at once to die.

For pride in being alive is what?
Is being what yourself are not,
Is being a world which must outlive
All you take from it or give.

285

Your Alter Egos, present, past,
Or future even, could not last
Did your word only prove them true;
Though you choose them, yet they chose you.

In and of the world and yet
Distinct from it, our task is set
To become Atlas while we can
And bear the world which made us man.

The windblown web in which we live
Presumes a yawning negative,
A nothing which cries out to see
A something flout its vacancy.

To singe the beard of the King of Spain
Was but a token; Tamburlaine
Found no more in his earthly crown
Than was allowed to Corydon;

And both demanded something more
Than their set piece of love or war,
Than what faint echoes drift to us
Of muffled drums or calamus.

Yet read between those lines and peer
Down through the mesh of gossamer
And you will sense the darkness which
Made either guttering candle rich;

And you, a would-be player too,
Will give those angry ghosts their due
Who threw their voices far as doom
Greatly in a little room.

IV

Come, my sheep, my goats, graze where the shoots are tender,
  Now I will sing of her
Who passed but once this way and never again till Judgement
  Day become Mayday too
And ribbons are round the Cross. Come where the grass is emerald;
  Battles were fought here once.

Come, my flocks, but shun the rusty wire, the tank-traps;
    Now I will sing of her
Whose shadow was taller than she and never till shadows have voices
    Dare I expect a reply
To the song I sung to her once. But come while the shadows lengthen,
    Graze your fill before night.

Come, this pipe is only on loan, I only a hireling,
    Yet, though my hire be due
And always unpaid, and my songs, heard by you only,
    Must needs be always unheard,
Come, my flocks, where this twilit wall still holds the noon-heat;
    Now I will sing of Her.

Areopagus

I

A tall story over a dark sanctum:
That Hebrew riddling in a land of olives
    Was an appetiser for a tired mind.
With a stone in it too. A sharp titillation
    With a snub, if not threat, in it too.

Never built on, not then nor since.
The saint on the run had a sword in his mouth
    And his feet on the rock were rock;
Iron faith in the city of irony.
    As it were scales had dropped in Damascus.

Outcrop of judgement. The foreign accent
Souring their salt. Beneath in the cave,
    Once avenging, later beneficent,
With tousled vipers, gravestone eyes,
    The Kind Ones turned in their sleep.

Limestone burning the feet, and opposite
Tiers of Pentelic, he whetted the blade
    Of the wit of his faith to slice their pagan
Prides to the quick; they nudged and doubted.
    Diamond cut diamond. Something new.

287

II

Spermologies fallen on stony ground. Stone of relentlessness, stone of
   crime,
Where hard words flew in the dark. Primaeval
Echoes of evil. A nuance, a noise,
As of Titans gurgling into the sink of the world.

And the torches hissed where now, ringed round with mountains,
Flow seas of electric light. New lamps for old;
Red eggs for Easter. Stones are rolled away
And caves are fallen in; yet raise your eyes
From these children with old faces, from these women
With handkerchiefs over their faces, from these hands
Which decimate time with beads, you still may glimpse
The child-eyed Fury tossing her shock of snakes,
Careering over the Parthenon's ruined play-pen.

Old testaments for new. New blood for old.
If Christ be beyond us They can be grasped who grasp;
We each have inherited curses and breed our own and not all
The gadarene jeeps nor all the taverna bouzoukis
Can utterly drown the pack that yelps on the scent.

Ech! Ech! Ooh! Ech! Ech!Oo-o-oh!
Hide if you choose in Stoa and Garden,
Your own crisp words will begin to hiss
In key with our torches, in step with our snakes,
And your own sharp eyes, at home to doubt,
Will blur with a greater despair: belief.

Ech! Ech! Ooh! Which is why Paul
Scouring the market found an altar
Clearly inscribed but between the words
Was the ghost of a Word who runs may guess,
Who runs from a fate unclear, unkind.

Unkind was early, clear was classic,
Now it was late. But for Paul was early
And the trumpet about to sound; the Virgin
Mother was one more daughter of Night,
She and her son not yet scaled down
To ikon or niche; like those other Virgins
Long brought down to classical earth.

Down to life-size. Poet and builder
Paid off the Avengers. Then came Christ
Speaking a sword that was red from his own
Lungs and his arms sprawled on the cross
To strangle the world; till bishop and builder
Gilded the nails, adjourned the verdict,
And boxed the cross in a square.

No nonsense for Pericles—nor for Byzantium;
The shapeless shapes were a whiff of the past
And the whale-mouthed arch the bones of the future,
So the words of Paul were swamped in rock
To hiss like the snakes that hissed in their sleep
On the heads of the sleepers, daughters of Night,
Drowned, disregarded, thought of as nonsense.

And yet not utterly. No long walls
Put out and cut off like feelers, no stings drawn.
No schools of rhetoric or resignation,
Not fez and hookah (there is no God but God),
Not tommy-gun and brochure (there is no god but Man),
Could cancel out Christ's death or prove the Furies dead.
Scale from the beam, beam from the eye, scales from the eye had
    dropped in Damascus
For a trap had snapped in a flash on a lonely dust-white road
While in a limestone cave the past was not dead but sleeping.

III

After anemones, after almond,
Pitiless heaven, enamelled sea;
The Furies plumped the grapes with blood,
Their living rock was the death of sea.
As Christ's dead timber fired by blood
Was to blossom bright as peach or almond.

The Unknown God? Judge or saviour?
The unknown goddesses—Cursing or kind?
Shall we have neither? Either? Both?
The dark prehistory of their kind
Hung over Jews and Greeks and both
Found, of their kind, a likely saviour.

Christ, if we could, having Christian fathers;
But Furies, if we must. For no

Life is for nothing, all must pay,
Yet what unknown is dread, we know
Can yet prove kind; our selves can pay
Our sons atonement for their fathers.

After the murder, after the trial,
Justice undone but honours new,
Who came to blight had stayed to bless
This folk; old fears were born anew
As hopes, and flock and crop could bless
The powers that put man's faith on trial.

The fierce pack bays no more; their note is new.

IV

Flying and ravening Curses, bark no more!
The blood of all the world lies doubtless at our door
But at whose not? These questions have been bruited, solved, unsolved
   before.

His mother's keeper? Leda brought to bed
Could have heard you even then, distantly howling; your red
Torches formed an early canopy over her grandson's head.

But, Saul called Paul, adjourn your day of doom.
Orestes too was acquitted. The body may be a tomb
Yet even the beggar's body is bread, is wine, is flowers in bloom;

Trundle back then that weight of sin from the grave.
With the cross hidden in the square, the Furies hidden in the cave
Ripening the corn, Christ too must have bodies too to save.

Nightmares are often just. This starlit court
None the less cut one just, one divine, impeachment short;
The plaintiffs foiled of blood emerged of fair, not ill, report—

Venerable ripeners of crop and flock,
Smiling on yeoman and bride, warding off blight and shock,
They made their haven for good beneath this judicial, this grim, rock.

Could we too lead our Furies to their shrine?
Forget them sprung from blood, remember them divine?
Nurses of fear and hope, come taste our honey, taste our wine!

Cock o' the north

But I am half a Scot by birth, and bred
A whole one, and my heart flies to my head . . .
DON JUAN

I

Bad Lord Byron went to the firing, helmet and dogs and all,
He rode and he swam and he swam and he rode but now he rode for
a fall;
Twang the lyre and rattle the lexicon, Marathon, Harrow and all,
Lame George Gordon broke the cordon, nobody broke his fall;
Mavrocordato, Colocotroni, faction, fiction and all,
All good fellows in fustanellas but all good fellows must fall.
Fall, fall, the kodjabashis! Snuff, douse, the Turkish moon!
Dollar credits with Barff and Hancock, conches in the sick lagoon!
Don John had fought Lepanto, Don Juan will dare it too;
Knaves and slaves are burning Sappho—hubble-bubble, hullabaloo!
'Flies and lice and fleas and thieves', Jeremy Bentham and gin—
Scusi!Scusi! Entusymusy! How did I ever get in?
In amidst this waste of marshes, waste of muskets, waste of breath,
In with the rogues, the cranks, the pirates, in and under, in at the death.
        The Pilgrim came down like a wolf in the cold,
            Kept from the door and trapped in the limelight,
        His tartan was faded, his nerves were old,
            But he knew a hawk from a handshake.
        Pepper trees drooping and mist on the swamp—
            Oh Meleager! Ah Meleager!
        Where is Leonidas? Has he struck camp?
            Where is my shield to be borne on?
Hail, hail, the conquering hero! Flaunt, vaunt, the hoplite's purse!
Rain on the roof and mud in the blood but everything might be
worse.
The London Committee drool in the City, Castlereagh turns to curse,
While we are deficient in men and munitions, still everything might
be worse.
Worse, worse, than stench and vermin, worse, worse, than sugary lies,
'Speculators and peculators'; Miltiades is coming,
The golden age is coming back, coming to life the poppied eyes,
Spring and Greece and glory—and Easter too—are coming.
        Easter is coming and the guns will boom:
            Christos anéste! Christos anéste!
        Scarlet flowers from a far-off tomb,
            Christos! Christos anéste!

291

II

The flattest place, it seems, in Hellas. A bad dream.
The sea gets never deeper, nor is it sea;
A thin mud line coalesces with the horizon.
Whose name was writ in bilge . . . A stilted hovel
Like a sick bird stood hunched in the lagoon,
Its thatchy feathers moulting. Stepping stones through pus
But the next step was where? Across the gulf
The mountains of the Morea seemed a mirage; to the east
What there remained of a river flowing from Calydon
Wept stones for Meleager. The boar was black
Like the after-life of an Ethiop; his tusks
Flashed curving through the forest like the Milky Way
And his small eyes were death. But not Meleager's;
His death came through fire, in his hour of triumph,
Through a fire some miles away. And miles behind, away,
Byron while shooting duck felt groping at his liver
The flames in Six Mile Bottom. You would never guess
This from his statue in the Garden of Heroes
Among the arranged trees and the marble clichés
And the small memorial cannon like staring infants
With lollipops in their mouths. You would never guess
From Greece who Veeron was. Across the gulf—
'*Hier stand, hier sass* Their Royal Highnesses . . .'
The marble bust of Clauss, benevolent distiller,
Guards his titanic vats, German epigonos
Who found Greece free and under a foreign king,
Frockcoats instead of turbans. Now in the heat
Missolonghi yawns and cannot close its mouth
And all its bad teeth show. The tired horizon
Remains a line of mud. In the plain around
The fruit trees, like his Souliots, wear white stockings,
The oleanders are pink and dry beside the river
Which weeps for Meleager. Crackle and hiss
On the hearths of Calydon and Kirkby Mallory.
Who had faced the brute, his life in the log—
But so far away—was burning away.

III

Close the vein! It is Easter Eve.
The long white candles wait to be lit,

The staring guns are agog to boom,
The boar is dark in the night of the wood,
The boar is dead in the glens of myth,
There is only a flame in the back of the mind
Consuming a log, the soft grey ash
Soft as, not grey as, the locks of hair
He hoarded in drawers. Close the vein!

Bruno and Millingen, close the vein!
The leech is black on the pale of the brow;
Poor me, poor Greece, there is my life to her!
My windows are misted within and without
Above the lagoon neither deep nor rolling;
Is this Greece Greece and is that sea sea
And what is there dear in the world? Adonis
He too went hunting boar and died
But the goddess loved him. Adonis *anéste*!

Afraid of the dark? Come and take light,
Where is your candle? I have no candle,
Only a sword. Which I have not used.

IV

Bards wha hae for Hellas bled—
   Oh Meleager, ah Meleager—
Anemones flourin' frae your blude
   When twa white queens focht owre ye!
Christ is wax, Adonis wax—
   Oh Cythereia, ah Cythereia!
The dumb tongues o' the candle wicks
   Haud ne'er a hint o' harvest.
A far cry here frae Aberdeen—
   Mither! Mither! Wae the Gordons!
Yon granite tours cam clatterin' doun
   I' the sunset waves o' Zante.
A far cry here frae Melbourne House—
   Dice in Almack's, flames in Moscow—
I' the year o' the stockin'-frame and waltz
   Wi' the price o' bread still risin'.
A far cry here frae the Grand Canal!
   That which once was! Breasts and eyebrows!
The vein is closed and the profit nil

And the rest is Barff and Hancock.
The rest is a nicht where nae rest is—
Oh Missolonghi, ah Missolonghi!
The dogs i' the nicht are ill at ease
For they snuff the boar i' the reed-banks.
His white tusks curve like a Turkish sword—
Back to the nightmare! Back to the nursery!
Our Lady o' Death has all assured
And her board is spread for Adonis.
The dried branch is itchin' to bloom—
Mither! Mither! *Crede Biron!*
Was it my fault you bore me lame
To a warld o' sharks and dandies?
To thae bricht lichts where licht is nane?
Christ gies licht but nae to pagans!
I maun burn my body to clear my een,
Yon withered bough maun blossom.
To fell yon boar means death by fire—
Calydon saved and Calydon ruined,
But the flame o' courage feeds on fear
And the halt mak lordly riders.
Qu'allais-je faire dans cette galère?
Was it for her sake, was it for my sake,
I flew like a bumblin' moth to the lure
O' the gutterin' lamp o' Hellas?
Open the vein, I maun gie her oil,
Oil from my guts an' oil from my marrow;
Yon leech is black as a ganglin' eel
I' the dour lagoons beneath me.
Yon boar is black as the nicht o' the heart
Wha bides my shaft and bodes my passin';
I maun gang my lane to wed my hurt,
I maun gang my lane to Hades.
The fire is low in Calydon hall—
Mither! Mither! Blaw the bellows!
My foreign doctors kill to heal
And the last licht leads to darkness.
Under the bed, look under the bed,
What is it growlin', what is it groanin'?
Thunder at sunset! What can it bode?
Is it mysel'? My sunset?
You may throw my brand in yonder fire—
Oh Meleager! *Crede Biron!*
I will hae the courage o' my fear
And blaze a path to silence.

Didymus

I

A million simmering kettles: in the Destroyer's shrine
The world is on the boil, bats in malodorous dark
Under a pyramid of writhing sculpture
That rams the destroying sky. But round the unsculptured lingam,
The restful purposeful indifferent phallus,
The bats like microbes stitch their hectic zigzag
Of black on black, of blind on blind, and dot
And carry and dot and carry and sizzle like seaweed
That reeks on the shore of the Infinite. While outside
The whole of India jinks and twitters too
Around her granite axis; so shrill yet so resigned,
Monochrome under her motley, monolith under her flimflams,
Mute column of black stone hung round with grace-notes.
Smoke from no visible fire; yet fire like a fir-cone
Nestles in Shiva's hand, the dainty embryo
Of all that is and the end of all, the core
That never moves nor melts yet holds the dance,
Innumerable limbs reduced to one
Black pencil of pure fire. Roses and sandalwood,
Red spittle on the flagstones of the temple,
Green flash of parrots, phosphorescent waves,
Caparisoned elephants and sacred bulls,
Crystal-gazers, navel-gazers, pedants,
Dazzling and jangling dancers, dazzling lepers,
Begging unfingered hands and mouthing eyes,
Faces on faces each like a blind end,
Lives upon lives bubbles of jewelled scum
Born every second and reborn regardless,
Who has come here against you? Slow of speech
With trouble in his eyes and tarry hands
And no sophistication and no caste,
Who has come here armed with two plain crossed sticks
To flout your banyan riot of dialectic?
Is it a prince whose veins run blue with magic?
Is it a sage whose water-divining mind
Will twitch to the smallest drop at the final nadir?
Is it a god who has more arms than yours,
More words, more shapes, more worlds, invincible avatar?
No; it is Doubting Thomas.

II

Nothing more simple. Among the tarnished
Mirrors of paddy and cocoanut palms,
Black-and-white turkeys in courtly fantails,
And no human beings but children,

Tiny and self-assured in whitewash
Stands a plain church, no frills, no gilt,
Among Portuguese names on wooden crosses,
The Church of the Little Mount;

Whitewashed also within—the barrel
Vault as hale as a barrel of flour.
But under the chancel there sleeps a crypt
Not so much crypt as cave;

And here, says the plaque, here in Madras
Before Madras or Madeira was heard of
Here was the hiding place of the saint
Who had left his faith to his hands.

His two hands only, only two—
What could they prove against Shiva and Krishna?
Or against the sweet-toothed jumbo-god
With his trunk in the bowl of candy.

Peter would have talked big and John
Have called forth a serpent out of the sherbet,
Paul would have matched them abstract with abstract
But this man, how could he start?

With his two hands and his cruse of doubt
Which never ran dry? And even doubting,
For those dark and sly and chameleon minds,
Was a technique they knew.

So, after days in the cave, of a night
He would sneak to the beach and watch the indifferent
Waves of the shark-ridden ocean and dream
Of nets that he used to mend

And of the man who spied him at it;
He could no longer remember his face

Nor most of his words, he could only remember
That his nets were repaired on time

And that so it began, a doubtful beginning,
His fisherman's hands were hardly right
For a preacher's gestures, he would have sooner
Saved them to tie strong knots.

Yet, staring out at the phosphorous wave-tops
And brushing away the eye-flies, Thomas
Thought of the Indian kings who never
Would raise a hand, having hands

Bought by the thousand for them, slaves
With enormous fly-whisks; and Thomas thought
Of the Indian gods who could sprout at pleasure
All the hands they might need.

And then he thought: I am proud, I have only
Two hands for all things, including the cross,
As have the coolies; it is my mission
To help their lack with mine.

And beside that sea like a sea on the moon
He clasped his hands to make sure they were only
Two and, finding them two but strong,
Raised them gently and prayed.

III

Oh but my doubt is a sea harsher than this that I see,
    Oh but my hands tremble fumbling the night,
To all of my questions I know the reply must be No;
    To me those tongues of fire were fire, not light.

Blessed are those who believe and ask no leave
    Of hand or eye, for whom all water is wine,
Who whatever the weight on the heart have the heart to wait
    For the clouds to lift—a gift that was never mine.

Whatever the clime, my task is ever to climb
    Foothills that never are mountains; this Indian sky

Is bowed with the dour monsoon and I doubt but soon
    All of my converts and most of my work must die.

I doubt that I have the least right to preach or write
    In the name of Christ, I doubt that my doubt can find
One hint that my terrible role could aspire to roll
    The stone from the door of the tomb of the Indian mind.

I doubt and I doubt; in a crumbling exposed redoubt,
    Enfiladed by heathendom, here to the end
I watch in the endless rain to herald the reign
    Of the Friend of Man—but can he be Thomas's friend?

Was he that once, the sole delight of my soul?
    My memory wilts in the heat. I was mending a net
When I sensed with a start that I was under his eye
    And he called my name; the rest of his words I forget.

Is he my friend still? No, perhaps. All that I know
    Is that each rice-farmer, snake-charmer, scavenger, merchant,
        mahout,
Each life in this land that is sore has the chance to soar
    To find and keep that friend. But, for myself, I doubt.

IV

The last light purples the mirrors of paddy, the tracks
Become dark rivers of peasants with brushwood on their heads,
Rivers which all day long flowed out of sight
Leaving the world to children. Now the palmtrees
Grow dark like gigantic fly-whisks and the church
A glimpse of white that might be a temple; though here
The lingam, could it be here, were only an axis
Abstracted from or imagined on space, while space
Shrinks to a granite hide-out and the world
Turns round that hollow kernel where all noise
Lies folded away like grave-clothes. Only a whisper
More tenuous than the shriek of one lost bat
Spins out like the one weak thread of one lost spider,
The ghost of the groping doubt of one lost man.
                Thomas, Thomas, were you right
                In your blindness to preach light?
                Cowering there in that dark crypt

With body and soul so ill equipped
And the Christ whom once you knew
Torn for ever from your view,
Thomas, Thomas, do you find
That out of sight means out of mind?
Out of sight . . . These millions, where do they vanish in the daytime?
These ants who thrust and haul the crumbs from Shiva's table
While Shiva's foot, as he dances, hangs above them,
Their life being merely between one step and the next,
One tap on the drum and the next. And the gospel of Thomas
Which grants each ant its worth is only by proxy
Since Thomas himself is a proxy, hawking a faith
That he knows should be theirs while he dare not assume it is his
Unless he confirm and remind himself by his hands
Caressing his walls of rock, batting the flies,
Or pressing them merely together, those hands that once
Were tested and proved, yet failed through needing a test.
          Thomas, Thomas, do you not
          Even yet repent your lot?
          Fisherman who left your boat
          To trawl for souls, nameless, remote,
          Which when you catch and lift them high
          Flash like mackerel and then die.
          What started this you know—but why?
          Thomas, Thomas, do not lie!
Liar? Not Thomas; he had too much doubt
And hair on the back of his hands, they looked so clumsy
Yet in the dark could tell new twine from old
And tell himself himself, they had taught him once
That a spirit was still a man, since when in his sleep
More than awake they grope as if under sea
To prove all men are spirit. Believing Thomas,
Apostle to the Indies! If never there,
The Indies yet can show in a bare church
On a bare plaque the bare but adequate tribute
To one who had thrust his fingers into the wounds of God.

Our sister water

I

World's best is water; in the megrims of parched
Towns where the sun's laugh drills into the occiput

Or in brown uplands where river beds parody
Bubbles with pebbles, rivers with rock.

Heart's best is water; behind the glaring
Stucco of faces, lost in wrinkles,
In clefts of rubbish and fluttering newspaper,
Might be a rivulet; heart's, world's best.

O my dear sister, my dear Sor Acqua,
Useful and humble and precious and chaste,
Might we, admiring no less than needing,
Name you not also spendthrift? Harlot?

Francis preached to the birds but Pindar
In a land still drier sung for the oligarchs,
Found no image to praise their virtue
Better than water, colourless, pure.

Yet, as we know, my wraith of the backstairs,
Underground whisperer, queen of mirage,
None has more ball-dresses, pheasant or kingfisher,
More golden armour, plate or chain.

Whose name was writ in . . . Keats was right;
They would wish on us hearts of oak, of iron,
Or even of gold—all crude things, tame,
To the wealth and whip and gamut of water.

Blind in the desert the palate shrills:
Wine is for luxury, milk for babes,
But for men dying water is all
To be wished. Is also the wish to live.

In gas, maybe, the world began
But in water we. Thales was right;
Stone can stand, steel thrust, but we
May dodge betwixt, may slither between;

Spinning our senses thin to diaphanous
Film over sand or marble slab,
Humping our passions in tidal waves,
Booming a cataract, tinkling a raindrop.

Water our core and water our trivia;
Here on this grid of cemented heat

300

We wilt at a table and order a Turkish
Coffee. To pay for. Water is free.

Water is free; she comes in a tumbler.
Coffee is charged for, comes in a cup,
A hot sweet thimbleful thick with grounds
But a tower of liquid light beside it

Which the sun coins and cool from ice
It spears the throat like an ice-cold sun.
The cup is a gulp of dregs, but double,
But triple our tumblers, turrets of water.

Sister! Look forth on the heat-crazed road;
Is that the sandstorm? Those dry daemonia,
Mark how they dance! But you, you can match them:
Jongleurs de Dieu, tumblers of God.

II

Back in the Seventeen-Seventies to Birmingham he came,
The Scot, John Watt, of combustion engine fame,
Having lived overlong in a hobside dream,
Murdering his sister Water, turning her to steam;
Then Watt, having got what he wanted most, her ghost,
Packed her off to Birmingham, his wee key post,
Where he and Matthew Boulton built a limbo dark and high
To blazon English locomotives black across the sky.

The great Soho foundry is there to this day;
From the thick black sand the red flames play,
The molten metal slops, trundled round by hand,
By the black hands on the barrows, in the thick black sand,
And a thick black laugh from a man you cannot see
Takes a pot shot at Watt and his point d'appui;
For Watt's soft spot was for things that puff and bray
But those rich red gutters make weighing machines to-day.

Now a metre of green being, as a Frenchman said,
Greener than a centimetre, if machines are dead
And a fortiori dry, the driest, deadest of the lot
Are these finicking machines which were not designed by Watt
And Watt may be turning, between disgust and rage,

In his grave which is the grave of the whole Steam Age,
Or else, all passion spent, may wink the other eye
From that grave which is so narrow, so dirty, so dry.

Water, Water, Watt! You dealt us mere steam;
Hard cash flowed but can dividends redeem
The desiccated banks, the clinker paths designed
To weld a mobile body to a bone-dry mind?
Water, Water, Watt! You were never in the South,
A dour northern hero with a dry northern mouth,
And your name is writ in steam over heaven—perhaps a blot
Here and there—but, in my ear-drum, were you ever thirsty,
    Watt?

III

Steam is a dry word; the best word is water
For artist and peasant however the sewers debase it,
Whatever foul acid may slur it. Best in the West
Squelching round ankles, dousing the nape of the neck,
Ringing the jackpot of colour out of the mountains;
Best in the large or best when a girl in a shawl
Barefoot and windblown staggers her way through the bog
With a bucket of windblown gold. Best in the East
Where humpbacked oxen maunder down a ramp
To brim the pitchers of the girls in saris,
Or in flat plats of paddy sprigged with green,
Or on the rulered page of a Moghul garden—
Cool marrow of marble spines; or in the endless
Plains in the gross monsoon with one white egret
Posed on a stump among red miles of soup,
Red miles of wheat to be. In large or little
And east or west the best. As on these marches
Of East and West where beneath this capheneion table
Pistachio shells lie dry as fag-ends, poor pink shells
That never savoured brine; and in the street,
Where dust of down-coming houses irks the nostrils,
Red mouths of water melons gape and slobber
Red in a cart of great green globes while women,
Dark handkerchiefs over dark glasses over dark eyes,
Like inquisitorial puppets fidget past
Towards some dry catechism. Look at the melons,
You wire-drawn fates, and wait! As Stephenson and Watt

302

For an opposite cause waited and watched the kettle
Boil itself dry, dry. As the chosen people
Waited while Moses raised his rod to Yahweh
Through a second of dry eternity; then split it
Into a gash of silver. Or as we wait
Now for a coffee—and the more grounds the better
To prove that crystal crystal, that water wet,
Which will be slapped in free. Great things in little:
A leaf from Moses' rod, a psalm of David,
Trapped in a tumbler. Japanese flowers. A magnum
Of light in liquid. Stand on your heads you fountains,
Be lifted up you long horizontal lakes,
Spout your trombones of silver and you seas
Balloon your whales in the sky, make Pegasuses
Of all your white and randy horses. In Pindar's
Land his word runs true. Water is best:
A miracle out of the rock, a royal flush in the hand,
A river nymph on the table. Tumbler, chameleon,
Clown, conjuror of God!

IV

Water is beginning, is end, is pure, is pure gift
Of always shifting ground as never ground can shift,
In which, being of which, having weltered once, to-day
Soul retains what body lost scrambling out of a bay,
Shackling itself in legs: our birthright which we sold
For a mess of lungs and limbs. Even now we contain an untold
Capacity for sliding, rippling, filtering under the limestone hill,
Moving in order under ice, charging in combers, lying still,
Reflecting faces, refracting light, transparent or opaque,
Can be wind-curled fountain, tigerish weir, garrulous rain or tongue-
     tied lake,
Can be all shapes or shapeless, assume all voices or none,
Can alchemise rock and pavement, flatter and fleece the sun,
Maraud and mime and bless. Such is water, such are we,
World's most variables, constant in our variability,
Termagants and trulls of froth, virgins in the naked heart,
Bombardiers of breaker and bore, who in the end sidle apart
Into still cells of crystal. As Keats in the end withdrew
To Rome and his own illness, left his sister Water a new
Name for her silver archives, Adonais, the maiden knight

Of the sensual world; and his sister, veiled in white,
Wrote it and traces it still with her finger. Water and we are alive,
We talk and twist, fill out all moulds, contrive
Inroads into the alien, raiding the solid black
Preserves of earth or assaulting air, yet must fall back
In the end and find our level absolved of earth and breath
In that bed we were conceived in, born in, the bed of ocean, of death.

The island

I

First the distant cocks. A hairfine
Etching on silence, antiphonal silver,
Far-flung nooses of glittering sound,
   A capstan chanty to launch the day,
While the young though time-honoured Early Riser
   Fingers and proves her way.

Then the donkeys; clumsily splicing
Coarser hausers—Haul away, bullies,
For all your grumps and catarrh. Be docile,
   Enter those golden shafts and heave
The chariot over the mountain, freighted
   Once more with a reprieve.

Next and together a gush of water
And gabble of Greek. The sluices are open,
Each to his runnel, down from the mountain,
   From thriftily hoarded dams of sleep,
It flows as arranged; we are back to daylight
   When men and plants drink deep.

Back to normal; the ghosts in the pinetrees
Have dwindled to lizards; primaeval brows
Lined with a myriad drystone terraces
   Smile in the sun; the welded blue
Of sea and sky is the tenure of legend;
   Far; near; true.

Always begun so. Cutting his capers
On mattock and needle, sun on the cypresses

Polishing cone-studs as in Homeric
    Times when he brassed the boss on the shield
Of some rough-hewn hero under the cypresses
    And held out fame in the field.

But then, as now, Sun was deceiver
Who promised no more than he could give
But than men could take, dangling before them
    Wealth, glory, freedom, life;
When Icarus flew too high that freedom
    Lopped his wings like a knife

And he fell by this island. Where the woodsmoke
Smelt as now, where the naked rocks
Were as naked then, where labouring wisdom
    Then as now, ready to leave
Things till to-morrow, asked of to-morrow
    No freedom, only reprieve.

II

Which still is much. Here in this mountain village
Favoured with trees, bareness above and below it,
Suspended over a sea which melts in a sky suspended
Over a little blue dome which melts, which melts in upper
And nether blueness: here, one might think, is a closed
Circle, cave of Calypso. No horizon
Beyond the sombre warmth of looseknit stones, beyond
The warmth of daily greetings—no horizon
Did not these whitewashed rooms among wine-gourds, goat-skins,
    ikons,
Include a letter or two with a foreign postmark
From Cleveland and Detroit, diners and luncheonettes,
From wholesale grocers, coffee jobbers, gobetweens,
Who proved there was a horizon when they crossed it
Yet still are sons and uncles. Hermes came from Olympus
Tipster and god of the market; these across the Atlantic,
Tides invading the tideless. Where was the land of the dead
Rise now the towers of life, the steel and concrete
Which scorn yet prop these cabins. Hermes parted the creepers
That screened the cave of the nymph, gave her his ultimatum
And left. As the sun will leave who is peeping now through the figtree
But also broods on Wall Street. The epithets of Homer

Were fixed, albeit capricious, including the compounds
With God in them, by dint of repetition
Or ignorance ringing true. As cockcrow and cicada
Argue that light will last. The timeworn baker,
Burnt out of Smyrna, smokes his hubble-bubble,
The grey stones breathe in sky, a slim and silent girl
Gathers salt from the sea-crags, green among green leaves
Figs, kid-soft purses, bulge, on low stone roofs
Figs, grapes, tomatoes, dry in the sun and sweat
Pastes the hair to the forehead, a tall woman
Strides out of Homer over the pine-needles, mule-droppings,
Holding a distaff while the swallowtail butterflies
Fly, or seem to, backwards. Seem to. Backwards.
The sluices were all closed hours ago; where the water
Tumbled the rocks are dry, our shadows are short in the sun,
Painters would find this innocent. If difficult.
Its blue too blue. And giving nothing away.

III

Gorged on red, green, purple, tomatoes, peppers, aubergine,
   The visitor lies among tattered shadows
Under a walnut tree where a high sun shines through the smooth green

   Leaves so unlike the leaves of Athens,
Those dusty rats' tails. An August siesta. Here, he feels, is peace,
   The world is not after all a shambles

And, granted there is no God, there are gods at least, at least in Greece,
   And begins to drowse; but his dreams are troubled
By the sawmill noise of cicadas, on and on—Will they never cease?

   Were he to count a thousand, a hundred
Thousand sheep, they would all be scraggy and stare at him with the
      stare
   Of refugees, outraged and sullen,

Who have no gap to go through, who even if free are free as air
   Long since exhausted. And the cicadas
Force, force the pace; a jaunty cavalcade of despair.

   Idyllic? Maybe. Still there is hardly
Such a thing as a just idyl. The sanguine visitor dreams
   And finds himself on the run with barking

Dogs at his heels who turn into wolves, into men, and each of them
  seems
 To be running in creaky shoes; before him
Brood vast grey rocks, turtle-shape, cottage-loaf, rubble of dried-up
  streams,

 Among which reigns the judge in his glory
In a wig like a dirty sheep, frightened himself, with a nerve in his face
 Ticking away, giving wisdom and warning

In the voice of a circular saw. Forcing the pace, forcing the pace,
 Did not a quick breeze scour the treeless
Dream and also the tree that shelters the dreamer, yet cannot efface

 The truth of his panic; these are no megrims,
This is the world and this island—a brown leaf clanks from the green
  tree
 Dry on dry ground like a subpoena—

And there are prisoners really, here in the hills, who would not agree
 To sign for their freedom, whether in doubt of
Such freedom or having forgotten or never having known what it
  meant to be free.

IV

Our shadows now grow long in the sun,
Not to be long in it. No horizon
All day for the brightness of sea and sky,
All night for their darkness. One by one
The clefts are closed and the colours run
And the olive groves turn muted velvet.

Later the water. Through his contrived
Miniature channel he dives and prattles
To puddle the powdery grooves; his voice
Breaks where the steep from which he dived
Turns level; but the earth revived
Feels young this evening, as this morning.

Our shadows walk on stilts, look old
As our ambitions, the sun is younger
Having no dreams; like a self-made god

307

Who mouths his mottoes, parades his gold,
But swaggers off with the facts untold,
The name on his cheque still wet behind him.

The water-talk ends; the scrawl on the sky
Smudges and fades, the upper and nether
Darknesses close, the night grinds small,
Gives nothing away; but frail and high
A new moon rides and the starved eye
Finds the full circle in the crescent.

Finds or seems to. Seems to. A full
Circle and full close. One donkey
Erupts, a foghorn, then runs down
Like a worn disc; and the moon's pull
On these dark seas comes weak or null
As the will and whims of a jilted goddess.

That gods are grudged the loves of men
Born proof against a life immortal
Calypso knew before Hermes spoke;
She sleeps alone in her cave since then
While the tired peasants in this glen
Lie upon planks, at least together.

Some who lived long on this poor soil
No more have part in it; their twilight
Falls eight hours later, their evening meals
Like their morning minds are soon on the boil
But where is their island wine and oil?
Where the slow concord of an island?

Slow. As life is. One by one,
Islands themselves, the stars move forward
In echelon, in grave pursuit
Of a routed, already returning sun
Who seems to be falling back, on the run.
Seems to. Back. Yet marches forward.

The round of dark has a lip of light,
The dams of sleep are large with daybreak,
Sleeping cocks are primed to crow
While blood may hear, in ear's despite,
The sun's wheels turning in the night
Which drowns and feeds, reproves and heartens.

Day of renewal

I

Do I prefer to forget it? This middle stretch
Of life is bad for poets; a sombre view
Where neither works nor days look innocent
And both seem now too many, now too few.
They told me as a child that ten was a ripe age
When presents must be useful; which was Progress
But I felt sad to end each fairy story,
Kept turning back to the first page.

Candles increased, then vanished. Where I was born,
Heckled by hooters and trams, lay black to the west
And I disowned it, played a ticklish game
Claiming a different birthplace, a wild nest
Further, more truly, west, on a bare height
Where nothing need be useful and the breakers
Came and came but never made any progress
And children were reborn each night.

Go west and live. Not to become but be.
Still that remains an ideal—or a pretence;
Death is, but life becomes, and furthest westward
The dead must lap fresh blood to recover sense
As Homer rightly thought. Birthdays come round
And the child graduates from milk to meat
And loses count of himself, finding and losing
Visions as quickly lost as found.

As time, so place. This day a year ago
Or thirty years lies rooted in one spot
Which in itself has changed but in our mind
Does not become but is; is what it now is not.
Thus for me Cushendun is war and frustrated
Love, Dieppe an astringent idyl, Lahore
Blood, cholera, flies, blank eyes, becoming forty:
Each birthday placed and each place dated.

Such and such my beginnings, launched and engined
With such and such a tackle of nerve and gland
And steered by such and such taboos and values,
My What and How science might understand

But neither the first nor last page tells the story
And that I am remains just that I am.
The whole, though predetermined to a comma,
Still keeps its time, its place, its glory.

II

Turn again, Whittington. Riding the surf
Of the winds of England far-off bells
Change and taunt you, change and tempt you:
Turn again, Whittington, your pocket full of milestones.
And so for all of us. Fits and starts,
Bronze tongues lost in a breaking wave,
Then clear on the crest. When his grimy bundle
Bred vaults of gold and his cat was dead,
Still the bells rang the same. Same changes.
Same. Is life. Changes. Is life.
One-Two-Three-Four-Five-Six-Seven-Eight:
This year, no year, ever, never, next time,
Eat your cake, have your cake, last time lucky,
Ace high, bottoms up, cut again, turn again,
This year, next year, a pocket full of plumstones,
All the white horses and—turn again, Whittington—
All the King's aldermen sweating on the bellropes
Cannot put together again, by no means whatsoever again,
What time and tide have parted—brickbats and dividends.
Orange flotsam, lemon jetsam, Tower Reach is bobbing with it
And never put together again. Bow bells and coster carts.
I'm sure I don't, the bell says, the great bell, the tenor bell
Booming out of the brine trough, swinging on the world's wheel,
Mouth up in ribaldry, I'm sure I don't, an oracle
For lord mayors and beggar boys, I'm sure I don't know!

And so for all of us. Bits and pieces,
Mayoral banquet and barefoot mile,
Here the self-licensed purr of a cat
And there the toasts, the commercial phrases:
This year? Next year? When will you pay me?
Ever and always. Long may he live!
But the clappers overlap in the waves
And the words are lost on the wind. Five farthings . . .
Five farthings for what? For turtles? Candles?
The great procession comes once a year

Like Christmasses, birthdays. Gifts and leases;
They all run out. As a man's wardrobe
Bulges with clothes he no longer wears
Or only on off days; turned again,
Turned and returned, darned and patched,
Stained with memories. Moth and clock
Have done their damn'dest. Ancient brogues
Caught in a wrinkled grin when the wind changed
Repeat their inglenook yarns, remember
Only one walk out of many; a hat
With a bent black brim remembers a funeral;
And white drills drill in India. Memories
Flitter and champ in a dark cupboard
While in a box among old tin whistles
And paper caps lie stubs of candles
Twisted, snuffed out, still in their holders,
Relics of Christmas, birthday butts.
Ding! Dong! Pussy's in the ding-dong!
Who put us here? The daily Why,
The birthday But. We are still children;
Don't Care was hung, Did Care was haunted;
Big A, Little A, Why's in the cupboard;
Why, say the children, is Why in the cupboard?
And what is that light at the top of the well?
Who'll pull us out? We want that light
At the top of the well. On my next birthday
Shall I get out? Or the one after next?
Or the next after that? Or the next after that?
Here come the candles; now can I do it?
The light up above us is one big candle.
To light us to what? To what, say the doubting
Children and stay but not for an answer.
Ding! Dong! What? Ding! Dong! Why?

III

Milestones. My own; small things lost in a vast
Forest of marble obelisks, private code-words
Drowned in a maelstrom of wavelengths. The lines are crossed;
The miles are a wrong number; the rivers are jammed
With angry logs on which in great spiked boots

Lumberjacks fight each other and when one falls
They stamp upon his face. While on the shore
The self withdraws to its third floor back, shakes out
Its fears, hopes, hungers, loves, its doubts and visions,
The small things that are its own; which tinkle, sparkle,
Then roll off into corners. What is own?
The corners maybe but the light they danced in
Came through the window, the same light that still
Gilds the murderous river, catches the spikes
On the boot that is raised to blind. So what is own?
One's birthday is a day that people die on—
Shorthand of wavering shadow on white icing
Scribbled by tiny candles. Thus for me
Being twenty-one was at home but seemed at large
For all the coming slump. And being thirty
Was London and the fear of growing old,
Also the fear of war. And being forty
Was an arm sore from the needle, a Tom Collins
In the garden of Faletti's with Lilac Time
Tinkling between the massacres, was Lahore
When all the lines were dead. And now I am forty-three,
At sea in the small hours heading west from the island
Where other massacres drove poor folk west
To make this Turkish delight, so soft and sweet
It lights up one's bad tooth. In the small dark hours
At sea this time and westwards—west to live
A small hour though my own. But next time? (What
Are those lights ahead? Already the port so loved
By Themistocles, great patriot and statesman,
Great traitor five years on?) But next time what?

IV

This year, last year, one time, ever,
Different, indifferent, careless, kind,
Ireland, England, New England, Greece—
The plumstones blossom in my mind.

A child inside me lights the beacons
Which spell both victory and defeat,
Candles that he cannot see
Around a cake he dare not eat.

Peasticks and dried pea-stalks and empty
Cartons, old letters and dead leaves;
My odd job conscience lights a bonfire
Which gasps and crackles, exults and grieves.

For all my years are based on autumn,
Blurred with blue smoke, charred by flame,
Thrusting burnt offerings on a god
Who cannot answer to his name.

And purged of flowers that shone before me
I find in roots beyond me, past
Or future, something that outlasts me
Through which a different I shall last.

Whitewash, pebbledash, beaverboard, brick,
Plane tree, neem tree, crabapple, pine,
Freehold, leasehold, trespasser, tenant,
All men's, no man's, thine, mine.

For no one person may found a city
As Cadmus knew who, bowed beneath
His lonely burden, prayed for helpers,
Then cashed that bond of dragon's teeth.

Born as we are in need of friends
We take our fears and sow the earth
Which burgeons with them, fully grown,
Too many for comfort, armed from birth.

Mentor, tempter, mistress, wife,
Helping, hampering, casual, dear,
Every dark furrow sprouts with eyes
And from each eye there shines a spear.

Hence mutual clashes where some fall,
None but a few survive to lay
The needed stones and light the fires
Which make and unmake every day.

To eat one's cake and have it? Perhaps
In the end we can; when no one flame
Shines less than all and through blown smoke
There drifts a god who needs no name.

Day of returning

I

Crouched upon sea-chiselled gravel, staring out and up at the sea,
  The gnarled and glorious twister, seasoned in danger, wept,
Thrusting his heart at that monstrous wall of water
  Beyond which somewhere was Ithaca.

Behind him the island was terraced, before him terrace on terrace of
    waves
  Climbed to the cruel horizon; though he was strong, he wept,
The salt tears blent and blurred with the salt spindrift
  While the salt of his wit grew savourless.

Behind him also, faintly curling out of the woods, a voice,
  Which once entranced, now pained him; instead of that too sweet
    song
He yearned for the crisp commands of laundry and kitchen
  Which his wife must be giving in Ithaca.

And again he rode his mind at the hurdles of ocean, counted the hours
  That would not pass, the waves that would not sleep, and wept
But not as of old when he half enjoyed the weeping
  For shared sorrows in company.

But this was not tragic, this was frustration; infertile as the foam
  That creamed around his sandals, listless as the hope
The sweet voice held out sometimes of an immortal
  Life, but life here, not Ithaca.

For here his bed was too soft and the wine never rough and the scent
    of the flowers
  Too heavy; here when he should have smiled he wept.
Better have stayed on that other island of lotus
  Smiling from pure forgetfulness.

Out and up at the sea. A stiff climb for a tired mind
  And nothing at the top; the terraces dissolved
In the clambering eye; while a voice sang on, destroying
  All heart, all hope, all Ithaca.

II

Home beyond this life? Or through it? If through, how?
Through as through glass—or through the nerves and blood?

We all are homeless sometimes, homesick sometimes,
As we all at times are godless or god-fearing—
    And what does that imply?

On scrubbed white deal two hands, red from the sink, are clenched
On the hope of an after-life; there is dirt in the cracks
Of the table and under the nails for all their scouring
And the golden walls of Jerusalem the Golden
    Have black cracks in them too.

Zion is always future. Just as Calypso's isle
Was always and too present, so out of time;
But home is seen and lived through time, the alarm clock
Rules from the kitchen shelf and the dog Argus
    Grows old and vexed with fleas.

On Sunday perhaps the alarm is stilled and the red hands
Reposed on a Sunday lap in the just-so room
Which does not exist on weekdays, where the Penates
Are no more jug nor clock but family photos
    Of a family not to the life.

Stiff collars and a harmonium. White and black. Stiff keys.
A creaking lock in gates of mother of pearl.
The street is curtained off that up and inwards
The mind may count the golden rungs, though Jacob
    Unseen limp down the street.

A stiff climb—and at the top? Will Wesley hand us a gold
Chalice of nectar—immortal and islanded life,
A home from home? But is it a window or mirror
We see that happiness in or through? Or is it
    Merely escape from the clock?

As Penelope never escaped. And, though her husband did,
He found that bliss a prison and each day
Wept as he watched the changing unchanging ocean
Beyond which lived his wife and the dog Argus
    And real people. Who lived.

III

But even so, he said, daily I hanker, daily
Ache to get back to my home, to see my day of returning

315

After those years of violent action—and these of inaction.
Always and even so. But I have no ship, no comrades,
Only my wits with nothing to grind on. Nectar, ambrosia,
Promise me nothing; the goddess no longer pleases me.
Who would be loved by a goddess for long? Hours which are golden
But unreal hours, flowers which forget to fall,
And wine too smooth, no wrinkles to match my own—
Who would be loved by a goddess who cannot appreciate
The joy of solving a problem, who never wept
For friends that she used to laugh with? I stare at the sea
Till that hard horizon rounds one great round eye
Hard as that of the Cyclops; this time I have no
Means of putting it out—and now I am really No Man
For my ears ring with a too sweet voice which never
Falters or ages. They call me crafty Odysseus;
I have used my craft on gods and nymphs and demigods
But it is time, high time, I turned it again
To the earth that bred it, a new threshing floor
Or setting up boundary stones, for even the best
Neighbours encroach—and I like to have someone to argue with
About my rights of grazing or wood-cutting; aye, it is time
I heard the bleat of my goats and smelt the dung of my cattle;
Here there is neither dung nor rights nor argument,
Only the scent of flowers and a too sweet voice which is ever
Youthful and fails to move me. Here could never be home,
No more than the sea around it. And even the sea
Is a different sea round Ithaca.

IV

They call me crafty, I robbed my brother,
Hoaxed my father, I am most practical,
Yet in my time have had my visions,
Have seen a ladder that reached the sky.
A smooth old man but when I was younger—
You noticed my limp, here, in the thigh—
I wrestled all night with God Eternal.

Which one can never do twice. And the ladder
I never saw that again either; presumably
It is there always if one could see it

And the shining messengers, busy as bees,
Go up and come down it searching for honey
In the hearts of men; they are hard to please,
Want only the best. But we know when they find it

Because we feel suddenly happy. For all that
One should not think too much about them; analysis
Cannot hit off what they want; it is better
To keep one's eyes on the earth and they
Can take their tithes when they choose, they are welcome,
But now is my home and here is my day
And my job is to father a chosen people.

A hard job but grateful. Laban exacted
Seven years of diligent bailiffry,
Then tried to cheat me; my wives, my children,
Proved jealous; followed the years of dearth
When Joseph was lost—but God had assured me
My seed should be as the dust of the earth
And Joseph and corn were found in Egypt.

Yet sometimes, even now, I have a nightmare,
Always the same, that the challenge has come again
In a stony place, in ultimate darkness,
And I feel my sinews crack in advance
And, because this time I know my opponent,
I know that this time I have no chance
Of holding my own. My own is nowhere;

And I wake in a sweat, still in the darkness
Which might be nowhere—but I am most practical,
I put out my hand to finger the darkness
And feel the nap of it, it is my own,
Enclosed by myself with walls and enclosing
My family; besides, the ache in the bone
Of my thigh confirms me that I am somewhere,

That I am home; no more a vagrant,
No more—except in flashes—a visionary,
No more a chooser, I have been chosen
To father the chosen, a full-time task—
With by-products perhaps such as shall we say honey—
Still on the whole I have little to ask
But that day should return, each day of returning.

The death of a cat

I

Since then, those months ago, these rooms miss something,
A link, a spark, and the street down there reproves
My negligence, particularly the gap
For the new block which, though the pile of timber
Is cleared on which he was laid to die, remains
A gap, a catch in the throat, a missing number.

You were away when I lost him, he had been absent
Six nights, two dead, which I had not learnt until
You returned and asked and found how he had come back
To a closed door having scoured the void of Athens
For who knows what and at length, more than unwell
Came back and less than himself, his life in tatters.

Since when I dislike that gap in the street and that obdurate
Dumb door of iron and glass and I resent
This bland blank room like a doctor's consulting room
With its too many exits, all of glass and frosted,
Through which he lurked and fizzed, a warm retort,
Found room for his bag of capers, his bubbling flasket.

For he was our puck, our miniature lar, he fluttered
Our dovecot of visiting cards, he flicked them askew,
The joker among them who made a full house. As you said,
He was a fine cat. Though how strange to have, as you said later,
Such a personal sense of loss. And looking aside
You said, but unconvincingly: What does it matter?

II

To begin with he was a beautiful object:
Blue crisp fur with a white collar,
Paws of white velvet, springs of steel,
A Pharaoh's profile, a Krishna's grace,
Tail like a questionmark at a masthead
And eyes dug out of a mine, not the dark
Clouded tarns of a dog's, but cat's eyes—
Light in a rock crystal, light distilled
Before his time and ours, before cats were tame.

To continue, he was alive and young,
A dancer, incurably male, a clown,
With his gags, his mudras, his entrechats,
His triple bends and his double takes,
Firm as a Rameses in African wonderstone,
Fluid as Krishna chasing the milkmaids,
Who hid under carpets and nibbled at olives,
Attacker of ankles, nonesuch of nonsense,
Indolent, impudent, cat catalytic.

To continue further: if not a person
More than a cipher, if not affectionate
More than indifferent, if not volitive
More than automaton, if not self-conscious
More than mere conscious, if not useful
More than a parasite, if allegorical
More than heraldic, if man-conditioned
More than a gadget, if perhaps a symbol
More than a symbol, if somewhat a proxy
More than a stand-in—was what he was!
A self-contained life, was what he must be
And is not now: more than an object.

And is not now. Spreadeagled on coverlets—
Those are the coverlets, bouncing on chairbacks—
These are the chairs, pirouetting and sidestepping,
Feinting and jabbing, breaking a picture frame—
Here is the picture, tartar and sybarite,
One minute quicksilver, next minute butterballs,
Precise as a fencer, lax as an odalisque,
And in his eyes the light from the mines
One minute flickering, steady the next,
Lulled to a glow or blown to a blaze,
But always the light that was locked in the stone
Before his time and ours; at best semi-precious
All stones of that kind yet, if not precious,
Are more than stones, beautiful objects
But more than objects. While there is light in them.

III

Canyons of angry sound, catastrophe, cataclysm,
Smells and sounds in cataracts, cat-Athens,
Not, not the Athens we know, each whisker buzzing

Like a whole Radar station, typhoons of grapeshot,
Crossfire from every roof of ultra-violet arrows
And in every gutter landmines, infra-red,
A massed barrage of too many things unknown
On too many too quick senses (cossetted senses
Of one as spoilt as Pangur Ban, Old Foss
Or My Cat Jeoffrey), all the drab and daily
Things to him deadly, all the blunt things sharp,
The paving stones a sword dance. Chanting hawkers
Whose street cries consecrate their loaves and fishes
And huge black chessmen carved out of old priests
And steatopygous boys, they all were Gogs and Magogs
With seven-league battering boots and hair-on-ending voices
Through which he had to dodge. And all the wheels
Of all the jeeps, trucks, trams, motor-bicycles, buses, sports cars,
Caught in his brain and ravelled out his being
To one high horrible twang of breaking catgut,
A swastika of lightning. Such was Athens
To this one indoors cat, searching for what
He could not grasp through what he could not bear,
Dragged to and fro by unseen breakers, broken
At last by something sudden; then dragged back
By his own obstinate instinct, a long dark thread
Like Ariadne's ball of wool in the labyrinth
Not now what he had played with as a kitten
But spun from his own catsoul, which he followed
Now that the minotaur of machines and men
Had gored him, followed it slowly, slowly, until
It snapped a few yards short of a closed door,
Of home, and he lay on his side like a fish on the pavement
While the ball of wool rolled back and down the hill,
His purpose gone, only his pain remaining
Which, even if purpose is too human a word,
Was not too human a pain for a dying cat.

IV

Out of proportion? Why, almost certainly.
You and I, darling, knew no better
Than to feel worse for it. As one feels worse
When a tree is cut down, an ear-ring lost,
A week-end ended, a child at nurse
Weaned. Which are also out of proportion.

Sentimentality? Yes, it is possible;
You and I, darling, are not above knowing
The tears of the semi-, less precious things,
A pathetic fallacy perhaps, as the man
Who gave his marble victory wings
Was the dupe—who knows—of sentimentality,

Not really classic. The Greek Anthology
Laments its pets (like you and me, darling),
Even its grasshoppers; dead dogs bark
On the roads of Hades where poets hung
Their tiny lanterns to ease the dark.
Those poets were late though. Not really classical.

Yet more than an object? Why, most certainly.
You and I, darling, know that sonatas
Are more than sound and that green grass
Is more than grass or green, which is why
Each of our moments as they pass
Is of some moment; more than an object.

So this is an epitaph, not for calamitous
Loss but for loss; this was a person
In a small way who had touched our lives
With a whisk of delight, like a snatch of a tune
From which one whole day's mood derives.
For you and me, darling, this is an epitaph.

Flowers in the interval

I

With you, pray not without you, trapped on the edge of the world
In the wind that troubles the galaxies, you my galactic
Marvel of ivoried warmth, with your warm hair curled
Over the cool of your forehead and your ambivalent
Tigercat eyes, which are amber and javelins, how,
How, my heart, did I dare to contrive this heartfelt
Artifice? Nonetheless, please take it now.

Without you once, in the wilderness, pondering years and years,
I heard thin strings in the air, came round a corner
On a quickset hedge of fiddlebows and my ears

Tingled because I was thinking of someone unknown to me
Who had pricked her finger and slept while the long nights grew
Into a tangle of quivering hands and gracenotes
Through which I plunged and found her—and she was you.

You, not anyone else; and your castle still stands there
But the thorns have blossomed, a young sun shines on the trumpets
And now there are rights of way since you have now made rare
Things common and very clean, a kind sun shines on the cabbage-plot
While a gay wind plays on the wheat, the plains are pearled
With dew and the willows are silver in wind—Can it possibly
Be the same wind that harries the ends of the world?

II

But to turn in on the world, you are all the places
That I have been in with you, blacked-out London,
Polperro's blue braided with gulls or Nephin
Striding beside us always on the right
While we were trudging west, you are the Tessin
Fuddled with oleanders, you are the crystal
Of the Venus Pool in Sark, you are Ménerbes
Anchored over the Midi, you are the comfort
Of Constable's mill in Suffolk, you are the miles
On miles of silence down Magilligan strand,
You are Marseilles on New Year's Eve with bottles
Parked at the crossings, you are the trolls' white limbs
Of Norway shagged with pineblack, you are the gentle
Green Stone Age forts of Dorset, and you are Greece
Armoured in Bronze Age light, you are Mycenae—
A gold mask in the darkness, you are the islands
With cyclamens and sheep bells or with the first
Flame of a single leaf on each black vine,
You are the folds of Hymettus, you are Delphi
(Eagle-colliding centre of the world)
Her ancient olives twisted into questions
Beneath the dead gymnasium, you are the air
Through which you flew to what was once Byzantium
Once Greek and once The City where un-Greek mists
Convey on belts across the Golden Horn
Cloth caps that fit poor Moslems, where Moslem domes
Rival the Holy Wisdom's, Moslem gravestones
Tilted like drunken chessmen still dare hint

At male and female forms, you are all these,
All these places. But also all the places
Where you have been without me; you are the Alps
Which crowned your early birthdays, you are Berlin
In ominous carnival, you are all the times
And places you were without me.

                                But still you,
In your own right and light; not anyone else.
For which, without or with me, I am grateful—
Without me yes, with me more yes. Because . . .

III

Because you intoxicate like all the drinks
We have drunk together from Achill Island to Athens,
Retsina or Nostrano, pops and clinks

Through snow or mist or mistral, aquavit
Or Château Neuf du Pape, from coloured inks
To the blood of bulls or sun-gods, dry or sweet,

Bitter or mild, armagnac, ouzo, stout,
Because, like each of these, you reprieve, repeat
Whether dry or sweet your newness, with or without

Water, and each one ray of you distils
A benediction and an end to doubt
Because your presence is all rays and rills;

Because your presence is baths of freesias, because
Your eyes are the gold-flecked loughs of Irish hills,
Your hands are Parvati and Millamant and what was

The earliest corn-and-fire dance is your hair,
Your stance is a caryatid's who seems to pause
Before she slips off, blandly unaware

Of the architrave on her head, because your moods
Are sun and water and because the air
Is burnished by you and the multitudes

Of humble moments answer to your voice
Like goldfish to a bell or sleeping woods
To a fresh breeze, because you make no choice

Unless you feel it first, because your laugh
Is Catherine wheels and dolphins, because Rejoice
Is etched upon your eyes, because the chaff

Of dead wit flies before you and the froth
Of false convention with it, because you are half
Night and half day, both woven in one cloth,

Because your colours are onyx and cantaloupe,
Wet seaweed, lizard, lilac, tiger-moth
And olive groves and beech-woods, because you scoop

The sun up in your hands, because your form
Is bevelled hills which neither crane nor stoop,
Because your voice is carved of jade yet warm

And always is itself an always new,
A pocket of calm air amidst a storm
And yet a ripple beneath all calms, a view

Into wide space which still is near; is you.

IV

In still grey dawn a delicate tendril
Climbs through the stillness, turns to song
And edging, dodging, through the grey,
Curling along, around, along,
Drops jasmine petals on the day
And adds one glint, one lift, to sunrise.

And so your voice. Through which forgotten
Ladies in wimple, ruff or hoop,
Bonnet or bustle, take the air
To join the shawled and kerchiefed troop
Of milkmaid, negress, vivandière,
Who sing when you sing, move as you do.

Of whom, thus launched, one rocks a firelit
Cradle beside a dying fire,
One wanders moonstruck on the fells,
One flirts and yields behind the byre.

And one, too proud to yield, repels
The taffeta phrases of her lover.

Thus Villon, Sidney, Campion, Purcell,
And all the unschooled anonymous Folk
Stand close behind you while you sing,
Restored by what their songs evoke
Through you and your interpreting,
Through you, your voice, your stance, your gesture.

So there you are, on a stage in a spotlight,
As here, on the edge of the world at home,
Making the absent present, awake
To the little voices of chalk and loam,
The lost tunes in the lonely lake
And the sunlit ghosts, receiving, giving.

Thus, when once more I round the corner,
I know your castle is also mine
And I know your dream defies the sands
Which count the minutes, I know the sign
That must let me in where your hair and hands
Are gay with the dawn, a waking beauty.

Like a walking dream. Like the first blossom,
Like a river fed from melting snow,
Like a leopardess with her cubs, like a bird
Returned from a land I did not know
Making unheard-of meanings heard
And sprinkling all my days with daylight.

And thus when the winds begin to whisper
Which lurk in the night and trouble space
I cross my fingers, grit my teeth,
And wait for the moment when your face
Appears from nowhere, as beneath
The frozen earth the bulbs burn upward.

The weathercock on the grey turret
Stirs in his sleep, the hedge of hands
Throws forth allegros in the sun
Which gilds and thwarts the dribbling sands
And green chords bind the barbican
While music tinkles from the hour-glass.

For you are there, are here, and nothing
Dare cancel that; you are my dear
With whom, pray not without, I live,
Incredibly ever-newly here
Each passing moment while you give
A timeless perfume to each moment.

XI

1953

Do I contradict myself?
Very well then I contradict myself . . . .

WALT WHITMAN

Prefatory note

In the autumn of 1938 I wrote a long occasional poem, *Autumn Journal*, hinged to that season. Its sequel, fifteen years later, though similarly hinged to the autumn of 1953 and so also by its nature occasional, is less so, I think, than its predecessor. *Autumn Sequel* contains a number of characters drawn from my personal friends. All these, for mythopoeic and other reasons, are represented under pseudonyms. Apart from allusions to the Old Masters, there are one or two to the works of my contemporaries, e.g. parody echoes of Yeats and William Empson. The last line but one of Canto XVIII is a quotation from Dylan Thomas.

Canto I

August. Render to Caesar. Speak parrot: a gimmick for Poll.
Castle your king in sand; as the dog days die,
I hate the grey void that crams the guts of the doll

And deplore each megrim and moan I scrawled on the sky
In my hand of unformed smoke those fifteen years
A-going, a-going, ago. I to I

Is not for that self and me; the long surge nears
The crumbling drawbridge and the tears of things
Will drown out his and mine and all such partial tears,

While the cracked voice calls Check, the sandfly stings,
The cage is ungilded, the Parrot is loose on the world
Clapping his trap with gay but meaningless wings.

Fifteen years—and enough. Plain or pearled,
Chequered or lacquered, I do not want them again;
Though golden curls in lockets come uncurled,

Put back no clock; clocks were made for men.
It is not time I resent, it is that the hand should stick
On a lie which the heart repeats again and again.

An autumn journal—or journey. The clocks tick
Just as they did but that was a slice of life
And there is no such thing. Our days are quick—

Quick and not dead. To lop them off with a knife
In order to preserve them seems pure fake;
Day upon day, dish upon dish, drum upon fife,

Means in itself nothing. To be or make
Means more than subtracting or adding. Rise from bed
Day after day, how do you know you wake?

You may be puppet or parrot, doll or dead.
Rhetoric? Why, no doubt. To contrive the truth
Or the dawn is the bloom and brief of days ahead,

In the teeth of ponce and newshawk, nark and sleuth,
Who deal in false documentaries. August fades,
Barbicans crumble, Caesar loses his youth,

But we shall find what we make in the falling glades
And be what we find in the evening; we shall contrive
A truth to jump the facts of the dour stockades

Garnished with heads that were never, not once, alive.
The Parrot cocks his poll but before he speaks
Let us gag him with human voices and not connive

In his perihypnotic pollosophy. Senseless beaks
May iterate what they will; remains for man
To give the lie to nostrum-peddling cliques

And tell what music, pipe what truth he can.
August fades but the voices bloom in the sere:
Thor and Krishna, Isis, Ariel, Pan,

Thundering, fluting, whispering; while Puck and Lear
Further the drive of life with voice on voice.
And those whom I have known, found strange and dear,

Gavin and Gwilym, and Aidan, Isabel, Calum, Aloys,
Devlin, Hilary, Jenny, Blundell, McQuitty, Maguire,
Stretton and Reilly and Price, Harrap and Owen and Boyce,

Egdon and Evans and Costa and Wimbush and Gorman: a choir
That never were all together; four of them now
Have left their stalls. Pan to the top of the spire

Where the weathercock sweeps them away; time will allow
Not Gavin nor Reilly nor Harrap nor Wimbush again
To be vocal or vital. A cradle swings on a bough

That had held a child who never from now till the utmost Then
Will need to be sung to sleep; that will be four
Uncalled for songs in the family trees of men.

Wimbush went last; last month he paid his score.
Stone. Stone. Stone. Stone. Stone.
He lived it and he died it—more and more,

Whether Hoptonwood or Hornton; he worked alone,
Chiselled his vision in a midland shed
Chip upon chip, undaunted and unknown,

Till this July he cast his home-made bread
On London's waters and was proud and gay
And took his pint next door, next day was dead,

Before a letter came from him to say
'I believe that pint you stood me saved my life'.
An empty mug and a cradle; already away,

The weathercock hustles him on, the winds are rife,
He vanishes through that revolving door in the sky
To no known point of the compass. Drum and fife

Triumphed through gilded arches this July
While Wimbush walked through one plain arch unseen
Leaving some dumb stone blocks for his goodbye.

And now it is August, fading what was green,
Forgetting what was death, jogging along,
Two plain, two purl, to end the Augustan scene

More sock than buskin, more cheap wine than song.
Shortly we must turn over an old leaf
To prove the year goes round while we go wrong.

Geraniums still bloom bright, no flowers for grief;
Still twice a week the Zoo keeps open late
Where flanks and shanks, that might be furs or beef

But for the grace of Man, still twitch and wait
Till the great wilds reconquer Regent's Park—
But the peaked hat stands always at the gate

And one accordion gypsifies the dark
And walls of glass between us and the apes
Reflect ourselves while shadows hoot and bark

And goats perch high on fabricated capes
And bears beneath them sleep depolarised
And night festoons them all with stars and grapes.

Those fifteen years ago when I devised
My journal within earshot of all this
(Lions, sea-lions, gibbons, unexorcised

333

Reproaches, emblems of the night's abyss)
I lay awake and listened on Primrose Hill
Indulging my own heart's paralysis,

Until they cut the trees down; Jack and Jill
Stood by to watch the grove make way for guns,
And heads rolled in the headlines, the world was ill.

And drab. Remembered in no orisons
Our poor velleities, we walked a stage
With real thunder off. The kites and duns

Forgathered on the billboards; page on page
Of jargon choked the drains; in the dark below
A gibbon whirled his clown-call at the age,

His touchstone at the pundits. Did we know
That when that came which we had said would come,
We still should be proved wrong? The black bureau

Of history where pale clerks do sum on sum
Carrying over and over, hides a door
At the end of its inmost passage, grained and glum

And marked In Exile, where stern eyes deplore
The minutes they correct and a stern pen
Proves lies are lies and politics a whore,

Yet can concede some virtue in those men
Who fight for their own chattels, burn or freeze
From pride which may be foolish, though folly again

Might have a tint of wisdom, as disease
Can foster courage; that all things are mixed
Or have two sides had taught Thucydides

How little, a precious little, in life is fixed:
On the one hand this but on the other that;
Justice must lie between and truth betwixt.

A cool head but no cynic. Like a gnat
He pricked the war-lords and the demagogues
But still could love his Athens. The black rat

Might spread bubonic plague to glut the pariah dogs
But he still loved the Pnyx, even while the blade
Of Damocles hung above it and thick fogs

Of fear and greed deluded and decayed
And made each fiery speech a fading ember.
May we at least, who watch this August fade

In zeppelin purple clouds, at least at last remember
How wise he was. The pimps appear to stand
On the right hand of God to greet September—

But, on the other hand, there is another hand.

Canto II

'On the other hand,' said Gavin—or could have said,
'This being now the month in which you were born,
You had better lump and like it; to be dead

Is really no alternative. Forlorn:
The very word come-hithered poor John Keats
But that was Fanny's fault. The Gates of Horn

Are good enough for me and the London streets,
And to hell with magic casements! Mark that seam
Which scales the rounded calf till the stocking meets

A wide expanse of thigh, a scoop of cream
Which would be tempting whipped. I have no time
For Belles Dames Sans Merci, I am on the beam

Which ends in real buttocks. The paradigm
That I have learnt consists of hooks and eyes
And buttons on the left. Reason and rhyme,

It seems to me, come back to breasts and thighs.'
So Gavin spoke, in the innocence of his lust,
Looking for troubles in a fond surmise

And doodling on his pad a buoyant bust
To more than round off Rubens; his undertone
On the other hand was drier, dust to dust,

Which I accepted. Only, had I known,
Gavin was due to meet his death by water
Far from all dust and women, sleeping alone.

Those were the days of blackout and dull slaughter;
Corvette or ark of bulrushes, each child
That could not speak was seeking Pharaoh's daughter

But Gavin's cradle sank and the dark defiled
Atlantic scrawled its flourish of cold foam
Above him, while on shore we drank our mild

And bitter, wondering when he would come home.
Until one day (I was living in Saint John's Wood
In one small cell of London's half empty comb)

His sister called and came upstairs and stood
Quietly and said quietly 'We have lost
Gavin'; a cobra spread an enormous hood

Over the window and a sudden frost
Froze all the honey left in the looted hive
While the white Dove revoked his pentecost,

Muting the tongues of fire. What was alive,
Wild, witty, randy, serious, curious, kind,
And boisterously loyal to his five

Senses and his one life, had now resigned
His quips and queries to the ocean bed
Deep out of sight and deeper into mind,

Into my mind for one. Gavin is dead
Ten years this autumn. Floods of printer's ink
Have drowned whole fleets of names since first we read

That name among the casualties; no chink
Of light between those lines, no need to keep
That cutting. Ancient history, one might think,

Runs into World War Two. A dive-bombed jeep
Is no less broken, or old, than a bronze wheel
From Agamemnon's chariot. Sleep, sleep,

336

You widows of Mycenae. The years reveal
The need for everydayness, for picking up
Such trivial threads, more durable than steel,

As Gavin himself had dropped. His poodle pup,
His period prints, the witchball on the stairs,
Were pillars of his temple. We'll take a cup

Of kindness yet with anyone who cares
Enough to remember, more than enough to forget.
The bars are open and a bright light glares

On brass and glass and bottle, the world is wet,
Gwilym has come to town, it is time to take
Our kindness, blindness, double. Yet. And yet?

This is the first of September; let us unmake
The dreary dog days and baptize the Fall,
The winds that exhilarate, the gold that drops in the lake.

Gwilym begins: with the first pint a tall
Story froths over, demons from the hills
Concacchinate in the toilet, a silver ball

Jumps up and down in his beer till laughter spills
Us out to another bar followed by frogs
And auks and porpentines and armadills.

For Gwilym is a poet; analogues
And double meanings crawl behind his ears
And his brown eyes were scooped out of the bogs,

A jester and a bard. Archaic fears
Dog him with handcuffs but this rogue's too quick,
They grab and he turns a cartwheel and disappears.

An artist needs to know some little trick,
Being always on the run. Malice and guilt,
Baton and mace and cosh and shooting stick,

Are always after him; an ugly silt
Chokes all his channels while the leering sand
Threatens what works he builds or might have built.

And worst of all is money. In the Grand
Hotel resides a spider who would like
The poet hamstrung and his art trepanned;

Gwilym, who knows this, stands alert to strike
All eight legs off and drown that spider's bag
In wells of glass or pewter, where blind pike

In the dark dregs may gulp it. Let money brag,
The poet will not be bought, he has powerful friends
Who are his own inventions—the one-eyed hag

Whose one is an evil eye, the maiden goddess who sends
Her silver javelin straight, the Knave of Fools
Who cocks his snook and blows his dividends,

The soldier with the nosebag who breaks the rules
Wide open, the mountain-moving oaf, the cook
Whose pies are singing birds, whose soups are schools

Of gambolling porpoises, the endearing crook
Who says his name is Noman, the talking fox,
The ropetrick man, the baldhead with the book

That is all question marks, the Jack-in-the-Box,
The Will o' the Wisp, the mermaid, the Man in the Moon,
And old Nobodaddy himself, high god of Paradox.

Such are our friends; we need them late and soon
To fight our false friends for us, we feel no shame
To sham dead while they do it; trombone, bassoon,

Ram's horn and ocarina pour out flame
To force the walls of Jericho and crown
One local conflagration with a name.

And so to-day, with Gwilym come to town
Like Saturn swathed in ring on ring of smoke,
The walls of Albany Street came tumbling down

With enough cries of Time to point the joke
While enough ash to fill a funeral urn
Dropped from his cigarette; a dwarfish folk

Crept out from under the counter and took their turn
Mumbling and gesturing their pagan lore
Till dolmens rose about us and a quern

Ground out red herrings and mustard sauce galore
Which flowed all over the borough of Marylebone
To prove that two and two do not make four.

That was one night; already Gwilym is gone
Carmarthenwards; September shakes her mat
Of hair like a wet dog whose tail replies Anon,

Anon, sir, while his ears go rat-tat-tat;
Throw him a stick, at once he's back in the pond
But may emerge the Devil for all that.

Mephisto loves the Fall, his clerks abscond
With all the green of nature and the green
Thoughts of young men who would stay young beyond

All common sense. The Devil is too mean
Not to exact his interest; falling leaves,
And each a last reminder of his spleen

Whose other name is Time. The young man grieves
To receive the account in red—red on the tree
Or on the evening sky. Under the eaves

Each nest hangs empty and the querulous bee
Prints her last testament in wax before
Jack Frost achieves his delicate filigree,

While, as Keats put it, shells and cells are more
O'er-brimmed and plumped, close wrought and overwrought,
But dumped in jars and baskets at that door

Which passes nothing that has not been bought,
Windfall or gift being counted here a crime.
Here in the Customs Office of Maiden-thought

Stands one dark officer. Whose name is Time.

Canto III

To work—To Beaconsfield. A suburban train
Squeezes me through the black wood of Saint John
By intestinal tunnels like a pain

That London would get rid of, on and on
Past West Hampstead where the backs are ill
With tired chrysanthemums and woebegone

Lace curtains, past the antennae of Wembley Hill
And Sudbury Hill, drab realms of television,
Till the blue roofs turn red and the houses spill

And become semi-detached, a smug decision;
Past heaps of coke and cosiness and blight
And lines of washing (subject for derision

To those who are all front), past poplars white
With wind, past hollyhocks that lurch and toss,
South Ruislip and West Ruislip, homes in flight

Eastward each weekday morning, the garden's loss
Being the Market's gain; whereas my train goes west
Crossing the stockbrokers at Gerrard's Cross

And passing one more golf course, shaved and dressed
With yellow flags but empty; on and on
Until we stop beneath Mount Everest.

We stop—and start. All Beaconsfield is gone,
Each slick red wall and roof, each dapper row
Of pompons and each deft automaton

Trimming the lawns, all are submerged below
The icefall tumbling from the Western Cwm
Above which deserts of unsounded snow

Brood, above which again one ominous plume
Flies from the crest of what was Peak Fifteen
Which even now knows fifteen brands of doom,

Twenty-nine thousand and two feet high, a clean
Rebuttal of the verities of Bucks
Where a projector clamps it on a screen

And I write words about it; gaps and rucks
Are smoothed away, the silences of ice
And solitudes of height washed out in flux,

A weir of whirling celluloid. What price
Should we demand for turning what was rare
Into a cheap couvade or proxy paradise,

Just one more travelogue to make the groundlings stare?
Groundlings will never see why Mallory answered why
Men should climb Everest: because it is there.

Which for so much would be the apt reply:
Why do we back a horse or fall in love,
Learn our calculus, play our trout, or die?

Are there? . . . . Where? . . . . Here? Beyond? Above?
Behind? Below? Between? The fact is this:
Tempted and tempter being hand in glove,

The target that we almost hoped to miss
Is what we hit and what we hate we pardon
And only kill what we have failed to kiss.

Once upon a time there was a garden
And once within that garden stood a tree
Whose fruit must ripen as its bark must harden

To bear the carved initials of you and me;
Cradle on cradle swings upon its boughs,
Coffin on coffin skulks beneath its lee.

Cicadas, above and hidden, chant or drowse,
A woodpecker taps. This has happened before. Beware,
The time returns to make, and to break, vows;

A glimpse of golden breasts, a mat of hair
Thrown back from the eyes; a naked arm in a ray
Of sunlight plucks an apple. Because it is there.

The woodpecker, like a typist, taps away
Relentlessly; the record must be kept
Though the same larceny happen day by day,

The original and the final sin. Inept
Professors may reduce it to a case
And prove that Eve who brooded, burned and wept,

Was merely maladjusted; Queen and Ace
Survive, whoever deals, as Ace and Queen.
No matter; time returns to break the Lhotse Face

In coldest Bucks. Ice pinnacle and ravine
Dare us to turn their terrors to a stunt
And let the millions see what some few dozen have seen.

Stopwatch and gum and scissors bear the brunt
But in the prop room there are crampons too
And windproofs and an ice axe; when you hunt

On ice you had better do what ice-men do;
The abominable snow queen keeps her code,
Thinks of herself and never at all of you,

So cut your steps with caution, a slow road
Is better than a quick crevasse; our aim
Is popularity, not palinode.

And careful with those rushes. Who can blame
The middleman for leaving some things out?
What's in a peak that is not in a name?

Middlemen all, we labour like devout
Lay brethren whom our Rule allows to talk,
Not knowing what the silence is about.

The reels are stowed away, a stump of chalk
Squeaks on a board and I am again despatched
Homewards by train while hooded Sherpas walk

Home to Tibet by sky, a sky much scratched
And patched with scree and glacier; on the ground
The small dolls' houses still are semi-detached

But about to detach completely; chasms abound
Under each plot and path; commuters hurrying back
Ought to be roped together—could a fit rope be found.

I leave them to their fate, enter again the black
Tunnel of gentle or was it headless John,
Suffering a little from my bivouac

At such high altitudes, my breath is gone,
My wits are going; I shall cure all this
Down there at my base camp in Marylebone.

The mild September evening blows a kiss
In ripples over the lake, a sky of peach
Explodes its pulp—a metamorphosis

That leaves a stone. And stony-grey trees reach
Down to the water where like landing craft
Low-draughted ducks whiten their wakes as each

Duck's whim directs but never land, a daft
Moorhen crosses their bows, its clockwork head
Going forward, backward, forward, while abaft

Over the silver shimmer and sombre lead
Sail two great swans, ghost-white, and between them two
Birds trying to be ghosts, still brown, still birds instead.

The whistles begin: from Clarence Gate to the Zoo
The lights go up on the road and down in the lake,
The deckchairs empty and the shades accrue,

The lovers untwine and rise, intertwine again and take
Their long abstracted exit, terriers bark
Hustled away on their leads while, like a sudden ache,

A harsh voice cries All Out—all out of Regent's Park,
Of Everest, of Eden—casts a doubt
If we were ever in. The whole massif is dark,

The one tree silent, one day (to-day) ruled out, all out.

Canto IV

To work. To my own office, my own job,
Not matching pictures but inventing sound,
Precalculating microphone and knob

In homage to the human voice. To found
A castle on the air requires a mint
Of golden intonations and a mound

Of typescript in the trays. What was in print
Must take on breath and what was thought be said.
In the end there was the Word, at first a glint,

Then an illumination overhead
Where the high towers are lit. Such was our aim
But aims too often languish and instead

We hack and hack. What ought to soar and flame
Shies at its take-off, all our kites collapse,
Our spirit leaks away, our notes are tame,

The castle is on the carpet, aisle and apse
Are shrunk to this small office where large files
Reproach me and a typewriter taps and taps.

Shorthand and a new ribbon; miles on miles
Of carbon copies rippling through the waste
Of office hours that no red light beguiles;

The Word takes shape elsewhere and carapaced
Administrators crouch on constant guard
To save it for good business and good taste.

A seven-figure audience makes things hard
Because they want things easy; as Harrap said
Suggesting I might make an air-borne bard

(Who spoke in parentheses and now is dead),
'On the one hand—as a matter of fact I should
Say on the first hand—there is daily bread,

At least I assume there is, to be made good
If good is the right expression; on the other
Or one of the other hands there is much dead wood

On the air in a manner of speaking which tends to smother
What spark you start with; nevertheless although
Frustration is endemic (take my brother,

He simply thinks me mad to bother so
With people by the million) nevertheless
Our work is aimed at one at a time, you know,

And by and large and at an approximate guess
If poets must live (perhaps I am wrong to think
They must but if they must) they might find this mess

No more a mess than wasting wits and ink
On scratching each other's backs or possibly eyes
Out or half out (no wonder they take to drink;

We might have one by the way) but it could arise
They found it in fact less messy; after all
Homer liked words aloud.' Harrap's blue eyes

Twinkled between the brackets, a silver ball
Darted about the pin-table as he leant
Over the bar. Remembering that Saul

Was also among the prophets and that the rent
Had to be paid and that what Harrap half
Or three and a half times said, he singly meant,

And that some grain is better than no chaff
And that there was a war on, I agreed
To join this new crusade; the Golden Calf

Mooed once and Pegasus whinnied. 'There will be need
For the moment of course,' said Harrap, 'for much work
Of a purely ephemeral kind; you will have to feed

The tall transmitters with hot news—Dunkirk,
Tobruk or Singapore, you will have to set
Traps for your neutral listeners, Yank or Turk,

While your blacked-out compatriots must be met
Half way—half reprimanded and half flattered,
Cajoled to half remember and half forget;

For that is propaganda. Bored and battered
And sleeping in long tubes like suspect germs
They must be told that what they once thought mattered

Still matters. It is not much; but Goebbels' terms
Of reference are worse. The time is ripe
For lame dogs jumping stiles and turning worms.'

Harrap ended; Herriot filled his pipe
(Who was going to be my boss) and Devlin, who
Was going to be my colleague, took his swipe

At both their dignities, the evening grew
Significant and inconsequent. Content
To find there was ephemeral work to do,

Ephemeral work I did. The skies were rent
And I took notes; delicate whippets of fire
Hurdled the streets, the cockney firmament

Ran with flamingoes' blood and Dido's pyre
Burnt high and wide and randy over the Thames
While a mixed metaphor of high-tension wire

Capsized, still clutching heaven by the hems
And ripping off a star. Devlin and I
Fished in this troubled air, our stratagems

Landed some strange old boots and other curious fry;
Thus in a concrete tank of formaldehyde
Beneath one bombed museum I cast a fly

And up there rose to take it, side by side
Bobbing and churning in the purple wave,
His stomach stripped for the scalpel, London's pride

Of late, the giant panda, and with grave
Eyes neatly closed and small wrists neatly crossed
The one exhibit the rescue squad could save

Of Hunter's own, who with such care and cost
Began this whole collection, an unborn
But eighteenth-century baby, groomed and glossed

Like a small soapstone Buddha, his clouts unworn
But hooded in half his cowl. I threw him back
In his tank; he seemed too odd a fish to adorn

A twentieth-century war. We changed our tack
And jinked through gutted shop and staring church
Prospecting for more relevant bric-à-brac,

Copy and yet more copy. Such research
Was much preformulated, yet we found
Some facts that left our blueprints in the lurch,

Some lines not broad enough nor numbers round
Enough to be scored on the slate or paid in the lump;
Maybe our formulae were not so sound,

Our big slick words due for the rubbish dump,
Maybe ideals were less than men; maybe
The pen was weaker than the stirrup pump.

Devlin and I continued; what we see
Is sometimes more than what we think we feel.
Our sights unfelt ourselves. In some degree

What mind has passed sheer stocks and stones repeal,
And both self-pity and self-conceit give way
To a pride that sprouts from stocks or stones or steel.

Thus humbled and exalted day by day
We scratched among the debris. The war flowed by
In short or medium waves with a disarray

Of initials, M.I.5, O.W.I.,
Of names, Metaxas or Mihailovitch,
Of doubts and queries, If and But and Why,

Provided and Supposing, Where and Which,
And most especially When: oh when would this
Thing start or that thing stop? We were always rich

In speculation, poor in synthesis,
But at last the whole thing stopped, the war was over,
And each prognostication of blight or bliss

Immediately out of date, the cliffs of Dover
Once more mere cliffs. As usual, Devlin sang
Folksongs, the Farmer's Boy and the Bold Drover

And the Foggy Dew, but they had lost their tang
Not being heard in danger, the sunset-tinted
Balloons were down, firemen's and airmen's slang

Like the Four Freedoms and other newly minted
Phrases would soon be obsolete and the wire
Stripped from the bathing beach and the blueprints unprinted

And democracy undressed. 'If you so desire,'
My employers said, 'this office will now return
To a peacetime footing where we might require

Your further service'. I could not discern
Much choice; it might in fact be better to give
Such service, better to bury than to burn.

I stayed. On my peacetime feet. There was little alternative.

Canto V

Hence these arrears, this filing cabinet crammed
With ancient history, scripts that blessed the Greek,
Polish or Czech Resistance, scripts that damned

The totalitarian state; we no longer speak
So confidently, those discs have been destroyed
Though the same actors' voices week by week

Still entertain the public with unalloyed
Accents, their owners as of old exalted
By a good notice, as of old annoyed

By the slightest fluff. Whatever else has halted,
Actors' careers go on and I sometimes think
That I am an actor too, that the Muse has defaulted

And left me an apparatus, rivet and link,
With nothing to link or rivet, and I lament
The maker I might have been; in half a wink

The eye can be put out. The hours I have spent
Nagged by those two black telephones on my desk
And signing my own name in dumb consent

To something or other or nothing seem burlesque
Beside the hours they could have been, the hours
Greek, Gothic, Roman, Norman, Romanesque,

Byzantine or Baroque, domes, spires or towers
But original work and timeless. Whereas I find
That timeless means the time one office hour devours,

A fact to which we might even feel resigned
Were we not spared the saving grace to take
Our mind off such mere time and time off from our mind

In idleness or image. We still can shake
The circulars out of our hair and dive clean through
These wells of ink to surface in a lake

Two hundred miles away, two hundred fathoms blue.
Which is exactly what, tipping the scales
Out of the window, I am about to do,

Leaving Buck Devlin to his Milesian tales,
Boss Herriot to his peace pipe and his port,
While for nine days I seek my own pipe dreams in Wales.

A nine days' wondering. A great black fort
Among pre-Christian mountains hides a girl
Whose footsteps bloom with clover, to consort

With whom is death unless a man can curl
In a ball like a hedgehog, swell to the sky like a tree,
Slip through the fingers like water, blithely twirl

Like the spindle of the Fates, an impossible He,
Fit lover for the Impossible who waits
Till he shall lightly stride the Irish Sea

And lightly glide between her granite gates
Having fulfilled his errand, and lightly place
Upon her granite table among the cates

And drinking horns in homage to her grace
And small prepayment for her love his own
Head on a charger. Though the years efface

Her memory and his and not one stone
Be left upon another, yet she still
Will wait for him, in these high mists, alone,

While still the clover blooms beneath her uncastled hill
And we drive past it dipping towards a bay
Into which Celtic myth and Roman leadmine spill

Their diverse dreams and losses. Across the way
But a long way there floats a different land
Where never a Roman came and to this day

The crooked is not made straight; as I well understand
Being born there. So here seems half way home,
One half of me approved and one half contraband;

But grass is no less green here or the dome
Of sky less trampled over by cavalcades
Of spluttering white-maned stallions free to roam

Our memories and our future. The wind braids
Long strands of brine together; tags of gorse
Assert their blazing truth as the bracken fades

And empty seats along the long sea front endorse
The turning of the year; my birthday has gone by
In a matter of autumn hours, a matter of course.

Thirty-two years ago the same Welsh sky
And sea in this same month beguiled a boy
Who, looking back on it, I note was I—

More or less I. Perhaps more: the years destroy
The courage of our ignorance. Perhaps less:
The tree of knowledge stands the test of joy

And evil strops our wits. It is no man's guess
If Eden would be tolerable; those small
Footprints in yellow sands of gentleness

Are long since washed clean out; the castles fall,
The sea once blue and green turns white and black
And shows its fangs and chews and spews its gall

While, capped and belled with surf, the secret Jack
Of Wrecks comes bladdering up the slithering shingle
To slap the dunes in the face with a wand of wrack

And crack his quips and set his bells ajingle
In a dance of sand and salt, and as he speaks
Our flesh goes gooseflesh and our earlobes tingle

Because he speaks of us; his long hair leaks
Into our minds and his great web-feet plash
Over our graves, making our bones antiques,

Our names as lost as flotsam. It would be rash
To charge this mer-clown with contempt of court
Seeing what Court employs him. Through the gash

And crumble of his mouth his words make sport
Of all that sinks or drowns, to each complaint
He blows his conch and flings a salt retort:

'You do not want to drown? It makes you faint?
Lose breath? Lose heart? Lose life? But, my good man—
For man you are, whether hero, sage or saint—

Such things were made to be lost. Live as you can
On land, your body is water, the earth you tread
Condemned to end in the puddle where it began,

Your mother's childbed was the ocean bed,
Your hands are unravelled flippers. What you wish
Is not what you think you wish but to be dead,

To be dissolved.' A shoal of jellyfish
Shimmered through Price's drawingroom as he spoke
And shivered into nothing. One great swish

351

Of seaweed, and a cruel comber broke
About the table legs in marbled scum,
And polypods and squids and deep sea folk

Burst in with longshore fife and deep-sea drum
And pennons and scarves of spindrift, agog to see
Their long suit proven and their kingdom come;

Conger and shark and blundering manatee
Fused all the lights in one last cataclysm
And turned us indoors out. A filigree

Of froth for just one moment made a prism
Before the darkness closed. It closed and all
The world was madness, panic, paroxysm . . .

And then it opened again. First a small
Quivering in the loins, and then a click
Brought Price's four walls back and on each wall

The lights were bright, the room as usual spick
And span, the trickster and his waves withdrawn
Though his dark waves and he hold more than one more trick.

But that can wait. Enclosed by trees and lawn
These walls enclose a meanwhile. Meanwhile we
Are here, not There; if we have lost a pawn

We have kept our queen, this is still land, not sea,
Still life, not death; the ceilings shake and laugh
With dogs' and children's feet; having lost the key

We have not locked the door, having lost both scrip and staff
We have kept our pilgrims' legs; though half the meaning fails
We still can double the surviving half

And put some flesh upon it. This is Wales,
A matter of flesh and rock. This is a room
Of living people. Nothing perhaps avails

Against the sea like rock, like doomed men against doom.

Canto VI

Everydayness is good; particular-dayness
Is better, a holiday thrives on single days.
Thus Wales with her moodiness, madness, shrewdness, lewdness,
    feyness,

Daily demands a different colour of praise;
And one day's levitation of saffron light
The next is a stolid field, a strip of baize.

So one day skulks indoors, a troglodyte
In a firelit cave equipped with drinks and books,
And one day catches mackerel, a thousand white

Excitements flapping on a thousand hooks,
And one day combs its hair with the west wind
And takes its pinch and sneezes gulls and rooks;

And all these days are wilful, not to be pinned
Down to a definite answer—What they appear
To resolve, they instantaneously rescind

By simply disappearing. The sly weir
Of sunset drags them down to merge together
Their separate bubbles, swamp the near and dear

With these nine rainbow days. A change of weather
Comes with our change of place, equinoctial gales
Chivvy our homeward train through backward heather

And rusting bracken; sleep with weighted scales
Cuts off our sight while unseen telegraph
Poles pursue their countermarch to Wales

With humming wires to which each joke or epitaph,
Bet, love or business, come as equal grist
All equally being words, whether grain or chaff,

And all those words flow westward into mist
While we move east to London, only to find
The wind has got there first shaking his fist

White to the knuckles over that bruised and blind
Great Wen, hustling its daytime out of sight,
Its tuliptime and playtime out of mind.

Already the Park is scribbled across with white
Goalposts and lines, winter's too simple script,
While empty deckchairs cast a cold grey blight

Over the cold grey lake. Where August visitors dipped
Their own amused reflections, late September
Ploughs up the mirror, has the dahlias whipped,

With a cold sneer anticipates November
And orders early nights, while sucking out
The curtains from our windows; we remember

Too well this chill and challenge; beak and snout
Tap at the panes and snuff beneath the floor
While in our dreams a garish roundabout

Grinds round with empty saddles, a battledore
Strikes at a broken-feathered shuttlecock
And misses, as we have struck and missed before.

Yes; we are back. Farewell ancestral rock,
We are back on London clay, promptly tomorrow
We must bow down to telephone and clock

And the small clayfoot gods from whom we borrow
Such small sums at such interest. A pound of flesh
To whom is neither flesh nor joy nor sorrow

But merely a pound in weight; their worldwide mesh
Lets no fish through, however small, but when
You try their fish shops, you find nothing fresh—

Or rather very little. Just now and then
Our lives elude their apathy and our work
Tastes like the work not of machines but men.

Which is our one encouragement. Through the murk
And mangle of modernity we know
There gleams one duty which we must not shirk,

One light we must keep lit. It may hardly show
Through the horrescent headlights of the press
And two world wars with their sick afterglow

And the auto-da-fé of nations; yet no less
It is and must be there. What it can give
To us or we to it we can only guess

But still must act upon that guess to live.
To burn the fingers keeping warm the heart
Is every man's own risk; and own prerogative.

So back into the streets; to make a start
Somewhere and once again, cross on the amber
Thrusting the dustman's truck and hangman's cart

And Boadicea's chariot off the camber,
Dodging the open drain where embryos leer
And the tall lamp-posts up which corpses clamber,

And churning through the tickertape that fear
And greed and lust have vomited axle-deep.
What is the news? Big business and small beer,

Meat and eggs expensive, life still cheap,
Divorce and juvenile crime, while peace on earth
Is muttered away by statesmen in their sleep.

In fact the usual. Birth but no rebirth,
Deaths that we cannot mourn and loveless love affairs,
One waste of traffic jams, one jam of dearth.

Earthquake or flood or napalm bomb: who cares?
The Parrot encores, the Doll has nothing to lose
Stuffing itself with nothing, the moving stairs

Move up and down crowded with empty shoes
All stepping into each other. The man in the street,
Whoever he is, assaults or sues or woos

Some shrinking shadow while the clocks repeat
Each other all over London, hand and dial,
Yet the one grace remains, we still can meet

Men's hands and faces also. Though denial
May please the Parrot and the Petrine cock,
Yet some still tell the truth in an hour of trial,

Say Yes instead of No. You need only knock,
There still are doors to open; somewhere hidden
Beneath our clay there lies our basic rock.

And many doors. Some may be woodworm-ridden,
Some with a whining hinge and sour with rust,
But still can answer if correctly bidden

By the simple magic word. As if a gust
Of spring blew through them they will bathe your head
In scent and light to banish doubt and dust

And bring to life what never had been dead.
Thus fifteen years ago I already knew
Several such doors and had not left unsaid

My Open Sesame and not a few
Interiors where the light was bright and heady
Had swung with a clash of cymbals into view;

Already I knew Owen, whose hair already
Was white, to whom the seasons give free choice
Of birds and butterflies, whose smile and stride were steady

And bound for Maiden Castle; and there was Boyce
Twinkling Greek wisdom in his potting shed,
And Calum with surf and heather in his voice,

And Gavin, who now is dead, and Wimbush, dead,
And Hilary with green fingers for works of art,
And Esther who stuck her black hair full of red

Roses and ran away, and Stretton who stood apart
Benignly silent, Aloys benignly bald,
And driving a spotted pig in a gimcrack cart

Egdon, the bad third son, the conjurer, the skald;
And there was Jenny too whose temper burst
In squibs and rockets and left her friends appalled

But left the night lit up. These were among my first
Welcomes; as yet I had not met Maguire
Whose Irish stories matched his Irish thirst,

Or Gwilym and Gorman, poets whose words inspire
Their vision, or Evans or Aidan or McQuitty,
Or Isabel in her turret of ice and fire,

Or Devlin the double bluffer or bluffly witty
And blandly bulking Herriot who could swallow
Every jack sprat and oyster in this city,

Or his friend Harrap (dead) whose words were hard to follow
But not his values, or Costa the painter, more
Quiet than other Greeks, who finding Paris hollow

Wedded Byzantium to his native shore
With a signet ring and with paints that emulate
Mosaic. None of these had I known before

My autumn journey ended in 'Thirty-Eight;
Nor had I known, above and apart from all,
Her for whom all my years were warned to wait,

Without whom spring would be empty, the Fall merely a fall.

Canto VII

A cloud of witnesses. To whom? To what?
To the small fire that never leaves the sky.
To the great fire that boils the daily pot.

To all the things we are not remembered by,
Which we remember and bless. To all the things
That will not even notice when we die,

Yet lend the passing moment words and wings.
The pigeons are ringed and ready; let them go—
Someone, not they, will need and read those rings

That clasp their coral legs, someone will know
Just possibly who sent them. Gavin could—
Sometimes, not always—or Gorman or Stretton, though

Sometimes, not always, they misunderstood;
Such thin and crumpled messages require
Deciphering, even when the light is good.

Still, let the pigeons go. Let needling spire
And reeking smokestack point and prick their flight
Dead straight and straight alive from shire to shire

To reach, with middling luck, their goal by night;
And we must wait to catch them when they land
And give them corn and water to requite

Their blithe annunciation (Mary's hand
Made half a move to bless, though unaware
What she was blessing; round its neck a band

Of colour was a covenant, and the air
Redeemed with rainbow; after the long storm
The ark was about to land, the weather was set fair).

How many miles to Christmas? On this warm
September morning need the Three Kings start?
There needs no time to which they must conform,

Only a star that sprouts in each man's heart,
One cannot spot it in the September sun,
It moves unseen, unknown, aloof, alive, apart,

Yet intimate. All other colours run,
All other guides abscond; its countless rays,
Could we but count them, would add up to One.

Then clutch that thread of light and seize the days
Opening; which, opening, will not let you out
But lead you in, to the blind heart of the maze

Where your antagonist waits, unknown, though all about
Him stand your too well known and too triumphant foes,
Each horned and crooked greed and spite and doubt

With small red virulent eyes which presuppose
Eternal malice; but behind them all
Stands the eternal bride like a half-opened rose

In a hedge of spears and horrors. Thus the ball
Of light has brought you in and you have brought
It back to her who gave it outside the wall

And now you find her, like a buried thought,
At this one inmost point where fights are always lost
Or drawn, yet serve their end simply by being fought.

Which Gavin knew, before the torpedo crossed
His path, and Maguire in Burma knew it too,
And Boyce, emending a corrupt and glossed

Text of Plotinus, knows it. Much ado,
Cynics may say, about nothing. But is it not
Nothing Itself from which all cynics grew,

Being always there to dog our steps and rot
Our guts and wits and soul? Give It its way,
We could not even plant the bergamot

Or call a spade a spade or make one day a day.
Thus Boyce, both classical scholar and gardener,
Alike in shelves and plots can plant a Yea

Against that obstinate No; there comes a stir
Alike among Greek roots and roots of flowers
When Boyce bends over them. Each blight and blur

And slur and slug and sheer hiatus cowers,
And garbled soil and pest-infested page
Become themselves, thanks to his cleansing powers,

While the great No-God winces. This is the age
He has made his own by making nothing in it
Appear worth while; we can throw down our gage

Regardless, this very minute, and every minute,
And fight him to the death, without expecting
That He will lose that fight. And yet He need not win it

Provided Boyce goes on manuring and correcting,
Provided Calum saves his Gaelic line in song,
Provided when the electors are electing

Devlin keeps interjecting jokes to prove them wrong,
Provided Owen still finds pleasure in a wren,
Provided Egdon gives to Snark and Dong

His kind attention still, provided when
The seas run high McQuitty still sets sail,
Provided Costa finds Byzantium again,

And Gwilym and Gorman the Unholy Grail
Of poetry, and Isabel a view
Of the dark side of the moon, and Maguire a hail-

Fellow-well-met-againship, and Stretton a cue
For speech and Evans for silence, and provided
They all keep finding—and making—something new

And rehabilitating the derided
And breaking out of the vacuum, breaking in
To heavens many-coloured and many-sided.

Then, given luck, the Antagonist need not win
And the Parrot will be struck dumb and we be quit,
Though only for the time being, of cosmic sin,

The time being what we make it. Bit by bit,
Brick by brick and tock by tick we build
Our victory over the clock; our Obiit

Cannot disprove our skill, if we were skilled,
Our lives if we ever lived. On a grave as wide
As the world there is no need to carve or gild

An epitaph; for neither time nor tide
Invalidates the lives and deaths of those
Who turned their cosmic guilt to cosmic pride.

So Fanfare for the Makers: who compose
A book of words or deeds who runs may write
As many do who run, as a family grows

At times like sunflowers turning towards the light,
As sometimes in the blackout and the raids
One joke composed an island in the night,

As sometimes one man's kindliness pervades
A room or house or village, as sometimes
Merely to tighten screws or sharpen blades

Can catch a meaning, as to hear the chimes
At midnight means to share them, as one man
In old age plants an avenue of limes

And before they bloom can smell them, before they span
The road can walk beneath the perfected arch,
The merest greenprint when the lives began

Of those who walk there with him, as in default
Of coffee men grind acorns, as in despite
Of all assaults conscripts counterassault,

As mothers sit up late night after night
Moulding a life, as miners day by day
Descend blind shafts, as a boy may flaunt his kite

In an empty nonchalant sky, as anglers play
Their fish, as workers work and can take pride
In spending sweat before they draw their pay,

As horsemen fashion horses while they ride,
As climbers climb a peak because it is there,
As life can be confirmed even in suicide:

To make is such. Let us make. And set the weather fair.

Canto VIII

Fair; not to say radiant. The Twentyfifth of September
Nineteen Hundred and Fiftythree begins in haze.
But clears to blue, though no one will remember

This undistinguished Friday; more pompous days
Will jockey it out of the straight. Its lack of pomp
Could neither parallel nor paraphrase

Those great occasions which subsume and swamp
Our wills and our ideals; this is merely
A day when strollers stroll and children romp

361

With a little extra enjoyment, when the clearly
Defined keeps clear but soft, when brick and stone
Are warmer and the blights of London nearly

Redeemed, her skies as yet not overblown,
Her river, though brown and crumpled, with a bright
Polish; the one small tug that plods upstream alone

Trails a long strand of smoke which, black as night,
Seems softer than fine wool. Millbank is debonair.
I gather the wool in my hand and turn to the right

Unravelling a gallery and there
Find that inside these pictures too the weather
Has stored its sunshine and remains set fair.

This master lived to be old but velvet and ostrich feather
And breast and thigh still pleased him and he could blend
The sensual and the serene, thick clod, gay light, together;

With the brush strapped to his wrist could still transcend
The pains and limits of his age and make
The tiny world he knew world without end.

Pagan? Materialistic? Crimson lake
Is more than matter, bilberries and cream
Can be a prayer or paean, nothing is too opaque

For paint to illuminate. When painters changed their theme
From myth to bistro, something mythical
Still dogged their hands like an abandoned dream

That dares come back in daylight; rational
Behaviour may ignore the cloven hoof
But hoofprints in the heart remain indelible.

Where science, ethics and politics stand aloof
The arts eat meat and paddle around in dung,
They tear off women's knickers and raise the roof

With thump and rump and kickshaw, they blow the bung
From the cask and the corpse from the casket, they mount the
    ladder
Of Jacob and toss it behind them rung by rung.

And the arts are unpredictable, like an adder
They sting you in the heel, like a drunken ape
They daub your belly and brow with woad and madder

And chop your logic by half and change your shape
And, when you might prefer a string quartet,
They give you a drum and muffle it in crape.

Minx or mother, old witch, young coquette,
And often as not a nun, the Muse will never
Conform to type, she uses a finer net

Than the fishing laws allow, she is not clever
So much as cunning, she often walks alone,
Sleep means as much to her as high endeavour,

And she can stare for hours at a polished stone
And see all heaven in the grain of a table;
At times she is monolingual, monotone,

At others mistress of the Tower of Babel;
She prefers the halt and the blind, the fanatical ones
And the simple-minded to the merely able,

She favours dying kings and setting suns
But also the egg that hatches, the lips that kiss,
She loves the drone of bees and the thud of heavy guns,

She will pirouette on a wire over the last abyss,
Is equally prone to cast the truth in your teeth
And slip it aside in a gabbled parenthesis.

Nor is she the best of employers; it being beneath
Her pride to pay on the day or sometimes at all,
She can pay a thousandfold with a funeral wreath.

Anyhow it is employment, stand or fall,
And all I am fit for now, which is saying little
But claiming almost everything; life may pall,

She can restore its savour; it may be brittle,
She can prevent it breaking; it may be blind,
She can touch and cure its eyes with clay and spittle.

So to the galleries: to escape mankind
By rediscovering it. As in the case
Of Devlin once who, scanning a deeply lined

Self-portrait hung in its usual silent place,
Said 'Think how many thousand pots of beer
And tots of schnapps have gone to make that face.'

The face of Rembrandt. One quick change of gear
And we were in reverse; as Devlin spoke,
The usual silence splintered on the ear,

The sober gallery filled with oaths and smoke,
The dark brown canvas filled and sailed away
To the low and rowdy countries of the Folk

Where Devlin feels at home; who even today
Can find in a Green Dragon or an Eel's Foot
Russet and drugget in their old array,

Islands of dung and dialect and soot
Where regional and rural craft endures
Though Transport House and Whitehall cry Caput!

From Snape to Clun, from Athelney to Bures,
Devlin has been the rounds to find what wall
Remains of local stone and still immures

A local memory, and has met with all
The autochthonous trades, the man who catches moles
Or dresses flies, who imitates the call

Of hares, the woodman cutting chestnut poles,
The saddler, dowser, badger, thatcher and wheelwright,
And all the others for whom the curfew tolls

Their banishment to inorganic night.
The Isle of Purbeck or the Forest of Dean,
The Isle of Ely or the Isle of Wight,

Devlin has been the rounds, knows the demesne
Of Norfolk turkey and of Suffolk Punch
And Lincoln Longwool, shares with the obscene

Long Man above Cerne Abbas his proud hunch
That England still is with us, the hands of each
Being rough with marl and sarsen, flint and clunch.

But London too is with us. The long reach
That outreached Cobbett drags us back on time
To the rule of desk and hooter, the black leech

Of the telephone bleeds us white, from the sublime
We step to the meticulous; too much reason,
Of means though not of ends, has spoilt our rhyme,

Unseasoned efficiency too much in season,
Communications too good, each subcommittee
Making our joys a trespass, our toys a treason.

'On the one hand', said the Master, 'it is a pity
Things should be so; on the other hand they are
So and not otherwise. In a modern city,

Too big to be called a city, the facts debar
The citizen much say in what is done
On his behalf or to him. This may jar

On some, it contents others. The average run
Of men prefer a safe but narrow scope,
A place but a small one in a lukewarm sun.

It was not always so. A limestone slope
In the fierce light of Athens in my day
Was crowded with the people's faith and hope,

And mine as well; we thought we could have our say
But the words, the roars, that filled our throats were not
Our own; Plataea and Melos had to pay

For the freedom of our ears. The days grew hot,
The Spartans hotter still, we wanted a high
Place in the solar zenith; what we got

Was the Syracusan quarries, the right to die
On a daily half pint of water. A word to the wise:
Such are political ends. And yet, I cannot deny

That, though Athenians died, Athens no longer dies.'

Canto IX

The Master closed the door. The unmodern words
In Exile stared us once more in the face
And stranded us in London. Broken sherds,

Long before Christ or Marx, had left us out of place
In twentieth-century England. With one glance
At a Pnyx rebuilt by Pugin, where the mace

Is back on the table, we take a different chance
On a different bauble in a lighter sphere,
A bauble, a bubble, a ballet fresh from France,

A match to be won on points. We watch and hear
A gay, genetic ritual. Two cells,
Ovals of light on the stage, appear and disappear

And dodge around each other; as one repels,
The other attracts, each with a nucleus
Half shadow and half body, a tale that tells

Itself by interruption; an incubus
Of straining catgut calls them to the verge
Of a bristling pit, then stops; for them, for us,

The sudden silence thwarts the cosmic urge.
Then the magic relents and starts again, they answer
Each other and half agree, overlap and agree and merge,

Created male and female, one the advancer
And one the advanced upon, but each in turn
Each, and the two made one, but each, or both, a dancer.

One cell from two—yet those two nuclei burn
To multiply for ever. Row on row,
As the house lights go up, a thousand bodies yearn

To be fertilized with rhythm, but Not So
The house lights say, going up; Go Out, they say,
Go home, go away, go anywhere, but go

Forth from this magic circle, which was play,
Not to be taken seriously. They drive
Us out, then go out too. The cells have melted away

In the black jelly of night, while we, once more alive
With a life of fallen insteps and surplus fat,
Once more are conscript workers in a hive

Which holds no dance or magic. That was that,
A bauble; and this is this, a Saturday night
Past closing time, an interim of flat

Refusal and discouragement; the white
Tiles in the public lavatory deny
The whiteness of the skirts that bloomed in flight.

And the stairs carry us down and we do not try
Even moving down to move; an endless file
Of faces flows up past us, brassy or coy or sly,

Boosting each gadget, gewgaw, stunt or style,
All with the same self-love; below in the long gut
Of London larger faces, equally vacant, smile

Us into and out of stations, minx and mutt
Welcome our passing millions, will keep on,
When far above the gates from the world above are shut,

Welcoming no one with the same foregone
Conclusiveness. Theirs is the age and theirs
The vast assurance of the automaton.

And now to get up and out; up similar stairs
With the faces moving down, but to find at last
At home, in the upper air, among gentler airs

Of things remembered, something not yet past
Which, lights or no lights, closing or no time,
Seems not yet undercut nor overcast,

Nor over nor under stated. Home is a prime
Number, a simple colour, a coloured word,
Which dare not be automatic. No posters climb

These stairs. This is a place where things unheard
Can be overheard; where, as tall stories tell,
We find the Singing Tree and the Talking Bird,

And what was lost when the ballet curtain fell.
Here too the curtain falls but, in this case,
Enfolds us in the centre of the cell

Which forms us, which we form, both time and space
Extended yet concentered in the dance,
A dance of before and after, a word of grace,

A name that makes things real. The small, dark hours advance
Anonymous tentacles to drag us down
But, given a house is home, we can seize the chance

Of riding out the night till the waking town
Rechristen itself and the larger hours explode
In burning trees and barking dogs while brown

And grey turn gold and silver, and the slow toad
Of London flashes the jewel in its head
And all the gears change up. Each new-born road

Restakes its claims to somewhere and the red
Pillar boxes redden to greet anew
The age-old resurrection of the dead.

Morning; and still September. But now the view
Burnishes into October, a misty sun
Mellows each capital and curlicue

Of Portland stone or stucco; one by one
The well-dressed trees of London change their dress
From stolid green to rust or cinnamon

Or gold-embroidered brocade; who have not yet said Yes
To the winds that are yet to come but come they will
To consummate our year in nakedness.

Meanwhile the Burning Bush. Meanwhile the still
Small voices of the mist. Meanwhile the slow
Toad hopping, stopping, starting, up the unending hill

To find at the crest a princess who long ago
They said would wait for him: another old
Wives' tale about young brides—but even so

Young brides believe it too, wait for their cold
And clumsy suitor to appear and change
Back to himself, and change the world to gold.

Dry rot and warts and pockmarks, scabs and mange
And toadlike clamminess; yet London can
Halloo her fancy still and let it range

And cast her diapason far as man.
Back to herself. To Latimer at the stake,
Fox in the gaming house. Back where her bones began

To take on flesh and prophesy; William Blake
And Bunyan tenant Bonehill Fields where high
Explosive rocked them lately. Rocked them asleep? Awake?

Coffins and cradles airwise. Rockabye,
Mein Prinzchen, little toad on the spinning top
That weaves a siren note through the breaking sky

And begins to tilt and stagger; should it drop,
What will become of you? Even a toad
Needs legs to hop with and some place to hop.

'What will become of me? The blasts forebode
Ruin it seems—as I seem—but instead
Of being what I seem, my hidden road

Will lead my hidden self to that hidden bed
Where She still waits; and should I die on the way,
Hers will remain the jewel in my head.'

An old wives' tale? Exactly. On a day
In Nineteen-Forty-One an old, old wife,
A groping ghost through mazes of decay

Created overnight rank, dank and rife,
Groped her way on and on and joined the queues
Of those that huddled in the rags of life,

And told me this. That year such tales were daily news.

Canto X

Daily news. And today? There is not so much to note.
Much talk in Cairo of the Suez Canal,
Much talk in Capetown of the Coloured Vote

(And Kaffirs have rallied sharply—Fal-de-lal!),
Much talk in Margate where the dextral faction
Of Labour has outplayed its left cabal,

Much talk throughout the world of action and reaction
And explanation centres and isotopes
And interzonal permits; for distraction

Much talk of football pools and Britain's hopes
On the greens of Virginia Water. Through the scrub
Of the daily press the daily reader gropes

For anyone still alive he has known in home or pub
Who may have cracked one twig or left one whiff
Of a pipe or a cigarette or even a stub

That is still alive. Thus today I peer and sniff
And glimpse through dark Nigerian undergrowth
The Ibos and Yorubas in a tiff

Which may turn bloody; though one should be loth
To laugh at that, I laugh, for it brings to mind
Evans who two months back had met them both

And painted them in laughter, being inclined
To a fine but primary palette. And I shuffle
The paper to Korea, where I find

The Indians and their prisoners in a scuffle—
And Evans again comes jaunting out of the wings
Like a truffle hound on the scent of a monster truffle,

With a poignant nose for copy, a voice that rings
The jackpot, a voice that walks, the born recorder
Of cabbages that are booby traps and kings

That preferably are boobies; all disorder
Appeals to Evans, a Celt, whom I have seen
Laughing his way across the dubious border

Between the convention and the fact, between
The alleged realities of black and white
And those fantastic worlds which are evergreen

And real worlds; worlds of delight and fright
That pile up random minute on random minute,
That ravish or scald the ear, caress or savage the sight

'To describe such things is a trade; once you are in it,
You cannot leave off', said Evans, 'and look where you land!
Out of this world!' said Evans, meaning In it.

Meaning for instance in India (where this canned
Report of Korea leads me). Evans and I
Were once with British and Indian soldiers, bland

But tired and nervous under an angry sky
With a stench of death from those already dead
And a stench of fear from those about to die,

And the refugee lorries waiting, but age-old dread
Had glued their feet to the road and no one moved
Till Evans, losing his temper, found his head

And bundling up one hag, with a grey face grooved
With age and raddled with blood and half an arm,
Hoisted her into a lorry and so disproved

That men were immovable objects; like a charm
The example worked, the bundles opened their eyes
And crawled to what feet they had. The sudden alarm

Of Evans' action seemed to galvanize
Both British and Indian officers, who now
Began to shift those bags of fear and flies

Which were men, women and children. This is how
I remember Evans, once when he did not laugh,
When the Land of Cockayne for once gave way to the Slough

Of Despond and he carried us through it. Remembering half
That scene I remember enough; and turn again
To find what else the editorial staff

Has chosen for today, what other shapes of men
Can be glimpsed between their handouts. And I read
That the Skins have reached Nairobi. Nine or ten

Young officers with blackthorn sticks proceed
To down their pints in my mind; that was Belfast
And early in the war and there was need

To watch the clock, the rounds were spinning past
And they had a train to catch. Inniskillings, fare ye well;
Dragoons or fusiliers. Maguire was about the last

To catch it; that was normal. Always he had to tell
One more tale for the road and across the road,
As he ended, I could hear the station bell.

He waved his blackthorn and went, the Army Code
Buttoned around him but his spirit gay
To reap the Indian corn that Krishna sowed

And drink the drinks that Omar put away.
The black train started as it had to start;
No matter, further stories a further day

And, as he always said, 'You cannot fart
Against the thunder'. Which is what Hobo said,
His friend with the broken nose; their ways were doomed to part.

Hobo stept on a landmine and is dead
In Sicily, while Maguire came back from the East
With brand-new jokes and jorums in his head.

And now without these two, Hobo deceased
And Maguire demobilized, the Skins have gone
To Kenya with their trousers smartly creased

And no clear notion what is going on
But the pipes playing farewell—and that is all
I need from today's paper: Automedon

And Achilles, fare ye well. I will make one ball
Of all this black and white to light the stove.
Summer time ends at midnight; dark will fall

Still earlier tomorrow. What we wove
We can unweave; in the hour the clock forgets
The winds deconsecrate the sacred grove

And the papers swallow their words and welsh on their debts
And quite a few people die. Today's hot news,
Blown cold along cold streets and parapets

Or trodden to sodden grey by shopping queues,
Will no longer mean whatever it might have meant
And, whatever amusement it gave, no longer amuse.

Summer time ends and good riddance. Trailer and tent
Have notice to quit, the daylight that stayed and stayed
At last has outstayed its welcome, we can assent

With a smile to its going. This same week puts paid
To the pleasure gardens in Battersea Park, dead leaves
And chill airs taunt the chinoiserie-bound parade,

The pavilions of coloured lights. Acrasia grieves
Her fluorescent joys, her papier mâché rocks,
Her arches that lead to nowhere, her unbound sheaves

Of imitation corn, her filigree box
Of knick-knacks and false bottoms, her swans in plastic
And all her inanimate creatures. Antirrhinums and phlox

Have yielded to candy floss, the heavy fantastic
Toes have tripped on a cocoanut, the last
Fun of the fair will snap with a snap of elastic

And all this summer's fandango be part of the past
With Vauxhall Gardens and Ranelagh. The smoke
Flies from the power house chimneys at half mast.

Pepys would note this in his diary, perhaps with a joke,
If he still kept a diary. Fancy's knell
Tinkles over the Thames and the bell-ringers are broke.

Fare ye well, momes and midgets. Fare ye well.

Canto XI

The golden guineas filter through the mist.
Farewell and hail: October waves her hand.
And (here beginneth the Ambiguist)

The art of falling is you cannot stand.
So fall, Pomona, with your breasts of apples
And fall, green ladies of the summer land,

Take to your moongrown rest in lofts and chapels
Before the long frost comes. A pencilled red
Cross on a broken wall that broken sunlight dapples

Will mark the window where you have gone to bed
And drawn the curtains. Legendary girls,
Sleep well and dream; it is your dreams that shed

Their aura on our loves; a string of pearls
Once worn and warmed by you preserves its glow
Though twined round real throats, through real curls,

In the realities of our long ago
Two or three decades back when what we knew
Lay subject still to what we did not know

And woman was El Dorado. The mere view
Of each untravelled ocean still could knock
Our knees together and our wits askew,

Standing like Cortez on a high dry rock
And fumbling for a name. The names emerge
And the young venturer, dizzy with the shock

And blinded by blue miles of glare and surge
Knows that he has been all but here before,
Here at this point of prospect, here at this void and verge.

But why Pacific? Mother or maid or whore,
This is that western sea where ships go down.
Think twice, Leander, trembling at the door,

Before you throw it wide and swamp the town.
What of it if you swam the Hellespont?
It is in Hero's love you are doomed to drown.

The names emerge. Whatever it is we want,
We christen lust to turn it into love;
Our church may be an arbour and our font

A flagon, still the bright myth floats above
And in the moment that the word is made
Woman, itself descends, a word, a dove,

While our dumb blood flowers in a cannonade
Of pentecostal voices. But not all
Names breathe out equal magic; some names fade

And some turn black and blacken our day and call
Our skeletons out of the cupboard. Byron invented
Haidee but did not marry her. A wall

Of wailing lies at the back of many a tented
Temple of Love; where men repent their folly
And the next wink repent that they repented,

While high among the bottle-glass Pretty Polly
Repeats 'I told you so', repeats that this
Is no fit age for lovelorn melancholy

But for brass tacks and cold analysis,
Repeats 'I told you so, I told you so, I am Pretty
Polly who knows that one peck makes a kiss'.

But what does one lost handkerchief make? The pity
Of it, Poll Parrot, the pity! The old song
Hums on the telephone wires all round the city

As the wronged lover does himself more wrong
Waking in Circe's room, where marmosets
Lurk in the curtains and a slobbering throng

Of hairy or scaly creatures gambols and upsets
The creams and trays and siphons of last night,
Then swarms up Circe's bed, being her pets,

And as the young man shrinks away, the white
Body beside him vanishes and leaves
The bed to him and the beasts, while the bitter bright

Day creeps under the door and under the eaves
Outside the sparrows yield to a louder bird:
'I told you so, I told you so', it grieves,

'I told you so' it cackles, as the blurred
Mirror comes clear and shows a different room
And shows to Circe's bedmate what occurred

Really between them there. This is one gloom
Too gloomy, too well known, and hers one name
Whose magic blackens to one gathering doom

That has its day for most men. To reclaim
The day before is impossible, and yet
Worse magic still can cause us greater shame

In other names we gladly would forget:
Jocasta, Medusa, Medea. The man who meets
Whom can too seldom guess whom he has met

Until it is too late. The best-lit streets,
The happiest rooms, can hide them; and it is our
Own innocence drags them between the sheets

And makes their evil potent. A dark tower
Shadows each house they live in but it is we
Who helped them build it, as the poisoned flower

Medea wore between her breasts was free
Of poison until Jason placed it there
To kill her children and his. The lovesick sea

Turns black and claims its wrecks and London's air
Reeks of Thebes or Colchis, while London brides
Unveil and show the serpents in their hair.

This is that greater doom which bodes and bides
Its time till it burst the clock. This is the point
In the crooked and narrow path where romantic love collides

With brute and practical hate; where a witch's oils anoint
Our hands with numbness and our eyes with pain.
The strings, my lady, are false. Each minute is out of joint.

There is something rotten there, down Lovers' Lane
Where we had chosen to walk; those other, more Roman, roads
Drawn with a ruler dead against the grain

Of the live country, ruled by colder codes,
Seemed even more broken down; most ambition,
Most service of God or man, had seemed the modes

Of some forgotten music, futile mission.
So off we went. Went arm in arm. With what?
And to what end? It might have been perdition,

Sometimes it was. Yet hells, however cold or hot,
Are not in fact for ever. At other times
Dawdling down that same lane we found a happier lot

Between wild hedges where the dogrose climbs
With Chloe or Nicolette, whose magic was white and pink
And no false note could spoil the varied chimes

We heard with them at midnight, when to think
Meant to feel and to feel meant to be
And being meant pure joy and no weak link

Impaired the daisy chain which a not impossible She
Had tied our hands and hers with. We did not call
On God or Time to free us; nor did we want a free

Hand, nor would we imagine a world at all
Outside our present chains. Nor did we know
That heavens, however green in leaf or gold in fall,

Are not for ever, and yet can be heavens even so.

Canto XII

Now to dissolve in port. I take the train
Through Biscuit Town and Didcot to the seat
Of learning which I sat in half in vain

When there was less to learn and more to eat;
The years like small dun oxen crash the ford
And I am spattered by their passing feet.

The Rowlandsonian chins which swept the board
Have swept themselves away, the Johnsonian wit
Trickles and fidgets where it roared and poured

And few young men are much impressed by it
(Or by the Good, the Beautiful, the True).
As always, the quadrangles are ill lit

But now the rooms are underheated too,
The proving mind begins to fail the prober,
The bonfires weave their dreamful doubtful blue,

The young have foundered in a drably sober
Slumber of regular work beneath the gnarled and yellow
Tree of knowledge. Oxford in October

Seems all dead stone (which here hath many a Fellow)
While Arnold's spires have spiked and burst their dream
And Bacon's Brazen Head has ceased to bellow

And many a thematist has lost his theme.
Knowing all this I let the porter take
Just half my ticket, leave just half the beam

In my good eye. Preferring half a cake
To too much bread, I leave the remembered station
And, headed for a contract and a steak,

Pass the small shop where once in June's elation
Esther bought whiteheart cherries; next I cross
The canal where Gavin and I held cosmic conversation

Becalmed in a hired canoe. Thus, gathering moss
Of sentimental memories, I roll on
Past walls of broken biscuit, golden gloss,

Porridge or crumbling shortbread or burnt scone,
Puma, mouldy elephant, Persian lamb,
And other modes of stone to the foregone

Conclusion of a business lunch; I am
Not what I was; twenty-five years ago
I studied the impromptu epigram

Which now I could not, would not. I have become slow
Though, possibly, more honest. If the Master
Of those who know so well that they do not know

Were to put out his hand of alabaster
And buttonhole me now, I would sham dead
Or, failing that, play dumb or, failing that, walk faster.

Faster and faster. Slower and slower. Red
Gowns glow through colder ages where poor scholars
Shiver and toss in garrets two to a bed,

Threatened by duns and daggers, drenched in squalors,
Their brains and bowels cluttered with the grist
Of nominalists or realists or lollers.

Exactly seven centuries of mist
Have rolled away since the first Chancellor died
Who wished Greek letters added to the list

Of the humaner studies and defied
The dead hand of the Church, though by his day
This church was already old; I step inside

Its littered sombre innards to survey
The damage of a recent fire; the black
Ribs of the roof with the slates fallen away,

The smell of wet charred woodwork, whisk me back
A dozen years to a dozen mornings after
In London where the latest air attack

Had so well stripped the flesh from strut and rafter
That twelve years on those bones look no less old
Than these bones here. Stony or leaden laughter

Spouts from the mouths of gargoyles, jackdaws scold
And the Parrot pinnacled high where a weathercock should be
In the intense inane begins to repeat 'I told

You so, I told you so; you would not agree,
Walter de Merton and William of Wykeham, but all
Your works are marked for ruin, believe you me,'

And anyway what does it matter? Where are Saucer Hall
And Peckwater Inn and Bocardo? Where are the grey
Friars and the black friars? Gone to the wall;

And the wall has gone—or is going with little delay.
Duns Scotus, William of Ockham and Roger Bacon,
Wycliffe and even Wolsey, have had their day;

The trivium and quadrivium are forsaken;
Dried up, broken, and sunk like the reefs of coral
That once, before the seas were overtaken

By land and plankton turned to vetch and sorrel,
Were all there was of Oxford. Parrot speak!
Everything flows. And dries. So runs that old Greek moral

Which Parrot loves to bandy week by week,
Millennium by millennium. And to fix
This better in your mind, where is the clique

That you yourself in Nineteen-twenty-six,
When you came up, belonged to? I myself?
Cherwell and Thames might now be Lethe and Styx,

Aesthete and Hearty, Ghibelline and Guelph,
To my self now. And the clique? My friends? Already some
Have become like books on a top or bottom shelf

That I never may read again; and one has become
A book I cannot, having been dropped in the sea,
And all that remain are changed. A horny thumb,

Not mine, has turned those pages. A lost key,
If it could open their rooms, would merely disclose
A pile of anchovy toast and a pewter pot of tea,

Both cold. And my own rooms? The staircase number shows
They are the same—but are they? This was where
The Lotus of the Absolute and the Rose

Of All the World bloomed in the smoke-blue air
Till someone opened the windows, made us switch
To gossip. Here came Egdon with his hair

And his theories falling over his eyes, a rich
If random prophet and pedlar, and here came
Stretton whose silences concealed an itch

For castles in the air, and Gavin always game
For some Gargantuan abbey where the nuns
Wear crimson hose and farthingales of flame

And do whatever they will in despite of wrynecked Huns
And baboon-like Ostrogoths. Remembering such
Strong talk over strong tea and Chelsea buns

Or over strong drink and nuts, I slightly touch
The lintel and move on; we had much to say
Which did not in the end add up to much,

Still, the equation worked out for the day.
Now Egdon lives across that same Atlantic
Where Gavin met his death, and perhaps his self, half way,

While Stretton has long dropped his corybantic
And abstract rituals, and for my part,
No longer the misunderstood romantic,

These days I put the horse before the cart,
Having found out through blight and blot and blunder
That, as Maguire would put it, one cannot fart

Even with the best intentions against thunder.

Canto XIII

Leaving the colleges then and their half-remembered
Hobsnobberies, which echoed my own voice,
I make my way through warmly umbered embered

Foliage to catch a bus in search of Boyce
Who lives in a village in a seasoned home,
Keeping his head and exercising choice

And titivating his garden. He knows that Rome
Absorbed rough wine and blood with the she-wolf's milk
And that the dogmas of each pompous dome

In Moscow, Washington, and places of that ilk,
Are largely based on some irrational urge
To make an old sow's ear seem brand-new silk

Full of hard cash or facts—though few of either emerge.
Boyce with his schooling in the humaner letters
Can spot the flaws in each inhuman purge

Or measure of false security, knows what fetters
Are forged in the name of freedom, still declines
To defer to politicians as his betters.

I find him among his books, his presence shines
Like a straight candle in a crooked world,
His eyebrows twinkle and the thoughtful lines

On the high forehead run true, his terrier lies curled
In its basket by the fire as he talks of kindly things
While the small sitting-room seems furred and furled

In warmth of mind and body; the autumn sings
In a small still voice outside, he remarks the frosts are late
And the leaves late on the trees; and after tea he brings

Me out to show me his garden with its straight
Borders and close-napped lawns and apple trees
And specially printed blooms which he can annotate

As well as his Greek texts; what the eye no longer sees,
As the twilight catches us out, some other sense
Divines—the huge chrysanthemums floating at their ease

Regardless of their stalks, and the optative tense
Of bulbs in beds that Boyce with his usual care and skill
Has made for their winter sleep. A damp and dense

Night descends and, descending Marston Hill,
We both return to Oxford, there to dine
In Wolsey's arrogant hall where frozen portraits spill

From either wall reflected lights in line
As if in some deep canal beneath the roof's high night
While the high table too lies gemmed with lights of wine

And voices like a host of rooks take flight
Confusedly up to the darkness. A Latin grace
Adjourns us to the Common Room, our white

Napkins clutched in our hands, to leisurely chase
Decanters round a table and leisurely knit
Our sentences plain and purl. This is a leisurely place

And almost a timeless one. The managerial writ
Here hardly seems to run; here nothing seems
In fact to run, however you hustle it.

The snuffbox glides around, the silver gleams
And it grows hard even to raise one's voice
To say that one must leave; the body dreams

While the lips move. Till in there comes Aloys
To take me to his flat and back to earth
And, half relieved, I say goodnight to Boyce

Sifter of seeds and words, guardian of worth,
Sage with a sense of humour. I pass the lodge
Into that outer world of death and birth

And grinding gears and hooters, the hodge-podge
In which we live and love. Aloys, who knows
No guile but relishes the simple dodge,

Offers me wine bought at a bargain, glows
Through all his massive body, his bald head,
Exchanging shop and gossip, a kind of prose

Resembling Chinese poems, a well read
Man with a gift of friendship, apt and able
In a courtly quiet way to gild the gingerbread

Of works and days. Aloys keeps a good table
This side the Yellow River and can match
Li Po or T'ao Ch'ien with cup and fable

And traveltalk and kindness and a batch
Of lines from Goethe or Rilke; a dignified
And diligent man, he can laugh at himself, detach

Himself from his work and stand outside, inside
His bald head, giving out. As here one night
He gave to our friend Aidan, once the pride

Of the Irish Republican Army, who could requite
Hard times with warmth, Aidan who twice had broken
Jail when condemned to die, now took delight

In breaking bread with Aloys, two soft-spoken
Men in a firelit room. Where now I stay
For this one night, tomorrow must be woken

In time to leave. Tomorrow, that is today,
Comes. On a college lawn I hear a sweeper's broom
Swishing inexorably the leaves away,

Monotonous as the pendulum of doom,
And taking one last stroll along the Turl,
Half savouring the mist and my own gloom

I pass the shop where Esther, a slim girl,
Chose herself roses for a ball and pass
The rooms where one young poet used to twirl

His inconclusions in a whisky glass,
A tall and tousled man who wrote short poems and died
This summer. Oxford trees weep leaves on Oxford grass

Suggesting a tag of Homer. Ghosts in jerkins ride
Clattering through the kennel, the debtor's bag
Swings from the high grilled window, I stand outside

This past but feel it. Save me, Lamb and Flag,
Pray for me, Eagle and Child, I feel as old and dry
As the splintered spines and shells in the coral rag

Of these obsolete city walls. Yes, it is high
Time to retreat to my stuccoed London house
Which is only a hundred and thirty years old. Goodbye,

Buttery, crypt, and quad. Cricket and mouse
May talk their heads off in you; for me, I have talked enough
And much too long ago here. Wood worm and wood louse

384

Can make what comment they will; I have other stuff
To pick my private holes in. Let Big Ben
Shout down Great Tom, let the train for Paddington puff

These puffball dreams away and remind me when
Is when and what is what, and spirit me home before
My middle or darker ages descend again.

So. I am back. Dead leaves around the door,
The windows lighter where the trees have moulted,
The yellow flowers in my windowboxes more

Advanced, or rather declined; the winds have bolted
Their fill of golden wafers, the park is damp,
My Lares and Penates have revolted

Against the time, demand their reading lamp
Sooner and extra blankets. Curtained, shuttered in,
Cramped in a chair and suffering thinker's cramp

I unthink youth and Oxford. A little pin
Drops in the back of my mind. The pin is out,
As the sergeant said; the battle must begin

All over again. As usual. To be devout
Or scholarly would help; with little learning
And less devotion, we can only scout

False images of either and, discerning
What light of reason or of love we can,
Light our own taper there and keep it burning

And thereby prove at least that man is man,
As most men guess they are though too few know it.
The proof may need big guns, but one who is in the van

And only has a grenade, the pin being out, must throw it.

Canto XIV

A battle? That is one way of looking at the matter;
Or it could be a Quest. While windblown moons embark
On seas of cloud and the winds of October scatter

The late night finals round the empty park,
Young men with dead leaves plastered on their shoes
Set out with scrip or briefcase through the dark,

Telling themselves that they have nothing to lòse
But not so sure what it is they stand to gain.
This very night they may cross the Bridge of Booze

Into the Castle Crapulous, or draw rein
In Queer Street where the doorways are baroque
And long shrill shadows flute their old refrain

'My dear! My dear! My dear!' and the luminous clock
At the end of the street has lost its hands and the night
Bulges with scents that please, with sounds that mock.

So some stay here for the night—and night is right,
Tomorrow they will be old—while some go on
To call on Potiphar's wife or the Moabite

Madames and so put out the light that shone
In the back of their mind this morning. Others clutch
Their amulets and wallets, and leaning on

The staff of Conscience and despising Dutch
Courage and drugs from Carthage or Cathay,
Look for the Church of Arc-lights where there is much

Too much light and much too much to say
And too loud speakers to say it; yet many trust
That show of fat white hands to point the way

To the Better Life for All. Away with dust and lust!
No lust grows here unless the lust for power.
'And though', the young men think, 'such power may be unjust,

We need a hand to guide us in this hour;
Another hour may be different'. So they flow
Into that blaze and blare of lies in flower

To join the worshippers, and do not know
That from now on there is no hour but this.
Words without end. Long live this Status Quo.

Still, some aberrant errants give a miss
To such Utopian Zions, turn about
Into the temple of Aesthetic Bliss,

That blind aquarium of chanting trout
And quivering fins and suckers. The glass walls
Reflect the inner lights and squeeze the outer out.

This temple has a thousand and one halls
And Scheherazade must tell her tale in each,
In each Pygmalion's mallet falls and falls,

His chisel chips and chips, his lips beseech
The marble to reply, till at last he knocks
His mistress into shape, but not yet into speech.

Pan with his pipe, Pandora with her box,
And Cinderella losing her slipper again
And Peeping Tom still fumbling with the locks

And Orpheus looking back and Penelope counting ten
Stitches and dropping twelve and Cuddie counting sheep
And Daniel singing in the lions' den

And Rip van Winkle still two thirds asleep
And Tristram two thirds mad, they all are here,
They all are here, uncertain whether to laugh or weep.

Weaving their way through whom, the young men persevere
Hoping to find what others find through science
Or perhaps through God; but their own eye and ear,

On which they place such innocent reliance,
Provide less certain standards as they drift
From concert hall to gallery in defiance

Of everything outside. Outside and inside shift
Into each other continually. No sieve,
Not even the finest in the world, can sift

Essence from accident; the muses give
Nothing for nothing; works of art, like men,
Must be at least a little impure to live,

And therefore accident-prone. No brush or pen,
Woodwind or strings, can pledge a constant truth
That may not lapse into untruth again.

But too few acolytes know this yet; some youth
Before some worthy's portrait may espy
Over that worthy's shoulder an uncouth

Shape which should not be there and, wondering why,
Dive through the gilded portals of the frame
Into the canvas itself and, passing by

The sitter in his robes of office, claim
A word with his hanger-on; who tries to escape
To that less conscious world from which he came

But the thick pigments hold him. He turns to gape
At the man who has caught him up to catch him out
As he is always caught, being not man but ape,

Being not able to smile, only to pout.
Whom the young man accosts: 'Why are you here?
Who are you? Are you my past? Are you my doubt?

My alter ego? My basic self? My fear?
Or even my future too?' The sad eyes blink;
He scratches first his arse and then his ear

But answers nothing. Hearing a distant chink
Of flint on flint the young man tries again:
'How was it that you missed the missing link

And stayed on the far side, so far from men?
Looking at whom, do you regret it now
Or are you glad we have passed beyond your ken?'

He drags one long black hand across his puckered brow
And with the other fumbles at a straw
Worldwearily as though the facts allow

No deviation from his tribal law,
And again answers nothing. The young man
Almost in desperation grasps his paw

And looks him in the eye—catch who catch can
What meaning skulks there: 'You whose explorations
Ended long epochs before ours began,

We still share one thing, life, which our human qualifications
Disqualify us for. Can you, whose face
Shows not a glimmer of such complications,

Tell us what life in your so pure and simple case,
Take it or leave it, really is? Oh what
Is life in the first, which is also the last, place?'

He twists the straw, failing to make a knot,
And answers nothing; but this time turns round
And lays one quavering finger on one spot

Where the oil-paint has worn thin; his interrogator, bound
By his own questing mind to follow every clue,
Tests it with one foot, both feet. The unsound

Canvas collapses and he tumbles through
Into a silence that vibrates, a scum
And scurry of life, a stillborn hullabaloo.

He has been here before; these rows of dumb
And swaddled bodies in this fetid air,
A distant judgment rumbling like a drum

Somewhere ten miles above. He climbs a spiral stair
Picking his steps among the mummied heads
(Tread softly because you tread on the dreams that are not there)

Until he comes where one small blue light sheds
Obscurity, one low mean tunnel crawls
Reluctantly away and shreds and shreds

Into still smaller tunnels with damper walls
Too low for him to pass. But pass *they* do
In helmets, masks, and mudstained overalls,

With bucket, pick and stretcher, a silent crew
Whose hectic energy seems all the more
Hectic because they are silent. They pass—but who

Are They? Has he, or not, been here before?

Canto XV

Been here before? Whether he has or no,
The question is: Must he be here for ever?
In this black labyrinth, this to and fro

Of meaningless activity, of clever
Means to some stupid end, this endless spate
Of highly organized yet blind endeavour.

Thus he debates with himself; but the debate
Already seems irrelevant, this is It,
His furthest fathom and his meanest fate,

His Sine Die and his Obiit,
His A.B.C. of silence. If the cap
Of invisibility appears to fit,

Why, he must put it on and close the gap
Between himself and this blind bustling nation
Who want no gaps. Or do they? A sudden clap

Of thunder sets their world in perturbation;
The workers seize their shovels, a faceless warder
Drawing the polished key of his vocation

Unlocks a door that is marked in red 'By Order:
Private: No Exit: Danger'. In they throng
Down one more long dark passage towards the border

Of everything they know, a path as blind as long,
Which ends in a blank wall. They hoist and poise
Their battering ram, the foreman's whistling thong

Lashes their shoulders and undreamt of noise
Engulfs their silent world as in they go
To the attack. On what? The tools that each employs

Must serve some end but what he does not know.
Let there be! was the order; in their fright
They missed the rest of it. Still, blow on blow

Has to be struck—for something. With all their might
They hack and scoop and batter, blink and rumble,
Till suddenly—let there be—and there is! A new thing. Light.

Appalled, the workers and their warders tumble
Back on themselves, the steel-clad troops begin
Arriving from the rear to rally or harry their humble

Fellows to finish the job; that small hole which lets in
That dangerous unknown light must let them out
Into an unknown world. The drudgery and the din

Continue, clods and clinkers clutter about,
The hole becomes first a window, then a wide
Doorway; the undergrounders burst and spout

And flood the green fields black on every side.
But this is merely the prelude. Now the guards
Of honour clack their mandibles, divide

Into two ranks and, starched as playing cards,
Await what comes—and what comes is their queen
Surrounded by her court of drones and bards

But ready to try her wings in the never seen,
Let alone flown in, sky. The masses cringe
And look away; she launches herself, the green

Earth swings away beneath her, a rainbow tinge
Catches and celebrates the unfolding gauze
While she ascends where steelbright rays impinge

Dazzlingly on her breastplate and the laws
Of the vaulted dark are lost in the vault of blue,
And on she flies and up, not knowing the cause

Though the poor cause has won his frail wings too
And already is gaining air. The grounded crowd
Crane their stiff necks and, not being able to woo

Themselves, admire this courtship, though endowed
With little erotic and less aesthetic sense;
While the young man among them, cowed and bowed

To their own size, stares upwards; one immense
And blinding heaven strikes him, he can feel
What myth takes shape above him. Pale and tense

He waits and they all wait; in wheel on wheel
And reel on reel the shining couple above
Ply their transparent wings of silk and steel

And high beyond the reach of lark or dove
At last embrace each other in mid air
And make, for the first and last time ever, love.

And the young man, while the dumb cohorts stare,
Knows that it is the last and slinks away,
Glad that he saw a miracle happen there

But sad to think the same must end today,
As perhaps all miracles do; the queen will shed
Her wings and there will be nothing more to say

Either of flight or light; these living dead,
These purposeful automatons below
Will take her back; everything has been said

Of love and freedom. It is time to go.
'Walk up! Walk up!' keeps clanking in his ear,
So up he walks—into a tent of snow.

The barker takes his money. 'All change here!'
The barker cries, 'Walk up! Walk up! Sit down!
None of the snows and shows of yesteryear

Ain't half a patch on this, least not for half a crown.
One at a time though, gentlemen. This ride
Is the best joyride ever known in town

But keep your mouth shut once you get inside
And don't you speak to no one, just hold tight,
Just let your sense of Whatnot be your guide

And, if you want to, you'll come out all right—
Unless you choose to stay there, one never knows,
I knew one chap what did, he had an uncommon white

Skin and pink eyes; still, I should hardly suppose
You'll find him in there now. All right, who's first?
You, sir? Paid your half crown? All right, sit tight, here goes!'

A hatch snaps open and shut. Precipitated, immersed
In a clinging dark, a rubbery blubbery duct,
Wormlike the young man slithers through its pursed

And elastic coils, its foiled and moiled and mucked
Byways, its miles of narrowness and juice
With no more room for his body than a plucked

Fowl wrapped in lard, he feels he must lose the use
Of every sense and limb, can hardly breathe,
Feels utterly alone, cannot deduce

His where or whatabouts, to squeeze and wreathe
Is all his locomotion, damply hot
Valves burst their abscess round him, stink and seethe

And suffocate, his mind begins to clot
Between his twisting legs. He remains alone.
Alone? But he suddenly feels that he is not—

And that he would rather be. Is this his own
Skin? It is not. This thing that moves as he
Moves is a separate thing, that hairfine monotone

Is not his voice and, though he cannot see,
He knows it cannot either. What does it say?
He makes his mind a blank and listens. 'Follow me!'

The weak voice says: 'Give up your feet of clay,
Give up your feet, your hands, your sex, your eyes, your brain,
And follow me—I am the only Way.

Some call it degeneration; to speak plain,
They call it so from envy. Let who can,
Adapt themselves as well. I know no pain,

I do no work for ever; in the van
Of nature I am I, who live both in
And on man's guts and so have conquered man.

Progress, my friend! Would you rather call it original sin?'

393

Canto XVI

The young man cannot answer. Is this life?
He asks himself—but dare not answer that.
The Quest has come to a standstill. Like a wife

The worm clings closer, closer, in the fat
And intestinal darkness. What night could be
Darker than this? His thought is answered pat

By the thin colourless voice: 'I cannot see
And would not if I could, but there are darker cells
Enclosing blinder lives. Guess where. Why, inside Me.

These lives, if life is what their action spells,
Could dance in millions on the point of a pin
And hold the keys to nine and ninety hells

Which so-called higher creatures suffer in.
They live far less than I, perhaps not at all;
The less they live, however, the more they win,

Which means the more you lose. Whether you call
Them organisms or chemicals, who cares?
If life means rising skywards but to fall,

Who would choose life?' The young man unawares
All but agrees—did not a voice outside
Come suddenly back to him. Through the dumb gut it blares:

'Just let your sense of Whatnot be your guide . . .
Just hold tight . . . If you want to . . .' That great voice
Cuts through the Gordian knot the worm has tied.

Unless you choose . . . You choose? 'Then I have choice!'
The young man cries; 'Most certainly I choose;
Choose to grow and decay, to weep and rejoice,

To be what I was and shall be.' The foul ooze
Begins to ooze, and the dark to melt, away;
Then, with dead leaves yet sticking to his shoes,

The young man spirals back into his day
Where it is still the Fall. But he is more
Than one day older, having found the Ne

Plus Ultra and learnt the worst. We could deplore
His weakness had we too, even you and I,
Not served our term in similar depths before

And proved as weak, and yet regained the sky
And the give and take of humanity. And yet
The Quest goes on and we must still ask why

We are alive, though no one man has met
A full or lucid answer; all we can do
Is answer it by living and pay the debt

That none can prove we owe. And yet those debts accrue
Which we must pay and pay but, what is odd,
The more you pay the more comes back to you.

Which some explain by reference to God
And others find an inexplicable fact,
But fact it is, as downright as a clod,

As unremitting as a cataract.
Remembering which, remembering that for ever
We are bound to live and give and make and act,

And that the blackest magic cannot sever
The Castle of the Grail from the land of men,
But also that the land of men is never

Free from the Blatant Beast, we turn again
From Red Letter days (or Black) to every day,
From Red Cross knights to Joe Maguire or Ben

McQuitty who lives in a ketch. Morgan le Fay
Cannot be always with us, the girls we know
Rarely put on white samite, even at their most gay.

The common writ still runs. Which being so,
One of ten million, I accept my dated
Located briefing; it is time to go,

In this case to East Anglia. The belated
Month is upon my heels; I take a bus
Into the night, feeling repatriated

If without reason (let who will discuss
The reasons for nostalgia) and my friend
Blundell escorts me from the terminus

To a thatched cottage whose long years commend
Their earth to earth beneath a dormered brow
While down the orchard naked trees transcend

Themselves with apples, acres under plough
Make succulent, sun-gilded gingerbread,
As Pebmarsh makes next morning Here and Now.

And now to Norwich, to the Maiden's Head
Known to the Pastons but unknown to me,
As all of Norfolk is and so, instead

Of being what today it ought to be,
Norwich up-ends its yesterdays together
And overlaps its faults; where we should see

Commercial travellers talking shoe for leather,
Dead Benedictine monks and Flemish weavers
Intrude, intruding mediaeval weather

(Today was the first frost) while cumbrous cogs and levers
Turn twenty geese on one enormous spit
At a great fire, and fires yet greater teach deceivers

Not to be Jews or Lollards, till further fires are lit
By Cromwell's roistering troops to burn the books
Of Rome; till a German fat man signs a chit

For yet more fires in Norwich. As one looks
From the Maddermarket to Bishopgate, a broth
Of history garnished by ten thousand cooks

Simmers around one; calamanco cloth,
Cobbles, copper, pewter and blown glass,
Serpents and bass recorders and the froth

Of home-brewed ale, canaries, and church brass
Boil over while Sir Garnet Wolseley rides
High on a swinging sign and pilgrims pass

North-west to Walsingham and the night confides
Kett to the hangman's rope. Across the river
The tanneries deal with twentieth-century hides

While we, who have just arrived, ramble and shiver
Through an uninhabited Close where faintly whining
Ghosts beg their banished Virgin to deliver

Their souls from what dark verdicts hold them pining
Through centuries of purgatorial nights.
Mediaeval walls of knapped wet flint are shining

In mediaevally dim electric lights;
We wonder, trying to hold our memories fast,
If seeing sights means merely claiming rights

In some maybe maudlin, maybe mortgaged past.
Meanwhile, half way between the town and gown,
Between the older legends and the last

New learning, sitting at ease and looking down
Upon the cryptic relic in his hand,
There broods the statue of Sir Thomas Browne

Whose major object was to understand
The microcosm, who managed by the way
To make our language dance a saraband.

A Norwich doctor, basking in the ray
Of his invisible sun, prepared to eat
Frogs with the French and let his fellows pray

According to their whim, his mind replete
With curious questions and exotic riches,
Sweet rarities and charities, his feet

Ready to lug his wits through miles of ditches
Collecting and collating facts; and yet
This more than learned man believed in witches

And thought it godless not to. Without let
Or hindrance strange things walked his house, were seen
Scratching about his door, such things as might be met

In Norwich again tonight. For tonight is Hallow-e'en.

Canto XVII

This was the night that specially we went down,
When we were small, to the kitchen where the cook,
A Catholic farmer's daughter from Fivemiletown,

Poked up the fire in the open range and took
Her apron off and dropped her crochet work
And dropped the apples in the tub and shook

The lamplight with her laughter; quiz and quirk,
Riddle and slapstick, kept the dark at bay
Though ghosts and goblins, we well knew, must lurk

No further off than the scullery and today
The bogs, the black domain of the Will o' the Wisp,
Had closed in round our house from miles away.

No matter; apples were sharp and nuts were crisp,
She practised divination with cups of tea
And we responded in a childish lisp

To what our future brides or grooms should be,
And cracking nut on nut were unaware
Of the god that grinned at us from the hazel tree.

An ancient Celtic world had filled the air,
The cropped black sow was lurking at the gate
To seize the hindmost, and the empty chair

That creaked was creaking from the unseen weight
Of some dead man who thought this New Year's Eve,
The Celtic world having known a different date.

The white ash dropped; the night kept up its sleeve
The Queen of Apples, the Ace of Fires, the Jack
Of Coffins, and one joker. Soon we should have to leave

The lamplight and the firelight and climb back
Into our small cold beds with a small cold
Wind that made the blind in the window clack

And soot fall down the chimney on to the six-months-old
Newspaper frill in the fireplace. Climbing asleep in the snow
Of the sheets I remembered again what I had been often told:

'Aye, you are here now—but you never know
Where you will be when you wake up.' I lay
Fearing the night through till the cock should crow

To tell me that my fears were swept away
And tomorrow had come again. So now I wake
To find that it is Norwich and All Saints' Day,

All devils and fancy spent, only an ache
Where once there was an anguish. The tall spire
In harsh grey rain stands grey while great gales shake

The trees of Tombland; every man's desire
Is washed away in what is a record fall
Of rain, as the gay colours of nave and choir

Were washed away long since. The church bells call
Forlornly from their cages within cages,
Oak beams within blind stone; a similar wall

Immures for each of us the Middle Ages
Of our own childhood; centuries of rain
Have made the colours run and swilled the pages

Whether of missal or chapbook down the drain
In one conglomerate pulp; the distant chimes
Have ceased to hold us in their tangled skein

Since we must have our worlds as in our times
And, if we once looked back, might turn to stone
Like all the saints. The reasons and the rhymes

Of Mother Church and Mother Goose have grown
Equally useless since we have grown up
And learnt to call our minds (if minds they are) our own,

And neither need a special spoon to sup
With the devil any more nor need to forage,
As lepers did, for scraps with clapper and cup;

We know no leper, or devil, remains in Norwich
And that, however rashly one proceeds,
One cannot burn one's mouth with cold plum porridge.

Knowing all which and having such few needs,
Having put childish things away and sprayed
Each man his own pet killer on those weeds

That yesterday were flowers, and having made
Each man his own renaissance, why should we
Still feel at times inept, inert, afraid?

Seven o'clock; night like a choppy sea
Rocks each high-masted church but one by one
The public houses welcome you and me,

The Woolpack, Adam and Eve, the Evening Gun,
The Horse Barracks, the Oakshades. You and I
Squashed on a settle feel the unseen sun

Within us thrusting through a stubborn sky.
Sir Thomas Browne was right and so was Dame
(Or Mother or Lady) Julian to descry

That life, in spite of all, is a flame and a pure flame.
Norwich gave both a place in which to live and think,
And both gave Norwich back some ends at which to aim.

In the small gaslit bar the workers clink
The time away till closing time; cajoled
By an open fire and dialect and drink

Served by a landlord eighty-four years old,
We put tomorrow off; tomorrow means
Return to London, the prosaic mould

In which our bright dreams cool. Tomorrow weans
Our backward-looking thoughts, snatches away
What few stray ears of corn our fancy gleans,

And hoots us into court, one further day
Of traffic lights to count, of moving stairs
To move on, of dull orders to obey.

Back. We are back; as London now prepares
Old guys to burn and poppies to remember
Dead soldiers with and soup for the Lord Mayor's

Banquet, all items proper to November
When Lord Mayors turn again at the last post
And small boys warm their hands to the last ember.

The year has chilled, our chill hands welcome roast
Chestnuts, the vistas of the Park are bleak,
The bank of blowsy dahlias, which engrossed

The view from our bedroom window just last week,
Is bare brown earth where gardeners are sowing
Minefields of tulip bulbs, the factories reek

With lethal fogs to come, the Thames is flowing
As dourly as the Wensum, summer has gone
Long since and middling cheap, autumn is going, going,

The hammer hangs and taunts the gems that shone
Only while they were worn. The auctioneer
Cries with the parrot's voice: 'Come on, Come on!

Any more offers for this tarnished year
Which even now at a pinch might take a polish?'
No; no offers from me. Let the gutter urchins jeer

The dying guy; let the breakdown gangs demolish
The gold pavilions; let the trees denude
Themselves and the abolitionists abolish

All summer's frills and freeholds, We, imbued
With devil-may savoir faire will lightly kiss
Our hands to what our minds have long eschewed

And turn to greet the winter. Could we miss
The coming months, we would not. Though by now
Some new star may have burst from time's abyss

Upon the Eastern skies, our skies allow
None but the usual quota of fixed stars
For us to journey by. Whether we disavow

Mystical signs or not, our life debars
Our living by the bread of heaven alone,
We still must chore our chores and clean our scars

And thus notch off these days that are small days but our own.
Tuesday the Third: to the dentist. Who explains,
As always, how my growth of gums and bone

Is something quite peculiar; with some pains
In both and in my mind, and having read
Reports that the maxillary remains

Of some so-called ape-woman, now proved dead
A million years in Africa, are delighting
The savants, my jaw too, I think, could shed

Some million years from now just as exciting
Light upon something; though, of course, even then
My teeth would not be typical and the writing

Of theses in a world devoid of men
Seems rash to bank on. Time must have a stop—
And so must this poor tooth, I will tell you when

You hurt me; these same teeth must grind and chop
And grit themselves from now till Saturday
The Seventh, when I will drop it all and drop

In at a sporting fixture. I wake gay
On Saturday the Seventh, search the morning
Paper for what the sporting writers say

About the opposing side and find a warning
That they are strong—with other warning cries
Of other kinds of danger; almost scorning

These latter (since it gives me no surprise
That Persia or Trieste has trouble still)
I read—and drop it all—that Gwilym lies

In a coma in New York and is seriously ill.

Canto XVIII

Lament for the Makers. Monday comes; at noon
Gwilym died in New York; if it was late
For his strange kind of poet, it was soon

For all who knew him and we need not wait
To meet his like; his like is seldom born,
Being admitted through the Ivory Gate

Where most must enter through the Gates of Horn.
Now all our childhoods weep and all our early
Loves, the deep-bosomed goddesses of corn,

The Celtic heroes playing chess or hurley,
The dancers in the nursery fire, the fauns
And satyrs at their ancient hurley-burley

Among the woods of Wales. A grey day dawns
For all of them, and for us. The Singing Tree has shed
Its leaves and once again the enamelled lawns

Of old Damoetas miss the measured tread
Of Lycidas. And we? Simply, we find it hard
To accept that it is Gwilym who is dead,

Whom we had seen so lately with a card
As usual up his sleeve, a cock in his eye:
A jester and a Quester and a bard,

One who would always throw the Parrot's lie
Back in its beak, who knew some mountains must be climbed
Because they are there—and also because they are high.

And so he cut his steps in the ice and rhymed
His way up slowly, slowly by a star,
While in his ears the bells of childhood chimed

And avalanches roared beneath him far
And the Three Kings went with him and the Three
Gold Shoemakers of Wales, who would not mar

A single stitch on a shoe, no more than he
Would botch a verse. He made his own sea-shells
In which to hear the voices of the sea,

And knew the oldest creatures, the owl that tells
How it has seen three forests rise and fall,
And the great fish that plumbs the deepest wells

Of Cambrian prehistory, yet all
The time Gwilym himself stayed young and gay,
A bulbous Taliessin, a spruce and small

Bow-tied Silenus roistering his way
Through lands of fruit and fable, well aware
That even Dionysus has his day

And cannot take it with him. Debonair,
He leant against the bar till his cigarette
Became one stream of ash sustained in air

Through which he puffed his talk. The nights were wet
And incomparably alive; only three weeks ago
We met him last—for the last time well met—

And that was this. Evans who used to know
Him at his Swansea school, Calum and Price,
Devlin and Gorman—and others, row on row—

Remember such well-meetings. On high ice
An ice-axe falls and flounders down a slope,
The last step has been cut, the last device

Devised, and we below must give up hope
Of seeing Gwilym again, he stays above
Somewhere upon the mountain while we grope

Our own way back. Something, snowflake or dove,
Follows us down with something in its beak,
A green sprig; a token. Of peace? Of love?

Tuesday the Tenth: we find it hard to speak
As yet without a catch; when we begin,
The mind is willing but the words are weak,

A pain of sorrow runs from throat to chin—
And then the wave recedes. Was it really I
Who felt like that just now? I cannot pin

It down, whatever it was, and am wondering why,
When in a wink whatever it was comes back
Like thunder out of a clear and placid sky

Stretching our nerves and notions on the rack
And scattering forth what long ago we hid,
The curtains rustle and the world grows black,

Brakes begin to squeal and wheels to skid—
Where were we? What was it you meant to ask?
And did we once see Gwilym plain? We did.

And heard him even plainer. A whole masque
Of tones and cadences—the organ boom,
The mimicry, then the chuckles; we could bask

As though in a lush meadow in any room
Where that voice started, trellising the air
With honeysuckle or dogrose, bloom on bloom,

And loosing bees between them and a bear
To grumble after the bees. Such rooms are still
Open to us but now are merely spare

Rooms and in several senses: damp and chill
With dust-sheets over the furniture and the voice
Silent, the meadow vanished, the magic nil.

I knew one other poet who made his choice
To sing and die, a meticulous maker too,
To know whom too made all his friends rejoice

In a hailfellow idyl, a ragout
Of lyricism and gossip; Reilly came
From Connaught, and brown bogwater and blue

Hills followed him through Dublin with the same
Aura of knowing innocence, of earth
That is alchemized by light. He was always game

For hours on hours of Rabelaisian mirth,
He too had a rolling eye and a fastidious ear,
He too was proud of his landscape and his birth,

Was generous and vague, would disappear
Blithely when he was wanted, would punctuate
The timetable with gaps, he too would down his beer

With gusto, and he too more often than not was late
To meet the prosy world, and he too died too soon.
But it is twelve years since that Irish gate

Clanged shut and this is different. A new moon
Has fallen like a meteor from the sky;
Sir Patrick Spens has wet his cork-heeled shoon

Once more and once more Arthur has passed by
In the slow barge and all who drew their breath
For the last time in ballad and saga die

Once more for the last time; in Gwilym's death
We feel all theirs and ours. Their flowers are stone,
Are rubble. Vanity, the Preacher saith,

Of Vanities—But Gwilym from his lone
Pulpit calls back: I see no emptiness
But fulness of all fulnesses my own

And everyone else's too. Deirdre plays chess
With Naisi, neither caring which will win,
For both of them are doomed and yet their doom may bless

Posterity, who always must begin
From the beginnings; Gwilym knew that well
And never stopped beginning; sink or sin,

Doubles or quits, he dared the passing bell
To pass him and it did. The Ass his brother
Now at long last can crop the asphodel,

Whose recent loads had made him limp and smother.
But, when you can risk a pound, why save a penny?
'After the first death there is no other.'

More power to the Makers. Of whom, he made as well as any.

Canto XIX

'All out!' the voices cry in the Park, 'All out!'
It is hardly time for tea but November trundles on.
We had forgotten what we were about,

Lost in the thorny paths of the Mabinogion,
Till the stern voices cried and now the stern
Door marked In Exile opens and upon

Our muddle breaks a verdict: 'If to burn
Be better than to rot and if the worst
Course be merely to die and not to earn

One's death, then other dead men may stand cursed
But not your friend, who always earned and burned.
If, on the other hand, what in the first

Place as one plain historian I discerned,
He played his part regardless of the whole,
By which I mean society, and spurned

The civic virtues, to assess his role
Seems not so easy. On the one hand this
But on the other that. And to condole

Should not condone. A just analysis
Would weigh the pros and cons; the cons are great.'
'Master', we answer, 'do not take amiss

That, with respect, we find you out of date.
There may be civic virtues still, they are not
Those which you cherished in your City State.

We share the word democracy but what
Is Demos now? A muse or two might play
His game at moments, but play cold and hot;

Those poets born all fire, what truck can they
Have with this huge and lukewarm monster, why
Should they remake their many-coloured day

In its ungendered image and decry
Their own clairvoyance for its book of rules?
Let Demos rule the streets, they own the sky.

Society and the whole? We are not such fools
As to equate the two.' The Master smiles
And answers: 'Even today it seems there are two schools

Of thought upon this subject; one reviles
The notion that any artist could fulfil
A conscious social role; the other files

Art in the civil service. Both are ill
Judged theories as I see it; but then my own
Society was unique—we paid the bill

For that in my own lifetime. To condone
Demos was not my object, though I hold
That Demos at his best supplied a temperate zone

In which the arts could flourish and unfold.
You would agree they flourished?' We agree,
But with a rider: 'Ivory and gold,

All the materials he could want, were free
To Pheidias till the goddess raised her spear
To dazzle navies over miles of sea,

Yet on that same Acropolis you appear
To have taken other statues, to our eyes
As beautiful, and used them all as mere

Rubble to plug your gaps.' In mild surprise
The Master answers: 'Then your eyes are wrong;
Those works were primitive, and our supplies

Of masonry were short, nor had we long
To fortify the citadel. After all
We were solid practical men.' A ghostly throng

Of too, too solid Athenians begins to bawl
Practical tactical words: 'Injustice pays.
Unless you knock your neighbours down, you fall.

Imperialism means the means to raise
Standards of life at home. What do we care
If Potidaea whines and Megara brays?

It is we who count. Let Mitylene dare
To revolt, let puny Melos dare to stay
Neutral, we have no sentiment to spare,

They and their like are merely in our way
And call out to be massacred. One vote
By Demos and self-interest wins the day

Over those pleas for mercy that connote
A failure to keep up to date.' 'Aye! Aye!'
Shouts Demos in his haste, and cuts each throat

In Melos. And the proposal they should die
Was brought by whom? None other than the friend
Of Socrates on whom all Athens placed such high

Hopes, who was such good company, a blend
Of vineleaf frolic and contriving wit,
And who turned out a traitor in the end.

'Master, if Athens was a so well-knit
Harmonious whole, where is your harmony here?
How does this typical Athenian fit

Into your pattern?' He replies: 'I fear
That pattern was dissolving long before
Alcibiades ruined it. Is that not clear

From my own history of the war, the war
Which broke both Athens and me?' He turns his back
And leaves us gaping at a famished door

Still marked In Exile, with not even a crack
Of violet light beneath it. The Eye of Greece,
Turned to a statue's eye, has lost the knack

Of vision; all the gold of the Golden Fleece
Will not put Phoebus Apollo back in the sky.
The war which broke us? Which war? Or which peace?

We wonder, staring in that hollow eye:
Are we in exile too? If so, all praise
To those in this strange land who still defy

Its brash new age and thus redeem our days
From uniform sterility. I read
In the evening paper that the opening phase

Of experimental bombing should proceed
Quite equably in Kenya, a big stick
Of bombs to make all terrorists take heed,

A bitter pill to make the forest sick
And vomit its black poison; so the paper
Assumes at any rate. But a dark thick

Miasma seeps between its lines, a vapour
Of fear and hate obscures the printed page,
Down its long columns devil-dancers caper

While rattles and dark drums foment a rage
Which neither all the leaders of Whitehall
Nor all the Fleet Street leaders can assuage.

Yes, history makes bleak reading after all
And exile is the place for it. I toss
This paper in the basket and instal

Thucydides on his shelf once more and cross
Once more from the public to the private sphere
Where waste and loss are felt as waste and loss

But where at least some balance of good is clear
And hollow sockets gleam once more with eyes
And living words revive the dying year.

It is the time when someone we know dies
That life becomes important; it is the same
Time that the leaves fall and the trees rise

In their own right, articulate as flame,
It is the same time that time is crime
And virtue all in one, when pride and shame

In their own time blend and transcend their time.

Canto XX

To Wales once more, though not on holiday now;
Glued to my seat, whirled down a ruthless track
To Wales once more, grasping a golden bough,

Key to the misty west. I am wearing black
Shoes which I bought with Gwilym in Regent Street
To travel to Drumcliff in, five years back;

Drumcliff was wet, those new shoes cramped my feet
At Yeats's funeral; they are not so smart
Nor yet so tight for Gwilym's. From my seat

I see my night-bound double, slumped apart
On a conveyor belt that, decades high
In emptiness, can neither stop nor start

But just moves on for ever till we die.
It is too late for questions; on this belt
We cannot answer what we are or why.

Unseen festoons of steam, of thought, may melt
Into the past, and passing lights suggest
Long rows of candled shrines where once we knelt;

Once is the operative word, the best
If least is to stay put and let each light
And thought fly east, the body still bound west,

Vacantly staring at the vacant night,
A world of space with yet so little room
To live in. But of a sudden I catch sight

Of one good presence, her, her without whom
I would not, could not, live; she too is there
Beside me on that moving belt of doom

That grinds through small dark stations of despair;
Until at last, stopping in one dark station,
We see a sudden flounce of light, a flare

Of gules and gold make an annunciation
As one lone engine shunts across a lighted
Window and scrolls of steam unscroll in wild oblation.

Then on to Swansea for the night, benighted
In black and barren rain. But night must end,
And ending banishes the rain. Delighted

Morning erupts to bless all Wales and send
Us west once more our sad but sunlit way
Through hills of ruddy bracken where each bend

In the road is another smile on the face of day.
We stop at random for a morning drink
In a thatched inn; to find, as at a play,

The bar already loud with chatter and clink
Of glasses; not so random; no one here
But was a friend of Gwilym's. One could think

That all these shots of whisky, pints of beer,
Make one Pactolus turning words to gold
In honour of one golden mouth, in sheer

Rebuttal of the silence and the cold
Attached to death. The river rolls on west
As proud and clear as its best years have rolled

And lands us at the village, which is dressed
In one uncanny quiet and one kind
Blue sky, an attitude of host to guest

Saying: Come share my grief. We walk behind
The slow great heaps of flowers, the small austere
And single laurel wreath. But the numbed mind

Fails to accept such words as tempt the ear—
The Resurrection and the Life; it knows
Only that Gwilym once was living here

And here is now being buried. A repose
Of sunlight lies on the green sloping field
Which should hold goats or geese. My fingers close

On what green thoughts this acre still can yield
Before we leave that deep, that not green, grave,
That letter to be superscribed and sealed

Now that it has no contents; wind and wave
Retain far more of Gwilym. What he took
From this small corner of Wales survives in what he gave.

The green field empties, with one tentative look
Backwards we move away, and then walk down
To where he lived on a cliff; an open book

Of sands and waters, silver and shining brown,
His estuary spreads before us and its birds
To which he gave renown reflect renown

On him, their cries resolve into his words
Just as, upon the right, Sir John's just hill
Looks now, and justly, Gwilym's. We leave the curds

And crimps of flats and channels and through the still
Evening rejoin the mourners. If a birth
Extends a family circle and glasses fill

Confirming its uniqueness and the worth
Of life, I think a death too does the same,
Confirming and extending. Earth to earth,

But to the whole of it. In Gwilym's name
We talk and even laugh, though now and then
Illusions (surely illusions?) rise, to shame

My reason. Three illusions. One: that when
We left that grassy field, we also left
Gwilym behind there, if not able to pen

One word, yet able perhaps to feel bereft
Or maybe to feel pleased that such a place
Remains to him. Then was it gift or theft,

This burial? More rational thoughts efface
Such whims, but the second illusion comes: perhaps
Gwilym has slipped off somewhere, into the grace

Of some afterlife where free from toils and traps
He revels for ever in words. These fancies too
Flicker like Will o' the Wistfuls, and collapse;

Since, even if an afterlife were true,
Gwilym without his body, his booming voice,
Would simply not be Gwilym. As I or you

Would not be I or you and, given the choice,
I, for one, would reject it. Last, the third
Illusion, which gives reason to rejoice

Or rather strong unreason: what we have heard
And seen today means nothing, this crowded bar
Was one of Gwilym's favourites, it is absurd

He should not join us here, it was always going too far
To expect him on the dot but, late or soon,
He will come jaunting in, especially as there are

So many of his friends here to buffoon
And sparkle with. However, if not tonight,
We need not wait for leap year or blue moon

Before we run across him. Moons are white
In London as in Wales and by tomorrow
We shall be back in London where the sight

And sound of him will be welcome, he may borrow
A pound or two of course or keep us waiting
But what about it? In those streets of sorrow

And even more of boredom, his elating
Elated presence brings a sluice of fresh
Water into dim ponds too long stagnating.

This is the third illusion, a fine mesh
Of probable impossibles; of course,
Of course, we think, we shall meet him in the flesh

Tomorrow or the next day, in full force
Of flesh and wit and heart. We close the door
On Wales and backwards, eastwards, from the source

Of such clear water, leave that altered shore
Of gulls and psalms, of green and gold largesse.
November the Twenty-fifth. We are back once more

In London. And will he keep us waiting? . . . Yes.

Canto XXI

The thirtieth inst., too soon the thirtieth ult.
I clear the in tray, feed the out, and leave
My twin black telephones alone to insult

Each other in my absence and deceive
My office with portentousness, pretending
That on this reach-me-down December's eve

There really is some urgent business pending.
However, I take the train, to take the floor
Beneath those dreaming spires, now condescending

To get their dreams refaced; Oxford once more,
But I am here to speak and spend one dreamless night
And then move on (I have been here before).

December dawns, with neither bark nor bite,
And I move on through lands I long had taken
My leave of, which had seemed, when out of sight,

To be also out of life but no; there is Wiltshire bacon
Still browsing in the fields; what I forsook
Continues on its own and fails to feel forsaken.

And so to Bath, which equally does not look
As though it had missed me since I was thirteen
And peopled it with Romans from the book,

At that time knowing nothing of salts and spleen,
Of Wits and clouded canes, for then as now
The Eighteenth Century and its Silver Mean

Were not my pet nostalgia. To avow
Myself Augustan works against my grain,
The powdered wig that boosts the pompous brow

Could make me boast my wiglessness and feign
Rusticity; and I would rather wear
My own if thinning hair and thereby gain

Something at least that I at worst can tear.
Not but what Bath beguiles me. Taste and measure
Of biscuit-coloured stone in curve and square,

The inference that life is either leisure
Or convalescence and that self-respect
Is not so much a duty as a treasure

And that due exercise of intellect
Denotes the gentleman and that, as Lord
Chesterfield put it, for the Life Correct

Each action at the ball or at the board
Or doubtless in the bed should always be
In minuet time: all this can afford

Me gentle pleasure, though not for long. For me
The Eighteenth Century, like Ovid's Rome,
Makes a fine show for sightseers to see

But never a context where I feel at home.
Yet let me take my Bath this winter day
In would-be minuet time through the foam

And steam of many bodies, a mixed display
Of history where the age of different ages
Seems relative, centurions at play

No older than those belles in their brocaded cages
Carried by stinking chairmen to leave cards
In one another's lodgings by slow stages.

Only the ground has risen. As regards
Tombstones, the Roman slabs lay snug below
In that built-over darkness which retards

Time while above them merchant, soldier, beau,
Left their own marble cards on the Abbey walls
In token that two centuries ago

Fresh from their banks and battlefields and balls
They each and all of them showed all the expected
Virtues of Christian gentlemen, paid calls

On those that were well off or well connected,
Men like themselves of a superior mind
Who never skimped their duties nor neglected

The chance of what their probity could find
In the City or Bengal; if they must die
And leave not a rack nor a pinch of snuff behind,

At least they would leave a fortune. Here they lie,
These worthy notables who knew no doubt
Of their own worth; under that well-groomed sky

Accomplishments were in, enthusiasm out,
Although to our mind perhaps it seems a pity
That prose and reason ran to fat and gout.

No matter; they were sensible and witty,
Were ornaments to England and enjoyed
This still to be enjoyed and ornamental city.

Gentlemen? Yes: but Christian? From the fan-vaulted void
Of this most secular church no dove descends.
And, since the phrase rings stale and much alloyed,

I leave these noble names to their own ends,
The Pumproom to its phantoms, and pursue
My course to where a mist of trees descends

Beneath a mouth of stone that drinks the view,
The great outriding Crescent. From a deep
Area suddenly something red and new

Claws at my thoughts and wakes again from sleep
The more vernacular, not so secular, things.
And in full berry too. Perhaps holly will be cheap

This Christmas. But in Bath this tree of red blood brings
An odd note in. Shepherds may chase a star
But what would Lord Chesterfield have made of the Three Kings?

Or even of King Arthur? I go by car
Tomorrow through Arthur's country to the Isle
Of Glastonbury; they say it is not far

But in one sense it is. Lord Chesterfield could smile,
He never laughed in his life. But the hermit laughed
Like a drunkard in his dream for a long and a gay while

The night that Lancelot died when, fore and aft
Crowded with angels, the abbey rode the storm
While Guinevere slept below and a great waft

Of spicery rose from the hatch and the cold night grew warm
And the dead began to live. Which is just what
The wits of Bath, for all their sense of form,

Could never have understood. For them a plot
Of flowers was something, like the plot of a play,
That had to be well contrived but the flowers were not,

And the play was not, the thing. They had their day
But starved it of the night. So pray desist,
You arbiters of tattle and Bohea,

Lords of cotillions and queens of whist,
Pray, pray desist from boasting, since in fact
Though there was much you gained there was also much you missed

And now goodbye; I am off to counteract
Your classic with some gothic. Let the bells
Of Wells ring Bath away, let the knights in the clock enact

Their cosmic ritual hourly while vast shells
Of groined and soaring stone echo the seas of God,
And let His gluttonous angels grab their ells

Regardless of that Georgian measuring rod
Which only thinks in inches; let your bevel
Curves become sharper and your evens odd,

Your tenors not so easy nor so level,
Your reasons not so simply based on Reason,
And, if it comes to the worst, let us have the Devil

Rather than mere negation. For the season
Today is mild, too mild, but old Jack Frost
Lurks in the graveyard. Kyrie Eleison.

Pity us for the follies we have lost;
Pity us for our learning, who can count
In light-years by the million, but not the cost

Of even a broken toy. The knights dismount
And let their horses wander where they will;
The Grail is gone but still one whispering fount

Of holiness keeps green the far-seen hill
Where Joseph of Arimathea planted a thorn
Plucked from a crown which, sharp and royal still,

Is said to blossom each time Christ is born.

Canto XXII

So this is Glastonbury. A green hill far away
Round as a lost round table; not a breath
Disturbs the too green grass where these grey ruins say

No more if even so much as the Preacher saith.
Bedivere, Arthur, Lancelot, Guinevere,
They left their names, their mark, and the mark is death.

No more or not so much. Arriving here
For the first time I feel a mild surprise
Not to feel more surprised; the fabulous mere

Is drained; the dreams that tilted in the eyes
Lie shivered in the sockets; glittering helms
And thundering hoofs are gone. This too green scene denies

That ever Arthur ruled those errant realms
Which no surveyor could map, where that unknown
Presence which undermines or overwhelms

(Presence or absence?) nibbled at his throne
Till all his knights began their new Quest, inward bound,
While he remained in the darkening hall, alone,

His elbows on a table which seemed as round
And as large as the world but empty. As for the Quest,
Most knights that year found less than they had found

At other times in a week, lacking the best
Equipment for this venture; all the points
Of the compass focused on one empty West

Where earthly feats were nothing. Stiff in the joints,
Numb in the soul, they rode but could not find
The light that feeds, the glory that anoints,

Maybe a light which they had left behind
These long years in a cradle, maybe a light
Striking them full in the face—but maybe they were blind.

Who knows? Having looked round this green and muted site
We drive some three miles off to visit one
Who in a different sense could be called a gentle knight,

Owen, who once was a walking belfry, the sun
Strode through his lips and boomed in his steps when first
At the age of ten I watched the wild flowers run

Into his fingers and all Dorset burst
In birdsong round his head, trill, twitter, chirp and chaff.
Whom now I find in a cottage, half immersed

In lameness, deafness, blindness. But the half
That still can greet me greets me full, the voice
Comes strong as a gong as ever, and the laugh

As deeply ingrained and warm. Rejoice, rejoice,
Was always Owen's motto; on two sticks,
He still repeats it, still confirms his choice

To love the world he lives in. Memory flicks
The pages over; this was my first master
Who taught me the names of butterflies and the tricks

Of Latin elegiacs; the dull plaster
Busts of the usual schoolroom came alive
And the dull schoolroom clock went faster, faster,

As Owen made the swallows loop and dive
From the high belfry louvers, and so brought
Us children to our senses. Which were five.

But that was the next door county and a thought
Or much thought more than thirty years ago;
All our small fish that caught small flies were caught

Themselves long since and Owen, who could throw
A fly with Izaak Walton, has long since
Had to lay by his tackle. Under a low

Ceiling he sits by the fire; only his words evince
One lasting love for worlds that are wide and green
Through which, through Arthur's land, he walks a prince

Of Arthur's line and through the distorting sheen
Of those enormous lenses I catch his eye
And we both know we know what we both mean.

And then I leave. Under a gentle sky
Bronze-wintered hedges, feathered fans of winter,
Old trees and grey stone roofs go swerving by,

One stockstill man on the road comes westward like a sprinter
And soon we are back in Wilts; and the downs climb
Where early man spent hours, spent weeks, upon a splinter

Of flint; and now I am back in my own early time
Where I spent days, spent years, learning to doubt
Whether I had not already passed my prime

Before I was even of age. Loping about
On these bare downs, the haunt of ancient man,
With the turf skin-deep and the chalk showing through and the
   knout

Of the hail-studded wind on each stud in my spine, I began
To feel I had never been young. It was here that asleep
In a high long panelled room from the time of Queen Anne

I once had the worst of my dreams, when climbing a steep
Down with my father, one clear and silent day, I went
Ahead of him towards the skyline, he could not keep

Up with me, being heavy; I climbed with my head bent
When suddenly on the skyline there stood a tall
Redcoat rigid as lead and the sky was rent

With the motley noise of a funfair, the brangle and brawl
Of hooters and concertinas and snatches of cockney song,
And I passed that towering sentry and crossed the rim with all

My premonitions on edge, and I looked down and a gong
Rang in my guts for time. Below me, cut in the dead
White chalk lay an amphitheatre packed with a holiday throng,

Tom, Dick, and Harry, peeping, dirty, red
In the face with shouting, bunting and paper caps,
While tiers and tiers below, where all the gangways led

Down to the round arena, newspaper scraps
Capered around the foot of three tall black
Crosses and through the noise I foresaw the world collapse

In my father's mind in a moment, who at my back
Was still coming up, coming up. This was the worst
Of my dreams and I had the worst of it, in the lack

Of my own faith and the knowledge of his, the accursed
Two-ways vision of youth. Childhood was left behind
In the limestone belt with Owen, and here in the first

Inhabited heights of chalk I could feel my mind
Crumble and dry like a fossil sponge, I could feel
My body curl like a foetus and the rind

Of a barrow harden round me, to reveal
Millennia hence some inkling of the ways
Of man before he invented plough or wheel

Or before England, still in her foetal daze
Of forest and fen, had cut the umbilical cord
That bound her to the Continent. It pays,

In adolescence, not to face that horde
Of Stone Age men, who never saw their names,
If they had names at all, pinned on a board

Or stitched on a cloth tab, and yet their claims
To worth are greater by an age-long chalk
Than any modern boy's, however good at games.

Such were the thoughts, the shadows, that used to walk
Beside me on these downs that carve the sky
With a clean indifferent sweep, such are the thoughts that baulk

My sense of value now as driving by
The gates of youth I see youth dawdle down,
Chalk on its shoes, to pass those gates where I

For five years kept on sidestepping the frown
Of an unrecording angel, till it occurred
To me that, whatever purpose or renown

May lie in a record, it remains absurd
To expect an angel to keep it for one, so
I began to keep it myself, word upon fumbling word.

Which was the easier, once I came to know
Gavin, Stretton, and Hilary, all of whom
Living those same years through in that same rut below

These timeless downs, found time enough and room
To keep their records too. When thus befriended,
We feel less need of angels; and our doom,

Though certain, seems—for a moment or two—suspended.

Canto XXIII

December continues mild. The rose garden
In Regent's Park continues full of roses
That look the softer as the rose trees harden

Their ever thinning bones. The feast one presupposes
Is rarely what one gets. That Christmas should be white
Is something we go on with, like false noses,

But neither the nose nor the season usually matches right.
And so this year, if Christ should be born again,
He will be born, in a sense, in our despite.

The bouncing robin and the shrinking wren
Will find no snow in which to shrink or bounce,
Nor will the stars mean much goodwill towards men.

The news continues mad, the bigwigs trounce
Each other, Science in her armoured huts
Sharpens her claws and bides her time to pounce,

And pessimism whines and optimism abuts
On lunacy and works and days grow weary—
Goodwill towards men my foot! I hate their guts;

Or lack of guts, corrupted by some theory
Or else, their theoretic sense asleep,
Jogging along from dreary point to dreary

Point till the birthright that we could not keep
Returns and stabs us in the back; even then
We are not much surprised, finding the death of sheep

As natural to us as the life of men.
Oh well; December continues mild, at least
We shall not suffer frost-bite in that pen

In which, when first we penned ourselves, we ceased
To have the right to complain. So here we are,
Prepared to huddle through, our ideas creased

Neatly from knee to ankle; somewhere far
From here three unwise men are making tracks
Though certainly not for home. Who thinks a star

Could lead one home? Those ice-cold bivouacs
Are not for us; why should we follow wild
Lights that refuse to let the soul relax

And, at the most, might lead us to a child?
Where is the sense of it? We had rather stay
Just where we are. December continues mild.

Green shoots come stabbing upwards day by day,
Though prematurely; while our premature
Yearnings to love or honour or obey

Something or other wilt in the impure
Air of Kings Log and Lud. This dying year
Could beg a mumming doctor for a cure

But not so many mummers doctor here
And Harley Street seems short of elecampane,
The humpenscrump that charmed some forebear's ear

Now makes the roast pigs caper in Cockayne
And ritual has been banished into dream
While we—we express ourselves. Ourselves in vain;

Who lose those selves by finding them, it seems,
And lose the others too, in our thick mists
Of introspection or in our own schemes

For their own good. We turn philanthropists
Forgetting human beings. But, although
We do our best, humanity resists.

For which may men be thanked. No vast bureau
Or consulting room can snuff their lights for good,
Even for their own good. Though burning low

They are not quenched and, though a fleecy hood
May mask their faces in the bleating pen,
I must withdraw my words; a tree is not dead wood,

A man in sheep's clothing may turn again
And shed his ticks, become once more a man.
So, after all, why not goodwill towards men?

Let then this season open like a fan
Or Japanese flowers in water; let surprises
Arrive by unexpected caravan

Or up the moving stairs in glad disguises
Or from the sky in a great sheet containing
Flesh, fowl and fish all colours, shapes and sizes,

Not common nor unclean. And these remaining
Days of December do surprise; one day
My son appears from nowhere, after straining

At gnats to swallow a camel, and goes his way
At once across the Atlantic, there to tackle
The problems of his nineteen years and pay

The tax on all the ages. Dry twigs crackle
Into new light and heat and burn the hurdled pen
Wide open, what was meant to cramp and shackle

Becomes a beacon and a warmth for men,
The Parrot is gagged, the isle is full of voices
Beyond a parrot's range; my daughter with her ten

Years reappears from nowhere, the house rejoices,
The dog stands on its head, a festive aura
Descends on Devlins, Gormans, Blundells, Prices, Boyces.

Whose mantelpieces begin to brim with flora
And fauna out of the past, Tithonus finds
Himself rejuvenated for Aurora,

And I slip off to where the unlettered hinds
And miners watch an oval ball cavort
In a huge roaring box, a black shirt grinds

A red shirt in the mud; the joy of sport
Identifies oneself with X or Y
Or even with that ball, which one minute gives short

Change with its bounce and at the next will fly
Madly beyond and over; while this crowd
Also is something to identify

Oneself with, lose oneself in, on one loud
Raised beach one pebble in fifty thousand, tinted
Pink by the sinking sun; those muddy but unbowed

Players are me, this crowd is me, that undinted
And indestructible mischievous ball is me,
And all the gold medallions ever minted

By sinking suns are mine. Beside a distant sea
A Phaeacian princess throws a coloured ball;
From Ancient Ireland comes the repartee

Of hurling sticks. This game links up with all
The ball games ever played; and looking back
To thirteen years ago this month I call

To mind New York and Isabel whom black
Waters had blotted out while I sailed far away
In a snaking laddering boat, an eastward doomward track,

With the survivors of the *Jervis Bay*
Absorbed in silent pingpong. Tit for tat
Went the tiny ball on the lurching table, grey

And silent men replied with bit for bat,
Tittle and tattle and rattle and battle; the word,
The last word perhaps was battle, and this was that.

Like bowls on Plymouth Hoe. Is it absurd
To have preferred at times a sport to works of art?
Where both show craft, at times I have preferred

The greater measure of chance, that thrill which sports impart
Because they are not foregone, move in more fluid borders.
Statues and even plays are finished before they start,

But in a game, as in life, we are under Starter's Orders.

Canto XXIV

December the Twenty-third: I visit the Ancient East
In the British Museum where as a little boy
Goggling with awe at blends of man and beast

That loomed and bellowed above me, giggling with joy
At names like Memphis and Thebes, I felt that beside
These monsters life-sized life-shaped things must cloy;

Nor did these seem unnatural, they complied
With early dreams of mine, which decades later
I felt again, watching the Sphinx deride

The lives on which she turned her back; the traitor
To life within us all reorientates
Himself with her to flout the world's creator

By brooding on the desert which negates
And abnegates for ever. So today
I seek my boyhood's favourite, her who hates

And punishes men with the skill of a cat at play
In a universe of mice, that sleek cat-headed
And hatchet-profiled goddess, to obey

Whom will not fill the bill, she must be dreaded
With the moon on her head and her tight skirt and her bland
Whiskers and small round breasts; our deep embedded

Lusts fear and fears lust after her, the land
Will run with blood if so she wills, and yet
She bears the key of life in her left hand.

And the whole story is other. We forget
That, when the world lay under water, one
Small hill of silt rose slowly through the fret

And froth of chaos, and the enlivening sun
Began all life on that pyramidal mound,
Since when each year sees all life rebegun

By flooding and ebbing Niles in the ransomed ground,
And every pyramid represents that first
Mud eminence; the Pharaohs may sleep sound

Inside and underneath, their sleep is nursed
By dreams of life, each tomb remains a token
Of resurrection; what the Sphinx has cursed

These pyramids redeem and what was broken
Has here been mended in these heaps of stones,
All flesh redeemed in stone, the first and last word spoken.

The Wisdom of the East? Was it mere bones
And riddles? Or did one of the Wise Men
Set out from here, from Egypt, all the groans

Of the builders' gangs behind him; in front, beyond his ken,
The groans of a woman in labour? Did he guess
That the Book of the Dead must be revised again?

Or one from Babylon? Did the memory press
Upon him of Gilgamesh who set out
To find a cure for death, through his distress

At having lost his friend, and through his doubt
Of all death-ridden life; who found the plant
Of everlasting youth but even then, without

Thinking, he laid it down—and the powers grant
No second thought; for in a tempting lake
He bathed himself while askew, askance, aslant,

A small dark hole released a small dark snake
That swallowed eternal youth; a moral which
Has weighed upon all Babylon since, an ache

In the back of the heart, a twitch in the nerve, an itch
In the front of the soul. So maybe those brick towers
Did send their man to Bethlehem with rich

Gifts; did he guess that there are other powers
Which do grant second thoughts? Or, further east
Again from where the mad monsoon devours

And at the same time nourishes, did some priest
Or rajah glimpse one star between those clouds and leave
That banyan maze where everything had ceased

Long since to be itself, where the god Shiv
Destroys while he creates and where his wife
One moment will reprieve, and next bereave,

With equal pleasure; there she squats, a knife
In one hand, in the other a bowl of rice,
Ready to end a famine or start a strife,

But always to be feared, one moment nice
And dainty as a bride, the next a blear
Fanged hag picking a corpse, her paradise

A choir of gibbering skulls, a grove of fear,
Of dense black rotting trunks that multiply for ever.
Did one of those Three Wise Men start from here?

If so, where were they bound for? Can we sever
Two thousand years ago from here and now,
Or Bethlehem from say Birmingham? I never

Can make of history what the dates allow
Or clamp historic places to the map;
Gas Street seems old as Memphis and the brow

The foundry worker mops beneath his cap
Seems wrinkled deep as Joseph's. By outmoded
Canals beneath black piles of slag and scrap

One still can find a stable. And if corroded
Iron makes room for steel and glass, what then?
Statistics in the end must be decoded

Into the works, and days, and lives of men
Who still are born and die. Profit and loss
Will not prevent the robin and the wren

Mourning the babes in the wood; no chromium gloss
Could ever disguise a manger, no transmitter,
Gantry or pylon dare replace the Cross.

No; not a white Christmas. It would be fitter
To sweep up all the snow from the Christmas cards
And stack it in this museum under the bitter

Gaze of the granite gods and among the shards
Of broken epochs; ours is merely breaking
And, as for real snow, in Russia perhaps the guards

Have some such on their boots in the raking, aching
Wind as they watch the firing squad prepare
For this day's task of making or remaking

Or perhaps unmaking history. Unaware
Of which event as yet, I leave these labelled blocks
To stand up straight or sit down straight and stare

At where great rivers should run and herds of kine and flocks
Of kites should fill this gallery; and I leave
The Roman busts in the next to dust their locks

And rub their elegiacs up and grieve
Over the fall of Rome, but meanwhile I
Must hurry home; tomorrow is Christmas Eve

And there are things to parcel and lay by
And baubles to hang up and tinsel stars
To constellate across a plaster sky.

So I come home; a mellow light debars
My chill and sallow thoughts, while she who is she
Who makes this home a home sets nenuphars

Afloat in every carpet and a tree
Ablaze in every room and the stocky dog
Stands on its head once more and a bumble bee

Bumbles in every saucepan and the fog
Is fooled and routed by an electric fire
Which masquerades for once as a Yule log

(Hauled to the hearth of every man's desire)
While I, brought up to scoff rather than bless
And to say No, unless the facts require

A neutral verdict, for this once say Yes.

Canto XXV

And today is Christmas Eve. Once more to work,
Once more to Norwich in a crowded train,
One brief commitment I would rather shirk

Had not my idle working days made plain
That I must work when other people idle,
And serve me right. But oh for elecampane

Now I am long in the tooth and cannot bridle
My thrusting paunch or halt my thinning hair;
Oh if some mumming bum of a quack would sidle

Rapidly up with a motley mockery air
To pull that long tooth out, a time-worn stunt
But so is Norwich itself; and now I am there

I find that both its lights and lacks affront
Both expectation and reminiscence. Was this
Poor hole in the night, where weary engines shunt,

The town where two months back I was prepared to kiss
Its flints from pure nostalgia? Never mind,
I have a job on hand and must not miss

The time or place; before I know it I find
Myself at a microphone with miles of flex
Twining around me and myself entwined

By headphones with the world and at the becks
And calls of each blind sound wave, but what most
I hear is one strange thing that taps and pecks

And pecks and taps, a woodpecker, a ghost,
A time signal in Eden. But before
It pins me like a bug to the last post

Or the first apple tree, they want no more
Rehearsal on the air and I can spend
The rest of the evening as I will, explore

The slapstick Market, the quiet Close, or bend
My hazel wand of fancy to the wells
Which, walled up far below, yet well up without end.

I am too late for dinner in my hotel's
Grill room but too late too for other things:
Where are the Middle Ages with their bells?

I go for a drink to the Woolpack; the name brings
The merchants back who built East Anglia's churches;
The shepherds back who came before the Kings.

In the bad weather of fancy a sheepthief lurches
Out of a miracle play; in a high mosaic
Contrived in Greece or Ravenna a white dove perches

Under the roof of the world while one archaic
Donkey pretends to listen but the talk,
Greek, Latin, Hebrew, Coptic, Aramaic,

Slides off his glossy back. I empty my glass and walk
Away through the damp mild weather of fact, a blur
Of a moon in the sky with never a bray nor a squawk

Nor a bleat of animal life nor even a rustic burr
But only cold canned music. This makes seven
Years since my Christmases could not incur

The charge of urbanization, without leaven
Of country smells or breathing beasts, without
That sense of open night which opens heaven

Even to those who are no way devout
Nor even wish to be. And it is nine
Since flying bombs and friendship drove me out

To Wiltshire for a three-days anodyne
With Harrap, who is dead. And now this year
I think of this year's deaths. Which in a sense are mine.

Harrap and Wimbush and Gwilym: what was near
Grows far and what was far this year has brought
Nearer by sheer destruction, in the drear

Wastes of Korea or the wastes of thought.
The Jack of Wrecks has trumped and burst the dykes
And hoards of persons have been sold and bought,

Their staring heads drip from the trademarked spikes
Of countless bridges under which the dark
And universal river rolls and strikes

The roots of all our houses. Pariahs bark
And jackals howl across the wincing earth;
The rod of hyssop and the Bloody Sark

Are swept away as relics of no worth
Along with the swaddling clothes. So here tonight
The last thing one might think of would be birth

And yet children are born; once more the light
Bursts through the shattered rafters and the prism
Contains all colours yet adds up to white;

And, in despite of ology and ism,
Barbicans crumble while the stable stands,
And one great catafalque and cataclysm

Condemns the live, revives the wasted lands.
On the one hand, Thucydides keeps saying—
And is struck deaf, struck dumb, by other hands

Already at work (who said no bells?) belaying
Our lives with bouncing ropes. Eight velvet sallies
Leap in the night, eight great bronze muzzles baying

The blurred moon fill the furred and cobbled alleys,
The dark sound tallies with our childhood rhymes,
Wild chimes remembered in December's valleys.

A jewel in his head, the slow toad climbs
The golden bed, the dead boar wreathes his chaps
In rosemary, thyme and bays to praise the times,

The dragon snaps and fools fling high their caps
And bells in the sky, a flounce and flower of folly,
While towering arches march to a stooping apse

Where dandled, candled, crowned in hoops of holly
The little nut tree bears its golden pear
And in hob-bobbing shadows long-tailed Colly

And wall-eyed Dobbin munch and breathe and stare
At what lies quite beyond them. Sinking, climbing,
The changes ring and range from here to There

Till jingling jangling booming clamouring roaming rhyming
Ascending dropping hammering blending changing chopping
Pealing reeling rambling, rumbling tumbling chiming

The last bell dies and I am asleep and dropping
Down to a silent world where a group of silent men
With goatskin hoods and crooks follow one never stopping

And ever silent star; the shepherds are here again
And I am sound and soundlessly asleep,
Silent beneath a peak in Darien.

The morning comes. Which is still night. I creep
Back to my job on hand under a clear-cut moon
While in the top of the sky the sky-plough ploughs its deep

Furrows across the ages. Perhaps it is not too soon
Nor yet too late to be merry. Now, once more
Haloed with headphones, through their crackle and croon

I eavesdrop on a distant summer shore
Where now it is nearly twilight. Somewhere there
Are Herriot and Evans; I deplore

And yet enjoy this commons of the air
Which closes such great gaps, yet also fails
To open such great vistas. Who is where,

I ask myself, and where are winter's tales
In this new global world? Meanwhile the Plough
Ploughs its own stars in deeper while the pails

Ring with the new day's milk and one still patient cow
Still stares beyond to where the skies are warning
That a new sun is rising and that now,

Take it what way you like, is really Christmas morning.

Canto XXVI

A morning bright as summer. The job on hand,
Our radio hook-up, has been hooked and landed
And I am down from the air and back on land

Or rather back on wheels, abstracted, stranded
In a seemingly empty train which saunters through
Unheard-of empty stations and a candid

And overquiet landscape. Is it true
That this is a special day? The telegraph poles
Endlessly filing past against the blue

Remind me that those wires connect with living souls,
Some few of whom I know; and as the long
And backward strand of memory unscrolls,

The slow wheels gather slowly to a song,
My private hook-up, and I start to send,
Wires or no wires, directions right or wrong,

My Christmas greetings out to friend on friend:
To Owen in Arthur's country, may his voice
Wrench from the stone that sword which none can bend;

And joy to Price my host in Wales, to Boyce
Beneath his reasoning spires, to Stretton saying
So much less than he knows, and to Aloys

Who will be with us tonight, to Devlin playing
The immortal Fool in Kent, to Calum and Aidan whom
The Gaelic language loves, to Gorman straying

Where words may will-o'-the-wisp him through their gloom
And glory, and to that other errant maker,
Egdon, who in America finds room

For thoughts of a Christian world or a Cornish acre,
And joy to Evans and Herriot far away,
To Isabel, Hilary, Costa, each a taker

Of pains that they may give, and a glad day
To Jenny with her three children, and to Maguire
Who makes Belfast in all its grime seem gay;

To all of these the fruits of their desire,
Likewise to many others, and to all
Their others cherishing whom their selves aspire

To something more than selfhood; let the wall
Of isolation crumble and the light
Break in, but also out, the black scales fall

From all their eyes together in one white
And final annunciation. With which prayer
The sky outside me changes and my sight

Changes to meet and greet this different air.
For now the pigeons are homing, each equipped
With some short message to repulse despair

And send the Parrot slinking, gagged and stripped,
With his killer's walk far off, while wells of words
Upbubble where the dowser's wand had dipped

And all the winter flowers in showers of birds
With rainbow necks and coral legs and rings
Of gay words round their legs; while some unknown hero girds

Himself once more for the Quest, and the whole train sings
Gladly, sadly, at once, this empty train.
Empty? It chugs and jogs and jolts and swings

And changes as the sky did; what was vain
And vacant becomes purposeful and full,
Crowded with past and future, joy and pain,

And, slow or fast, no one can ever pull
The communication cord; this train goes on,
Unravelling its endless strand of wool

Like Ariadne's ball which led the wan
And doubtful Theseus through the empty maze.
Empty? What little light there was, it shone

On faces he remembered; all his days
And still more all his nights in silence followed
His quickening steps as after long delays

He went to meet that monster which had swallowed
So much of him already. Thus attended
By eyes, not voices, through the unhallowed hollowed

Long lanes of rock he twisted and descended
To find his level and untwist his fate.
So I today, equally undefended,

Not knowing if we are running fast or late,
Walk through this empty train. Empty? To my surprise
Each carriage is full of creatures that look me straight,

If straight is the right word, between the eyes.
But who or what? Some of them should be dead,
Yet here they sit four-square in full disguise

Of life. The wrongs that I have done, thought, said,
Stare back at me. Some of them should be men,
But why are their hands like claws, their eyes an acrid red?

Must I now run this gauntlet over again?
Over and over again? I stumble past
In the lurching train and slowly count to ten

Before I dare to glance at another carriage; aghast
I mark a huddle of men with coloured skins
Had they not lost their skins in the scorch and blast

Of new and clever bombs; and now the train begins
To drum a different note. Why am I here?
And the pat cliché answers: For your sins.

Each meanness, blight, spite, doubt, guilt, hate, remorse and fear
Fills carriage after carriage. Blank-eyed refugees,
Starved children, faceless freaks, appear and reappear,

Each window sweats with horror and disease
In carriage after carriage. Till the train
Changes its note once more; not that all these

Do not remain on board, will not remain
With me further than London. Still, I find
There are other passengers too who can regain

Something of what was lost; one flapping blind
Reveals one old and snubnosed Greek who takes
The hemlock, smiling and with passport signed

In Exile sits next door another Greek who makes
A virtue of necessity; next door
I glimpse an open face, inspired, which might be Blake's,

And carriage after carriage opens more
Inspiriting faces to me, here some sage
And there some Lord of Misrule misruling as before,

Here some young maker in his Maker's rage
And there some mother of ten who having borne
And reared all ten now smiles at her old age.

So it goes on, the train goes on, the horn
Of horror sounds no longer; I can smell
A waft of frankincense, maybe this morn

Is really Christmas, maybe (who can tell?)
The Kings are on this train. All that I know
Is that good will must mean both will and well

And that, crowded or empty, fast or slow,
This train is getting somewhere. I return
To my own seat and wait and, also serving, go

Irrevocably forward. To discern
The future is not easy since those fires
That warm us are the selfsame fires that burn

Our guts, and since the wood of our desires
Consists of single yet entangled trees
Which maybe form a wood the world requires

But yet a wood which none distinctly sees
Or fully finds his way in. This being true,
I wait unmoving, moving by degrees

Towards home where waits one person which is you
Who takes the ancient view that life is holy.
Meanwhile, to bring me nearer to that view,

This train approaches London. Quickly. Slowly.

XII

1952—1956

To Hedli

The days running into each other, but oh the distance
   between!
The march or rout of events grows blurred in printer's ink
With all those public fears which bruise our minds;
Yet, whatever stooge and pundit think they think,
You know, as I know, that their catchwords mean
Far less than what in time the timeless vagrant finds.

To the public

Why hold that poets are so sensitive?
A thickskinned grasping lot who filch and eavesdrop,
Who enjoy ourselves at other men's expense,
Who, legislators or not, ourselves are lawless,
We do not need your indulgence, much less your pity;
With fewer qualms, we have rather more common sense
Than your Common Man, also of course more freedom,
With our burglars' and gunmen's fingers, our green fingers.
So, crude though we are, we get to times and places
And, saving your presence or absence, will continue
Throwing our dreams and guts in people's faces.

To posterity

When books have all seized up like the books in graveyards
And reading and even speaking have been replaced
By other, less difficult, media, we wonder if you
Will find in flowers and fruit the same colour and taste
They held for us for whom they were framed in words,
And will your grass be green, your sky be blue,
Or will your birds be always wingless birds?

April Fool

Here come I, old April Fool,
Between March hare and nuts in May.
Fool me forward, fool me back,
Hares will dance and nuts will crack.

Here come I, my fingers crossed
Between the shuffle and the deal.
Fool me flush or fool me straight,
Queens are wild and queens will wait.

443

Here come I, my clogs worn out
Between the burden and the song.
Fool me hither, fool me hence,
Keep the sound but ditch the sense.

Here come I, my hair on fire,
Between the devil and the deep.
Fool me over, fool me down,
Sea shall dry and devil shall drown.

Here come I, in guts and brass,
Between the raven and the pit.
Fool me under, fool me flat,
Coffins land on Ararat.

Here come I, old April Fool,
Between the hoar frost and the fall.
Fool me drunk or fool me dry,
Spring comes back, and back come I.

Dreams in middle age

Sooner let nightmares whinny, if we cannot
Retrieve our dreams of dalliance. Gloom or green,
We have been drowned or blinded, we have seen
Our springtime lady in her ringtime arbour,
We have been turned to stone or flown through chanting trees,
We have been present at the Crucifixion.
Such make have been our dreams—but what are these?

The debris of the day before; the faces
Come stuttering back while we ourselves remain
Ourselves or less, who, totting up in vain
The nightlong figures of the daylong ledger,
Stick at a point. Our lives are bursting at the seams
With petty detail. Thus we live, if living
Means that, and thus we dream—if these are dreams.

No, sooner let the dark engulf us. Sooner
Let the black horses, spluttering fire, stampede
Through home and office, let the fierce hands feed

Our dying values to the undying furnace.
The watch will stop and mark the red cross on the door
And cry 'Bring out your dead!' at any and every moment,
Unless we can be ourselves—ourselves or more.

Sailing orders

Gangway or Curtain Up! Then forth
We move—white horses, amber lights—
Towards coral islands of first love
Where makebelieving boy and girl
Assume the music of the spheres.

Assume, consume. . . . The music fades,
The curtains and the gangways fall,
We vanish, boy and girl no more,
Since every ocean ends in port—
And yet beliefs are still to make.

And yet beliefs are still to make;
Whip your sea white or flood your stage,
All loves are first, the islands rise
Preposterous, the concentric spheres
Hum round the soul whose age is youth.

Age with the bit between the teeth,
Youth in the amber lights of age;
All ports have oceans in their eye
And stage and quay retain their hands
To raise our gangways, curtains, hopes.

1956

Donegal triptych

I

Broken bollard, rusted hawser,
Age-old reasons for new rhyme,
Bring forward now their backward time:
The glad sad poetry of departure.

445

But arrival? Go your furthest,
The Muse unpacks herself in prose;
Once arrived, the clocks disclose
That each arrival means returning.

Returning where? To speak of cycles
Rings as false as moving straight
Since the gimlet of our fate
Makes all life, all love, a spiral.

Here for instance: lanes of fuchsias
Bleed such hills as, earlier mine,
Vanished later; later shine
More than ever, with my collusion.

And more and mine than ever, the rumpled
Tigers of the bogland streams
Prowl and plunge through glooms and gleams
To merge their separate whims in wonder;

While the sea still counts her sevens
And the wind still spreads his white
Muslin over the strand, and night
Closes down as dense as ever.

But who has turned the screw? We are further
Off. Or is it deeper in?
All our ends once more begin,
All our depth usurps our surface.

Surface takes a glossier polish,
Depth a richer gloom. And steel
Skewers the heart. Our fingers feel
The height of the sky, the ocean bottom.

Yet the cold voice chops and sniggers,
Prosing on, maintains the thread
Is broken and the phoenix fled,
Youth and poetry departed.

II

Acid and ignorant voice, desist.
Against your lies the skies bear witness;

Forgotten words in wafts of mist
Come home to roost, forgotten silence

Will drown your logic fathoms deep,
For age means change and change renewal,
And herds of immemorial sheep
Will find new gaps to break through always,

While high in the west one wool-white cloud
Marks a yet thornier gap and greater
Through which our fathers, dying proud,
Broke out like rams and left their houses

Like pyres from which blue smoke was caught
In upward spirals, carefree omen
For our own selves whose life-size thought
Of death must spiral westward, upward.

Therefore salute to our own selves,
To our brother the Ass, our sister Water,
And the seal that broods on bookless shelves
Who knows no answer, asks no question.

And salute to our uncle, the Knave of Storms
Who wolfs the stars and gulps the Atlantic,
Who cares not a wreck for means and norms
But winnows nerve and brain to spindrift.

And salute to our bride, our Bride in the Moon
Who brings the tides of the world for dowry,
Lightening our threshold late and soon
But never there when we draw the curtain.

III

Which being so, which beauties being evanescent but also recurrent,
And Fate, frustrating, fulfilling, turning the screw,
It is good to pause on the turn, look back on the glittering silent spiral
Of time in a timeless moment where the nether blue meets the upper
    blue.

For now the music will start once more, the trout stream chirp and
    gurgle,

Stiff reeds and soft leaves whisper, sea-gulls cry,
And in black bog-cuttings lambs call to their blackfaced mothers,
And on black wet roads a mouth-organ start once more with its
   Why? Why?

Which it is good to ask provided the question is sung, and provided
We never expect an answer. Who could live
If he knew it all in advance? No, let the rain keep sifting
Into the earth while our minds become, like the earth, a sieve,

A halfway house between sky and sea, being of the water earthy,
And drenched in echoes of our earlier lives
Before we flippered ourselves ashore when our first and last horizon
Was a steelbright sea cut round and sharp with the first of carving
   knives.

So now from this heathered and weathered perch I watch the grey
   waves pucker
And feel the hand of the wind on my throat again,
Once more having entered solitude once more to find communion
With other solitary beings, with the whole race of men.

A hand of snapshots
The Left-Behind

Peering into your stout you see a past of lazybeds,
A liner moving west, leaving the husk of home,
Its white wake lashing round your pimpled haycocks.
Drink up, Rip MacWinkle. The night is old.

Where can you find a fire that burns and gives no warmth?
Where is the tall ship that chose to run on a rock?
Where are there more fish than ever filled the ocean?
Where can you find a clock that strikes when it has stopped?

Oh, poverty is the fire that burns and gives no warmth.
My youth is the tall ship that chose to run on a rock.
Men yet unborn could more than fill the ocean,
And death is the black clock that strikes when it has stopped.

My glass is low and I lack money to fill it,
I gaze on the black dregs and the yellow scum,
And the night is old and a nightbird calls me away
To what now is merely mine, and soon will be no one's home.

1954

The Back-Again

Back for his holiday from across the water
He fishes with spinners or a rubber eel,
Fishes for mackerel or pollock, but also for something
That he remembers now more by the feel
Of the jigging line than by how it looked when landed.

If it was ever landed. Sitting beside his father,
Whose eyes are smoored with distance, he talks of crops
And weather but would prefer to talk of something
For which he has no words. Till the talk stops
And the fire inside and the rain outside are silent.

And his thoughts return to the city as he fingers
His city tie, thinking he has made good,
Gone up in the world, on the whole, were it not for something,
Intuited perhaps though never understood,
Which flitted through this room around his cradle.

So, on his last day, walking beside his brother,
Whose dog like a black thought streaks through ditch and fence
Rounding up sheep, he sees in his brother a sudden something:
An oaf, but an oaf with dignity and the sense
That it is a fine day if it rains only a little.

1954

The Gone-Tomorrow

Two years high by the world wide,
It scatters pebbles on every side,
It takes two hands to cake or cup,
It pulls the tails of puss and pup.

And the blaze of whins, the smell of turf,
The squelch of mud, the belch of surf,
The slop of porridge, the squawk of gulls,
Enter that smallest of small skulls.

Which some day, skull and nothing more,
Will lie in a box on a foreign shore;
Nor will those empty sockets be,
Like seashells, mindful of the sea.

For mottled fields and marbled foam,
Cries of birds and smells of home,
Will all have vanished and the skies
Have lost their blue like those blue eyes.

1954

The Once-in-Passing

And here the cross on the window means myself
But that window does not open;
Born here, I should have proved a different self.
Such vistas dare not open;
For what can walk or talk without tongue or feet?

Here for a month to spend but not to earn,
How could I even imagine
Such a life here that my plain days could earn
The life my dreams imagine?
For what takes root or grows that owns no root?

Yet here for a month, and for this once in passing,
I can imagine at least
The permanence of what passes,
As though the window opened
And the ancient cross on the hillside meant myself.

The Here-and-Never

Here it was here and now, but never
There and now or here and then.
Ragweed grows where a house dies

Whose children are no longer children
And what you see when you close your eyes
Is here and never: never again.

Here it was coming and going, but never
Coming the same, or the same gone.
New York is not so far by post,
Yet the posted photograph seems only
The twitch of a corpse, the gift of a ghost,
The winter of a spring that shone.

Here it was living and dying, but never
Lifelong dying or dead-alive.
Few were few but all knew all,
The all were few and therefore many,
Landscape and seascape at one's call,
The senses five or more than five.

So now, which here should mean for ever,
And here which now is the Now of men,
They come and go, they live and die,
Ruins to rock but rock to houses,
And here means now to the opened eye
And both mean ever, though never again.

Wessex guidebook

Hayfoot; strawfoot; the illiterate seasons
Still clump their way through Somerset and Dorset
While George the Third still rides his horse of chalk
From Weymouth and the new salt water cure
Towards Windsor and incurable madness. Inland
The ghosts of monks have grown too fat to walk
Through bone-dry ruins plugged with fossil sea-shells.

Thou shalt! Thou shalt not! In the yellow abbey
Inscribed beneath the crossing the Ten Commandments
Are tinted red by a Fifteenth-Century fire;
On one round hill the yews still furnish bows
For Agincourt while, equally persistent,
Beneath another, in green-grassed repose,
Arthur still waits the call to rescue Britain.

Flake-tool; core-tool; in the small museum
Rare butterflies, green coins of Caracalla,
Keep easy company with the fading hand
Of one who chronicled a fading world;
Outside, the long roads, that the Roman ruler
Ruled himself out with, point across the land
To lasting barrows and long-vanished barracks.

And thatchpoll numskull rows of limestone houses,
Dead from the navel down in plate-glass windows,
Despise their homebrewed past, ignore the clock
On the village church in deference to Big Ben
Who booms round china dog and oaken settle
Announcing it is time and time again
To plough up tumuli, to damn the hindmost.

But hindmost, topmost, those illiterate seasons
Still smoke their pipes in swallow-hole and hide-out
As scornful of the tractor and the jet
As of the Roman road, or axe of flint,
Forgotten by the mass of human beings
Whom they, the Seasons, need not even forget
Since, though they fostered man, they never loved him.

1955

The rest house

The thick night fell, the folding table unfolded,
The black men cooked a meal on the thatched verandah,
The hissing lamp had hypnotised the lizards
That splayed their baby hands on the wired window
While crickets fiddled and sizzled to drown the river
Who, bowling his agelong bias out of Uganda,
Was curdling and burbling his nightlong way to the rapids
Tipsy with goggled hippo and drifting lilies.

And on the dark the voices of unknown children,
So shrill they might be white, sifted and splintered
And shivered away till, noisy lamps extinguished,
The bed beneath the ghostly netting beckoned

To chrysalid or sepulchral sleep. But such
Was now the river's dominance that he filtered
Through even the deepest sleep, weaving his journey
Out of too little history into too much.

1955

Beni Hasan

It came to me on the Nile my passport lied
Calling me dark who am grey. In the brown cliff
A row of tombs, of portholes, stared and stared as if
They were the long-dead eyes of beasts inside
Time's cage, black eyes on eyes that stared away
Lion-like focused on some different day
On which, on a long-term view, it was I, not they, had died.

1955

Return to Lahore

Along and back the creamed arcade
The tall scared Sikh had paced and paced,
Beyond the asylum of the hotel
The Five Rivers had run to waste
With rivers of men's blood as well,
While on the lawn the coloured lights
And tawdry band jollied the nights
A little along, a little back.

'So long! Come back!' So back I come
To find Lahore a matter of course,
At peace and dull. The sober lawn
Regrets the Punjab Boundary Force
(Which, like the drinks, has been withdrawn).
Town of the Moghuls, town of fear,
Where is your cyclist with the spear
Who lurked so long, who looked so back?

Along and back, along and round:
Maybe the cyclist killed the Sikh,
Maybe Jahangir in his tomb,
Though slow and dead, inspired the quick
To gems of fury, flowers of doom.
No matter: this remains Lahore,
Oxcarts and tongas, as before,
Jingling along or lumbering back.

1955

Visit to Rouen

Where she was burned the early market
Deploys its batteries of green;
Only the carrots mimic flame
And all the voices are without.

In hairdressers' and drapers' windows
They drape and crimp five hundred years
Of what was not concerned with dress,
Of what was of the earth, devout.

Westward the cranes look down their noses
Like seahorses, the steamers cry
Between green hills, eastward the bombs
Have made the cathedral graft a skin.

So, between glamour and big business,
Picture postcards and brass tacks,
This town exists upon the surface—
Yet such a surface can wear thin.

And show us gulfs of joy and horror
And bring a name to life, remind
Trader and tripper, bell and siren,
That Joan heard voices from within.

1956

Time for a smoke

Sitting once more outside the British Museum,
Behind me seekers for truth perusing a bottomless well,
I wonder on which floor in the building opposite
When I was a small boy and it a hotel
I stayed and, waiting for the gates to open,
Ran upstairs, trying to beat the lift;

Which was neither good manners, they said, nor good for the heart.
I turn to my left and Queen Victoria's gift,
An Easter Island idol, looks back through me
And I turn to my right and an Easter Island idol
Looks back, over my head. We remain apart
While behind us a million books wait to be opened;

Still, I have time for a smoke. Striking a match,
My mind knows less about it than my hand
To which this town means merely rough and smooth,
Means moving handrails, knobs, revolving glass,
Or the swing doors behind me which just now
It thrust to let its appended torso pass

From the room where buckets knock on the rim of the well;
But the child come down in the lift which he failed to beat
Prefers to linger here with pigeons and sparrows
For whom neither truth nor falsehood, heaven nor hell,
Holds any purport, who have no regrets,
No ideals and no history—only wings.

Jigsaws

I

What ghosts of cuckoo-spit and dew
Veil those fields that once I knew?
And, in my absence, who dare sleep
In beds where once I counted sheep,
Counted and counted and forgot
Where I was—and now am not?

But not to be where once I was
Casts doubt on that same spot, because
Being somewhere now where I am not
It seems no longer that same spot;
The view, without myself to view,
Is gone, like cuckoo-spit and dew.

II

Property! Property! Let us extend
Soul and body without end:
A box to live in, with airs and graces,
A box on wheels that shows its paces,
A box that talks or that makes faces,
And curtains and fences as good as the neighbours'
To keep out the neighbours and keep us immured
Enjoying the cold canned fruit of our labours
In a sterilised cell, unshared, insured.

Property! Property! When will it end?
When will the Poltergeist ascend
Out of the sewer with chopper and squib
To burn the mink and the baby's bib
And cut the tattling wire to town
And smash all the plastics, clowning and clouting,
And stop all the boxes shouting and pouting
And wreck the house from the aerial down
And give these ingrown souls an outing?

III

The gulf between us and the brutes,
Though deep, seems not too wide. Their games,
Though played with neither bats nor boots,
Though played with neither rules nor names,
Seem motivated much as ours—
Not mentioning hungers lusts and fears.

Cow flicking tail, cat sharpening claws,
Dolphin a-gambol, bird a-wheel—
Transpose our hands to fins, to paws,

To wings, we more or less can feel
The same as they; the intellect
Is all we add to it, or subtract.

The iceberg of our human lives
Being but marginal in air,
Our lonely eminence derives
From the submerged nine-tenths we share
With all the rest who also run,
Shuddering through the shuddering main.

IV

Fresh from the knife and coming to,
I asked myself could this be I
They had just cut up. 'Oh no, not you,
Certainly not!' came the reply;
'The operation must have veered
Off course, had not some nameless stranger
Entering your body volunteered,
Hand in glove, to share your danger.'

But hand in glove! one cell from two!
I thought, when stronger, I must ask
Who is this, ramifying through
My veins, who wears me like a mask—
Or is it I wear him? One week
Later I found that I could spare
The strength to ask, but did not speak.
That stranger was no longer there.

V

Although we say we disbelieve,
God comes in handy when we swear—
It may be when we exult or grieve,
It may be just to clear the air;
Let the skew runner breast the tape,
Let the great lion leave his lair,
Let the hot nymph solicit rape,

We need a God to phrase it fair;
When death curls over in the wave
Strings may soar and brass may blare
But, to be frightened or be brave,
We crave some emblem for despair,
And when ice burns and joys are pain
And shadows grasp us by the hair
We need one Name to take in vain,
One taboo to break, one sin to dare.
What is it then we disbelieve?
Because the facts are far from bare
And all religions must deceive
And every proof must wear and tear,
That God exists we cannot show,
So do not know but need not care.
Thank God we do not know; we know
We need the unknown. The Unknown is There.

Easter returns

Easters of childhood heaped in motley shards—
    Unloose no ribbons, loose no bells!
Why rake and sieve what time discards?
    All the grey steeple tells
Is that the cock may veer, but never crow.

Did we then after all, two nights ago
    (Or was it two thousand years?) mistake
The sound we thought we heard? For though
    Lies can keep liars awake,
To be denied, truths must be first believed.

Further, who failed last Friday to feel grieved,
    What right have we to this day's joy?
Whether our childhood stand deceived
    Or not, the years destroy
What happened in the garden, bliss or pain.

Movable feasts. A stuck-in-the-rut refrain.
    Ribbons grow faded, clappers cracked.
What to the child was loss or gain—
    Who knows? was never fact.
Movable? asks the man; you mean removed.

And yet, whether our childhood stand disproved
　　Or not, the myth returns, the stone
Is rolled away once more, the grooved
　　Sad earth still finds her own
Resurrection in corn. As man can find
The same green shooting from the wounded mind.

1956

The other wing

Rat-tat-tat-tash of shields upon Ida
Among pellmell rocks and harum-scarum
Ibex and tettix; willy-nilly
The infant cried while the tenterhook heaven
Cranes through the cracks of its blue enamel
To spot the usurper but metal on metal
Drowns him and saves him, drowns and saves.

Who later, enthroned in his talk-happy heaven,
Felt suddenly harassed, a sky-splitting headache
With nothing to cause it—and out of that nothing
Hard-eyed and helmeted vaulted a goddess;
A shuttle flew like a clacking fish,
A long spear flew, and the journeymen artists
Weighed her in stone, wooed her in stone.

Or in bronze or chryselephant; hence these muted
Miles of parquet, these careful lights,
This aquarium of conditioned air,
This ne plus ultra. Ultra? But yes,
Gentlemen, first on the left beyond these
Black-figure vases there lies a red
Letter or birth day, another wing . . . .

Where are two grubs: one like a sentry
In a tall box, at attention, lagged in his
Mummicose death-dress; one much smaller
Lagged against life—he too has a Mary
But never a Martha to tidy the stables,
Poor Tom o' Bethlehem, only a Mary,
An ox and an ass, a nought and a cross

Whose ways will cross, over and over,
The centuries unwinding the swaddling
Bands and the death-bands; the long thin pupa
Always must wait for the small round one,
Deaf till the warm voice cure him, but Tom
Condemned to another, a haunted, wing,
For all his fire poor Tom's a-cold.

1952

The burnt bridge

So, passing through the rustic gate,
He slammed it to (it broke in two)
As he took quick strides to tempt his fate
And the world ahead was daylight.

But when he reached the haunted coombe,
Glancing left, glancing right,
On either ridge he glimpsed his doom
And the world ahead was darkness.

He slept aloft on a sarsen stone
Dreaming to, dreaming fro,
And the more he dreamt was the more alone
And the future seemed behind him.

But waking stiff and scrambling down
At the first light, the cramped light,
The wood below him seemed to frown
And the past deployed before him;

For his long-lost dragon lurked ahead,
Not to be dodged and never napping,
And he knew in his bones he was all but dead,
Yet that death was half the story.

Still he clambered through the barbed-wire fence
Into the wood and against his will
And the air in the wood was dark and tense,
The world was tense and tortured.

So on he went and the wood went on,
With boughs a-creak, with birds a-croak,
But where, thought he, had his dragon gone?
Where had he gone and wherefore?

Yet he picked his steps and the wood passed by,
The world drew breath, the sun was safe,
When a shining river caught his eye
With a bridge and a shining lady.

She stood where the water bubbled bright
On the near bank, the known bank;
He took her hand and they struck a light
And crossed that bridge and burnt it.

And went to the west, went hand in hand,
(And hand in hand went song and silence)
Till they thought they saw the golden strand
Of the sea that leads to nowhere.

But was it strand? Or was it sea?
As near they came it went as far.
Dragons? she said, Let dragons be;
Those waves ahead are shoreless.

So, far they came and found no shore,
The waves falling, the night falling,
To board a ship sunk years before,
And all the world was daylight.

The tree of guilt

When first we knew it, gibbet-bare
It scrawled an omen on the air,
But later, in its wealth of leaf,
Looked too lush to hang a thief;

And from its branches muffled doves
Drummed out the purchasable loves
Which far below them were purveyed
On credit through the slinking shade.

461

And what a cooing trade was done
Around that tree-trunk anyone
Could guess who saw the countless hearts
Carved in its bark transfixed with darts;

So entering this enchanted zone
Anyone would add his own
Cut neatly with a pocket knife,
There for his life and the tree's life.

And having thus signed on the line
Anyone claimed his anodyne
And, drinking it, was lulled asleep
By doves and insects, deep and deep,

Till he finds later, waking cold,
The leaves fallen, himself old,
And his carved heart, though vastly grown,
Not recognizably his own.

The dove's is now the raven's day
And there is interest yet to pay;
And in those branches, gibbet-bare,
Is that a noose that dangles there?

House on a cliff

Indoors the tang of a tiny oil lamp. Outdoors
The winking signal on the waste of sea.
Indoors the sound of the wind. Outdoors the wind.
Indoors the locked heart and the lost key.

Outdoors the chill, the void, the siren. Indoors
The strong man pained to find his red blood cools,
While the blind clock grows louder, faster. Outdoors
The silent moon, the garrulous tides she rules.

Indoors ancestral curse-cum-blessing. Outdoors
The empty bowl of heaven, the empty deep.
Indoors a purposeful man who talks at cross
Purposes, to himself, in a broken sleep.

1955

462

Figure of eight

In the top and front of a bus, eager to meet his fate,
He pressed with foot and mind to gather speed,
Then, when the lights were changing, jumped and hurried,
Though dead on time, to the meeting place agreed,
But there was no one there. He chose to wait.
No one came. He need not perhaps have worried.

Whereas today in the rear and gloom of a train,
Loath, loath to meet his fate, he cowers and prays
For some last-minute hitch, some unheard-of abdication,
But, winding up the black thread of his days,
The wheels roll on and make it all too plain
Who will be there to meet him at the station.

1956

Death of an old lady

At five in the morning there were grey voices
Calling three times through the dank fields;
The ground fell away beyond the voices
Forty long years to the wrinkled lough
That had given a child one shining glimpse
Of a boat so big it was named Titanic.

Named or called? For a name is a call—
Shipyard voices at five in the morning,
As now for this old tired lady who sails
Towards her own iceberg calm and slow;
We hardly hear the screws, we hardly
Can think her back her four score years.

They called and ceased. Later the night nurse
Handed over, the day went down
To the sea in a ship, it was grey April,
The daffodils in her garden waited
To make her a wreath, the iceberg waited;
At eight in the evening the ship went down.

1956

Visitations

I

Never so lithe in the green dingle,
Never so ripe in the grown hay,
The ghosts of pastoral tease and mingle
With darker ghosts from that dark day
Which means our own. Your own? say they;
How can you prove your minds are single
Or, muted words from worlds away
Setting both ears and nerves a-tingle,
Tell what your ears and nerves obey?

Never so young in their green fettle,
Never so glad in their gleaned light,
Never so proud in pulse and petal,
So much themselves in despite of spite,
Look, they come back; and, burning bright,
Turn roof and tree to dazzling metal
Transmuting all our greys to white
And, when our night begins to settle,
Divulge their day to shame our night.

Never so innocent of lying,
Never so gay in blood and bone,
Never with more that is worth the buying,
Never with less for which to atone,
Never with pipes as truly blown
They pipe us yet where birds are flying
Beyond the ridge to lands unknown
Where we, once come, could boast when dying
We had not always lived alone.

II

When the indefinable
Moment apprises
Man of Its presence,
Shorn of disguises

Himself in his essence
Combines and comprises
The uncombinable.

With cabbage-whites white
And blue sky blue
And the world made one
Since two make two,
This moment only
Yet eras through
He walks in the sun
No longer lonely.

When the unobtainable
Seeming-disdaining
Vision is captured,
Beyond explaining
He can but, enraptured,
Accept this regaining
The unregainable.

With straws in the wind
And stars in the head
And the grail next door,
Though the wind drop dead
And the thresholded sentry
Forbid—let him tread
By the light in his core,
He still finds entry.

When the undreamable
Dream comes clearer
And all things distant
Newer and nearer,
All things existent
Grow suddenly dearer—
Wholly redeemable.

III

The merman under the Plough,
The mermaid under the Southern Cross,
Each on a lonely rock with none but gulls to talk to
And each, he thinks, she thinks, unable to cross

That line to which their constellations bow,
Dissect in mirrors their own eyes and lips
And, to kill time, make wrecks of unknown ships.

The merman under the Pole,
The mermaid under the Southern Cross,
Each staring hard and long as though to outstare the ocean,
He wills, she wills, himself, herself, across
That emptiness to some less empty goal,
But, tiring eyes reflecting failing will,
Focus once more on ships, and time to kill.

The merman under Orion,
The mermaid under the Southern Cross,
Each suddenly, stars apart, grown mindful of their freedom,
He flings, she flings, himself, herself, across
The desert (desert lioness and lion)
And swimming north and south, as both divine,
Still never cross, but meet upon the Line.

1955

IV

Man woman and child
Being each unique
(Their strength and weakness),
Yet some to some
Who glance or speak
Would seem to come
Having more uniqueness;
Come less defiled
Whether strong or weak;
Come more unique
Man woman or child.

King, queen and clown
Having each his day
For fame or laughter,
Yet some who came
That selfsame way
Seem never the same
As those came after
Or lost their crown

Before them. They
Keep each their day,
King, queen and clown.

Live man and dead
Being each unique
(Their pain and glory),
Yet some will have left
By force or freak
To us the bereft
Some richer story;
Their say being said,
They still can speak
Words more unique,
More live, less dead.

V

When the stranger came out of the night
Asking for bread and water
And, according to our lights and the moon's light,
We laid the table on the terrace,
Suddenly all of us felt a waft of danger,
Oddly blended with comfort from that stranger.

Though he spoke quite ordinary words,
Words of whence and whither,
And, according to our view or even a bird's
Eye view, was nobody special,
We felt a shiver in the scalp which seemed like fear—
And yet we wanted him to linger here.

So when he slipped off into the night
Thanking us for his supper
And then, by the moon's light and his own light,
Added that he was an angel,
We were a little, but not so much surprised;
For we had known him always, we realized.

VI

The gull hundreds of miles below him—
    Was it the Muse?
The cloud thousands of miles above him—
    Was it the Muse?
The river intoning his saga over and over,
The siren blaring her long farewell to Dover,
The grasshopper snipping scissors in the clover—
    Were they the Muse or no?

So those who carry this birthright and this burden
Regardless of all else must always listen
On the odd chance some fact or freak or phantom
Might tell them what they want, might burst the cordon
Which isolates them from their inmost vision.

The cradle thousands of years behind him—
    Was it the Muse?
The coffin a headstone's throw before him—
    Is it the Muse?
The clock that is ever impeding, ever abetting,
The bed that is ever remembering, ever forgetting,
The sun ever rising and setting, unrising, unsetting—
    Are they the Muse or no?

So those endowed with such a doom and heirloom
When others can be carefree must be careful
(Though sometimes, when the rest are careful, carefree),
Must wait for the unimmediately apparent
And grasp the Immediate—fairly or unfairly.

The world one millimetre beyond him—
    Is it the Muse?
The soul untold light years inside him—
    Is it the Muse?
The python of the past with coils unending,
The lion of the present roaring, rending,
The grey dove of the future still descending—
    Are they the Muse? Or no?

1955

VII

And the Lord was not in the whirlwind.
He sat in the cave looking out and the cave was the world;
Or he sat in his office with in-tray and out-tray
While nobody, nothing, came in but typed memoranda
Although through the curtainless window the wind was twirling the
    gas-drums
And whipping all London away into interstellar negation—
But the Lord was not in the whirlwind.

And the Lord was not in the atom.
He sat in a bar looking in (and the bar was the world)
On a high metal stool between intake and outlet
Still breathing in, breathing out, but nothing and no one
Passed the swing-doors while he waited and watched his tumbler
    erupting
A genie that grew like a mushroom, deleting the Words of Creation—
But the Lord was not in the atom.

Yet after all that or before it
As he sat in the cave of his mind (and the cave was the world)
Among old worked flints between insight and hindsight,
Suddenly Something, or Someone, darkened the entrance
But shed a new light on the cave and a still small voice in the silence
In spite of ill winds and ill atoms blossomed in pure affirmation
Of what lay behind and before it.

XIII

1957—1960

. . . age iam meorum
finis amorum . . .

Apple blossom

The first blossom was the best blossom
For the child who never had seen an orchard;
For the youth whom whisky had led astray
The morning after was the first day.

The first apple was the best apple
For Adam before he heard the sentence;
When the flaming sword endorsed the Fall
The trees were his to plant for all.

The first ocean was the best ocean
For the child from streets of doubt and litter;
For the youth for whom the skies unfurled
His first love was his first world.

But the first verdict seemed the worst verdict
When Adam and Eve were expelled from Eden;
Yet when the bitter gates clanged to
The sky beyond was just as blue.

For the next ocean is the first ocean
And the last ocean is the first ocean
And, however often the sun may rise,
A new thing dawns upon our eyes.

For the last blossom is the first blossom
And the first blossom is the best blossom
And when from Eden we take our way
The morning after is the first day.

Invocation

Dolphin plunge, fountain play.
Fetch me far and far away.

Fetch me far my nursery toys,
Fetch me far my mother's hand,
Fetch me far the painted joys.

And when the painted cock shall crow
Fetch me far my waking day
That I may dance before I go.

Fetch me far the breeze in the heat,
Fetch me far the curl of the wave,
Fetch me far the face in the street.

And when the other faces throng
Fetch me far a place in the mind
Where only truthful things belong.

Fetch me far a moon in a tree,
Fetch me far a phrase of the wind,
Fetch me far the verb To Be.

And when the last horn burns the hills
Fetch me far one draught of grace
To quench my thirst before it kills.

Dolphin plunge, fountain play.
Fetch me far and far away.

The riddle

'What is it that goes round and round the house'
The riddle began. A wolf, we thought, or a ghost?
Our cold backs turned to the chink in the kitchen shutter,
The range made our small scared faces warm as toast.

But now the cook is dead and the cooking, no doubt, electric,
No room for draught or dream, for child or mouse,
Though we, in another place, still put ourselves the question:
What *is* it that goes round and round the house?

1958

Notes for a biography

I

An oranges (sweet) and lemons (bitter) childhood:
Voices of duty or magic; the first cuckoo;
The longing back and aspiring forward; the double
Feeling that all is new and that all has happened before.

For example, there was a shore
(Oh catnap-happy, catacomb-haunted childhood)
Where head-down first he brooded on pebble and limpet,
Then raised his head to gulp the world entire—

Bumpers of foam and fire,
The horizon carving his guts like a Turkish sword
(Oh gay fire-walking, sad sword-swallowing childhood)
Leaving an ache in his guts and a troubled night.

Call it despair or delight
(Or both), it went. The ringers in St. Clement's
Rang their bells down and under the arch of hands
He escaped, or was carried away, from those ups and downs of child-
  hood.

II

Splinters under the nails, weals on the buttocks,
Schooled to service (or was it a pride of class?)
He graduated at length to a land of babus and banyans
And fought their topsyturvy and held the pass
And was just, so he thought; but lonely.

Until the pass was sold (or was it redeemed?)
And he, who had been so homesick, went home reluctant,
Among his own kind a stranger—and one who dreamed
Of a million strangers who fawned or looked askance,
Yet kept his life worth living.

For now, in the heart of his family, under a night
That knew no jackal or tomtom, he would feel
A ghostly net close round him outside which

Were office, children, wife, and the next well-caloried meal,
But inside which was India.

So the small hours filled with bugs and lathi charges
While the questions hammered away: Had it been strength
Or weakness what he had done and what his rulers had done?
After years of this he arrived at a peace of mind to which
He had graduated at length.

III

White rolling battlements on rumbling lead,
A waste of brine which left him thwarted, blinded,
These waves reminded him of love because
All seas are cruel, spendthrift, endless—or was
It that no love remained of which to be reminded?

So other scenes, which once were scenes of longing
Filled with the absence of one person, now
Revert to sheerer emptiness; the thronging
Memories only serve to witness how
Absent has grown the feeling of her absence.

And yet no doubt, ten years or twenty on,
Scars almost lost and the blood grown cooler, kinder,
Things will come back to him that were never gone
And the shifting sea will stand for permanence,
Wave upon wave, reminder upon reminder.

IV

To the Lords of Convention'—The horses went by
In the racket and dust of the chukker and I
Could assume in my youth that the system was sound
And the world little more than one great polo ground.

But the years they went past and I noticed a change:
The world had grown larger and out of my range.
With the horses gone out and ideas come in,
Where we thought we had ended they bade us begin.

But before we had hardly begun to revise
Those age-old assumptions that clouded our eyes,
What had been in the background now came to the fore
And we found once again that the world was at war.

Then the Lords of Convention they rose up and spoke:
'Your values are senile, your system is broke;
You may still talk of duty but we talk of power,
So open the atlas, for this is the Hour.

Now follow our pointer; look, here is Japan
Where man must now make what he chooses of man,
And these towns are selected to pay for their crime—
A milestone in history, a gravestone in time.'

When I first read the news, to my shame I was glad;
When I next read the news I thought man had gone mad,
And every day since the more news that I read
I too would plead guilty—but where can I plead?

For no one will listen, however I rage;
I am not of their temper and not of this age.
Outnumbered, outmoded, I only can pray
Common sense, if not love, will still carry the day.

V

Lavender blue for love, lavender green for youth—
Never is time to retire.
Let me buy one more bunch and hold myself straight as I can
Not out of pride but out of respect for the truth,
For the gorgeous, though borrowed, fire
Which shone on my cradle and warmed my heart as a man.

Street-cries under my window. Who will buy?
Never is time to retire.
Age and arthritis have crippled me, even so
I will respond to the blue and green in the cry
And purchase all I desire
For just a few pennies or annas, one gesture before I go.

Lavender green for youth, lavender blue for love—
Never is time to retire.
I have had both and unstinted and now, whatever

Doubt may rise from below or terror brood from above,
I will stand as if under fire
With a sweet-smelling bunch in my hand, face to face with Never.

The slow starter

A watched clock never moves, they said:
Leave it alone and you'll grow up.
Nor will the sulking holiday train
Start sooner if you stamp your feet.
   He left the clock to go its way;
   The whistle blew, the train went gay.

Do not press me so, she said;
Leave me alone and I will write
But not just yet, I am sure you know
The problem. Do not count the days.
   He left the calendar alone;
   The postman knocked, no letter came.

O never force the pace, they said;
Leave it alone, you have lots of time,
Your kind of work is none the worse
For slow maturing. Do not rush.
   He took their tip, he took his time,
   And found his time and talent gone.

Oh you have had your chance, It said;
Left it alone and it was one.
Who said a watched clock never moves?
Look at it now. Your chance was I.
   He turned and saw the accusing clock
   Race like a torrent round a rock.

Il piccolo Rifiuto

Impatient with cripples, foreigners, children,
As though they were midges or wasps he refused
Jam on his bread or to walk in the shrubbery.
Crutch and giggle and guttural accent

Were left in the air. He was disabused
Of a world not his, his birth certificate
Faded behind his eyes, his eyes
Blinked as the jets dived on the jampot
He had not ordered and harpy-wise
The insect world grew breasts and talons
And wogs and wops kept babbling and mad
Children went on a spacelark and God
Began to limp and deep in the bad
Shrubbery shrubs that should be ever
Green turned brown. He asked for a stone
But the waiter offered him bread in yiddish.
No, he repeated, I never ordered
Jam, God damn you, leave me alone.

The Messiah

(a memory of 1940)

In Portsmouth, New Hampshire, plugged with morphia,
Cranked up on my hospital bed to see through the window,
I watched in a building one hundred yards away
A light flashing on and off in a window,
Half an hour maybe between the flashes,
And I split in two, one naïve, one know-all:
What's going on over there?

           Why, don't you know, they are smelting.
(*Pause*). But who is?

           The great new surgeon of course.
(*Pause*). New Surgeon?

           Greatest surgeon in the world;
A completely new technique. How odd that you haven't heard of him.
I'm afraid I've not.

           But he's also the new Messiah.
(*Longer pause*). The what?

           A new mutation of man,
He knows the answers to everything.

           Everything?
           Yes, except
He cannot cure himself. It's very sad, you know.
(*Pause*). What is so sad?

479

He's a refugee from Europe.
(*Pause*). But so are many.
Of course, but he is sadder;
He's lost his name, you know.
(*Pause*). He's lost his name?
Yes, whenever one has to introduce him,
To prove who he is, you see, or that he is,
All he can do is hiccup. See where that light is flashing—
Just be quiet and listen and you may hear him hiccup.
I listened and did and began to hiccup too
And the night nurse came in and gave me another shot.
The building that flashed the light was the Maternity Ward.

The Atlantic tunnel

(*a memory of 1940*)

America was ablaze with lights,
Eastward the sea was black, the ship
Black, not a cigarette on deck;
It was like entering a zigzag tunnel.

Old Irish nuns were returning home,
So were young men due for the call-up,
So were the survivors from the *Jervis Bay*;
The tunnel absorbed us, made us one.

But how many miles or days we did not
Know we were one, nor how many waves
Carried in code the words to prevent,
The words to destroy. We were just passengers,

As on this ship, so on our own
Lives, passengers, parasites, never
Entrusted with headphones or signals and out of
The code, yet not in the clear. The tunnel

Might be about to collapse, this whole
Zigzag might be a widening crack
Which led to the bottom before Belfast
Or Liverpool gave us reluctant welcome.

Meanwhile the dark ship rolled, a ball
Prattled and spun on a rolling table;
The sailors from the *Jervis Bay*
Called the score, were otherwise silent.

Homage to Wren

(a memory of 1941)

At sea in the dome of St Paul's
Riding the firefull night,
Fountains of sparks like a funfair,
We patrolled between the inner and outer walls,
Saw that all hatches were screwed down tight
And felt that Sir Christopher Wren had made everything shipshape.

Then went on deck with the spray
Of bombs in our ears and watched
The fire clouds caught in our rigging, the gaudy signals:
London Expects—but the rest of the string was vague,
Ambiguous rather and London was rolling away
Three hundred years to the aftermath of the plague,

And the flames were whippeting, dolphining, over the streets,
The red whale spouting out of submerged Londinium
And Davy Jones's locker burst wide open
To throw to the surface ledgers and lavatory seats
And all the bric-à-brac of warehouses and churches
With bones and ghosts and half-forgotten quotations.

Then the storm subsided and it was dawn, it was cold,
I climbed to the crow's nest for one last look at the roaring foam,
League upon league of scarlet and gold,
But it was cold so I stretched out my hands from the drunken mast
And warmed my hands at London and went home.

Rites of war

So, Fortinbras; Alas is now the keyword here.
A waste you say? Yet graced with swagged and canopied verse,
All tragedies of kings having wings to raise their gloom

(Even as the lights go down the crowns come up) but you, sir,
Have seen far more of gore without this pomp, have heard
Your dying soldiers cry though not in iambics, not
In any manner of speech to reach the future's ear,
Their death being merely breath that ceased and flesh that slumped
As both, it is true, must do ten years, ten centuries, hence,
On a cutprice night, not a flight of angels near to sing
Their souls to whatever rest were best if souls they had.
Still, at this stage and age before, if ever, we read
The story, the glory, in full of your Polack wars and the long
List of your dead—you said a waste, did you not?—we also
Trust for the future's sake you will take your immediate cue,
That curtain, that certain line—and the last chance to boot
For Fortinbras to pass. Go, bid the soldiers shoot.

1958

Jericho

Oh the sun stood still above the Passport Office
And Joshua remembered Moses.
They chewed gum, they sweated gore,
Their visas were refused once more
And the Tables of the Law were broken again.

And the sun stood still above the Law Courts in Fleet Street
And Joshua remembered Moses.
Adulteries and libels both
Got bogged in medieval sloth
And the Tables of the Law were broken again.

And the sun stood still above the hard courts in Hampstead
And Joshua remembered Moses.
Refugees from worlds away
Worked out their loneliness in play
And the Tables of the Law were broken again.

And the sun stood still above the Stock Exchange
And Joshua remembered Moses.
Thousands of ants in pinstriped pants
Went back upon their tracks like ants
And the Tables of the Law were broken again.

And the sun stood still above the dome of Paul's
And Joshua remembered Moses.
The fires were out from the war we lost,
Also the fires of Pentecost,
And the Tables of the Law were broken again.

And the sun stood still above Notting Hill Gate
And Joshua remembered Moses.
The Caribbean in spite of cosh
And flick-knife wouldn't come out in the wash
And the Tables of the Law were broken again.

And the sun stood still above the Ministry of Defence
And Joshua remembered Moses.
Neither sense nor conscience stirred,
Having been ultimately deterred,
And the Tables of the Law were broken again

Yours next

Fruit machines and pin tables—
Someone has got to pay for the round.
Only release the spring, the ball
Will scurry, the coins will clatter and all
That was ill lost may well be found.

Contract and lease and marriage lines—
Someone has got to pay for the round.
Only sign on the line and all
The gains you doubt may come on call
And rate one farthing in the pound.

Stake and faggot and gas chamber—
Someone has got to pay for the round.
Only press the button and all
The springs will twang, the heads will fall,
And yet, whatever drinks are downed,
Someone has got to pay for the round.

Dark age glosses

on the Venerable Bede

Birds flitting in and out of the barn
Bring back an Anglo-Saxon story:
The great wooden hall with long fires down the centre,
Their feet in the rushes, their hands tearing the meat.
Suddenly high above them they notice a swallow enter
From the black storm and zigzag over their heads,
Then out once more into the unknown night;
And that, someone remarks, is the life of man.
But now it is time to sleep; one by one
They rise from the bench and their gigantic shadows
Lurch on the shuddering walls. How can the world
Or the non-world beyond harbour a bird?
They close their eyes that smart from the woodsmoke: how
Can anyone even guess his whence and whither?
This indoors flying makes it seem absurd,
Although it itches and nags and flutters and yearns,
To postulate any other life than now.

on the Grettir Saga

The burly major they denied
The Victoria Cross because of his drinking habits,
Blown up soon after, for some reason reminds me
Of the strong man of Iceland who also died
Under the frown of the safe men, cooped in an islet
With a festering leg and a bad record:
An outrageous outlaw, his mind ill equipped,
His temper uncertain, too quick with his weapons,
Yet had done the scattered farms some service,
Also had made people laugh, like the major
Raising his elbow in the mess at 'Pindi;
But, unlike the major, Grettir was cursed,
Haunted by eyes in the dark, on his desolate
Rock on the fringe of the Arctic knew
The fear no man had ever induced in him,
And thus awaited his doom. Whereas
The major, who also was doomed, slept sound
And was merely cursed by the curse of his time.

on the Njal Saga

The tall blonde dabbing scent behind her ears
And throwing over her shoulder her Parthian curse
To leave her lover facing the world defenceless
Calls up the picture through one thousand years
Of a tall blonde with her hair to her waist, exulting
Over her husband with his bow-string cut
Because he had begged one strand of her hair to mend it.
'Yes indeed, my hair could save your life now—But
Do you remember that slap you gave me once?'
So Gunnar stood with the roof off over his head
And his enemies closed in. She watched and smiled.
Almost reluctantly they left him dead
And they and she thus left a legacy
Of many deaths to come—man, woman and child—
And one great saga casting from those dark
Ages a lighthouse ray, a reminder that even then,
For all the spite and hatred and betrayal,
Men had the nobler qualities of men.

on the Four Masters

The light was no doubt the same, the ecology different:
All Ireland drowned in woods. Those who today
Think it a golden age and at Glendalough
Or Clonmacnois let imagination play
Like flame upon those ruins should keep in mind
That the original actual flames were often
Kindled not by the Norsemen but by the monks'
Compatriots, boorish kings who, mad to find
Loot to outride each other's ambition, would stop
At nothing—which so often led to nothing.
Which is even—tell it not in the Gaelic League—
True of the High King Brian whose eighty years,
Caught in a web of largely his own intrigue,
Soured him with power and rusted him with blood
To let him die in a tent on a cold Good Friday
To earn his niche. And yet he earned his niche.
The last battle was his; maybe the sun came out

Before the defeated Norseman struck him, before
History endorsed the triumph and the rout.
The light was no doubt the same—and just as rich.

Indoor sports

Darts

Begin and end with a double. He places his feet
Square apart on the rubber mat. I bet I shall end
As always on double one. The squeaking chalk
Subtracts, subtracts. . . . What did I tell you? And why
Is it the hardest bed? Singles are useless
And there is no going back.
                              He flicks his wrist,
Hardly looking, and wins.

Shove halfpenny

On the field of elm or slate the lines are far too close;
The brass discs knock each other out of place.
You need a glancing blow with the ball of the thumb;
One disc can knock another one into place
With skill and join her there. No, not like that;
Like this.
          You see. Both safely between the lines.
With skill, as I said. And luck.

Vingt-et-un

Stay, twist, or buy. Ace is eleven or one.
Not really much scope for skill, I could play this game in my sleep;
Still, talking of sleep, it too can pass the time.
Yes, what do you think? I'm going for five and under;
I ought to twist but I'll buy.
                                The small cards fall;
I'm buying again, I ought to be bust, but there—
It paid me not to twist!

Crossword puzzles

Ninety-nine down: a one-letter word meaning something indefinite.
The indefinite article or—would it perhaps be the personal pronoun?
But what runs across it? Four-letter word meaning something
With a bias towards its opposite, the second letter
Must be the same as the one-letter word.
                                                    It is time
We left these puzzles and started to be ourselves
And started to live, is it not?

Idle talk

Flightily falling words like yellow
Leaves are blown into coigns of memory;
The little trees of our youth are bare
While on tall steel masts the big words bloom

To put in the shade, and to shame, our idle
Gossip, to fill our skies with a smell
Like an open drain: ratchet and fang,
Weirds of our children, man-eating flowers.

And yet we continue, frivolous, garrulous,
Plotting our chatter, planting our annuals—
Anecdote, limerick, tittle-tattle, chestnut—
But, come full circle, the leaves are green.

And, come full circle, the chestnut candles
Abide the spark of tapered wit,
While the rotten compost of hackneyed phrase
Reprieves the captive, feeds the future.

For, whether to find oneself or find
Those other selves through whom one lives,
The little words that get in the way
Can also pave the way for a wish.

Shop-talk, club-talk, cliché, slang—
The wind that makes the dead leaf fall
Can also make the live leaf dance,
Though the green of this was the green of that

And all our gems have been worn before
And what we intend as new was never
Not used by someone centuries back
Or by oneself some weeks before.

In despite of which, though the First Garden
Is supposed to be closed to all for ever
The innocence that our days outmode
Seems no more innocent than that

Adam achieved when, holding the half-
bitten, already half-forgotten,
Fruit in his hand, he looked at Eve
And, wholly forgetting Eve herself

As he had known her till that moment,
Looked and felt for the same three words
Which he had uttered time and again
But never like this, and said: 'I love you'.

Country week-end

I

Coffee leaps in a crystal knob
Chugs and glints while birds gossip;
We have been here a thousand years
Nor yet have reached the age of gas.

And a thousand years of songbirds' bones
Are pasted in these cottage walls,
While a thousand years of harvest mice
Wait for our cat to pounce the next.

Outgoing heirlooms: cups and plates,
Nettle and colt's foot, elder hedge,
Blackthorn beyond, then field on field,
And then the skyline; then the sky.

Not ready yet? It takes its cue,
Boils over, and the rats in the thatch
Boil over too, while children's laughter
Rattles the plates and scares the birds,

As once it did when plates were wood,
Coffee unknown and fields unhedged,
Though then as now the sky was ours
Of which our souls were part and parcel,

Tied with blue ribbon or coarse twine.
But rat and bird are settling back
As, eggspoon poised, the youngest child
Assumes this day his lasting life.

Not ready yet? For what may spill
Or shine or pipe or pounce? This world,
Ingrown, outgoing, soon outgone,
Stays ours. We are ready now as then.

II

Forth from a sack of fishing-reels and deck-quoits
Emerge the stubborn boots which once,
Part of my Home Guard outfit, hammered sparks
From Regent Street but are rusticated now

To aid yet another makebelieve, to seal
The countryside with hobnails, while my walk
Becomes a countryman's. As if discomfort
Around the feet could loose and lift the mind.

Boots also link us with the world of folk-tales:
What third son setting forth to bilk an ogre
Or pluck a bride from her redoubt of thorn
Ever wore shoes? I also need my beanstalk—

Hand me that dibble. That the earth is good
Stands trial this week-end. Let it get under
My finger-nails, add weight to what I have read
And wish to think I feel; and to my boots.

Even blisters help, which these same plodhoofs gave me
In the Constable country on an Easter Monday;
It was Nineteen-Forty-Four and the day was full
Of cowslips, birds and beer, but the night, we knew,

Would be full of southbound bombers and a moon
Of which one old farm-labourer raising his eyes
From a pint that might have been a ball of crystal
Said: 'You know, we call this Monty's Moon.'

III

Wild grass in spate in a rainy wind,
We have come from London to stay indoors
With paraffin on our hands, our eyes
Watching through glass the trees blown east.

As if hypnotised, as if this wet
Day were the sum and essence of days
When such spinning shafts of steely water
Struck to numb, or revive, the mind.

As once in a low-slung floating island,
Hardly afloat that day, Tiree,
We stopped indoors in the small hotel
And a young Glaswegian in broad checks

Told our fortunes while sniggering faces
Froze in surprise and fear as the cards
Kept turning up and the rain kept falling.
Or as once, in an Irish island, the turf

Hissed in the fire and I felt marooned
In a whitewashed room in a world of water
Part rain, part brine, where one small ark
Was casting off to find Atlantis,

But I did not dare embark. Or as often,
Much further back, a child I pressed
My nose against the streaming pane
That framed the road to the neighbouring graveyard

On which with luck could be seen beneath
The sodden trees the huddled mourners
At a slow squelch behind the box
Crossing the pane, through the rain darkly.

And so today as these different windows
Blotch and weep in Southern England
Our defences, both of stone and skin,
Seem weak to hold this peace inside

Four walls—Worth what compared with that
First element, those fluent spears?
Spearmen or not, ourselves, in dreams,
This element, once ours, though lost,

In dreams may still be fought and wooed;
So let this rain keep falling, let
This wind from the west be backed by waves
On which the mind can embark anew.

IV

Here too, as in my childhood, twilight
Means pouring in and turning up,
Striking a match, lighting a wick,
A ritual for the hands, a pause

Between the light which, we were always
Told, was not good enough to read by,
And this new light which needed watching
And which, whether good enough or not,

Made print and content both seem different.
So now these oil lamps make a different
Evening from our usual, span
A gap of decades, calling back

Bustling dead women with steady hands,
One from Tyrone and one from Cavan
And one my mother; the soft lights marched
Nightly out of the pantry and spread

Assurance, not like the fickle candles
Which gave the dark a jagged edge
And made it darker yet, more evil,
Whereas these lamps, we knew, were kind

Like good Penates, from their globes
Or tasselled tents conferring peace
Even on the Lays of Ancient Rome.
Just so my reading of middle age

Reads better in this light, without
The chance of a failure at the main
Or a short, without—what matters more—
That sameness governed by a switch

Which could epitomise our times
Where everything, not only light
But food and freedom, thought and life,
Can be switched on just so—or off.

So now it is time. Decant the oil,
Turn up the wick. Call it escape
Or what rude name you like—or call it
A good deed, rather a good night:
One good night in a naughty world.

Nature notes

Dandelions

Incorrigible, brash,
They brightened the cinder path of my childhood,
Unsubtle, the opposite of primroses,
But, unlike primroses, capable
Of growing anywhere, railway track, pierhead,
Like our extrovert friends who never
Make us fall in love, yet fill
The primroseless roseless gaps.

Cats

Incorrigible, uncommitted,
They leavened the long flat hours of my childhood,
Subtle, the opposite of dogs,
And, unlike dogs, capable

Of flirting, falling, and yawning anywhere,
Like women who want no contract
But going their own way
Make the way of their lovers lighter.

Corncrakes

Incorrigible, unmusical,
They bridged the surrounding hedge of my childhood,
Unsubtle, the opposite of blackbirds,
But, unlike blackbirds, capable
Anywhere they are of endorsing summer
Like loud men around the corner
Whom we never see but whose raucous
Voices can give us confidence.

The Sea

Incorrigible, ruthless,
It rattled the shingly beach of my childhood,
Subtle, the opposite of earth,
And, unlike earth, capable
Any time at all of proclaiming eternity
Like something or someone to whom
We have to surrender, finding
Through that surrender life.

Sleeping winds

North

The wind was curled in a ball asleep in a tree
With a young man cutting a heart on the bark;
Something came into the absence of mind of the wind,
He threw off the green and yawned himself over the sky;
The young man also grew to the height of a cloud
And was loud and rapid and free and never to die.

East

The wind was slumped on a charpoy in the bazaar,
Her breasts heavy with history; something crept
Slily under her sari at dead of noon
And while the city slept she craved for water
And jumped to her feet and brushed the flies from her eyes
And took her pitcher and ran to the well of her own monsoon.

West

The wind lay still on the deck of Brandan's ship
While the sailors tried to rouse her; she never stirred
Till Brandan joined his hands and, coincidence or not,
She got on her knees and filled her lungs and put
Her lips to the sail and puffed. The long-lost ship
Flew home and into legend like a bird.

South

The wind had hidden his head in a pit in the sand
Of an uncrossable desert; something slid
Into his lack of ear, he gradually uncurled
Like a king cobra, rose and spread his hood
And swayed in time with what the charmer piped,
In time with Time, to wreck or bless the world.

The park

Through a glass greenly men as trees walking
Led by their dogs, trees as torrents
Loosed by the thaw, tulips as shriekmarks
(Yelps of delight), lovers as coracles
Riding the rapids: Spring as a spring
Releasing the jack-in-a-box of a fanfare.

Urban enclave of lawns and water,
Lacquered ducks and young men sculling,
Children who never had seen the country
Believing it this while those who had once
Known real country ignore the void
Their present imposes, their past exposes.

South and east lie the yellowed terraces
Grandiose, jerrybuilt, ghosts of gracious
Living, and north those different terraces
Where great white bears with extensile necks,
Convicted sentries, lope their beat,
No rest for their paws till the day they die.

Fossils of flesh, fossils of stucco:
Between them the carefully labelled flower beds
And the litter baskets, but also between them
Through a grille gaily men as music
Forcing the spring to loose the lid,
To break the bars, to find the world.

The lake in the park

On an empty morning a small clerk
Who thinks no one will ever love him
Sculls on the lake in the park while bosomy
Trees indifferently droop above him.

On the bank a father and mother goose
Hiss as he passes, pigeons are courting,
Everything mocks; the empty deck-chairs
Are set in pairs, there is no consorting

For him with nature or man, the ducks
Go arrowheading across his bows
Adding insult to absence, his mood
Disallows what the sun endows.

The water arrows are barbed; their barbs,
Corrugated like flint, can start
No Stone Age echoes in his mind
And yet they too might pierce his heart.

Dogs in the park

The precise yet furtive etiquette of dogs
Makes them ignore the whistle while they talk

In circles round each other, one-man bonds
Deferred in pauses of this man-made walk
To open vistas to a past of packs

That raven round the stuccoed terraces
And scavenge at the mouth of Stone Age caves;
What man proposes dog on his day disposes
In litter round both human and canine graves,
Then lifts his leg to wash the gravestones clean,

While simultaneously his eyes express
Apology and contempt; his master calls
And at the last and sidelong he returns,
Part heretic, part hack, and jumps and crawls
And fumbles to communicate and fails.

And then they leave the park, the leads are snapped
On to the spiky collars, the tails wag
For no known reason and the ears are pricked
To search through legendary copse and crag
For legendary creatures doomed to die
Even as they, the dogs, were doomed to live.

Sunday in the park

No sunlight ever. Bleak trees whisper ironies,
Carolina duck and Canada goose forget
Their world across the water, red geraniums
Enhance the chill, dark glasses mirror ironies,
The prams are big with doom, the walkers-out forget
Why they are out, London is lost, geraniums
Stick it out in the wind, old men feel lost
But stick it out and refugees forget
Pretences and grow sad while ironies
Frill out from sprinklers on the green veneer
That screens the tubes in which congested trains
Get stuck like enemas or ironies
Half lost between the lines while dachshunds run
Like centipedes and no one knows the time
Whatever foreigners ask it. Here is Sunday:
And on the seventh day He rested. The Tree
Forgets both good and evil in irony.

Windowscape

Green skeletons of fish, they swim across the pale
Blue wind, acacia leaves. The summer is turning stale,
The panes are dusty, the birds are silent, this whole
Suburb is lost in the dream of one lost soul
Who looking outward marks a road where no one lives
And feeling backward craves a gift that no one gives.
This is Number One The Grove, the shops are far and dear,
Window-cleaner and postman call just once a year
And never a priest. Looking up and out from his room he sees
An aerial on a roof, a pattern of crossed keys,
Crossed bones that are failed fingers. He pauses never to think
The pause is one long trance of an eye that cannot blink,
The eyelids being sewn up; the pause is a failed flow
Of a mind that does not even know that it does not know.
Thus he looks up and whether he has been fed
Or not he does not know, feels neither alive nor dead,
Has neither diary nor menu, form nor fate,
Nor can look down to see what is left on the plate.
So many fingers to cross, so many windows to clean,
So many summers to bone. And yet those bones are green.

Solstice

How did midsummer come so soon,
The lean trees racing into lush?
He had turned his back one moment, then turned
And took it full in the face—the gush
Of green, the stare of blue, the sieve
Of sun and shadow, the wish to live.

And what was nowhere now was here
And here was all and all was good;
Between the lines the words were strange
Yet not to be misunderstood.
The glad flowers talked with tongues of flame
And who was he was not the same.

Nor was there question who was she
For whom his years were blessed to wait,

Whose opening eyes to him were now,
As his to hers, an open gate,
One entrance to one constant song.
How can midsummer stay so long?

Indian village

Whatever it is that jigs and gleams—
Flickering lizard, courting bird—
For which I could not, had I even
One hour to implement my dreams,
Concoct one new and apposite word,
Might yet prove heaven this side heaven,

Viz. life. Euripides was right
To say 'whatever glints' (or dances),
Thus answering those who mark the spot
Meticulously in black and white
And who, contemptuous of the chances,
Divorce the ever from the what.

So here, beneath this pepperpot temple,
Black buffalo eyedeep in the pond,
The sunset purples walls of mud
While hard and gnarled grow smooth and simple
And hunkered peasants gaze beyond
Their hookahs at that orb of blood

Which founders towards its rising day,
A one-eyed starer with a knife,
A ranter flushed with fire and wine;
When we shall also rise and say
A small piece but our own, and life,
Whatever it is, must leap and shine.

Jungle clearance Ceylon

In a manmade lake at first light
Cruising between the tops of bleached

Skeleton trees we waited for elephant
Coming to drink. They never came
But, focusing in, on each bare branch
Of the bonewhite trees we marked a pelican
Frozen to fossil, looking down
Its beak in contempt of human beings
Who had drowned a valley to found a town—
Power and water for human beings
In the thick of the bush. In the thin of the trees
The pelican perched as though in a glass
Case where the wind could never blow
Nor elephant come to drink nor human
Beings presume in the grey dawn
To press a button or throw a switch
To slap the west on the back of the east
In spite of archaic and absent elephant
In spite of archaic and present pelican
In spite of themselves as human beings.

Half truth from Cape Town

Between a smoking fire and a tolling bell
When I was young and at home I could not tell
What problems roosting ten miles to the west
Waited like vultures in their gantried nest
Till Prod should tumble Papish in the river.
I could not tell. The bell went on for ever.

Now through the swinging doors of the decades I
Confront a waste of tarmac, a roaring sky;
The Southern Cross supplants the Useful Plough—
But where are Livingstone and his Lion now?
That cross was raised to mark this safe hotel
Between the goldmines and the padded cell.

In each glib airport between here and you
As the loudspeaker speaks the ants pour through,
Some going north into their past and some
South to this future that may never come,
But all engrossed to that same point that good
Ants would die to get to if they could.

So here I rest, with Devil's Peak above,
Between a smoking fire and a calling dove,
Its voice like a crazy clock that every ten
Minutes runs down, so must be wound again;
And who is all but come or all but gone
I cannot tell. The dove goes on, goes on.

Solitary travel

Breakfasting alone in Karachi, Delhi, Calcutta,
Dacca, Singapore, Kuala Lumpur, Colombo, Cape Town,
But always under water or glass, I find
Such a beginning makes the day seem blind.

The hotels are all the same, it might be pawpaw
Instead of grapefruit, different flowers on the table,
But the waiters, coffee-coloured or yellow or black,
All smile, but, should you smile, give nothing back.

And taking coffee alone in the indistinguishable airports,
Though the land outside be empty or man-crammed, oven or icebox,
I feel the futility of moving on
To what, though not a conclusion, stays foregone.

But the Customs clamour, the stamp is raised, the passport
Like a chess game played by mail records the latest
Move of just one square. Which is surely seen
By the black bishop and the unsleeping queen.

And so to the next hotel to the selfsame breakfast,
Same faces of manager, waiter, fellow-traveller,
Same lounge or bar whose test-tube walls enfold
The self-indulgent disenchanted old.

Time and the will lie sidestepped. If I could only
Escape into icebox or oven, escape among people
Before tomorrow from this neutral zone
Where all tomorrows must be faced alone. . . .

Old Masters abroad

Painfully grinning faces like dogs' or
Inattentive like cats' all over
The static globe affect to be lectured
By the singing birds of unknown England.

Shakespeare flaunts his codpiece at dhoti,
Ditto at sari, Pope with his clouded
Cane conducts the dancers of Bali,
The lesser celandine sprouts in Lagos.

And the skylark crying 'Bird I never!'
Routs parrakeet, hornbill, kookaburra,
While the nightingale puts on spurs in Hampstead
To rip the guts from the decadent bulbul.

Wee sleekit courin' timorous warthog!
Tirra lirra by Kabul River!
The elmtree bole is in tiny leaf but
Not for long because of the termites.

At Bablockhythe the stripling Ganges
Burns on her ghats the scholar gypsy,
There's a deathly hush on the rocks of Aden,
Nine bean rows rise in the Kalahari.

The faces listen or not. The lecturers
Mop their memories. All over the static
Globe the needle sticks in the groove.
It is overtime now for the Old Masters.

Icebergs

If icebergs were warm below the water
One would not wince at their jagged tops;
Lifting and dipping on the swell
They still might signal all was well.

But icebergs are cold in the dark water,
Cold their base as white their crest,
And those who dive to check the fact
Can find no signal to retract.

There are no words below the water,
Let alone phrases, let alone
Sentences—except the one
Sentence that tells you life is done

And what you had of it was a mere
Ninth or tenth; the rest is sheer
Snub to those who dared suppose
Icebergs warm below the water.

Vistas

Emerging from aeons of ocean on to the shore
The creature found itself in a roadless
Forest where nothing stretched before
Its lack of limbs but lack of hope
Until the trees, millennia later,
Parted to grant it greater scope.

Emerging from miles of tunnel into a plain
The train finds itself in a foreign
Beatitude. Creeping fog and rain
And deafmute fears are left behind;
The stuttering grub grows wings and sings
The tune it never thought to find.

Emerging from years of lacking into a love
The Self finds itself in predestined
Freedom. Around, below, above,
Glinting fish and piping birds
Deny that earth and truth are only
Earth, respectively, and words.

Variation on Heraclitus

Even the walls are flowing, even the ceiling,
Nor only in terms of physics; the pictures
Bob on each picture rail like floats on a line
While the books on the shelves keep reeling
Their titles out into space and the carpet

Keeps flying away to Arabia nor can this be where I stood—
Where I shot the rapids I mean—when I signed
On a line that rippled away with a pen that melted
Nor can this now be the chair—the chairoplane of a chair—
That I sat in the day that I thought I had made up my mind
And as for that standard lamp it too keeps waltzing away
Down an unbridgeable Ganges where nothing is standard
And lights are but lit to be drowned in honour and spite of some dark
And vanishing goddess. No, whatever you say,
Reappearance presumes disappearance, it may not be nice
Or proper or easily analysed not to be static
But none of your slide snide rules can catch what is sliding so fast
And, all you advisers on this by the time it is that,
I just do not want your advice
Nor need you be troubled to pin me down in my room
Since the room and I will escape for I tell you flat:
One cannot live in the same room twice.

Reflections

The mirror above my fireplace reflects the reflected
Room in my window; I look in the mirror at night
And see two rooms, the first where left is right
And the second, beyond the reflected window, corrected
But there I am standing back to my back. The standard
Lamp comes thrice in my mirror, twice in my window,
The fire in the mirror lies two rooms away through the window,
The fire in the window lies one room away down the terrace,
My actual room stands sandwiched between confections
Of night and lights and glass and in both directions
I can see beyond and through the reflections the street lamps
At home outdoors where my indoors rooms lie stranded,
Where a taxi perhaps will drive in through the bookcase
Whose books are not for reading and past the fire
Which gives no warmth and pull up by my desk
At which I cannot write since I am not lefthanded.

Hold-up

The lights were red, refused to change,
Ash-ends grew longer, no one spoke,

The papers faded in their hands,
The bubbles in the football pools
Went flat, the hot news froze, the dates
They could not keep were dropped like charred
Matches, the girls no longer flagged
Their sex, besides the code was lost,
The engine stalled, a tall glass box
On the pavement held a corpse in pickle
His ear still cocked, and no one spoke,
No number rang, for miles behind
The other buses nudged and blared
And no one dared get out. The conductress
Was dark and lost, refused to change.

Restaurant car

Fondling only to throttle the nuzzling moment
Smuggled under the table, hungry or not
We roughride over the sleepers, finger the menu,
Avoid our neighbours' eyes and wonder what

Mad country moves beyond the steamed-up window
So fast into the past we could not keep
Our feet on it one instant. Soup or grapefruit?
We had better eat to pass the time, then sleep

To pass the time. The water in the carafe
Shakes its hips, both glass and soup plate spill,
The tomtom beats in the skull, the waiters totter
Along their invisible tightrope. For good or ill,

For fish or meat, with single tickets only,
Our journey still in the nature of a surprise,
Could we, before we stop where all must change,
Take one first risk and catch our neighbours' eyes?

The wiper

Through purblind night the wiper
Reaps a swathe of water

On the screen; we shudder on
  And hardly hold the road,
All we can see a segment
Of blackly shining asphalt
With the wiper moving across it
  Clearing, blurring, clearing.

But what to say of the road?
The monotony of its hardly
Visible camber, the mystery
  Of its far invisible margins,
Will these be always with us,
The night being broken only
By lights that pass or meet us
  From others in moving boxes?

Boxes of glass and water,
Upholstered, equipped with dials
Professing to tell the distance
  We have gone, the speed we are going,
But never a gauge nor needle
To tell us where we are going
Or when day will come, supposing
  This road exists in daytime.

For now we cannot remember
Where we were when it was not
Night, when it was not raining,
  Before this car moved forward
And the wiper backward and forward
Lighting so little before us
Of a road that, crouching forward,
  We watch move always towards us,

Which through the tiny segment
Cleared and blurred by the wiper
Is sucked in under the axle
  To be spewed behind us and lost
While we, dazzled by darkness,
Haul the black future towards us
Peeling the skin from our hands;
  And yet we hold the road.

The wall

Face to the wall and behind him
The room full of well-wishers.
But what, they said, can we do?
He has abdicated, his life is behind him.

The bed had known birth and death;
Where was the wall had once been a window.
Now all the light is behind him.
The wall is a blind end.

No, they said, no doctor.
Nor priest. What is the use?
There is not even a window
For body.or soul to look through.

But, as they spoke, their voices
Faded away while the wall
Grew nearer so that he heard
Different voices beyond it,

Singing. And there was light
Before him as through a window
That opens on to a garden.
The first garden. The last.

The snow man

His memory was shaped by forgetting
Into a snowman, handful by handful;
In the end two pebbles for eyes and a cherrywood
Pipe clamped in the thinlipped mouth.

But was this fellow really his past,
This white dummy in a white waste?
While the censor works, while the frost holds,
Perhaps he will pass—but then he will pass.

Yesterday was a dance of flakes
Waltzing down, around, and up,
But today is lull and smudge, today
Is a man with a pipe that will not draw.

Today is a legless day with head-on
Idiot eyes, a stranded deaf
Mute in a muted world. This lump
Is what he remembered when he forgot,

Already beginning to dribble. Tomorrow
Comes the complete forgetting, the thaw.
Or is it rather a dance of water
To replace, relive, that dance of white?

The truisms

His father gave him a box of truisms
Shaped like a coffin, then his father died;
The truisms remained on the mantelpiece
As wooden as the playbox they had been packed in
Or that other his father skulked inside.

Then he left home, left the truisms behind him
Still on the mantelpiece, met love, met war,
Sordor, disappointment, defeat, betrayal,
Till through disbeliefs he arrived at a house
He could not remember seeing before,

And he walked straight in; it was where he had come from
And something told him the way to behave.
He raised his hand and blessed his home;
The truisms flew and perched on his shoulders
And a tall tree sprouted from his father's grave.

The blasphemies

The sin against the Holy . . . though what
He wondered was it? Cold in his bed
He thought: If I think those words I know
Yet must not be thinking—Come to the hurdle

507

And I shall be damned through thinking Damn—
But Whom? But no! Those words are unthinkable;
Damn anyone else, but once I—No,
Here lies the unforgivable blasphemy.
So pulling the cold sheets over his head
He swore to himself he had not thought
Those words he knew but never admitted.
To be damned at seven years old was early.

Ten years later, his Who's Who
No longer cosmic, he turned to parody—
Prayers, hymns, the Apostles' Creed—
Preening himself as a gay blasphemer,
But what is a practical joke in a world
Of nonsense, what is a rational attitude
Towards politics in a world of ciphers,
Towards sex if you lack all lust, towards art
If you do not believe in communication?
And what is a joke about God if you do not
Accept His existence? Where is the blasphemy?
No Hell at seventeen feels empty.

Rising thirty, he had decided
God was a mere expletive, a cheap one,
No longer worth a laugh, no longer
A proper occasion to prove one's freedom
By denying something not worth denying.
So humanism was all and the only
Sin was the sin against the Human—
But you could not call it Ghost for that
Was merely emotive; the only—you could not
Call it sin for that was emotive—
The only failure was not to face
The facts. But at thirty what are the facts?

Ten years later, in need of myth,
He thought: I can use my childhood symbols
Divorced from their context, Manger and Cross
Could do very well for Tom Dick and Harry—
Have we not all of us been in a war
So have we not carried call it a cross
Which was never our fault? Yet how can a cross
Be never your fault? The words of the myth,
Now merely that and no longer faith,
Melt in his hands which were never proved

Hard as nails, nor can he longer
Speak for the world—or himself—at forty.

Forty to fifty. In ten years
He grew to feel the issue irrelevant:
Tom Dick and Harry were not Christ
And whether Christ were God or not
And whether there were a God or not
The word was inadequate. For himself
He was not Tom or Dick or Harry,
Let alone God, he was merely fifty,
No one and nowhere else, a walking
Question but no more cheap than any
Question or quest is cheap. The sin
Against the Holy Ghost—What is it?

Bad dream

The window was made of ice with bears lumbering across it,
    Bears the size of flies;
The ceiling was one great web with flies cantankering in it,
    Flies the size of men;
The floor was riddled with holes with men phutscuttering down them
    Into the jaws of mice.

Outside there were no other houses, only bedizened hoardings
    With panties prancing on them
And an endless file of chromium-plated lamp posts
    With corpses dangling from them
And one gaunt ruined church with a burglar alarm filibustering
    High and dry in the steeple.

Here then the young man came who wanted to eat and drink,
    To play, pray, make love;
Electronic voices nagged at him out of the filtered air,
    The eyes on the hoarding winked;
He knocked at the door of the house, the bears buzzed and the flies
    Howled to him to come in.

Inside he found a table laid for two, a mirror
    Flanking the double bed,

On the night table a scent spray, a tin of biscuits, a bible,
  A crucifix on the wall
And beside it a comic postcard: all this he carefully noticed
  And then he noticed the floor

Bomb-pocked with tiny holes, from one of which there rose
  One tiny wisp of white.
He watched as it clawed the air two inches from the floor
  And saw it for what it was,
The arm of a girl, he watched and just could hear her voice
  Say: Wait! Wait till I grow.

And the arm grew and he wished to bend and clutch the hand
  But found he could no more move,
The arm grew and the fingers groped for help, the voice
  That had grown with the arm, the voice
That was now a woman's about to be saved or lost was calling
  For help. He could not move.

Then everything buzzed and boomed. The chaps outside on the lamp
    posts
  Hooted, broke wind, and wept,
Men the size of flies dropped down his neck while the mansized
  Flies gave just three cheers
And he could not move. The darkness under the floor gave just
  One shriek. The arm was gone.

Good dream

He woke in his usual room, decided
Feeling completely awake to switch
The reading lamp on and read—but where
Is the switch? No switch no light. No light
No chapter nor verse. Completely awake
He gropes for the switch and finds the book
He left in the dark but what is a book
Left in the dark? He feels the book
Suddenly gently taken away
By someone's hand and a warm voice
Begins, beginneth, aloud in the dark:
Here beginneth the first chapter—
But it wasn't the first, he was half way through.

No, says the voice, *the first chapter*
At the first verse in the first voice,
Which is mine, none other's: Here beginneth—
But I tell you, he says, I was half way through,
I am completely awake, I can prove it;
Where is the switch? I will show you the place
Half way through.
                              There is no switch,
The voice replies; *in the beginning*
Is darkness upon the face of the earth
In which you must wait for me till I
Show you the place not half way through
But just begun, the place you never
Knew was here.
                              But I know this place,
It is my usual room, except
The switch has gone.
                              The switch was never
There to start with; which is why
You refuse to wake.
                              But I am completely
Awake, I told you.
                              You will tell me
Once you are. Here beginneth—
I tell you this is my usual room;
I can put out my hand from the bed and feel the . . .
Yes?
    The wall—but I can't. Where
Has the wall gone? My bed was against it.
What was against it?
                              Why is your voice
Moving away? Why do I hear
Water over it?
                              There is water
Between us, I am here on the bank,
You will have to row.
                              Row?
                                        What
Is a boat for? I am here on the bank.
But I need light to row.
                              No.
No light until you reach this bank.
Feel for your oars.
                              Here are my oars.
Then loose that rope. Are you ready? Row.

Here beginneth. . . .
                            He dips his oars
And knows the walls receding, hears
The ripples round the chair legs, hears
Larksong high in the chimney, hears
Rustling leaves in the wardrobe, smells
All the smells of a river, and yet
Feeling, smelling, hearing, knowing,
Still cannot see. This boat has no
Switch. No switch no light.
                            No light?
Pull on your oars. I am here.
                            He pulls.
Splutter of water, crackle and grinding
Of reeds and twigs; then bump. The hand
That stole the book that was left in the dark
Comes out of the dark, the hand that is hers,
Hers, none other's, and seizes his
To help him on to the bank.
                            'And God
Said Let there be light'.
                            His usual room
Has lost its usual walls and found
Four walls of sky, incredible blue
Enclosing incredible green enclosing
Her, none other.
                    Completely awake.

Selva oscura

A house can be haunted by those who were never there
If there was where they were missed. Returning to such
Is it worse if you miss the same another or none?
The haunting anyway is too much.
You have to leave the house to clear the air.

A life can be haunted by what it never was
If that were merely glimpsed. Lost in the maze
That means yourself and never out of the wood
These days, though lost, will be all your days;
Life, if you leave it, must be left for good.

And yet for good can be also where I am,
Stumbling among dark treetrunks, should I meet
One sudden shaft of light from the hidden sky
Or, finding bluebells bathe my feet,
Know that the world, though more, is also I.

Perhaps suddenly too I strike a clearing and see
Some unknown house—or was it mine?—but now
It welcomes whom I miss in welcoming me;
The door swings open and a hand
Beckons to all the life my days allow.

All over again

As if I had known you for years drink to me only if
Those frontiers had never changed on the mad map of the years
And all our tears were earned and this were the first cliff
From which we embraced the sea and these were the first words
We spread to lure the birds that nested in our day
As if it were always morning their dawnsong theirs and ours
And waking no one else me and you only now
Under the brow of a blue and imperturbable hill
Where still time stands and plays his bland and hemlock pipe
And the ripe moment tugs yet declines to fall and all
The years we had not met forget themselves in this
One kiss ingathered world and outward rippling bell
To the rim of the cup of the sky and leave it only there
Near into far blue into blue all over again
Notwithstanding unique all over all again
Of which to speak requires new fires of the tongue some trick
Of the light in the dark of the muted voice of the turning wild
World yet calm in her storm gay in her ancient rocks
To preserve today one kiss in this skybound timeless cup
Nor now shall I ask for anything more of future or past
This being last and first sound sight on eyes and ears
And each long then and there suspended on this cliff
Shining and slicing edge that reflects the sun as if
This one Between were All and we in love for years.

XIV

1961—1963

To Mary

Forgive what I give you. Though nightmare and cinders,
The one can be trodden, the other ridden,
We must use what transport we can. Both crunching
Path and bucking dream can take me
Where I shall leave the path and dismount
From the mad-eyed beast and keep my appointment
In green improbable fields with you.

Soap suds

This brand of soap has the same smell as once in the big
House he visited when he was eight: the walls of the bathroom open
To reveal a lawn where a great yellow ball rolls back through a hoop
To rest at the head of a mallet held in the hands of a child.

And these were the joys of that house: a tower with a telescope;
Two great faded globes, one of the earth, one of the stars;
A stuffed black dog in the hall; a walled garden with bees;
A rabbit warren; a rockery; a vine under glass; the sea.

To which he has now returned. The day of course is fine
And a grown-up voice cries Play! The mallet slowly swings,
Then crack, a great gong booms from the dog-dark hall and the ball
Skims forward through the hoop and then through the next and then

Through hoops where no hoops were and each dissolves in turn
And the grass has grown head-high and an angry voice cries Play!
But the ball is lost and the mallet slipped long since from the hands
Under the running tap that are not the hands of a child.

1961

Déjà vu

It does not come round in hundreds of thousands of years,
It comes round in the split of a wink, you will be sitting exactly
Where you are now and scratching your elbow, the train
Will be passing exactly as now and saying It does not come round,
It does not come round, It does not come round, and compactly
The wheels will mark time on the rails and the bird in the air
Sit tight in its box and the same bean of coffee be ground
That is now in the mill and I know what you're going to say
For all this has happened before, we both have been through the mill,
Through our Magnus Annus, and now could all but call it a day
Were it not that scratching your elbow you are too lovely by half
So that, whatever the rules we might be supposed to obey,
Our love must extend beyond time because time is itself in arrears
So this double vision must pass and past and future unite
And where we were told to kowtow we can snap our fingers and laugh
And now, as you watch, I will take this selfsame pencil and write:
It does not come round in hundreds of thousands of years.

1962

Round the corner

Round the corner was always the sea. Our childhood
Tipping the sand from its shoes on return from holiday
Knew there was more where it came from, as there was more
Seaweed to pop and horizon to blink at. Later
Our calf loves yearned for union in solitude somewhere
Round that corner where Xenophon crusted with parasangs
Knew he was home, where Columbus feared he was not,
And the Bible said there would be no more of it. Round
That corner regardless there will be always a realm
Undercutting its banks with repeated pittance of spray,
The only anarchic democracy, where we are all vicarious
Citizens; which we remember as we remember a person
Whose wrists are springs to spring a trap or rock
A cradle; whom we remember when the sand falls out on the carpet
Or the exiled shell complains or a wind from round the corner
Carries the smell of wrack or the taste of salt, or a wave
Touched to steel by the moon twists a gimlet in memory.
Round the corner is—sooner or later—the sea.

1961

The suicide

And this, ladies and gentlemen, whom I am not in fact
Conducting, was his office all those minutes ago,
This man you never heard of. There are the bills
In the intray, the ash in the ashtray, the grey memoranda stacked
Against him, the serried ranks of the box-files, the packed
Jury of his unanswered correspondence
Nodding under the paperweight in the breeze
From the window by which he left; and here is the cracked
Receiver that never got mended and here is the jotter
With his last doodle which might be his own digestive tract
Ulcer and all or might be the flowery maze
Through which he had wandered deliciously till he stumbled
Suddenly finally conscious of all he lacked
On a manhole under the hollyhocks. The pencil
Point had obviously broken, yet, when he left this room
By catdrop sleight-of-foot or simple vanishing act,

To those who knew him for all that mess in the street
This man with the shy smile has left behind
Something that was intact.

1961

Perspectives

The further-off people are the smaller. Grandparents,
Homeric heroes and suffering Bantu
Are nothing in size to the tax-collector
Or the dentist breathing fire on one's uvula.

So the stunted commissionaire bulks larger
Than the massive magnate at the turn of the stairs
While the coffin entering by the west door
Screens the chancel and dwarfs the altar.

Yet sometimes for all these rules of perspective
The weak eye zooms, the distant midget
Expands to meet it, far up stage
The kings go towering into the flies;

And down at the end of a queue some infant
Of the year Two Thousand straddles the world
To match the child that was once yourself.
The further-off people are sometimes the larger.

1961

Château Jackson

Where is the Jack that built the house
That housed the folk that tilled the field
That filled the bags that brimmed the mill
That ground the flour that browned the bread
That fed the serfs that scrubbed the floors
That wore the mats that kissed the feet
That bore the bums that raised the heads
That raised the eyes that eyed the glass
That sold the pass that linked the lands
That sink the sands that told the time

That stopped the clock that guards the shelf
That shrines the frame that lacks the face
That mocked the man that sired the Jack
That chanced the arm that bought the farm
That caught the wind that skinned the flocks
That raised the rocks that sunk the ship
That rode the tide that washed the bank
That grew the flowers that brewed the red
That stained the page that drowned the loan
That built the house that Jack built?

Here, to begin with, is the world
That breeds the race that claims the right
That makes the pace that makes the race
That bursts the tape that rings the bell
That drees the weird that scoops the news
That stews the tea that stales the smut
That gluts the guts that loathe the lights
That light the path that probes the maze
That traps the days that dodge the wolf
That haunts the door that bears the box
That gulped the bills that swelled the debt
That bent the back that caused the pain
That warped the mind that steered the feet
That took the road that climbed the hill
That boasts the yew that chills the ground
That grows the grass that chokes the flowers
That brewed the red that decked the bank
That bears the slab that wears the words
That tell the truth that ends the quest:
Where is the Jack that built the house?

1961

Pet shop

Cold blood or warm, crawling or fluttering
Bric-à-brac, all are here to be bought,
Noisy or silent, python or myna,
Fish with long silk trains like dowagers,
Monkeys lost to thought.

In a small tank tiny enamelled
Green terrapin jostle, in a cage a crowd

Of small birds elbow each other and bicker
While beyond the ferrets eardrum, eyeball,
Find that macaw too loud.

Here behind glass lies a miniature desert,
The sand littered with rumpled gauze
Discarded by snakes like used bandages;
In the next door desert fossilized lizards
Stand in a pose, a pause.

But most of the customers want something comfy—
Rabbit, hamster, potto, puss—
Something to hold on the lap and cuddle
Making believe it will return affection
Like some neutered succubus.

Purr then or chirp, you are here for our pleasure,
Here at the mercy of our whim and purse;
Once there was the wild, now tanks and cages,
But we can offer you a home, a haven,
That might prove even worse.

1962

Flower show

Marooned by night in a canvas cathedral under bare bulbs
He plods the endless aisles not daring to close an eye
To massed brass bands of flowers; these flowers are not to pluck
Which (cream cheese, paper, glass, all manner of textile and plastic)
Having long since forgotten, if they ever knew, the sky
Are grown, being forced, uprooted.

Squidlike, phallic or vulvar, hypnotic, idiotic, oleaginous,
Fanged or whaleboned, wattled or balding, brimstone or cold
As trout or seaweed, these blooms, ogling or baneful, all
Keep him in their blind sights; he tries to stare them down
But they are too many, too unreal, their aims are one, the controlled
Aim of a firing party.

So bandage his eyes since he paid to come in but somehow forgot
To follow the others out—and now there is no way out
Except that his inturned eyes before he falls may show him
Some nettled orchard, tousled hedge, some garden even

Where flowers, whether they boast or insinuate, whisper or shout,
Still speak a living language.

1961

In lieu

Roses with the scent bred out,
In lieu of which is a long name on a label.
Dragonflies reverting to grubs,
Tundra and desert overcrowded,
And in lieu of a high altar
Wafers and wine procured by a coin in a slot.

On the podium in lieu of a man
With fallible hands is ensconced
A metal lobster with built-in tempi;
The deep-sea fishermen in lieu of
Battling with tunny and cod
Are signing their contracts for processing plankton.

On roof after roof the prongs
Are baited with faces, in saltpan and brainpan
The savour is lost, in deep
Freeze after freeze in lieu of a joint
Are piled the shrunken heads of the past
And the offals of unborn children.

In lieu therefore of choice
Thy Will be undone just as flowers
Fugues, vows and hopes are undone
While the weather is packaged and the spacemen
In endless orbit and in lieu of a flag
The orator hangs himself from the flagpost.

1961

The taxis

In the first taxi he was alone tra-la,
No extras on the clock. He tipped ninepence
But the cabby, while he thanked him, looked askance
As though to suggest someone had bummed a ride.

In the second taxi he was alone tra-la
But the clock showed sixpence extra; he tipped according
And the cabby from out his muffler said: 'Make sure
You have left nothing behind tra-la between you'.

In the third taxi he was alone tra-la
But the tip-up seats were down and there was an extra
Charge of one-and-sixpence and an odd
Scent that reminded him of a trip to Cannes.

As for the fourth taxi, he was alone
Tra-la when he hailed it but the cabby looked
Through him and said: 'I can't tra-la well take
So many people, not to speak of the dog.'

1961

The grey ones

Crouched beneath a snowbound sky
Three grey sisters share an eye;
Before they lose it and forget
Ask the way to Never Yet,

Which might be Once Upon a Time,
Golden Age or Perfect Crime,
Kingdom Come or Free for All,
No past, no future and no fall.

Bandied round from face to face
One lonely eye in frozen space
Skewers the perspectives of the mind
Till what you wished you fear to find,

Which might be what your childhood swore
Lay shrined beyond the haunted door
Or might be where your mentor seems
To misdirect you to in dreams.

Every such what and where betwixt
Your fact and fancy stays transfixed
By that one unremitting stare
Which cancels what you never were,

Who might have been a prince of Troy,
A lord of song, a roaring boy,
Or might have been an idiot mild
Who meets his match in every child,

For all which persons lacking proof
The three grey sisters wait aloof;
They chew the cud, they pass the eye
And check the client next to die,

Who might be in some mountain cup
Where climbers meet it struggling up
Or might be in some Eastern town
Where most men take it lying down

Sprawled against the Gates of Doom
Whence all kebabs and cockstands come
On which stands guard for ever more
A beggar with a flaming sore.

1961

After the crash

When he came to he knew
Time must have passed because
The asphalt was high with hemlock
Through which he crawled to his crash
Helmet and found it no more
Than his wrinkled hand what it was.

Yet life seemed still going on:
He could hear the signals bounce
Back from the moon and the hens
Fire themselves black in the batteries
And the silence of small blind cats
Debating whether to pounce.

Then he looked up and marked
The gigantic scales in the sky,
The pan on the left dead empty
And the pan on the right dead empty,
And knew in the dead, dead calm
It was too late to die.

1961

Spring cleaning

The cripple aches in his lost limb,
The old man cries for a dropped dummy,
Dawn comes up with muted strings,
Spring rides high in a bailiff's van.

Blain and dazzle together, together
Magnolia in bloom and holly in berry
In the writing desk where nothing is written
Lurk latchkeys, counterfoils and lockets.

The stopnetting sags, the molehills rise,
Typewriters ring, opinions wilt,
Towers of pennies for spastic children
Wobble and crash while the tills ring

The Rites of Spring. Over the sticks
High horses crash, under the water
Black fingers pick at the ocean bed,
The whole flat smells of hot cross buns.

Peace and rumours of peace. Mechanical
Brains compute the chances. Jets
Trace on the skies their ads and prayers:
Let someone soon make all things new.

In spruce new wards new mothers shriek,
New vacuum cleaners run amuck,
New deaf incapsulated souls
Gaze out at noisy birds of dawn;

While on a pillar in the sands
A gaunt man scours his plinth and hauls
His empty basket up and cries:
Repent! It is time to round things off.

                                        1961

Another cold May

With heads like chessmen, bishop or queen,
The tulips tug at their roots and mourn

In inaudible frequencies, the move
Is the wind's, not theirs; fender to fender
The cars will never emerge, not even
Should their owners emerge to claim them, the move
Is time's, not theirs; elbow to elbow
Inside the roadhouse drinks are raised
And downed, and downed, the pawns and drains
Are blocked, are choked, the move is nil,
The lounge is, like the carpark, full,
The tulips also feel the chill
And tilting leeward do no more
Than mimic a bishop's move, the square
Ahead remains ahead, their petals
Will merely fall and choke the drains
Which will be all; this month remains
False animation of failed levitation,
The move is time's, the loss is ours.

1962

The pale panther

The sun made a late and lamented
Spring. Yellow teeth tore
The ribs of my roof. The giraffe
Necks of blind lamp posts bent
To lick up turds and print.
Beyond the electric fence
One tiny tractor stalled.

Milkman, milkman, your empties
Are all to collect; do not wait
Till they jive on the steps, you surely
Know about bugs in the sun,
Runways in rut, control
Towers out of touch, and burns
Whose gift is not to cure.

As for you, airman, your empties
Are broken test tubes or shards
Of caddis, it is too soon
To order replacements according

To the state of play since the green
Lies in shadow now and the tractor
Stalled when the sun stopped play.

1962

Réchauffé

The food on the walls of the dark tombs
Awaits the dragoman whose torch
Will warm it when the deep freeze burns
In the highpitched dried-date voice. By turns
These live men filing past inspect
These dead that serve by turns the painted
Food on the walls of the dark.

The hands on the ends of the sun's rays
Are like small paddles or bats to pat
Piedog and priest on the head and give
Pharaoh and land the chance to live,
Yet even the most sun-worshipping king,
Praise though he will, must also dread
The hands on the ends of the sun.

The dams on the breast of the mad Nile
Secure both budget and mind: what once
Could either prove too scarce or full
Stands docile now like a ringed bull
And yet who knows what sudden thrust
In the guts, what gripe in the mind, might burst
The dams on the breast of the mad?

1961

Ravenna

What do I remember of my visit to Ravenna? Firstly,
That I had come from Venice where I had come from Greece
So that my eyes seemed dim and the world flat. Secondly,
That after Tintoretto's illusory depth and light
The mosaics knocked me flat. There they stood. The geese
Had hissed as they pecked the corn from Theodora's groin,

Yet here she stands on the wall of San Vitale, as bright
As life and a long shot taller, self-made empress,
Who patronised the monophysites and the Greens
And could have people impaled. There was also and thirdly the
    long-
Lost naval port of Caesar, surviving now in the name
In Classe: the sea today is behind the scenes
Like his Liburnian galleys. What went wrong
With Byzantium as with Rome went slowly, their fame
Sunk in malarial marsh. The flat lands now
Are ruled by a sugar refinery and a church,
Sant' Apollinare in Classe. What do I remember of Ravenna?
A bad smell mixed with glory, and the cold
Eyes that belie the tesselated gold.

1961

Constant

Too many curds on the meat, too many dark cloth caps
On the conveyor belt that twice a day
Spans the Golden Horn, too much history
Tilting, canting, crawling, rotting away,
Subsiding strata where ghosts like faults, like mites,
Reminders of stagnation or collapse,
Emerge into the mist. After Athens
This place seems of the North, a halfway house
To Tomi or Kiev; the visitors' eyes
Play spillikins with minarets, a louse
Lurks in a banned fez, the bubbles rise
From someone drowned in a sack an age ago,
The Fourth Crusade dissolves in loot and rape,
Theologians, eunuchs, tipsters, goldsmiths, grow
Like fungi out of the walls, this game is high,
Caught between Roman and Turk a dream takes shape
And becomes Constant, known to sailor and exile
For its red lamps and raki, while the sky
Red with repeated fires, accidental or designed,
Sags like a tent over riot and ruin and one
Who calmly, having other things in mind,
Bears on his palm the Church of the Holy Wisdom.

1961

October in Bloomsbury

Edwardian pillar boxes wait for Edwardian letters; the Museum
Spreads its dead hands wide, a pigeon scores an outer
On a scholarly collar, the menu in the pub says Butter Beans Greens
    Peas,
Black men and schoolchildren rummage for culture, the tutelary
    spirits are hard to please,

Those epicureans who haunt the lawns, whose amputated delicate
    fingers tingle,
Whose delicate eyelids are dropped for ever not to be pained by the
    great new institutes,
Who sometimes even when out of mind become what we miss most,
In the callbox lifting a receiver warm from the ear of a ghost.

Now the parking meters picket and pick the Georgian locks and
    invisible
Meters tall as the yellowing trees docket and dock our history,
Though Charles James Fox unconcerned in a bath towel sits on his
    arse in Bloomsbury Square
While plane tree leaves flop gently down and lodge in his sculptured
    hair.

1962

New Jerusalem

Bulldoze all memories and sanctuaries: our birthright
Means a new city, vertical, impersonal,
Whose horoscope claimed a straight resurrection
Should Stimulant stand in conjunction with Sleeping Pill.

As for the citizens, what with their cabinets
Of faces and voices, their bags of music,
Their walls of thin ice dividing greynesses,
With numbers and mirrors they defy mortality.

So come up Lazarus: just a spot of make-up
Is all you need and a steel corset
And two glass eyes, we will teach you to touch-type
And give you a police dog to navigate the rush hour.

With all this rebuilding we have found an antidote
To quiet and self-communing: from now on nobody
Strolling the streets need lapse into timelessness
Or ponder the simple unanswerable questions.

Wheels upon wheels never moving, Ezekiel
Finds himself in a canyon of concrete;
Cage upon cage, Daniel goes feeling
From one to the next in search of a carnivore.

But, that Babel may rise, they must first work downward
To subliminate previous and premature foundations.
Bulldozer, dinosaur, pinheaded diplodocus,
Champ up forgotten and long-dry water-pipes.

1962

Charon

The conductor's hands were black with money:
Hold on to your ticket, he said, the inspector's
Mind is black with suspicion, and hold on to
That dissolving map. We moved through London,
We could see the pigeons through the glass but failed
To hear their rumours of wars, we could see
The lost dog barking but never knew
That his bark was as shrill as a cock crowing,
We just jogged on, at each request
Stop there was a crowd of aggressively vacant
Faces, we just jogged on, eternity
Gave itself airs in revolving lights
And then we came to the Thames and all
The bridges were down, the further shore
Was lost in fog, so we asked the conductor
What we should do. He said: Take the ferry
Faute de mieux. We flicked the flashlight
And there was the ferryman just as Virgil
And Dante had seen him. He looked at us coldly
And his eyes were dead and his hands on the oar
Were black with obols and varicose veins
Marbled his calves and he said to us coldly:
If you want to die you will have to pay for it.

1962

The introduction

They were introduced in a grave glade
And she frightened him because she was young
And thus too late. Crawly crawly
Went the twigs above their heads and beneath
The grass beneath their feet the larvae
Split themselves laughing. Crawly crawly
Went the cloud above the treetops reaching
For a sun that lacked the nerve to set
And he frightened her because he was old
And thus too early. Crawly crawly
Went the string quartet that was tuning up
In the back of the mind. You two should have met
Long since, he said, or else not now.
The string quartet in the back of the mind
Was all tuned up with nowhere to go.
They were introduced in a green grave.

1962

Birthright

When I was born the row began,
I had never asked to be a man;
They never asked if I could ride
But shouted at me 'Come outside!',
Then hauled the rearing beast along
And said: 'Your charger, right or wrong.'
His ears went back and so did I,
I said 'To mount him means to die',
They said 'Of course'; the nightmare neighed
And I felt foolish and afraid.
The sun came up, my feet stuck fast,
The minutes, hours, and years went past,
More chances missed than I could count,
The stable boys cried: 'Time to mount!'
My jaw dropped and I gaped from drouth:
My gift horse looked me in the mouth.

1962

Children's games

Touch me not forget me not, touch me forget me,
Throw salt over your shoulder when you walk under a ladder,
Fly away, Peter, they are waiting in the Vatican,
Come back, Paul, to your Macedonian runaround.

Hop scotch and somersault ring a ring of raspberries.
Who shall we send to fetch her away? Touch wood and turn again.
I'm the king of the barbican, come down you dirty charlatan.
When you see a magpie put salt upon her tail.

He knows I know you know catchum
Nigger by his whatnot round and round the launching site.
Boar's tusks and phonies say the bells of Saint Adonis,
Up Guards and Jenkins and all fall down.

The grand old Duke of York is just about to turn about,
Keep your fingers crossed when Tom Tiddler's ground is over you,
I'll beat you in a canter say the bells of Atalanta;
Touch me not forget me, touch me forget me not.

1962

Tree party

Your health, Master Willow. Contrive me a bat
To strike a red ball; apart from that
In the last resort I must hang my harp on you.

Your health, Master Oak. You emblem of strength,
Why must your doings be done at such length?
Beware lest the ironclad ages catch up with you.

Your health, Master Blackthorn. Be live and be quick,
Provide the black priest with a big black stick
That his ignorant flock may go straight for the fear of you.

Your health, Master Palm. If you brew us some toddy
To deliver us out of by means of the body,
We will burn all our bridges and rickshaws in praise of you.

Your health, Master Pine. Though sailing be past
Let you fly your own colours upon your own mast
And rig us a crow's nest to keep a look out from you.

Your health, Master Elm. Of giants arboreal
Poets have found you the most immemorial
And yet the big winds may discover the fault in you.

Your health, Master Hazel. On Hallow-e'en
Your nuts are to gather but not to be seen
Are the twittering ghosts that perforce are alive in you.

Your health, Master Holly. Of all the trees
That decorate parlour walls you please
Yet who would have thought you had so much blood in you?

Your health, Master Apple. Your topmost bough
Entices us to come climbing now
For all that old rumour there might be a snake in you.

Your health, Master Redwood. The record is yours
For the girth that astounds, the sap that endures,
But where are the creatures that once came to nest in you?

Your health, Master Banyan, but do not get drunk
Or you may not distinguish your limbs from your trunk
And the sense of Above and Below will be lost on you.

Your health, Master Bo-Tree. If Buddha should come
Yet again, yet again make your branches keep mum
That his words yet again may drop honey by leave of you.

Your health, Master Yew. My bones are few
And I fully admit my rent is due,
But do not be vexed, I will postdate a cheque for you.

1962

Sports page

Nostalgia, incantation, escape,
Courts and fields of the Ever Young:
On your Marks! En Garde! Scrum Down! Over!
On the ropes, on the ice, breasting the tape,

533

Our Doppelgänger is bounced and flung
While the ball squats in the air like a spider
Threading the horizon round the goalposts
And we, though never there, give tongue.

Yet our Doppelgänger rides once more
Over the five-barred gates and flames
In metaphors filched from magic and music
With a new witch broom and a rattling score
And the names we read seem more than names,
Potions or amulets, till we remember
The lines of print are always sidelines
And all our games funeral games.

1962

The habits

When they put him in rompers the habits
Fanned out to close in, they were dressed
In primary colours and each of them
Carried a rattle and a hypodermic;
His parents said it was all for the best.

Next, the barracks of boys: the habits
Slapped him on the back, they were dressed
In pinstripe trousers and carried
A cheque book, a passport, and a sjambok;
The master said it was all for the best.

And then came the women: the habits
Pretended to leave, they were dressed
In bittersweet undertones and carried
A Parthian shaft and an affidavit;
The adgirl said it was all for the best.

Age became middle: the habits
Made themselves at home, they were dressed
In quilted dressing-gowns and carried
A decanter, a siphon, and a tranquilliser;
The computer said it was all for the best.

Then age became real: the habits
Outstayed their welcome, they were dressed
In nothing and carried nothing.
He said: If you won't go, I go.
The Lord God said it was all for the best.

1962

Greyness is all

If black were truly black not grey
It might provide some depth to pray
Against and we could hope that white
Would reach a corresponding height.

But, as it is, we melt and droop
Within the confines of our coop;
The mind stays grey, obtuse, inert,
And grey the feathers in the dirt.

If only some black demon would
Infuse our small grey souls we could
At least attempt to break the wire
That bounds the Gadarene hens' desire.

But, as it is, we needs must wait
Not for some demon but some fate
Contrived by men and never known
Until the final switch is thrown

To black out all the worlds of men
And demons too but even then
Whether that black will not prove grey
No one may wait around to say.

1962

As in their time

(i)

They were so mean they could not between them
Leave one tip behind them; the others

Tipped so wildly it made no sense,
When the cold computer gathered the leavings
It broke about even, made no sense.

(ii)

Polyglot, albeit illiterate,
He stood on a crumbling tower of Babel
Cured of heredity, and though
His idol had a brain of clay
He could not read the cuneiform.

(iii)

She believed in love, but was it
Her self or her role believed?
And was it believed and not
Professed or envied? Lastly,
Was it love she believed in?

(iv)

He was the man you thought
And I thought too was me
That never was on land
Or sea but in fact was at home
On both and never was.

(v)

Year by year these old ladies had saved
For the sake of their nieces and decade by decade
For their great-nieces and greater-nephews
Till the inflation left them nothing
To leave to the heirs that were dead before them.

(vi)

He had clowned it through. Being born
For either the heights or the depths

He had bowled his hoop on the level
Arena; the hoop was a wheel
Of fire but he clowned it through.

(vii)

She had her mind on the main
Drain. When it all was over
She could maintain that the point
Was the main but the point was the drain
Was no more on the main than herself.

(viii)

For what it was worth he had to
Make a recurring protest:
Which was at least a gesture
Which was a vindication
Or excuse for what it was worth.

(ix)

He was to be found in directories,
Admiring asides and footnotes,
Flowers by request. When he entered
A room it at once was a morgue
To tip people off he had entered.

(x)

Citizen of an ever-expanding
Universe, burning smokeless fuel,
He had lived among plastic gear so long
When they decided to fingerprint him
He left no fingerprints at all.

(xi)

She was a bundle of statistics, her skin
Creamy with skinfood, *and* she knew the lingo,
So that when she entered the bush she was entirely
Camera-conscious. For all that the cannibals
Ate her one day they had nothing else to do.

(xii)

As a child showed promise. No need to push him,
Everyone said. Then came the drought
And after that, on his twenty-first birthday,
A cloud no bigger than a god's hand
And after that there was no need to push him.

1962

This is the life

Down the rock chute into the tombs of the kings they grope these
    battling sandalled
Elderly ladies in slacks and a hurry, their red nails clutching at hiero-
    glyphics,
Down to the deep peace of the shelter, everything found, cuisine and
    service,
All the small ochred menials and livestock discreetly in profile, every
    convenience
Laid on free so that they may survive in the manner to which they are
    accustomed,
Gracious in granite—this is the life—with their minds made up for ever
    and the black
Sarcophagus made up ready for the night, they can hide their heads
    under the graveclothes
And every day in the dark below the desert will be one of both in-
    dependence and thanksgiving
So they never need worry again as to what may fall out of the sky
But whenever they want can have a Pharaoh's portion of turkey and
    pumpkin pie.

1962

Budgie

(for Robert MacBryde)

The budgerigar is baby blue,
Its mirror is rimmed with baby pink,
Its cage is a stage, its perks are props,
Its eyes black pins in a cushionette,
Its tail a needle on a missing disc,
Its voice a small I Am. Beyond
These wires there might be something different—
Galaxy on galaxy, star on star,
Planet on planet, asteroid on asteroid,
Or even those four far walls of the sitting room—
But for all this small blue bundle could bother
Its beak, there is only itself and the universe,
The small blue universe, so *Let me attitudinize,*
Let me attitudinize, let me attitudinize,
For all the world is a stage is a cage
A hermitage a fashion show a crèche an auditorium
Or possibly a space ship. *Earth, can you hear me?*
Blue for Budgie calling Me for Mirror:
Budgie, can you hear me? The long tail oscillates,
The mirror jerks in the weightless cage:
Budgie, can you see me? The radio telescope
Picks up a quite different signal, the human
Race recedes and dwindles, the giant
Reptiles cackle in their graves, the mountain
Gorillas exchange their final messages,
But the budgerigar was not born for nothing,
He stands at his post on the burning perch—
I twitter Am—and peeps like a television
Actor admiring himself in the monitor.

1962

Memoranda to Horace

I

Aere perennius? Dissolving dialects.
Flaccus, why trouble now to be lapidary,
Knowing posterity, let alone unable

539

To scan or follow you, neither will be able,
Let alone yours, to cope with language,
Being confined to the usual and frozen
Channels, communicants in frozen sperm,
Caught between cosmic and comic radiation,
Against which world we have raised a monument
Weaker and less of note than a mayfly
Or a quick blurb for yesterday's detergent?

Yet (another paragraph) I should correct myself
Though not for myself or my time but for the record:
Fame you no longer presumed on than pontifex
And silent Vestal should continue daily
Climbing the Capitol. Whether that proviso
Has been properly kept seems open to question
Even though a coiffed and silent figure
Has been seen by some on Michelangelo's piazza
With eyes turned down on the past. Yet your image
'More lasting than bronze' will do: for neither
Sulphuric nor other acid can damage,
Let alone destroy, your Aeolian measures
Transmuted to Latin—*aere perennius*.

II

Returned from my far-near country, my erstwhile,
I wonder how much we are defined by negatives,
    Who have no more seen the Bandusian
Spring than have you the unreadable Atlantic,

You to whom seraph and gargoyle were meaningless
And I to whom Roman roads are a tedium
    Preferring the boreens of a country
Rome never bothered her ponderous head about.

So what have we, Flaccus, in common? If I never
Boasted a Maecenas, you never summarised
    Life from Rockefeller Centre
And if you never moved in a Christian framework

I never moved in a pagan; for that matter
I no more found Tir na nÓg than you

The Hesperides, yet vice versa
If you never found Tir na nÓg, then I never

Found the Hesperides. It looks as if both of us
Met in the uniqueness of history a premise
    That keeps us apart yet parallel,
The gap reducible only by language.

It is noisy today as it was when Brutus
Fell on his sword, yet through wars and rumours
    Of wars I would pitch on the offchance
My voice to reach you. Yours had already

Crossed the same gap to the north and future,
Offering no consolation, simply
    Telling me how you had gathered
Your day, a choice it is mine to emulate.

III

'Or with the tangles' as one of our own said
And another called it 'intense' but admiringly 'levity',
    This in the Nineteen-Thirties
Had you, Flaccus, been alive and improbably
    Tempted by the Party would as usual
        Have served as a second string.

Yes, Augustus had to arrive in a sealed train
And you had to praise him and even think you meant it
    The way you meant it for Regulus;
Yet we can guess between politics and personal
    Ties what making your expected
        Bow you really preferred,

Slipping away to Lalage. There in the shade
Of an ilex you could forget the triumphal arches
    And the rigged votes; the repetitive
Cicadas endorsed your sleep after lovemaking
    From which deliciously laughing
        She woke and gave you a phrase,

Which you dressed out in nonsense, that old yarn
Of the routed wolf, and yet today in London

When all the loudspeakers bellow
'Wolf repeat Wolf!' I can find asylum,
   As you did, either in language
     Or laughter or with the tangles.

IV

Though elderly poets profess to be inveterate
Dionysians, despising Apollonians,
   I find it, Flaccus, more modest
To attempt, like you, an appetitive decorum.

Contraptions in ear or mouth or vagina,
To you known neither as aid nor indignity,
   Assist yet degrade a generation
For whom quality has long been in pawn to security.

Which you, though they called you a time-serving parasite,
Must understand, though even your period
   Never foresaw such appalling
Stress upon mere irredeemable quantity.

So now, when faced by a too well evacuated
Sanatorium or mildewed junkshop,
   The point is never to recognize
Any preconception: let commonplace be novelty.

Which you, had they called you a legacy hunter,
Would yet have agreed, no matter how the market
   Jittered: the point was to recognize
The unborn face and the nigger in the woodpile.

Both of which gifts, whether non-recognition
Or pre-recognition, can serve us two thousand
   Years after yours as an antidote
To the poison of time and manoeuvre a compromise

With horrible old fellows, glazed and jowly,
Who were the ones we always avoided
   Yet soon to be resembled albeit
Our juniors resemble ourselves in avoidance.

Flaccus, there are creatures for you over-Gothic
Met only by twilight, who daylong dozing
By night are too wary: to these I am grateful,
To Cocksnook, Lilith and Harum Scarum.

With whom to hobnob is a mortification
Of self-respect, one's precious identity
Filtered away through what one had fancied
Till now were one's fingers, shadows to shadows.

Which yet means relief from the false identity
Assumed in the day and the city, the pompous
Cold stereotype that you in your period
Tried to escape in your Sabine farmhouse.

Which even for you was somewhat to archaize—
Much more then for us for whom Lares, Penates,
And all their kind are nothing but rhetoric,
Funerary urns from the supermarket.

But how strange to think that degenerate goblin
And fetch have outlasted your classics; at twilight
I go to my tryst, the sky was dirty
All day, there is snow to come, there are monsters

To come and corrupt me, it is almost cosy,
The sly paw gripping the lapel, the hurried
Old lag's tip in the lobby: 'Plead guilty
Before they acquit and adopt you'. *Lusisti*

Satis—remember? Likewise but otherwise
To opt out now seems better than capitulate
To the too-well-lighted and over-advertised
Idols of the age. Sooner these crepuscular

Blasphemous and bawdy exchanges; and even
A second childhood remembering only
Childhood seems better than a blank posterity,
One's life restricted to standing room only.

1962

Star-gazer

Forty-two years ago (to me if to no one else
The number is of some interest) it was a brilliant starry night
And the westward train was empty and had no corridors
So darting from side to side I could catch the unwonted sight
Of those almost intolerably bright
Holes, punched in the sky, which excited me partly because
Of their Latin names and partly because I had read in the textbooks
How very far off they were, it seemed their light
Had left them (some at least) long years before I was.

And this remembering now I mark that what
Light was leaving some of them at least then,
Forty-two years ago, will never arrive
In time for me to catch it, which light when
It does get here may find that there is not
Anyone left alive
To run from side to side in a late night train
Admiring it and adding noughts in vain.

January, 1963

Goodbye to London

Having left the great mean city, I make
Shift to pretend I am finally quit of her
Though that cannot be so long as I work.
   Nevertheless let the petals fall
   Fast from the flower of cities all.

When I first met her to my child's ear
She was an ocean of drums and tumbrils
And in my nostrils horsepiss and petrol.
   Nevertheless let the petals fall
   Fast from the flower of cities all.

Next to my peering teens she was foreign
Names over winking doors, a kaleidoscope
Of wine and ice, of eyes and emeralds.
   Nevertheless let the petals fall
   Fast from the flower of cities all.

544

Later as a place to live in and love in
I jockeyed her fogs and quoted Johnson:
To be tired of this is to tire of life.
　　Nevertheless let the petals fall
　　Fast from the flower of cities all.

Then came the headshrinking war, the city
Closed in too, the people were fewer
But closer too, we were back in the womb.
　　Nevertheless let the petals fall
　　Fast from the flower of cities all.

From which reborn into anticlimax
We endured much litter and apathy hoping
The phoenix would rise, for so they had promised.
　　Nevertheless let the petals fall
　　Fast from the flower of cities all.

And nobody rose, only some meaningless
Buildings and the people once more were strangers
At home with no one, sibling or friend.
　　Which is why now the petals fall
　　Fast from the flower of cities all.

1962

Off the peg

The same tunes hang on pegs in the cloakrooms of the mind
That fitted us ten or twenty or thirty years ago
On occasions of love or grief; tin pan alley or folk
Or Lieder or nursery rhyme, when we open the door we find
The same tunes hanging in wait as when the weather broke
In our veins or the golden bowl in our hands; they show
Frayed edges here and there or loss of nap but like
Chameleons can adapt to whatever sunlight leaks
Or thunderstorms impend or ghosts of long love strike.
Hence when the coffinlike cradle pitched on the breaking bough
Reveals once more some fiend or avatar, we reach
For one of those wellworn tunes; be it purgatory or hell
Or paradise even, circumstances allow
This chain of simple notes the power of speech,
Each tune, each cloak, if matched to weather and mood, wears well
And off the peg means made to measure now.

1962

545

Coda

Maybe we knew each other better
When the night was young and unrepeated
And the moon stood still over Jericho.

So much for the past; in the present
There are moments caught between heart-beats
When maybe we know each other better.

But what is that clinking in the darkness?
Maybe we shall know each other better
When the tunnels meet beneath the mountain.

1962

Thalassa

Run out the boat, my broken comrades;
Let the old seaweed crack, the surge
Burgeon oblivious of the last
Embarkation of feckless men,
Let every adverse force converge—
Here we must needs embark again.

Run up the sail, my heartsick comrades;
Let each horizon tilt and lurch—
You know the worst: your wills are fickle,
Your values blurred, your hearts impure
And your past life a ruined church—
But let your poison be your cure.

Put out to sea, ignoble comrades,
Whose record shall be noble yet;
Butting through scarps of moving marble
The narwhal dares us to be free;
By a high star our course is set,
Our end is Life. Put out to sea.

From a recent manuscript: ? 1963

XV
Translations

Three odes of Horace

I

Solvitur Acris Hiems (I.4)

Winter to Spring: the west wind melts the frozen rancour,
   The windlass drags to sea the thirsty hull;
Byre is no longer welcome to beast or fire to ploughman,
   The field removes the frost-cap from his skull.

Venus of Cythera leads the dances under the hanging
   Moon and the linked line of Nymphs and Graces
Beat the ground with measured feet while the busy Fire-God
   Stokes his red-hot mills in volcanic places.

Now is the time to twine the spruce and shining head with myrtle,
   Now with flowers escaped the earthy fetter,
And sacrifice to the woodland god in shady copses
   A lamb or a kid, whichever he likes better.

Equally heavy is the heel of white-faced Death on the pauper's
   Shack and the towers of kings, and O my dear
The little sum of life forbids the ravelling of lengthy
   Hopes. Night and the fabled dead are near

And the narrow house of nothing, past whose lintel
   You will meet no wine like this, no boy to admire
Like Lycidas, who today makes all young men a furnace
   And whom tomorrow girls will find a fire.

               c. 1936-8: from *The Earth Compels.*

II

Aequam Memento (II.3)

   A level mind in crooked times
   Preserve, preserve; nor in better fortune
     Dash into rash self-glory,
     My brother bound for death—

   Whether your life be a string of doldrums
   Or whether you loll on days of festa

At a private fête champêtre
With a bottle of vintage wine.

Towering pine and silver poplar—
Why do they intermingle their friendly
　　Shade? And why do these cantering waters
　　Jockey their way through winding banks?

Here is the place for wine and perfume
And the too fleeting bloom of the rose
　　While Time and Chance and the black threads
　　Of the three Fates give chance and time.

You must leave the estates you bought, the house
You built, which yellow Tiber washes,
Leave them—and all that pinnacled wealth,
　　Your work, will fall to another master.

If rich and of ancient lineage, it makes
No odds; no odds if born a beggar
　　You lived your life in the foulest slum,
　　Victims all of the pitiless Reaper.

All of us briefed the same; for all of us
Our lot is rattled like dice and sooner
　　Or later will fall and embark our souls
　　On the packet boat to eternal exile.

From a radio programme, October 8th, 1956

III

Carpe Diem (I.11)

Do not, Leúconoé, seek to inquire what is forbidden, what
End the gods have assigned to you or to me; nor do you meddle with
Astrological numbers. What shall arise count to your balance if
God marks down to you more winters—or perhaps this very one is the
Last which now on the rocks wears out the fierce Mediterranean
Sea; but be wise and have wine, wine on the board, prune to a minimum
Long-drawn hopes. While we chat, envious time threatens to give us
　the
Slip; so gather the day, never an inch trusting futurity.

? Summer, 1963; *from a manuscript*.[1]

[1] A different, less satisfactory, version was used in radio programmes, October 8th, 1956, and March 24th, 1963.

Four medieval Latin poems

I

Jam Lucis Orto Sidere

(Anonymous: sixth century?)

Now that first light has filled the sky
We humbly pray to God on high
That in our actions of the day
He keep us from the things that slay;

And also may he hold in check
Those angry tongues that rail and wreck,
And all our greedy eyes restrain
From drinking deep of beauties vain.

May he make pure our inmost heart,
May worldly Folly thence depart;
With rules of fasting for our guide
May we subdue our carnal pride.

So that, when day has been and gone
And God-appointed night comes on,
Having all worldly lusts abjured
We may sing praises to the Lord.

From a radio programme, August 11th, 1963

II

Corona Virginum
(Sigebert of Liège: d. 1112)

Lo the blessed assembly of virgins!
Gertrude, Agnes, Prisca, Cecilia,
 Lucia, Petronilla, Thecla,
  Agatha, Barbara, Juliana,

And many whose names to me are either
Unknown or, known, too long to mention,
 Who were made worthy of God's blessing
  By their own pure and believing spirit

551

With which to school them and guide their footsteps
Putting behind them joys terrestrial
  While in the body beyond all bodily
    Usage they led the lives of angels.

These now roaming those green celestial
Meadows search for becoming garlands,
  Plucking at will the roses of passion
    And the lilies of love, and love's violets.

From a radio programme, August 11th, 1963

III

Ut Quid Iubes, Pusiole

(Godescalc: ninth century)

What is it, child, you ask of me?
Something, my lad, that cannot be:
a song, a song of jubilee,
when I'm an exile forced to flee
  far to the sea.
How can you ask a song of me?

More likely, sad one, it would be
a dirge that, lad, you heard from me.
A wail would come more easily
than songs of love's philosophy.
  O cease your plea.
How can you ask a song of me?

And rather, ladling, I would see
my little brother piously
make lamentation here with me,
letting his voice and mine agree
  in misery.
How can you ask a song of me?

You know, despite your tyranny,
young godling that I hold in fee,
how in my exiled agony
embittered days and nights I see
  despairingly.
How can you ask a song of me?

You know, my lad, the history
of Israel's harsh captivity
in Babylon. Men wept to be
torn past Judaea's boundary
   by God's decree.
How can you ask a song of me?

Their hearts were far from psalmody;
the exiles brooded rightfully.
How could they raise a chant of glee
with only foreign eyes to see?
   Could song be free?
How can you ask a song of me?

But since you will not cease your plea,
my comrade in fidelity,
to Son and Father whom we see
dividual in deity
   I bend my knee.
This theme can wake my exstasy.

Lord, you have known how bitterly
almost two years I've learned to be
an exile here beside the sea.
Far have I come, but could not flee
   my destiny.
I pray in all humility.

One theme can wake my ecstasy.
My lad shall hear it sung by me.
On lips, in heart, one symphony,
by day or night, eternally,
   this song will be
my praise, O king of piety.

                        From a typescript: ? 1963

IV

Meum Est Propositum

('*Archipoeta*': twelfth century.)

Seething in my inmost guts with corrosive anger
I must now address my heart words of bitter rancour:

Being formed of air and froth, lacking stone and mortar,
I am like a leaf the winds toss to every quarter.

Granted that a man of sense, set upon endurance,
Knows that building on a rock makes the best insurance,
Foolish fellow that I am, I am like a flowing
Stream that, ever changing place, knows not where it's going.

Like a ship without a crew drifting hither thither,
Like a bird on aery roads flying God knows whither,
Quite immune to lock and key, quite immune to fetters,
Craving for my kind I join troops of drunks and debtors.

Weighty principles, for me, are not worth my money,
What I love is light-o'-love, sweeter far than honey;
Let but Venus give commands, easy 'tis to follow,
Venus who eschews the heart that is cold and hollow.

Down the primrose path I trip, green and salad fashion,
Virtue mine anathema, vice my only passion;
Less in love with heavenly joys than with pleasures sinful,
Dead in soul I save my skin, grant it many a skinful.

Hard enough it is and more, looking at a virgin,
To control what wanton thoughts from one's nature burgeon;
Being young how can we heed such restrictive motions
When the sight of velvet skins fills us with emotions?

Gambling in my list of sins forms the second heading;
But when gambling leaves me stripped both of shirt and bedding,
Frozen though my flesh may be, in my mind I'm sweating,
Then it is that verse and song find their best begetting.

Third and last but far from least taverns must have mention
Which have never lacked, nor shall, most of my attention,
Till the holy angels come and my eyes discern 'em
Singing for the dead their long *requiem aeternam*.

My proposal is to die somewhere in a tavern,
Liquor near my dying lips gaping like a cavern;
Then will all the angels sing, in most joyful chorus:
'May the Lord look kindly on this old drunk before us!'

From a radio programme, August 11th, 1963

Three poems in defeat

(From the French of Louis Aragon)

I

The Lilacs and the Roses

O months of blossoming, months of transfigurations,
May without a cloud and June stabbed to the heart,
I shall not ever forget the lilacs or the roses
Nor those the Spring has kept folded away apart.

I shall not ever forget the tragic sleight-of-hand,
The cavalcade, the cries, the crowd, the sun,
The lorries loaded with love, the Belgian gifts,
The road humming with bees, the atmosphere that spun,
The feckless triumphing before the battle,
The scarlet blood the scarlet kiss bespoke
And those about to die bolt upright in the turrets
Smothered in lilac by a drunken folk.

I shall not ever forget the flower-gardens of France—
Illuminated scrolls from eras more than spent—
Nor forget the trouble of dusk, the sphinx-like silence,
The roses all along the way we went;
Flowers that gave the lie to the soldiers passing
On wings of fear, a fear importunate as a breeze,
And gave the lie to the lunatic push-bikes and the ironic
Guns and the sorry rig of the refugees.

But what I do not know is why this whirl
Of memories always comes to the same point and drops
At Sainte-Marthe . . . a general . . . a black pattern . . .
A Norman villa where the forest stops;
All is quiet here, the enemy rests in the night
And Paris has surrendered, so we have just heard—
I shall never forget the lilacs nor the roses
Nor those two loves whose loss we have incurred:

Bouquets of the first day, lilacs, Flanders lilacs,
Soft cheeks of shadow rouged by death—and you,

Bouquets of the Retreat, delicate roses, tinted
Like far-off conflagrations: roses of Anjou.

II

The Unoccupied Zone

Cross-fade of grief to nothingness,
The beat of the crushed heart grew less,
The coals grew white and lost their gleam;
Drinking the wine of summer's haze
In a rose-castle in Corrèze
I changed this August into dream.

What could it be that of a sudden
Brought an aching sob in the garden,
A voice of low reproach in the air?
Ah not so soon, ah do not wake me;
This merest snatch of song must take me
Out of the barracks of despair.

I thought for a moment that I heard
In the middle of the corn a blurred
Noise of arms—a theme that sears.
Whence did this theme return to me?
Not carnations nor rosemary
Had thus retained the scent of tears.

By hook or crook I had got relief
From the dark secret of my grief
When lo—the shadows redivide;
My eyes were only on the track
Of apathy that looks not back
When September dawned outside.

My love, within your arms I lay
When someone hummed across the way
An ancient song of France; my illness
At last came clear to me for good—
That phrase of song like a naked foot
Rippled the green waters of stillness.

From *New Writing and Daylight*, 1943

III

Richard Coeur-de-Lion

If the universe is like this gaol where now
At Tours in France we are as prisoners penned,
If strangers put our clover under plough
If day today is empty of an end.

Must I mark up each hour upon a chart
As time to hate, who never had the will?
One has no home now—even in the heart,
O my country, are you my country still?

Not for me now to watch the swallow fly
Who speaks to heaven a language under ban
Nor watch the unreliable cloud go by,
Old ferryman of dreams that have had their span.

Not for me now to say what I am thinking
Nor hum this air that haunts my heart and brain;
I cannot face the silence without shrinking
And sunlight is as ill as fog or rain.

They are brute force and we are only legion;
You sufferers, we know where we belong.
Why make the night a yet more sombre region?
A prisoner can still compose a song,

A song as pure as running water, white
As bread before the war, a song to rise
Above the manger clear into the night
And high enough to catch the shepherds' eyes.

O all the shepherds, sailors, and Wise Men,
Carters and dons and butchers and the race
Of image-makers, tricksters with the pen,
And queues of women in the market-place,

People in business and commercial roles,
Men who make steel or textiles, also men
Whose job in life is scaling telegraph poles
And the black miners—all shall listen again.

All Frenchmen are Blondel, in each he sings:
Whatever name we called her at the start
Freedom—like a whispering of wings—
Answers the song of Richard Lionheart.

From *Aragon, Poet of Resurgent France,*
ed. Hannah Josephson and Malcolm Cowley (1946)

The legend of the dead soldier

(From the German of Bertolt Brecht)

And as the war in its fifth spring
Gave no inkling of peace,
The soldier drew the logical conclusion
And died a hero's death.

But the war was not yet over,
And therefore the Kaiser was vexed
That his soldier had died so soon,
It struck him as premature.

The summer crept over the graves
And the soldier was already asleep.
Then came along one night a Mil-
itary Medical Mission Extraordinary.

The Medical Mission proceeded
To visit God's Own Acre,
And with consecrated spades they ex-
cavated the fallen soldier.

The doctor overhauled him thoroughly—
Or rather, that is, what was left of him—
And the doctor found that the soldier was O.K.,
His injuries being occupational.

And at once they abducted the soldier.
The night was blue and beautiful:
Anyone who took his tin hat off
Could have seen the stars of home.

And because the soldier stinks of decay
A priest hobbles in front
Who swings a censer above
In order to stop him stinking.

Ahead the band with tow-row-row
Plays a rollicking march,
And the soldier, in accordance with instructions,
Goosesteps high from his arse.

And brotherly-wise two medical
Orderlies hold him up;
Otherwise he would collapse in the mud—
And that is strictly forbidden.

They painted his winding sheet with the three
Colours—the black–white–red—
And carried it before him; the colours
Prevented one seeing the filth.

A gentleman in morning dress,
Equipped with an athlete's chest,
Led the way; as a German
He was quite au fait with his duty.

So they took him, playing a tow-row-row,
Down the dark arterial road,
And the soldier staggered along
Like a flake of snow in a storm.

And as they passed through the villages
All the women were there.
The trees made a bow, the full moon shone,
And every one cried 'Hurrah'.

With a tow-row-row and welcome home!
And woman, dog and priest!
And right in the middle the dead soldier
Drunk as a drunken ape.

And as they passed through the villages
No one was able to see him;
You could only have seen him from above—
And up there is nothing but stars.

The stars are not always there,
The red dawn is a-dawning.
But the soldier, in accordance with instructions,
Goes to a hero's grave.

From a typescript, n.d. : ? c. 1958

List of pieces excluded by MacNeice from his *Collected Poems 1925–1948*
though published in earlier volumes

BLIND FIREWORKS (*Gollancz, 1929*):

Inaugural Rant
Child's Terror
Child's Unhappiness
A Conventional Serenade
Spring
A Serene Evening
Gardener Melancholy
Sailor's Funeral
Corpse Carousal
Sunset
Neurotics
Song in the Back of the Mind
Bound in Stupidity and Unbound
Homo Sum
The Court Historian (A Satirical Composition)
This Tournament
A Lame Idyll
Coal and Fire
Falling Asleep
The Humorous Atheist Addresses his Humorous Maker
Cynicism
The Sunset Conceived as a Peal of Bells
Γνῶθι σεαυτόν
Adonis
Old Maid
Harvest Thanksgiving
A Classical Education
Evening Indoors ii
Senescence
The Sea
Middle Age
Adam's Legacy
Twilight of the Gods

POEMS (*1935*):

Insidiae
Trapeze

POEMS (*Random House, 1937*):

Sonnet
For Services Rendered (repr. as 'Thank You' in *The Earth Compels*)

THE EARTH COMPELS (*1938*):

Solvitur Acris Hiems (Horace, Odes I.4)
Rugby Football Excursion

THE LAST DITCH (*Cuala Press, 1940*):

To Eleanor Clark
Here in this Strange Room
The Bulletins
Running away from the War
Eastward Again (repr. as 'Clonmacnois' in *Plant and Phantom*)
The Sky is a lather of Stars (repr. as 'Cushendun Again' in *Plant and Phantom*)
Primrose Hill
Departure Platform (repr. in *Plant and Phantom*)
Suicide (repr. in *Plant and Phantom*)

COLLECTED POEMS, 1925–1940 (*Random House, 1941*):

The Gates of Horn
Octets i, iii, iv, v, viii and ix
Men of Good Will
Coming from Nowhere
Ballade on an Old Theme
Ballade for Mr. MacLeish
Ballade in a Bad Temper
Ballade of Dirty Linen
Ballade for King Canute
The Sense of Smell

PLANT AND PHANTOM (*1941*):

Picture Galleries
The Expert (Novelettes vi)
Exile
O'Connell Bridge

SPRINGBOARD (*1944*):

Sentries

HOLES IN THE SKY (*1948*):

Week-end

Variant Titles

Save where otherwise stated the titles given in *Collected Poems 1925–1948* have been adopted in this edition.

Alternative Title	*Title in this edition*
A Cataract conceived as the March of Corpses (*Blind Fireworks*)	River in Spate
A Night (*Blind Fireworks*)	Nocturne
Beginning of a Comic-Delirious Drama (*Blind Fireworks*)	Mahavveray
Books, do not look at me (*The Earth Compels*)	Sand in the Air
Candle Poems (*Blind Fireworks; Collected Poems 1925–1948*)	Candles (*Eighty-Five Poems*)
County Sligo (*Plant and Phantom*)	Sligo and Mayo
Cradle Song (*Plant and Phantom*)	Cradle Song for Eleanor
Epilogue (*Letters from Iceland; The Earth Compels*)	Postscript to Iceland
Impermanent Creativeness (*Blind Fireworks*)	Breaking Webs
In Sligo the Country was soft (*The Last Ditch*)	Sligo and Mayo
Letter to Graham and Anne Shepard (*Letters from Iceland*)	Letter to Graham and Anna
Octets (*Plant and Phantom*)	Entered in the Minutes ii, iii and iv
Only let it form (*The Earth Compels*)	The Brandy Glass
On Those Islands (*I crossed the Minch; The Earth Compels*)	The Hebrides
Postscript (*Springboard*)	When we were Children
Reminiscences of Infancy (*Blind Fireworks*)	Trains in the Distance
Song (*Poems*, Random House, 1937)	The Sunlight on the Garden
The Coming of War (*The Last Ditch; Plant and Phantom*)	The Closing Album
The Merman (*Eighty-Five Poems*)	Visitations iii
The Muse (*Eighty-Five Poems*)	Visitations vi
The Old Story is True (*The Last Ditch*)	The Old Story
The Universe (an Excerpt) (*Blind Fireworks*)	Genesis
Three Poems Apart (for X) (*The Last Ditch*)	Trilogy for X

Index of Titles

Index of First Lines

567